Plato's *Timaeus*

Brill's Plato Studies Series

Editors

Gabriele Cornelli (*Brasilia, Brazil*)
Gábor Betegh (*Cambridge, United Kingdom*)

Editorial Board

Beatriz Bossi (*Madrid, Spain*)
Luc Brisson (*Paris, France*)
Michael Erler (*Würzburg, Germany*)
Franco Ferrari (*Salerno, Italy*)
Maria do Ceu Fialho (*Coimbra, Portugal*)
Mary-Louise Gill (*Providence, USA*)
Debra Nails (*Michigan, USA*)
Noburu Notomi (*Tokyo, Japan*)
Olivier Renaut (*Paris, France*)
Voula Tsouna (*Santa Barbara, USA*)

VOLUME 5

The titles published in this series are listed at *brill.com/bpss*

Plato's *Timaeus*

Proceedings of the Tenth Symposium Platonicum Pragense

Edited by

Chad Jorgenson
Filip Karfík
Štěpán Špinka

BRILL

LEIDEN | BOSTON

This is an open access title distributed under the terms of the CC BY-NC-ND 4.0 license, which permits any non-commercial use, distribution, and reproduction in any medium, provided no alterations are made and the original author(s) and source are credited. Further information and the complete license text can be found at https://creativecommons.org/licenses/by-nc-nd/4.0/

The terms of the CC license apply only to the original material. The use of material from other sources (indicated by a reference) such as diagrams, illustrations, photos and text samples may require further permission from the respective copyright holder.

Swiss National Science Foundation

L'étape de la prépresse de cette publication a été soutenu par le Fond national Suisse de la recherche scientifique.

Library of Congress Cataloging-in-Publication Data

Names: Symposium Platonicum Pragense (10th : 2015 : Prague, Czech Republic) | Jorgenson, Chad, editor. | Karfík, Filip, editor. | Špinka, Štěpán, editor.
Title: Plato's Timaeus : proceedings of the tenth Symposium Platonicum Pragense / edited by Chad Jorgenson, Filip Karfík, Štěpán Špinka.
Description: Leiden ; Boston : Brill, 2021. | Series: Brill's Plato studies series, 2452–2945 ; volume 5
Identifiers: LCCN 2020042177 (print) | LCCN 2020042178 (ebook) | ISBN 9789004436060 (hardback) | ISBN 9789004437081 (ebook)
Subjects: LCSH: Plato. Timaeus—Congresses.
Classification: LCC B387 .S965 2015 (print) | LCC B387 (ebook) | DDC 113—dc23
LC record available at https://lccn.loc.gov/2020042177
LC ebook record available at https://lccn.loc.gov/2020042178

Typeface for the Latin, Greek, and Cyrillic scripts: "Brill". See and download: brill.com/brill-typeface.

ISSN 2452-2945
ISBN 978-90-04-43606-0 (hardback)
ISBN 978-90-04-43708-1 (e-book)

Copyright 2021 by the authors, except where stated otherwise. Published by Koninklijke Brill NV, Leiden, The Netherlands.
Koninklijke Brill NV incorporates the imprints Brill, Brill Hes & De Graaf, Brill Nijhoff, Brill Rodopi, Brill Sense, Hotei Publishing, mentis Verlag, Verlag Ferdinand Schöningh and Wilhelm Fink Verlag.
Koninklijke Brill NV reserves the right to protect this publication against unauthorized use. Requests for re-use and/or translations must be addressed to Koninklijke Brill NV via brill.com or copyright.com.

This book is printed on acid-free paper and produced in a sustainable manner.

Contents

Preface   VII
Acknowledgments   IX

Genos, chōra et guerre dans le prologue du *Timée-Critias*   1
    Tanja Ruben

Die grosse Rede des Timaios – ein Beispiel wahrer Rhetorik?   22
    Lucius Hartmann

Panteles zōion e *pantelōs on*: Vita, anima e movimento intellegibile nel *Timeo* (e nel *Sofista*)   49
    Francesco Fronterotta

How to Make a Soul in the *Timaeus*   70
    Luc Brisson

Planets and Time: A Timaean Puzzle   92
    Karel Thein

The Day, the Month, and the Year:
What Plato Expects from Astronomy   112
    István M. Bodnár

Bodies and Space in the *Timaeus*   131
    Ondřej Krása

Does Plato Advance a Bundle Theory in the *Timaeus*?   149
    George Karamanolis

Matter Doesn't Matter: On the Status of Bodies in the *Timaeus* (30a–32b and 53c–61c)   169
    Gerd Van Riel

An Unnoticed Analogy between the *Timaeus* and the *Laws*   187
    Marwan Rashed

What is Perceptible in Plato's *Timaeus*?   213
   Filip Karfík

Plato on Illness in the *Phaedo*, the *Republic*, and the *Timaeus*   228
   Gábor Betegh

Responsibility, Causality, and Will in the *Timaeus*   259
   Chad Jorgenson

Index Locorum   275

Preface

The papers collected in this volume were originally presented within the framework of the *Tenth Symposium Platonicum Pragense*, which was held in Prague from November 12th to 14th, 2015. The symposium brought together Plato scholars from across Europe, representing a variety of traditions and methodological approaches. The aim was to foster a comprehensive discussion of the *Timaeus*, covering both well-established scholarly problems and less-studied topics and passages.

The arrangement of the individual contributions reflects, so far as possible, the thematic arrangement of the dialogue. Hence, Tanja Ruben opens the volume with "*Genos, chora* et guerre dans le prologue du *Timée*," showing how the narrative of the war against Atlantis anticipates themes from the main cosmogonical narrative, while Lucius Hartmann in "Die grosse Rede des Timaios—ein Beispiel wahrer Rhetorik?" focuses on the status of Timaeus' speech as an example of true rhetoric in the Platonic tradition.

The next four contributions focus on the discussion of the World Soul and astronomy in the first part of the *Timaeus*. In "*Panteles zōion* e *pantelōs on*: vita, anima e movimento intelligibile nel *Timeo* (e nel *Sofista*)," Francesco Fronterotta raises the question of the status of the so-called "intelligible animal," upon which the cosmos is modelled, drawing on evidence from the *Sophist* in order to explain in what sense it can possess life and movement. Luc Brisson's contribution, "How to Make a Soul in the *Timaeus*," guides the reader step by step through the difficult passage on the creation and structure of the World Soul. Karel Thein shifts the focus to astronomy with his "Planets and Time: A Timaean Puzzle," arguing—against the traditional interpretation—that it is not time, but rather the planets themselves that are the "moving image of eternity." Keeping with this theme, István Bodnár's "The Day, the Month, and the Year: What Plato Expects from Astronomy" reflects on the uses and limitations of astronomy in the *Timaeus* and the *Republic*.

From there, the focus shifts to the discussion of the receptacle in the second part of Timaeus' speech. Ondřej Krása's contribution, "Bodies and Space in the *Timaeus*," tackles the question of how this mysterious "third kind" relates to the more familiar Platonic concept of becoming. In "Does Plato Present a Bundle Theory of Substance in the *Timaeus*?" George Karamanolis uses contemporary philosophical tools to raise questions about the identity and structure of physical objects in the *Timaeus*' ontology. Gerd Van Riel closes this section with "Matter Doesn't Matter: On the Status of Bodies in the *Timaeus* (30a–32b and

53c–61c)," in which he raises the thorny question of whether the Timaean receptacle can be identified with matter and whether this is important.

The final group of articles focuses on the more eclectic third section of the *Timaeus*. Marwan Rashed examines the intermediary status of *mathēmata* between being and becoming in the *Timaeus* in "An Unnoticed Analogy between the *Timaeus* and the *Laws*," arguing that it provides a clear model for understanding the intermediary status of the city of the *Laws*. Filip Karfik asks "What is Perceptible in Plato's *Timaeus*?", exploring the relationship between sensible properties and the mathematical structures in which they are grounded. Finally, the volume closes with two papers on Plato's account of illness: Gábor Betegh's "Plato on Illness in the *Phaedo*, the *Republic*, and the *Timaeus*," which provides a comprehensive reassessment of the Platonic conception of illness, and Chad Jorgenson's "Responsibility, Causality, and Will in the *Timaeus*," which takes up the problem of vice as a form of psychic illness and its consequences for human and divine responsibility.

The Editors

Acknowledgments

The Tenth Symposium Platonicum Pragense was organised by the Czech Plato Society with the support of the University Centre for the Study of the Classical and Medieval Intellectual Tradition, Charles University, Prague. We would like to express our gratitude for the financial support of both institutions. We are very grateful to Gabriele Cornelli and Gábor Betegh for including the volume in the Brill Plato Studies series. Our sincere thanks go to Brill's anonymous referee for valuable comments on the manuscript, which helped us to improve it, as well as to Brill's editorial stuff for its unfailing assistance. We owe a debt of thanks to Máté Herner who compiled the *Index locorum*. Finally, it is a pleasure to acknowledge the generous support of the Swiss National Science Foundation, which made it possible to publish the volume in Open Access at Brill. Marwan Rashed's contribution "An Unnoticed Analogy between the *Timaeus* and the *Laws*," published previously in French in *Études philosophiques* 181, 2018/1, 115–138, could only be included in the print version of our volume, with the permission of Humensis.

Genos, chōra et guerre dans le prologue du *Timée-Critias*

Tanja Ruben

Abstract

This article defends the claim that Critias' discourse in the prologue of the *Timaeus* (20d–26e) introduces not only his own discourse about Atlantis in the *Critias*, but also that of Timaeus on the origin of the cosmos and the human being. In both cases, the concepts of *genos* ("family," "genus," "species"), *chōra* ("territory"), and *war* play a role. There are thus thematic links between the two discourses: the genealogies, the description of the territory of Ancient Athens, and the evocation of its war against Atlantis are taken up and transposed to the cosmic level in Timaeus' discourse, especially in the second part, where he describes the genesis of the four kinds of perceptible particles in the *chōra* (48a–68d).

Keywords

Plato – *Timaeus* – *Critias* – genealogy – *chōra* – receptacle

1   Introduction

Le philologue ou l'historien qui lit le début du *Timée* et le *Critias* parce qu'il s'intéresse au récit intrigant de l'Atlantide et à ses modèles littéraires ou historiques se heurte inévitablement au problème suivant : pour raconter la meilleure cité en guerre, pourquoi est-il nécessaire de commencer par le commencement, et d'exposer d'abord sur plus de 65 pages de l'édition Estienne la naissance du cosmos et des hommes, avant de relater enfin, et pas même jusqu'au bout, la guerre athéno-atlante ? Quelle est la fonction du discours cosmogonique et anthropogonique de Timée dans le plan annoncé par Critias à la fin du prologue ? Serait-il impossible de prononcer un discours sur la guerre de la meilleure cité sans celui de Timée ?

La question se pose dans l'autre sens au philosophe qui prend la peine de lire d'abord le long prologue imbriqué avant de se lancer dans le discours « philosophique » de Timée : si Platon avait l'intention d'exposer sa conception du cosmos et de la constitution psychique et physique de l'homme au moyen d'un récit cosmogonique et anthropogonique, pourquoi l'a-t-il encadré par un récit de guerre (inachevé) entre deux cités « mythiques » ? Le prologue du *Timée* serait-il davantage qu'un prologue au *Critias* ? Si oui, qu'apporte-t-il de plus à la compréhension du discours de Timée sur le cosmos et sur l'homme ?

Ces deux questions sont évidemment liées : d'une part, du point de vue du projet discursif, le discours de Timée devrait préparer celui de Critias le jeune. Comme ce dernier l'explique lui-même en présentant à Socrate le « menu » du festin de paroles, Timée est censé lui fournir les êtres humains, nés dans un cosmos nouveau, pour peupler l'ancienne Athènes, qui est la « vraie » Athènes primordiale, désormais identifiée à la meilleure cité (27a2–b6). La cosmogonie et l'anthropogonie exposées par Timée ont leur fin dans la politogonie qui est l'objet du discours de Critias. A cet égard, le discours de Timée forme un long prélude – comparable aux *Hymnes homériques* ou à la *Théogonie* – au discours d'inspiration iliadique de Critias. D'autre part, si on lit le *Timée-Critias* comme une unité dialogique, le discours de Timée se trouve au centre. Or, comme dans la *République*, c'est au centre qu'apparaissent les concepts philosophiques les plus novateurs, même si, du point de vue discursif, la partie centrale n'est qu'une digression. Si donc le prologue du *Timée-Critias* est vraiment un prologue, il n'introduit pas seulement les personnages mais aussi la thématique de la suite dialogique tout entière.

C'est pourquoi il me semble intéressant et important d'examiner en quoi le prologue du *Timée-Critias* prépare et éclaire aussi le discours de Timée. Ainsi peut-on montrer que la cité récapitulée par Socrate au début du prologue (17c1–19b2) ne rappelle pas seulement au lecteur la *kallipolis* de la *République*, mais qu'elle anticipe également la description de l'homme dans le discours de Timée (en particulier 69c5–72d3). L'homme y apparaît en effet, du point de vue de sa constitution physique et psychique, comme une cité en miniature : Timée réduit de nouveau en petits caractères la cité que Socrate, dans la *République*, avait fait naître en paroles pour examiner en gros caractères la justice humaine (368c7–369b4). Ici, je me suis toutefois proposé la tâche plus difficile de trouver des liens thématiques entre le récit de Critias dans le prologue et le discours de Timée qui lui fait suite. Ceux que j'ai repérés se tissent autour de trois mots clés : *chōra* (« terre civique », « territoire »), *genos* (« famille », « genre » ou « espèce ») et guerre.

1.1   *Le vœu de Socrate*

L'ouverture du *Timée-Critias* inscrit les discours qui y sont prononcés dans le cadre d'une hospitalité discursive : Timée, Critias et Hermocrate sont invités à rendre à Socrate un don sous la forme d'un discours équivalent au discours que celui-ci leur avait offert la veille. En guise d'aide-mémoire, Socrate récapitule brièvement son discours qui portait sur la meilleure cité et le genre d'hommes devant la constituer. Suit une comparaison par laquelle il essaie d'expliquer à ses trois hôtes ce qu'il éprouve face à la cité qu'il a parcourue la veille avec eux : sa cité lui donne l'impression de manquer de quelque chose, un peu comme des êtres vivants beaux (ζῷα καλά) mais immobiles nous donneraient envie de les voir bouger, plus exactement de les voir exécuter une lutte athlétique (19b4–c1). La comparaison permet à Socrate de formuler son vœu pour la suite du festin : de même que, face à de beaux êtres vivants immobiles, on a envie de les voir bouger et lutter, de même il aimerait voir la meilleure cité en pleine guerre :

> Ἡδέως γὰρ ἄν του λόγῳ διεξιόντος ἀκούσαιμ᾽ ἂν ἄθλους οὓς πόλις ἀθλεῖ, τούτους αὐτὴν ἀγωνιζομένην πρὸς πόλεις ἄλλας, πρεπόντως εἴς τε πόλεμον ἀφικομένην καὶ ἐν τῷ πολεμεῖν τὰ προσήκοντα ἀποδιδοῦσαν τῇ παιδείᾳ καὶ τροφῇ κατά τε τὰς ἐν τοῖς ἔργοις πράξεις καὶ κατὰ τὰς ἐν τοῖς λόγοις διερμηνεύσεις πρὸς ἑκάστας τῶν πόλεων (19c2–8).

> J'aimerais entendre quelqu'un raconter que ces luttes que soutient une cité, elle les affronte, elle aussi, contre d'autres cités, en entrant en guerre comme il faut et en se montrant, pendant la guerre, digne de la façon dont elle a été éduquée et élevée, aussi bien en pratique dans ses actes qu'en paroles dans ses négociations avec chacune des cités[1].

Socrate souhaite donc que ses trois hôtes prononcent pour lui un discours qui montre la meilleure cité en guerre, de telle sorte qu'à travers ses actions et ses discours, elle fasse valoir sa belle éducation. La meilleure cité a en effet été créée en paroles pour exceller dans la guerre. Les lignes suivantes (19d3–e8) suggèrent que Socrate s'attend à un discours mimétique qui, d'un point de vue formel, rappelle l'*Iliade* avec son alternance de discours et d'actions héroïques, sauf que les héros ne sont désormais plus un Achille ou un Hector mais les gardiens de la meilleure cité et leurs commandants. Socrate a attribué à ces gardiens une nature « à la fois impulsive et amie de la connaissance » (ἅμα μὲν θυμοειδῆ, ἅμα δὲ φιλόσοφον, 18a5), puis a décrit leur éducation et leur genre de vie (18a9–19a5). Il se montre convaincu que Timée, Critias et Hermocrate – qui sont à la fois philosophes et politiques, puisqu'ils partagent la même nature et

---

[1] Mes traductions des passages grecs s'inspirent de celles de Rivaud, *Platon. Œuvres complètes*, tome X, *Timée-Critias*, et de Brisson, *Platon. Timée. Critias*.

la même éducation que les héros qu'ils sont censés représenter – sont les seuls capables d'offrir un tel discours guerrier (19e8–20b7).

Avant d'examiner ce que propose Critias pour répondre au vœu de Socrate, il convient de rappeler brièvement comment naît la guerre dans la *République*. On comprendra ainsi mieux quel rôle jouent la *chōra* et la naissance d'un *genos* humain dans la réalisation de ce vœu.

1.2   *La naissance de la guerre dans la* République

La guerre apparaît au livre II, au moment où l'on passe d'une cité frugale et saine à une cité malade qui vit dans le luxe (372a–373e). La cité que Socrate et Glaucon viennent de construire en paroles est née du constat que la division du travail permet plus aisément aux êtres humains de pourvoir à leurs besoins de nourriture, de vêtements et d'abri (369b5–371e11). Les hommes et les femmes y mènent une vie modeste et se contentent d'une nourriture végétarienne, faite de pain et de galettes accompagnés de sel, d'olives, de fromage, d'oignons et de légumes bouillis, et de figues, de pois chiches, de fèves, de baies de myrtes et de glands rôtis au feu comme dessert (372a5–372d3). Selon Glaucon, une telle cité rurale, qui se nourrit de glands, couchée sur un lit de feuilles, fait penser à « une cité de pourceaux » (ὑῶν πόλιν, 372d4). Dans une cité humaine, on s'attendrait, selon lui, à une certaine qualité de vie, comprenant notamment une nourriture plus variée, avec de la viande et de vrais desserts ainsi qu'une culture de table digne de ce nom (372d7-e1). Socrate accepte de modifier son tableau et de laisser la cité saine qu'il vient de construire pour une cité luxueuse (τρυφῶσαν πόλιν, 372e3) qu'« il faut donc remplir d'une masse de choses et d'une quantité de gens » (ὄγκου ἐμπληστέα καὶ πλήθους, 373b3–4) : lits, tables et autres meubles, viandes, desserts, parfums, hétaïres, peinture et broderie, or et ivoire ; puis chasseurs, artistes et artisans de toutes sortes, ou encore pédagogues, nourrices, cuisiniers, bouchers, porchers et autres serviteurs (373a–c). Cependant, une cité qui dépasse la limite des nécessités vitales pour se livrer à l'acquisition illimitée de richesses (ἐπὶ χρημάτων κτῆσιν ἄπειρον, ὑπερβάντες τὸν τῶν ἀναγκαίων ὅρον, 373d9–10) a besoin d'une *chōra* (le terme apparaît en 373d4) plus étendue pour faire paître son bétail et semer des céréales. C'est pourquoi elle commence à transgresser ses frontières et à retrancher des parcelles de territoire appartenant aux cités voisines. La cité luxueuse fait la guerre pour étendre sa *chōra*, qui est comme son corps, et, ce faisant, enfle (φλεγμαίνουσαν πόλιν, 372e8)[2]. L'examen de ce passage de

---

[2] Pour une analyse détaillée des genres de vie de la cité de pourceaux et de la cité luxueuse dans la *République* II 372a-373e, voir Campese et Canino, « La genesi della *polis* », chap. II « La città dei maiali » (307-317) et chap. III « Polis tryphosa » (318-332).

la *République* nous apprend que la guerre naît donc au moment où une cité essaie d'élargir sa *chōra* aux frais d'une autre cité. Par conséquent, pour revenir au prologue du *Timée*, qui veut répondre au vœu de Socrate et montrer la meilleure cité en train de faire la guerre devra lui donner une *chōra* et définir les limites de celle-ci par rapport aux *chōrai* des cités voisines. C'est seulement ainsi qu'elle pourra entrer dans une guerre (défensive) contre une autre cité[3].

Par ailleurs, si l'on prend au sérieux la remarque de Glaucon sur la cité de pourceaux, des deux cités – saine ou luxueuse – seule la dernière est vraiment humaine[4]. Sous certains aspects, en effet, la vie paisible et saine des hommes et des femmes de la première cité de Socrate rappelle celle des êtres humains sous le règne de Cronos dans le récit du *Politique* (271d–e) : chacune des espèces vivantes, dont les êtres humains, formait alors un troupeau gardé séparément par une divinité, si bien qu'il n'y avait ni guerre (πόλεμος) ni guerre civile (στάσις)[5]. Ici, comme dans la *République*, les humains-animaux se distinguent des êtres humains actuels par l'absence d'activité belliqueuse. Or la guerre est aussi ce qui fait la différence entre les humains et les dieux ; car on a tort de croire que les dieux luttent et se font la guerre, comme Socrate l'explique un peu plus loin quand il entreprend de censurer les récits d'Homère et d'Hésiode (378b8–e3, cf. aussi *Critias* 109b1–5). La guerre apparaît seulement avec le genre (γένος) humain : la genèse de la guerre et celle des êtres humains vont de pair. Avec l'entrée en guerre de la cité construite en paroles par Socrate commence donc le temps propre au genre humain. Outre le fait qu'il faut pouvoir délimiter la *chōra* de la meilleure cité et celle(s) de ses adversaires, qui veut la montrer en guerre devra déterminer sa place dans la lignée généalogique des êtres vivants. Comme on le verra à propos du récit de Critias, ces deux exigences sont liées :

---

3 Bien que la guerre reste un mal qui ne pourra jamais être éradiqué, la cité, selon Platon, devrait viser la paix. C'est pourquoi l'ancienne Athènes (que Critias identifie avec la meilleure cité) excelle dans une guerre *défensive* contre l'Atlantide, alors que celle-ci, en proie à une envie illimitée de richesses, mène une guerre offensive contre les anciens Athéniens et les autres cités grecques. Sur l'attitude de Platon à l'égard de la guerre (et de la paix), voir Cambiano, « La pace in Platone e in Aristotele », et Brisson, « Platon face à la guerre ».

4 A juste titre, Campese et Canino, « La genesi della *polis* », 307–308, observent que les hommes de la première cité mènent une vie frugale et rurale mais non sauvage, puisqu'ils se nourrissent d'aliments cuits. Pour être précis, il faudrait donc parler non pas d'une « cité animale » mais d'une « cité d'animaux domestiques » (comme le sont les cochons justement).

5 La notion des pâtres divins en rapport avec la paix apparaît également dans le *Critias* 109b6–7 et dans les *Lois* IV 713c2–e3. Cf. aussi la vie modérée et paisible que mènent les survivants du déluge dans les montagnes au livre III 678e–679e des *Lois*. Sur les ambiguïtés de l'âge d'or chez Platon, voir Vidal-Naquet, *Le chasseur noir. Formes de pensée et formes de société dans le monde grec*, 361–380. Dans le récit du *Politique*, constate-t-il, « [l]e paradis de l'âge d'or est, en définitive, un paradis animal » (373).

le discours généalogique est toujours aussi un discours géographique et politique, ou mieux « chôrologique »[6].

Prononcer un discours sur la meilleure cité en train d'exécuter des mouvements de guerre, comme le souhaite Socrate, signifie donc tenir compte de deux choses qui semblent corrélées : la naissance d'un *genos* humain (distinct des *genē* des dieux et des animaux) et la *chōra* de la cité, c'est-à-dire sa « terre civique » ou son « territoire » (délimité par rapport aux *chōrai* des cités voisines).

1.3   La réponse de Critias au vœu de Socrate

Regardons maintenant comment Critias s'y prend dans le prologue du *Timée-Critias* pour répondre à Socrate. A peine celui-ci a-t-il exprimé son vœu d'entendre un discours montrant la meilleure cité en guerre que Critias se saisit de la parole pour lui présenter, au nom des trois hôtes du jour, « un discours certes très étrange, et pourtant tout à fait vrai » (λόγου μάλα μὲν ἀτόπου, παντάπασί γε μὴν ἀληθοῦς, 20d7–8). Ce discours, rapporté d'Egypte par Solon, raconte la guerre entre l'ancienne Athènes et l'Atlantide, et, à condition que l'on identifie la meilleure cité avec l'ancienne Athènes, répondrait parfaitement aux attentes de Socrate. C'est du moins ce dont Critias essaie de convaincre Socrate dans le prologue. Son propos présente la structure suivante :

1. La transmission du discours « absolument vrai » sur la guerre athéno-atlante à l'intérieur du *genos* de Critias le jeune (20d7–21d8)
2. Le récit de Critias l'ancien (21e1–25d6) racontant le voyage de Solon en Egypte et résumant le discours d'un très vieux prêtre égyptien (22b4–25d6). Ce dernier peut être divisé en trois parties :
    a) La « vraie » généalogie de la cité d'Athènes (22b4–23d1)
    b) La production du *genos* des anciens Athéniens dans la *chōra* attique et son organisation politique (23d4–24d6)
    c) La *chōra* immense des Atlantes dans « la vraie mer » et la guerre qu'ils ont menée contre les anciens Athéniens, suivie de leur défaite et de leur disparition (24d6–25d6)

---

6   Graf, « Zwischen Autochthonie und Immigration : Die Herkunft von Völkern in der Alten Welt », 71, remarque à propos du récit généalogique des descendants de Pyrrha et de Deucalion, transmis dans le *Catalogue des femmes* : « Die Analyse zeigt, was dieser Mythos von den Ahnen der griechischen Stämme leistet. Er ist ein Mittel, die Geographie des griechischen Festlandes zu denken. In einer Epoche, in der es keine Karten gibt und keine schriftlichen Schematismen, mit denen man etwas derart Kompliziertes wie die vielen Völker Griechenlands ordnen kann, zeichnet er eine völkergeographische Karte ». De même Fowler, « Genealogical Thinking, Hesiod's *Catalogue*, and the Creation of the Hellenes », 1 : « For those within the system a genealogy is a map. They can read its signs. To the names are attached stories, thousands of them ; collectively they gave the listeners their sense of history and their place in the world ».

3. La remémoration de l'ancien discours par Critias le jeune (25d7–26c5) et sa proposition de transposer la meilleure cité de Socrate « dans la réalité » en l'identifiant avec l'ancienne Athènes (26c5–26e1)

On peut constater que les généalogies et les descriptions géographiques et territoriales liées aux termes grecs de *genos* et de *chōra* jouent un rôle important tout au long du propos de Critias. La nouveauté ici, par rapport au passage du livre II de la *République*, c'est le problème de la « vérité » ou de la « réalité » (ἀλήθεια), qui surgit là seulement au livre III en rapport avec le « noble mensonge » racontant la naissance, de la *chōra*, d'un corps de guerriers parfaits (414b8–415d2).

Dans ce qui suit, j'examinerai d'abord le rôle des généalogies et des descriptions « chôrologiques » et leur rapport avec la guerre dans le discours du prêtre égyptien (22b4–25d6). J'essaierai ensuite de montrer en quoi ce discours prépare le deuxième discours de Timée (48a7–68d7), consacré à la genèse de corpuscules perceptibles qui se déroule dans la *chōra*, cette troisième espèce d'être que le philosophe de Locres est contraint d'introduire (cf. 48e2–49a6, 52a8–52d4). Cela me permettra de comparer, dans une troisième partie, les combats guerriers de ces corpuscules à ceux entre l'ancienne Athènes et l'Atlantide. Pour finir, j'aimerais soulever la question de la vérité en rapport avec les discours généalogiques et « chôrologiques » du prêtre égyptien et de Timée.

2   Généalogies et « chôrologie » dans le discours du prêtre égyptien

Afin d'inciter les prêtres de Saïs à parler de l'origine de leur cité (περὶ τῶν ἀρχαίων, 22a4–5), l'Athénien Solon tient ce que l'on pourrait appeler un discours « archéo-mytho-généalogique » : il cherche à remonter jusqu'aux premiers ancêtres panhelléniques et même humains de sa propre cité, Deucalion et Pyrrha, puis, avant le déluge, Niobé et Phorôneus, que l'on appelle le premier homme, et il tente de calculer leurs années de vie (22a4–b3). Le prêtre lui répond à son tour par un discours généalogique, qui a pour but de lui révéler la « véritable » origine (ἀρχή) de sa cité, Athènes. Il se moque gentiment du discours de Solon, en l'assimilant à des histoires pour enfants (παίδων βραχύ τι διαφέρει μύθων, 23b5) que se raconte un peuple à peine alphabétisé, pour enchérir aussitôt, en repoussant la « véritable » origine des Athéniens bien plus haut dans le temps, avant d'autres déluges qui auraient précédé celui de Deucalion, le seul connu des Grecs. Plus loin, il la situe exactement 9000 ans auparavant (cf. 23e4–5). C'est à cette époque qu'aurait vécu en Attique même, non encore ravagée par les déluges, sinon le premier genre humain, en tout cas le plus beau et le meilleur qui ait jamais vu le jour :

Τὰ γοῦν νυνδὴ γενεαλογηθέντα, ὦ Σόλων, περὶ τῶν παρ' ὑμῖν ἃ διῆλθες, παίδων βραχύ τι διαφέρει μύθων, οἳ πρῶτον μὲν ἕνα γῆς κατακλυσμὸν μέμνησθε πολλῶν ἔμπροσθεν γεγονότων, ἔτι δὲ τὸ κάλλιστον καὶ ἄριστον γένος ἐπ' ἀνθρώπους ἐν τῇ χώρᾳ παρ' ὑμῖν οὐκ ἴστε γεγονός, ἐξ ὧν σύ τε καὶ πᾶσα ἡ πόλις ἔστιν τὰ νῦν ὑμῶν, περιλειφθέντος ποτὲ σπέρματος βραχέος, ἀλλ' ὑμᾶς λέληθεν διὰ τὸ τοὺς περιγενομένους ἐπὶ πολλὰς γενεὰς γράμμασιν τελευτᾶν ἀφώνους (23b3–c3).

En tout cas, les généalogies concernant les gens de chez vous que tu viens, Solon, de passer en revue, diffèrent bien peu des récits des enfants. Car d'abord, vous ne gardez le souvenir que d'une seule submersion de la terre, alors qu'il y en a eu beaucoup auparavant. En outre, le plus beau et le meilleur genre (*genos*) du temps des hommes, vous ignorez qu'il est né chez vous, dans votre territoire (*chōra*) ; c'est d'eux que vous descendez, toi et l'ensemble de la cité qui est aujourd'hui la vôtre, parce que jadis un peu de semence s'en est conservée. Mais vous en avez perdu le souvenir parce que, pendant de nombreuses générations, les survivants sont morts sans avoir fait entendre leur voix à travers des écrits.

Notons que l'identification des citoyens de la meilleure cité de Socrate avec ce *genos* humain exceptionnel, que Critias le jeune propose tout à la fin (26c7–26d5), ne les prive pas de leur nature paradigmatique, mais les rend humains : d'êtres vivants (ζῷα) – beaux mais immobiles, pour reprendre les mots de Socrate – les citoyens de la meilleure cité deviendront « le plus beau et le meilleur *genos* du temps des hommes » (τὸ κάλλιστον καὶ ἄριστον γένος ἐπ' ἀνθρώπους, 23b7).

Dans la deuxième partie de son discours, le vieux prêtre explique que ce genre humain excellent est le produit commun de trois divinités : Gê, Héphaïstos et surtout Athéna (23d6–e2). Celle-ci a recueilli de Gê et d'Héphaïstos le rejeton (τὶ σπέρμα, 23e1) de la future cité d'Athènes et l'a nourri (ἔθρεψεν, 23d7) et éduqué (ἐπαίδευσεν, 23d7). En réalité, le prêtre ne révèle ici à Solon (l'Athénien !) rien d'autre que le récit sacré (ἱερὸς λόγος) du festival des Panathénées, en marge duquel Socrate rencontre Timée, Critias et Hermocrate (cf. 21a2–3 et 26e3–4). Ce récit raconte la naissance d'Erichthonios (ou d'Erechthée), l'enfant de Gê, fécondée par Héphaïstos épris d'Athéna, et son éducation par la déesse tutélaire de la cité[7].

---

[7] La version traditionnelle de ce récit se retrouve entre autres dans Hom. *Il.* II, 546–551 ; Eur. *Ion* 266–274 et Ps.-Apollod. III, 14, 6. Voir à ce propos aussi Parker, « Myths of Early Athens », surtout 193–197, et Bonnard, *Le Complexe de Zeus. Représentations de la paternité en Grèce ancienne*, 81–88 (avec de nombreuses indications bibliographiques).

L'éducation qu'Athéna a donnée à ce nouvel être est sa constitution politique (πολιτεία)[8]. Le prêtre poursuit en effet en décrivant l'organisation politique de l'ancienne Athènes au moyen de lois (νόμους, 23e5 et 24a2) qu'il induit à partir de celles encore en vigueur à Saïs, la cité-sœur de l'ancienne Athènes. Ces lois prescrivent une séparation stricte des différents groupes socio-politiques : 1) le *genos* des prêtres, 2) le *genos* des artisans, des bergers, des chasseurs et des paysans, et enfin 3) le *genos* des combattants hoplitiques (24a4–24b7). Cette division en trois *genē* fonctionnels rappelle, bien sûr, celle de la meilleure cité de Socrate, même si celle-ci ne connaît pas de *genos* de prêtres spécialisés en astronomie (ou bien en astrologie ?), mantique et médecine (24b7–c3)[9]. Le prêtre clôt ainsi sa description de l'organisation politique de l'ancienne Athènes :

> Ταύτην οὖν δὴ τότε σύμπασαν τὴν διακόσμησιν καὶ σύνταξιν ἡ θεὸς προτέρους ὑμᾶς [= τοὺς Ἀθηναίους] διακοσμήσασα κατῴκισεν ἐκλεξαμένη τὸν τόπον ἐν ᾧ γεγένησθε, τὴν εὐκρασίαν τῶν ὡρῶν ἐν αὐτῷ κατιδοῦσα, ὅτι φρονιμωτάτους ἄνδρας οἴσοι· ἅτε οὖν φιλοπόλεμός τε καὶ φιλόσοφος ἡ θεὸς οὖσα τὸν προσφερεστάτους αὐτῇ μέλλοντα οἴσειν τόπον ἄνδρας, τοῦτον ἐκλεξαμένη πρῶτον κατῴκισεν (24c4–d3)[10].

> C'est donc alors, après vous [= les Athéniens] avoir entièrement divisés et organisés les premiers, que la déesse a choisi et peuplé la région (*topos*) où vous êtes nés, apercevant que là l'heureux mélange des saisons allait produire les hommes les plus raisonnables. Etant donné que la déesse aime la guerre et le savoir, c'est la région (*topos*) qui devait produire des hommes lui ressemblant le plus qu'elle a choisie et peuplée d'abord.

---

8   Cf. Plat. *Ménex.* 238c1 : πολιτεία γὰρ τροφὴ ἀνθρώπων ἐστίν, « car la constitution politique nourrit les êtres humains ».

9   Dans son résumé du discours de la veille, Socrate ne mentionne explicitement que deux *genē* : celui des paysans et des autres arts (τέχναι) et celui des défenseurs de la cité (17c6-8) ; plus loin, il nomme les commandants et commandantes de la cité (τοὺς ἄρχοντας καὶ τὰς ἀρχούσας, 18d8-9), mais ne sait s'ils forment ou non un *genos* séparé de celui des défenseurs.

10 Vu le contexte, διακόσμησις et διακοσμέω doivent se référer à la « division » des Saïtiques et des anciens Athéniens en γένη. Quant à κατῴκισεν en 24c5, je pense qu'il se construit (comme en 24d3) avec τὸν τόπον (24c6) comme objet direct et a le sens de « peupler/coloniser la région ». C'est pourquoi et pour mieux mettre en valeur la structure annulaire (κατῴκισεν ἐκλεξαμένη τὸν τόπον – τόπον[...]τοῦτον ἐκλεξαμένη[...]κατῴκισεν), j'ai supprimé, après κατῴκισεν, la virgule qui se trouve dans l'édition d'Oxford de John Burnet (1902). Pour les différents sens du verbe κατοικίζω, cf. Casevitz, *Le vocabulaire de la colonisation en grec ancien. Etude lexicologique : les familles de* κτίζω *et de* οἰκέω – οἰκίζω, 168–173.

Si le passage 23d6–e2 rappelle le récit sacré des Panathénées, ces lignes-ci évoquent plutôt la version démocratique des rhéteurs, qui vantaient la naissance de l'ensemble des citoyens-soldats athéniens de la *chōra* même de la cité, qui les aurait nourris et élevés comme une mère et où ils habiteraient depuis toujours en autochtones[11]. Cela ressort plus clairement du passage parallèle du *Critias* :

[…] Ἥφαιστος δὲ κοινὴν καὶ Ἀθηνᾶ φύσιν ἔχοντες, ἅμα μὲν ἀδελφὴν ἐκ ταὐτοῦ πατρός, ἅμα δὲ φιλοσοφίᾳ φιλοτεχνίᾳ τε ἐπὶ τὰ αὐτὰ ἐλθόντες, οὕτω μίαν ἄμφω λῆξιν τήνδε τὴν χώραν εἰλήχατον ὡς οἰκείαν καὶ πρόσφορον ἀρετῇ καὶ φρονήσει πεφυκυῖαν, ἄνδρας δὲ ἀγαθοὺς ἐμποιήσαντες αὐτόχθονας ἐπὶ νοῦν ἔθεσαν τὴν τῆς πολιτείας τάξιν (109c6–d2).

[…] Héphaïstos et Athéna, qui ont un naturel commun, à la fois parce qu'ils sont frère et sœur, issus d'un même père, et parce que l'amour pour le savoir et pour l'art les a orientés dans la même direction, reçurent tous deux en partage pour cette raison un seul lot, ce territoire-ci (*chōra*), puisqu'il était naturellement approprié et favorable à l'excellence et à la raison, et après y avoir produit comme autochtones des hommes bons, ils leur ont mis dans l'esprit l'ordre constitutionnel.

Les deux passages montrent que la beauté et l'excellence guerrière et philosophique du *genos* athénien ont deux causes. La première est naturelle : la *physis* du *topos*, la « région »[12], et de la *chōra*, le « territoire »[13], où le *genos* athénien a grandi. Comme d'autres dans le *Critias* (111e1–5, 112e2–6), ces deux

---

11 Cf. Lys. 2 (*Épit.*), 17 ; Isocr. 4 (*Panég.*), 24–25 et 12 (*Panath.*), 124–125 ; Dém. 60 (*Épit.*), 5 et le pastiche dans Plat. *Ménex.* 237b2–c3 et 237e2–238a5. Voir aussi le noble mensonge dans la *République* (414b8–415d2), variante platonicienne de cette idéologie athénienne. Pour les deux versions (aristocratique et démocratique) du récit, cf. Loraux, *Les enfants d'Athéna. Idées athéniennes sur la citoyenneté et la division des sexes*, 35–73. Pour les aspects nourriciers et maternels de la terre civique (χώρα, mais aussi γῆ et χθών) voir Georgoudi, « Gaia/Gê. Entre mythe, culte et idéologie ».
12 Pradeau, « Être quelque part, occuper une place. ΤΟΠΟΣ et ΧΩΡΑ dans le *Timée* », 376 : « Τόπος signifie une région géographique, qualifiée par un trait caractéristique (morphologique ou climatique). Par exemple, une région élevée, ou bien une région du Nord, ou encore un lieu tempéré ».
13 Ibid. 376–377 : « Χώρα signifie le territoire ou la région *de la* cité, d'un peuple. C'est un terme qui désigne une réalité géographique, mais précisée et circonscrite par son appartenance à une unité politique. A la différence de τόπος, χώρα est toujours nommée d'après un sujet (c'est le territoire de la ville d'Athènes, ou le territoire sur lequel vivent les Lydiens) » (italiques de l'auteur).

passages suggèrent en effet qu'il existe une relation étroite entre d'une part le *topos* et la *chōra* et d'autre part l'excellence physique et psychique d'un *genos* humain, c'est-à-dire sa beauté et sa raison (*phronēsis*) qui se manifestent dans son amour de la guerre et du savoir. Plus le climat est équilibré et la terre fertile, mieux les hommes « poussent ». A l'inverse, si le climat change et que le territoire perd de sa fertilité, les hommes deviennent moins beaux et moins raisonnables. Ainsi, au cours des neuf millénaires écoulés depuis l'ancienne Athènes, de nombreux déluges ont-ils provoqué l'érosion de la *chōra* attique, qui ressemble désormais au corps squelettique d'un malade (cf. *Critias* 111a6–b7), ce qui en dit long sur l'état physique et psychique de la cité au moment où Critias le jeune parle, vraisemblablement au début de la guerre du Péloponnèse (entre 430 et 425)[14]. De l'ancienne *chōra* plus étendue et plus riche, il ne reste plus que des indices, que Critias énumère patiemment dans le dialogue qui porte son nom (110d4–112d3)[15].

La deuxième cause de la beauté et de l'excellence du *genos* athénien est artificielle : la division en groupes fonctionnels (γένη) et l'organisation politique (τὴν διακόσμησιν καὶ σύνταξιν, 24c4) de ce *genos* nouveau-né par sa déesse tutélaire, Athéna, qui lui a donné des lois (νόμοι). Dans le passage du *Critias*, il est dit qu'Héphaïstos et Athéna ont introduit dans l'esprit des autochtones athéniens l'ordre constitutionnel (ἐπὶ νοῦν ἔθεσαν τὴν τῆς πολιτείας τάξιν, 109d2). C'est cette législation qui fait de l'ancienne Athènes « à tout point de vue de loin la mieux gouvernée » (κατὰ πάντα εὐνομωτάτη διαφερόντως, 23c6). C'est parce qu'elle se distinguait par sa beauté et sa raison naturelles d'une part, par sa perfection constitutionnelle d'autre part, qu'elle a su l'emporter dans la guerre contre l'envahisseur atlante.

3 Généalogie et « chôrologie » dans le deuxième discours de Timée

Selon le « menu » du festin de paroles que Critias propose à Socrate en 27a2–b6, Timée va prononcer un discours qui commence par la genèse du cosmos et s'achève avec la naissance des hommes (ἀρχόμενον ἀπὸ τῆς τοῦ κόσμου γενέσεως,

---

14 Date dramatique selon Brisson, *Platon. Timée. Critias*, 72 et 332.

15 Que les conditions géographiques et climatiques d'un pays déterminent la constitution physique et psychique de ses habitants est une thèse défendue dans le traité hippocratique *Des Airs, des Eaux et des Lieux*, voir en particulier les chap. 12–13 ; 15–16 (§ 1–2) ; 23 (pour l'influence du climat) et 24 (pour celle de la nature du sol) avec la notice de Jouanna, *Hippocrate*, tome II, 2ᵉ partie : *Airs, Eaux, Lieux*, 60-64. Cf. aussi Hérodote II 77, 3 et IX 122, 3 ; Platon *Lois* V 747d–e ; Pradeau, *Le Monde de la politique. Sur le récit atlante de Platon*, Timée (17–27) *et* Critias, 248–256.

τελευτᾶν δὲ εἰς ἀνθρώπων φύσιν, 27a5–6), afin de fournir à Critias les ressources humaines pour peupler l'ancienne Athènes. Il est donc présenté comme un discours généalogique et composé ainsi :
1. Le premier discours (27c1–47e2) qui expose l'œuvre de l'intellect (*nous*) : cosmogonie, théogonie et anthropogonie (première partie)
2. Le deuxième discours qui expose ce qui relève de l'*anankē*, la « contrainte » (48a7–68d7) :
    a) La *chōra* précosmique remplie d'empreintes sans proportion ni mesure (48e7–53a8)
    b) La genèse des quatre *genē* de corpuscules perceptibles et de leurs espèces dans et à partir de la *chōra* (53b1–68d7)
3. Le troisième discours qui est une combinaison des deux autres (69a6–106b7 dans le *Critias*) : anthropogonie (deuxième partie) et thériogonie

La genèse du genre humain s'inscrit dans le projet général du démiurge de fabriquer un monde complet, représentant les idées comprises dans l'idée générique qu'est le vivant intelligible (39e3–40a2). Ces idées sont au nombre de quatre correspondant à autant d'espèces (γένη ou εἴδη) d'êtres vivants, destinés à peupler respectivement le ciel (les dieux), les airs (les oiseaux), les eaux (les poissons et autres animaux aquatiques) et la terre (les animaux pédestres et terrestres). Le vivant intelligible vers lequel l'artisan divin dirige son regard et dont il se sert comme modèle est décrit comme « le plus beau des [êtres vivants] intelligibles et à tout point de vue parfait » (τῷ τῶν νοουμένων [ζῴων] καλλίστῳ καὶ κατὰ πάντα τελέῳ, 30d1–2). De par sa beauté et sa perfection mais aussi de par son immobilité en tant qu'idée stable et inébranlable, ce vivant intelligible rappelle les beaux êtres vivants (*zōa kala*) immobiles auxquels Socrate a comparé la meilleure cité, exposée la veille en paroles. En tant qu'unité comprenant des *genē* ou *eidē* d'êtres vivants différents, il évoque la cité elle-même qui est divisée en *genē* fonctionnels. De fait, l'artisan divin se trouve face à une tâche similaire à celle que Socrate a confiée à ses trois interlocuteurs : comment mettre en mouvement cet être vivant ? Comment passer d'un vivant immobile à un vivant mobile ? Plus particulièrement, comment produire un genre humain qui soit capable de se mouvoir et, le cas échéant, de défendre sa cité par la guerre ?

Comme pour la meilleure cité, la mise en mouvement de ce vivant intelligible comporte un aspect généalogique et un autre, « chôrologique ». Dans le premier discours de Timée (27c1–47e2), qui explique l'œuvre de l'intellect (νοῦς) divin en faisant abstraction de la contrainte (ἀνάγκη) et de la troisième espèce d'être qu'est la *chōra*, l'aspect généalogique est prépondérant. Mais à partir du deuxième discours (48a7ss.), lorsque Timée est forcé de tenir compte en outre des effets de la contrainte dans la genèse du cosmos, les deux aspects sont présents conjointement. C'est ce deuxième discours, où entre en jeu la *chōra* comme nouvelle espèce ontologique, qui m'intéresse ici, car il présente certains parallèles avec le discours du prêtre égyptien. Comme le discours du prêtre, il combine, en effet, les deux aspects : généalogique, car Timée essaie d'expliquer la genèse de corpuscules perceptibles, et « chôrologique », dans la mesure où cette genèse se fait dans un « territoire », qui sert à la fois de réceptacle et de nourrice, la *chōra*.

Avant la fabrication du cosmos par le démiurge, le feu, l'air, l'eau et la terre étaient « sans proportion ni mesure » (ἀλόγως καὶ ἀμέτρως, 53a8) dans la *chōra* précosmique. Puis, le dieu s'est mis à les organiser :

> Ὅτε δ' ἐπεχειρεῖτο κοσμεῖσθαι τὸ πᾶν, πῦρ πρῶτον καὶ ὕδωρ καὶ γῆν καὶ ἀέρα, ἴχνη μὲν ἔχοντα αὑτῶν ἄττα, παντάπασί γε μὴν διακείμενα ὥσπερ εἰκὸς ἔχειν ἅπαν ὅταν ἀπῇ τινος θεός, οὕτω δὴ τότε πεφυκότα ταῦτα πρῶτον διεσχηματίσατο εἴδεσί τε καὶ ἀριθμοῖς (53b1–5).

> Lorsque l'univers commençait à être ordonné, d'abord le feu, l'eau, la terre et l'air présentaient certes quelques empreintes d'eux-mêmes mais se trouvaient entièrement dans l'état où se trouve vraisemblablement tout lorsqu'un dieu en est absent ; ce qui était alors par nature ainsi, il [= le dieu] l'a donc d'abord 'configuré' à l'aide de formes et de nombres.

Ces lignes montrent qu'il faut distinguer deux phases dans la genèse (γένεσις) du feu, de l'air, de l'eau et de la terre : d'abord, leur genèse, dans la *chōra* précosmique, sous forme d'empreintes ou de traces d'eux-mêmes (ἴχνη ἔχοντα αὑτῶν ἄττα, 53b2), c'est-à-dire de la nature (φύσις) et des propriétés (πάθη) qu'ils auront plus tard dans le cosmos et qui les rendront perceptibles pour l'homme (devenir traité dans le deuxième proème, en particulier 52d4–53a7). Puis, leur genèse à proprement parler, résultat de leur « mise en ordre » (διάταξιν, 53b8) par le dieu qui les a « configurés » (διεσχηματίσατο, 53b4) en leur attribuant les figures géométriques (σχήματα) que sont les quatre polyèdres (thème du deuxième discours, en particulier 53c4–56c7).

Comme la genèse de l'ancienne Athènes, celle du feu, de l'air, de l'eau et de la terre dans leur état cosmique a donc deux causes : l'une naturelle, l'autre artificielle. De même qu'Athéna a recueilli le rejeton né de Gê et d'Héphaïstos dans la future *chōra* attique, de même le démiurge a travaillé avec ce qui était né spontanément et naturellement dans la *chōra* précosmique, à savoir les empreintes du feu, de l'air, de l'eau et de la terre. Ensuite, il a formé ces empreintes au moyen de belles figures géométriques et ainsi engendré les quatre principaux *genē* de corps primaires tels que nous les percevons maintenant dans le cosmos, le feu, l'air, l'eau et la terre. De manière comparable, la déesse a formé le rejeton né de Gê et d'Héphaïstos en lui donnant un excellent ordre constitutionnel et a ainsi produit le meilleur et le plus beau *genos* humain qui ait jamais vu le jour.

Comme la genèse du *genos* des Athéniens, celle des quatre *genē* de corpuscules est racontée sans référence aucune à un modèle intelligible. En effet, l'existence du feu, de l'air, de l'eau et de la terre intelligibles semble être requise pour rendre compte de l'apparition des empreintes dans la *chōra* précosmique (cf. 51b6–52d4), mais non pour expliquer leur « configuration » au moyen des polyèdres. Ceux-ci sont désignés comme des éléments et des semences (cf. στοιχεῖον καὶ σπέρμα à propos de la pyramide, 56b5), de sorte que la mise en forme des empreintes s'apparente à des semailles ou à un engendrement plutôt qu'à la production d'un objet artisanal, qui se fait d'après une paradigme intelligible. Il semble en effet que les quatre *genē* de corpuscules soient engendrés par le dieu de manière artificielle, et non artisanale, au moyen de ces semences élémentaires dans la matrice-réceptacle et terre-mère qu'est la *chōra* précosmique. De fait, dans le deuxième discours on ne trouve ni le terme *dēmiourgos* désignant le dieu comme artisan, ni le verbe correspondant[16].

Le rapprochement de la genèse des corpuscules dans la *chōra* précosmique avec celle de la cité d'Athènes se justifie aussi parce que les noms par lesquels Timée tente de saisir la troisième espèce d'être – « nourrice » (τιθήνη, 49a6 et 52d4–5 ; τροφὸν καὶ τιθήνην, 88d6), « mère » (μήτηρ, 50d3 et 51a4–5) et « terre civique » (χώρα, 52a8 et 52d3), même celui de « réceptacle » (ὑποδοχή, 49a6 et 51a5)[17] – appartiennent tous au champ lexical de l'imaginaire de l'autochtonie athénienne auquel faisaient précisément allusion les deux passages cités plus haut (pp. 8–9).

4 Guerre des corpuscules, guerre des cités

A l'instar du *genos* des Athéniens, les quatre *genē* de corps primaires sont également destinés à combattre. Chaque espèce de corpuscules occupe en effet par

---

16   En 59a5, *dēmiourgos* désigne le feu comme « artisan produisant de l'hétérogénéité » dans l'eau.

17   Le terme *hypodochē* peut qualifier la matrice ; cf. Aristote, *Gén. des anim.* 4, 764b32–33. Voir aussi le participe *hypodexamenē* désignant la *chōra*-mère dans le *Ménexène* de Platon (237c2–3).

nature une *chōra*[18] et un *topos*[19] propres dans le cosmos en raison de l'action « sismique » de la nourrice du devenir qui les sépare selon leur similitude (52d4–53a7 et 57b7–c6). Toutefois, la rotation de l'univers presse les plus petits dans les interstices laissés par les plus grands (58a2–b5). Si un corpuscule pénètre dans la *chōra* d'un autre *genos* de corpuscules, soit il dissout les corpuscules qu'il heurte, soit il est lui-même dissous dans ses triangles constitutifs. A l'exception des triangles de terre, ces triangles peuvent se recomposer en un ou plusieurs corpuscules d'un autre genre[20]. Ces mouvements et transformations des corpuscules sont décrits dans le passage 56c8–57b7 avec un lexique guerrier : Timée emploie les verbes « cerner » (περιλαμβάνω, cf. περιλαμβανόμενον, 56e3 ; περιλαμβανόμενα, 57a7–b1), « lutter » (μάχομαι, cf. μαχόμενον, 56e4 ; μάχηται, 57a6 et 57b4), « l'emporter » (κρατέω, cf. κρατηθέντος, 56e6 ; κρατοῦντος, 57b2), « vaincre » (νικάω, cf. νικηθέν, 56e4 ; νικηθέντα, 57b6). L'occurrence de tels verbes permet de laisser aux notions de *topos* et de *chōra*, même dans ce contexte physique, leur signification géographique et politique courante et de les traduire par « région » et « territoire » respectivement, plutôt que par « lieu » et « place » comme l'a proposé Jean-François Pradeau[21].

Tant que le cosmos accomplira sa révolution sur lui-même, les luttes entre les corpuscules ne cesseront pas en raison de la contrainte qui dicte leurs mouvements et leurs transformations. La guerre entre les corpuscules a été intégrée comme un élément constitutif du cosmos, tout comme les guerres permanentes – déclarées ou non – entre les cités font partie du monde grec[22]. Au contraire, la guerre entre l'Atlantide et l'ancienne Athènes s'est terminée par la victoire définitive de cette dernière (25b5–c6), suivie de la disparition des deux adversaires : le corps des combattants athéniens dans la terre d'où ils sont issus, et l'île de l'Atlantide et leurs habitants dans la mer, rendant ainsi la mer extérieure inaccessible (25c6–d6). A l'époque de Solon ou de Critias le jeune, la *chōra* atlante n'existe plus et la *chōra* athénienne, on l'a déjà noté, a été érodée par de nombreuses pluies torrentielles.

---

18   Cf. χώραν ταῦτα ἄλλα ἄλλην ἴσχειν, 53a6–7 ; cf. κατὰ γένη διαχωρισθέντα ἕκαστα, 58a3 ; εἰς τὴν αὑτοῦ χώραν, 79d5–6.

19   Cf. κατὰ τόπον ἴδιον, 57c3 ; πρὸς τοὺς ἑαυτῶν τόπους, 58b8 ; εἰς τὸν ἑαυτοῦ τόπον, 60c1.

20   Pour les détails, voir Brisson, *Platon. Timée. Critias*, 301.

21   Pradeau, *Le Monde de la politique*, 291, distingue trois usages (physique, géographique et figuré) de *topos* et de *chōra* dans les dialogues platoniciens ; selon leur usage physique « *topos* signifie le *lieu*, l'endroit où se trouve quelque chose, et *chōra* la *place* qu'occupe une chose, ou qu'elle abandonne (elle 'fait place') en se déplaçant » (italiques de l'auteur). Cf. aussi Pradeau, « Être quelque part, occuper une place. ΤΟΠΟΣ et ΧΩΡΑ dans le *Timée* », 380 et 388ss. Pour l'usage géographique de ces deux termes, voir ci-dessus les notes 12 et 13.

22   Cf. Platon, *Lois* I 625e5–626a5 (où parle le Crétois Clinias).

Si l'on compare la deuxième et troisième partie du récit de Critias l'ancien dans le prologue (23d4–25d6) au deuxième discours de Timée (48a7–68d7), on peut remarquer que Critias évoque une évolution du monde inverse de celle de Timée. Cela se reflète dans l'ordre dont chaque phase est traitée dans le discours (cf. les plans des discours donnés ci-dessus p. 6–7 et 12) : Timée décrit d'abord la *chōra* précosmique, cette troisième espèce d'être difficile et obscure, qu'il est forcé d'introduire pour expliquer la perception sensorielle et dont il essaie d'éclairer la puissance naturelle (δύναμιν καὶ φύσιν, 49a4–5). Ensuite seulement, il peut expliquer comment y naissent, grâce à l'œuvre ordonnatrice du démiurge, à partir des empreintes désordonnées, les quatre *genē* de corpuscules (et leurs nombreuses espèces) que nous percevons maintenant dans le cosmos. Au contraire, Critias commence par la naissance et l'organisation politique du *genos* des anciens Athéniens. Elles ont eu lieu dans un temps antédiluvien, où la *chōra* attique était encore intacte et belle (cf. *Critias* 110d4–111e5) et l'espace marin, situé au-delà des colonnes d'Hercule, toujours ouvert à la navigation. Ce n'est que tout à la fin de son récit que fait irruption, à la fois dans son discours et dans le monde civilisé et ordonné de l'*oikoumenē* la puissance royale (δύναμις βασιλέων, 25a6) de l'Atlantide. Au moment où la cité insulaire commence la guerre, son immense territoire a subi de nombreuses transformations et fait plutôt penser à la *chōra* précosmique où « tout cela se trouvait sans proportion ni mesure » (πάντα ταῦτ' εἶχεν ἀλόγως καὶ ἀμέτρως, 53a8). Neuf millénaires plus tard, la terre civique des Athéniens se retrouve dans le même état. Quand Critias parle, elle ne présente plus que des restes de sa fertilité et de sa splendeur passées. Elle aussi ressemble désormais à la *chōra* précosmique, « lorsqu'un dieu en est absent » (53b3–4).

5   Le statut de vérité de l'ancien discours de Critias le jeune

Pour répondre au vœu de Socrate et mettre la meilleure cité en mouvement sinon dans les faits, du moins dans un discours, la notion d'*alētheia*, « vérité » et « réalité », joue un rôle aussi important que celles de *genos* et de *chōra*. Il se pourrait bien qu'il y ait un rapport entre la vérité du discours et ses aspects généalogiques et « chôrologiques ».

La vérité du « discours certes très étrange et pourtant tout à fait vrai » (λόγου μάλα μὲν ἀτόπου, παντάπασί γε μὴν ἀληθοῦς, 20d7–8) proposé par Critias est étroitement liée à son parcours dans le temps généalogique et dans l'espace géographique et politique. D'une part, Critias le jeune tient ce discours de son grand-père homonyme, Critias l'ancien, qui l'avait lui-même entendu de Solon, un parent et ami de Drôpidès, son arrière-grand-père (20d7–21a3).

La transmission continue de ce *logos* d'une génération à l'autre au sein de la famille (γένος) de Critias le jeune[23] semble, du moins pour ce dernier, une garantie de sa vérité. Ajoutons que les citoyens de Saïs, située dans le delta du Nil, où Solon a appris ce récit, sont eux-mêmes en quelque sorte apparentés aux anciens Athéniens, car leur cité a été fondée par la déesse Athéna sous le nom de Neïth (21e1–7, cf. 23d4–e2). D'autre part, ce discours « parfaitement vrai » provient d'Egypte, terre (χώρα) qui n'est jamais ravagée par les pluies diluviennes et qui est protégée des incendies par les crues du Nil (22d5–6 et e2–4). C'est un pays où rien n'est jamais détruit et tout reste intact, un pays de lettrés où rien ne s'oublie et tout se conserve, un pays de vieillards où les gens ne rajeunissent jamais dans leur âme. C'est là que sont documentés et archivés depuis des lustres tous les événements et tous les savoirs extraordinaires du monde (22e4–23a5), si bien que le discours d'un très vieux prêtre qui vit dans un tel territoire ne saurait être « un récit d'enfants » (παίδων μῦθος), mais seulement un « discours vrai » (λόγος ἀληθής). Le long récit de l'origine généalogique et géographique de ce *logos* est donc essentiel pour la véracité que Critias cherche à lui conférer.

Voyons maintenant brièvement quels rôles jouent les notions de *chōra* et de *genos* pour la transposition (μεταφορά) de la meilleure cité dans la réalité (ἐπὶ τἀληθές, 26d1). Après avoir résumé le contenu du discours du prêtre égyptien, Critias propose à Socrate de transposer la meilleure cité, élaborée en paroles, dans la réalité (μετενεγκόντες ἐπὶ τἀληθές, 26c8–d1), ce qui permettrait de répondre parfaitement à son vœu :

> Τοὺς δὲ πολίτας καὶ τὴν πόλιν ἣν χθὲς ἡμῖν ὡς ἐν μύθῳ διῄεισθα σύ, νῦν μετενεγκόντες ἐπὶ τἀληθὲς δεῦρο θήσομεν ὡς ἐκείνην τήνδε οὖσαν, καὶ τοὺς πολίτας οὓς διενοοῦ φήσομεν ἐκείνους τοὺς ἀληθινοὺς εἶναι προγόνους ἡμῶν, οὓς ἔλεγεν ὁ ἱερεύς. πάντως ἁρμόσουσι καὶ οὐκ ἀπᾳσόμεθα λέγοντες αὐτοὺς εἶναι τοὺς ἐν τῷ τότε ὄντας χρόνῳ (26c7–d5).

> Les citoyens et la cité que, toi, tu nous décrivais hier comme dans un récit (ὡς ἐν μύθῳ), en les transposant maintenant ici dans le réel (ἐπὶ τἀληθές), nous allons faire comme si celle-là était celle-ci, et les citoyens que tu as imaginés, nous prétendrons que ce sont nos vrais ancêtres, ceux dont parlait le prêtre. Ils concorderont entièrement et nous ne détonnerons pas en disant qu'ils sont ceux qui existaient en ce temps-là.

---

23   Platon lui-même appartenait à cette famille : sa mère, Périctionè, était la fille de Glaucon, un oncle de Critias le tyran, que j'identifie avec Critias le jeune ; cf. Brisson, *Platon. Timée. Critias*, 328.

Critias invite Socrate à considérer « cette cité-là » (ἐκείνην, 26d1) – la meilleure cité – comme identique avec « cette cité-ci » (τήνδε, 26d1) – l'Athènes actuelle –, et d'identifier les citoyens conçus par Socrate (τοὺς πολίτας οὓς διενοοῦ, 26d2) avec « ceux-là » (ἐκείνους, 26d2), c'est-à-dire les Athéniens d'autrefois, vrais ancêtres de ceux qui vivent à présent (τοὺς ἀληθινοὺς προγόνους ἡμῶν, 26d2–3).

La transposition dans la réalité s'opère donc sur deux plans, spatial et temporel. Du point de vue spatial, la meilleure cité sera localisée à Athènes même, là où se déroule le dialogue entre Socrate, Critias, Timée et Hermocrate. D'un point de vue temporel, les habitants de la meilleure cité seront projetés dans un temps très reculé et identifiés avec les lointains ancêtres des Athéniens actuels, dont Socrate et Critias ici présents. La cité sera donc inscrite non pas dans le *hic* et *nunc*, mais dans le *hic* et *tunc*, c'est-à-dire transposée ici même dans la *chōra* d'Athènes et en même temps identifiée du point de vue généalogique avec un *genos* athénien d'un passé fort lointain. Ou bien, comme le dit Critias un peu plus tard, il s'agit de « faire [des citoyens-gardiens de la meilleure cité de Socrate] des citoyens de cette cité-ci, puisqu'ils sont les Athéniens d'autrefois » (ποιῆσαι πολίτας τῆς πόλεως τῆσδε ὡς ὄντας τοὺς τότε Ἀθηναίους, 27b2–3). L'identification de la meilleure cité à l'ancienne Athènes et la transposition dans la réalité qu'elle implique font d'elle une cité dont on peut dire où, quand et de quels parents elle est née, une cité qui peut être située d'un point de vue tant « chôrologique » que généalogique. En outre, cela en fait une cité qui n'existe pas seulement dans mais aussi en dehors du discours. A la différence de l'Atlantide, engloutie à tout jamais dans l'Océan et confinée dorénavant à sa seule existence intradiscursive, la cité d'Athènes a une double existence, intra- et extradiscursive. Dès lors, l'identification de la meilleure cité avec l'ancienne Athènes que Critias propose à Socrate signifie pour elle davantage qu'une simple transposition dans un espace et un temps intradiscursifs : elle l'inscrit également dans un territoire et un temps généalogique extradiscursifs. La meilleure cité est ainsi doublement transposée dans la réalité, celle du *logos alēthēs* rapporté d'Egypte par Solon et celle de l'Athènes du temps de Critias le jeune, et elle est mise en rapport tant avec le passé qu'avec le présent.

Comme certains lecteurs modernes, Critias comprend donc le vœu de Socrate comme un souhait de voir sa cité réalisée dans l'« Histoire », d'entendre un discours qui aille au-delà de la *mimēsis* fictionnelle d'un récit de guerre[24].

---

24 Cf. p. ex. Hadot, « Physique et poésie dans le *Timée* de Platon », 115 : « Il [Socrate] aimerait bien qu'on lui montre sa Cité idéale cette fois en action, autrement dit qu'on la retrouve dans l'Histoire » ; Detienne, *L'écriture d'Orphée*, 169–170 : « Socrate voudrait qu'on lui

Si le discours de Critias est « vrai » (ἀληθής) par opposition à ce que Socrate a raconté « comme dans un récit » (ὡς ἐν μύθῳ), s'il ne s'agit justement pas d'un récit façonné (μῦθος πλασθείς, cf. 26e4), c'est du fait qu'il est un discours « chôrologique » et généalogique qui enracine la cité dans un territoire propre et la situe dans le temps humain à la fois dans et en dehors du discours. Une fois une *chōra* et une généalogie humaine intégrées dans le récit de Socrate, celui-ci se transforme en un *logos alēthēs*.

Timée, quant à lui, est moins affirmatif : pour son discours cosmogonique et anthropogonique, il n'aspire qu'à la vraisemblance. Son *eikōs logos*, « discours vraisemblable » – qu'il appelle aussi *eikōs mythos*, « récit vraisemblable »[25] – occupe une place au (juste) milieu entre le récit de Socrate et le discours vrai de Critias. Il n'empêche que l'intégration de la *chōra* et des *genē* de corpuscules augmente aussi la vérité de son discours. Pour son deuxième discours, Timée revendique en effet davantage de vraisemblance que pour le premier (cf. μηδενὸς ἧττον εἰκότα, μᾶλλον δέ, 48d3).

A cet égard, son premier discours, qui raconte l'œuvre de l'intellect, se rapproche du récit « idéaliste » de Socrate, récapitulé au début du prologue. Le deuxième discours, par contre, qui décrit l'œuvre de la contrainte, fait écho au discours « réaliste » de Critias. En d'autres termes, d'un point de vue narratif, le monde où sont nées l'ancienne Athènes et l'Atlantide et où a eu lieu la guerre qui les opposait, évoqué dans le récit du prêtre égyptien, prépare celui dans lequel sont nés les différents genres de corpuscules dont les mouvements obéissent à la contrainte. C'est un monde où les dieux, certes, ne sont pas absents mais où ils n'œuvrent pas comme artisans[26].

---

montre, en projection privée, la cité idéale telle quelle, mais en action, en branle. [...] Plus précisément, que pourraient être les exploits, les *áthloi*, de la cité idéale ? Que devient la *Kallípolis* jetée dans les eaux rapides de l'Histoire ? ». Pour un aperçu de la discussion autour du statut de vérité et du genre littéraire du récit de l'Atlantide dans le *Timée-Critias*, on peut se référer à Brisson, *Platon. Timée. Critias*, 313–325 ; Gill, *Plato : The Atlantis Story*, (introduction), et Gill, *Plato's Atlantis Story : Text, Translation and Commentary*, 1–48 ; Pradeau, *Le Monde de la politique*, 66–110 ; Vidal-Naquet, *L'Atlantide. Petite histoire d'un mythe platonicien*.

25   En comparaison des nombreuses occurrences de l'expression *eikōs logos*, *eikōs mythos* n'apparaît que trois fois (29d2, 59c6 et 68d2) dans le discours de Timée.

26   Je remercie Jakub Jirsa, Filip Karfík, Štěpán Špinka de m'avoir invitée à présenter ces réflexions sur le prologue du *Timée-Critias* au dixième *Symposium Platonicum Pragense*, organisé par leurs soins en novembre 2015. Un grand merci aussi à Kelly Harrison pour sa relecture attentive.

Works Cited

Bonnard, Jean-Baptiste. *Le Complexe de Zeus. Représentations de la paternité en Grèce ancienne.* Paris : Publications de la Sorbonne, 2004.

Brisson, Luc. *Platon. Timée. Critias.* Paris : Flammarion, 1992, quatrième édition 1999.

Brisson, Luc. « Platon face à la guerre ». *Cahiers d'Etudes Lévinassiennes* 14 (2016) : 34–44.

Cambiano, Giuseppe. « La pace in Platone e in Aristotele ». Dans *La Pace nel mondo antico* (Atti del Convegno Nazionale di Studi, Torino 9-10-11 Aprile 1990). Sous la direction de Renato Uglione. Torino : Associazione Italiana di Cultura Classica, 1991, 97–114.

Campese, Silvia et Lucia Loredana Canino. « La genesi della *polis* ». Dans *Platone. La Repubblica.* Sous la direction de Mario Vegetti. Napoli : Bibliopolis, 1998–2007, Vol. II, 285–332.

Casevitz, Michel. *Le vocabulaire de la colonisation en grec ancien. Etude lexicologique : les familles de* κτίζω *et de* οἰκέω – οἰκίζω. Paris : Klincksieck, 1985.

Detienne, Marcel. *L'écriture d'Orphée.* Paris : Gallimard, 1989.

Fowler, R. L. « Genealogical Thinking, Hesiod's *Catalogue*, and the Creation of the Hellenes ». *Proceedings of the Cambridge Philological Society* 44 (1998) : 1–19.

Georgoudi, Stella. « Gaia/Gê. Entre mythe, culte et idéologie ». Dans *Myth and Symbol I : Symbolic phenomena in ancient Greek culture* (Papers from the first international symposium on symbolism at the University of Tromsø, June 4–7, 1998). Sous la direction de Synnøve des Bouvrie. Bergen : The Norwegian Institute of Athens, 2002, 113–134.

Gill, Christopher. *Plato : The Atlantis Story.* Bristol : Classical Press, 1980.

Gill, Christopher. *Plato's Atlantis Story : Text, Translation and Commentary.* Liverpool : University Press, 2017.

Graf, Fritz. « Zwischen Autochthonie und Immigration : Die Herkunft von Völkern in der Alten Welt ». Dans *Anfänge.* Sous la direction de Detlev Clemens et Tilo Schabert. München : W. Fink, 1998, 65–93.

Hadot, Pierre. « Physique et poésie dans le Timée de Platon ». *Revue de Théologie et de Philosophie* 115 (1983) : 113–133.

Jouanna, Jacques, éd. et trad. *Hippocrate.* Tome II, 2ᵉ partie : *Airs, Eaux, Lieux.* Paris : Les Belles Lettres, 1996.

Loraux, Nicole. *Les enfants d'Athéna. Idées athéniennes sur la citoyenneté et la division des sexes.* Deuxième édition. Paris : Seuil, 1990.

Parker, Robert. « Myths of Early Athens ». Dans *Interpretation of Greek Mythology.* Sous la direction de Jan Bremmer. London : Croom Helm, 1987, 187–214.

Pradeau, Jean-François. « Être quelque part, occuper une place. ΤΟΠΟΣ et ΧΩΡΑ dans le Timée ». *Les études philosophiques* 1 (1995) : 375–399.

Pradeau, Jean-François. *Le Monde de la politique. Sur le récit atlante de Platon*, Timée (17–27) *et* Critias. Sankt Augustin : Academia, 1997.

Rivaud, Albert. *Platon. Œuvres complètes*. Tome x. *Timée-Critias*. Paris : Les Belles Lettres, 1925.

Vidal-Naquet, Pierre. *Le chasseur noir. Formes de pensée et formes de société dans le monde grec*. Troisième édition. Paris : La Découverte, 2005.

Vidal-Naquet, Pierre. *L'Atlantide. Petite histoire d'un mythe platonicien*. Paris : Les Belles Lettres, 2005.

Die grosse Rede des Timaios – ein Beispiel wahrer Rhetorik?

Lucius Hartmann

Abstract

The great cosmological speech of Timaios points in comparison to similar written texts of the 4th century to a number of peculiarities, and even inside the corpus Platonicum the text appears singularly. These remarkable features can be explained by the consequent application of the philosophical rhetoric – the soul conducted by words –, conceived by Platon mainly in the dialogs *Gorgias* and *Phaedrus*. The most important criteria are knowledge (especially of ideas), a good structure with the definition of central terms, the application of a scientific psychology and a critical attitude to the value of written texts. Timaios, as an exceptionally gifted astronomer, a politically successful orator and a true philosopher meets these requirements nearly perfect.

Keywords

Plato – *Phaedrus* – *Gorgias* – *Timaeus* – rhetoric – psychology

1 Eigentümlichkeiten der Rede

Liest man Platons Dialog *Timaios* und vergleicht die darin enthaltene grosse Rede des Timaios mit den Reden anderer Autoren des 5. oder 4. Jahrhunderts vor Christus, kann man zahlreiche Eigentümlichkeiten erkennen.[1]

So geht der Rede erstens ein dialogisches Einleitungsgespräch voraus, in welchem der Redner ebenso wie die drei Zuhörer – im Vergleich zu zeitgenössischen Reden ein geradezu verschwindend kleines Publikum – charakterisiert werden und der Vortrag der Rede motiviert wird. Und in der Fiktion des

---

1 Kurzfassung der Dissertation, die im Februar 2016 an der Universität Zürich angenommen und 2017 unter dem gleichen Titel publiziert wurde, vgl. Hartmann *Die grosse Rede des Timaios – ein Beispiel wahrer Rhetorik*. Angesichts der Kürze des Beitrags wird weitgehend auf Begründungen verzichtet, ebenso auf eine intensive Auseinandersetzung mit der Forschung. Als Übersetzungen wurden verwendet: Susemihl (zeno.org) für den *Timaios* und Georgii (zeno.org) teilweise für den *Phaidros* (markiert mit *).

Timaios wird die Rede kurz nach Beginn sogleich wieder unterbrochen, um den Zuhörern die Möglichkeit zu geben, ihre Zustimmung zu äussern (*Tim.* 29d).

Zweitens beginnt Timaios seine Ausführungen sehr atypisch mit einem Anruf der Götter (27c), den man sonst höchstens in der Dichtung noch findet.[2]

> ΤΙ. Ἀλλ', ὦ Σώκρατες, τοῦτό γε δὴ πάντες ὅσοι καὶ κατὰ βραχὺ σωφροσύνης μετέχουσιν, ἐπὶ παντὸς ὁρμῇ καὶ σμικροῦ καὶ μεγάλου πράγματος θεὸν ἀεί που καλοῦσιν· ἡμᾶς δὲ τοὺς περὶ τοῦ παντὸς λόγους ποιεῖσθαί πη μέλλοντας, ἦ γέγονεν ἢ καὶ ἀγενές ἐστιν, εἰ μὴ παντάπασι παραλλάττομεν, ἀνάγκη θεούς τε καὶ θεὰς ἐπικαλουμένους εὔχεσθαι πάντα κατὰ νοῦν ἐκείνοις μὲν μάλιστα, ἑπομένως δὲ ἡμῖν εἰπεῖν. Καὶ *τὰ μὲν περὶ θεῶν ταύτῃ παρακεκλήσθω*.[3]

> (Timaios:) Traun, lieber Sokrates, tun doch das wohl alle, die auch nur ein wenig Überlegung besitzen: *rufen* doch sie alle wohl beim Beginne eines jeden Unternehmens, mag es nun geringfügig oder bedeutend sein, stets *einen Gott an*. Und wir, die wir gar über das All zu sprechen im Begriffe sind, nämlich inwiefern es entstanden ist oder aber unentstanden von Ewigkeit war, müßten ja ganz und gar den Verstand verloren haben, wenn wir nicht *die Götter und Göttinnen anrufen und von ihnen erflehen* wollten, daß es uns gelingen möge, das Ganze vor allem nach ihrem Sinne, sodann aber auch in Übereinstimmung mit uns selber darzulegen. Und so mögen denn *die Götter* eben hierum *angerufen sein*.
> *Tim.* 27c f.

Drittens wird die Rede vom Autor gleichzeitig als *mythos* und als *logos* bezeichnet und oszilliert damit zwischen dieser Antithese der griechischen „Aufklärung".[4] Die Grenzen der menschlichen Erkenntnis und die Überlegenheit der Götter werden von Timaios in seiner Rede explizit thematisiert (29c f.), und dadurch scheint er seine Ausführungen grundsätzlich zu relativieren.

> Ἐὰν οὖν, ὦ Σώκρατες, πολλὰ πολλῶν πέρι, θεῶν καὶ τῆς τοῦ παντὸς γενέσεως, μὴ δυνατοὶ γιγνώμεθα πάντῃ πάντως αὐτοὺς ἑαυτοῖς ὁμολογουμένους λόγους καὶ ἀπηκριβωμένους ἀποδοῦναι, μὴ θαυμάσῃς· ἀλλ' ἐὰν ἄρα μηδενὸς ἧττον παρεχώμεθα *εἰκότας, ἀγαπᾶν χρή*, μεμνημένους ὡς ὅ λέγων ἐγὼ ὑμεῖς τε οἱ κριταὶ φύσιν

---

[2] Inhaltlich nahe ist z.B. Empedokles' naturphilosophisches Gedicht *Peri physeōs* (DK 31 B 3).
[3] Alle griechischen Texte sind dem TLG entnommen.
[4] Mythen werden auch den „modernen" Sophisten zugeschrieben: Prodikos (Xenophon, *Mem.* II 1.21–34) und Protagoras (Platon, *Prot.* 320c ff.).

ἀνθρωπίνην ἔχομεν, ὥστε περὶ τούτων τὸν εἰκότα μῦθον ἀποδεχομένους πρέπει τούτου μηδὲν ἔτι πέρα ζητεῖν.

Wenn ich daher, mein Sokrates, trotzdem daß schon viele vieles über die Götter und die Entstehung des Alls erörtert haben, nicht vermögen sollte, eine nach allen Seiten und in allen Stücken mit *sich selber übereinstimmende und ebenso der Sache genau entsprechende Darstellung* zu geben, so wundere dich nicht; sondern wenn ich nur eine solche liefere, die um nichts minder als die irgend eines anderen *wahrscheinlich ist, so müßt ihr schon zufrieden sein* und bedenken, daß wir alle, ich, der Darsteller, und ihr, die Beurteiler, von nur menschlicher Natur sind, so daß es sich bei diesen Gegenständen für uns ziemt, uns damit zu begnügen, wenn *die Dichtung* nur *die Wahrscheinlichkeit* für sich hat, und *wir nichts darüber hinaus verlangen dürfen.*

Tim. 29c f.

Viertens wirkt die Darstellung von komplexen mathematischen und naturwissenschaftlichen Zusammenhängen und Erkenntnissen in einer derart langen Rede fürs 4. Jahrhundert bereits anachronistisch, da sie ihre Parallelen eigentlich nur in geschriebenen Texten (z.B. der Medizin) findet.

Doch nicht nur neben den zeitgenössischen Reden scheint der *Timaios* auffallend, sondern auch innerhalb von Platons Werk. Wie kommt es, dass sich Sokrates (zwar nur als Zuhörer) mit einer naturphilosophisch geprägten Erklärung unserer Welt beschäftigt, einem Thema, von dem er sich gemäss eigener Aussage im *Phaidon* nach seinen schlechten Erfahrungen mit Anaxagoras (*Phd.* 97b ff.) längst gelöst hat und von dem er der *Apologie* zufolge gar nichts versteht (*Apol.* 19c)?

Weiter vertritt Timaios ganz eindeutig das Prinzip des *eikos* (*Tim.* 29c f.), ein von Platon überaus kritisch eingeschätztes Beweisverfahren der sophistischen Rhetorik.

πρὸ τῶν ἀληθῶν τὰ εἰκότα εἶδον ὡς τιμητέα μᾶλλον

(Sokrates:) <Gorgias und Teisias> erkannten, dass das Wahrscheinliche mehr als das Wahre geschätzt werden müsse.

Phdr. 267a6 f.

Schliesslich scheint auch die Länge der Rede nicht unproblematisch: Im *Gorgias* droht Sokrates seinem Gesprächspartner Polos, er werde sich aus dem Gespräch zurückziehen, wenn Polos weiterhin der *makrologia* fröne (*Gorg.* 461d f.), und ebenso will Sokrates den Dialog mit Protagoras abrupt beenden, wenn dieser seine Antworten nicht kürzer fasst (*Prot.* 334c ff.). Unter diesen Voraussetzungen wirkt es seltsam inkonsequent, dass Timaios' viel längere Rede Sokrates nicht im Geringsten zu stören scheint.

Umgekehrt präsentiert Platon – hauptsächlich in seinem Dialog *Phaidros* – eine Reihe von Kriterien für eine wahre, philosophische Rhetorik als Gegenstück zur traditionellen, sophistischen Rhetorik.[5] Es stellt sich daher die Frage, ob sich unter diesen Prämissen die Eigentümlichkeiten des *Timaios* besser verstehen lassen und ob der *Timaios* allenfalls sogar als ein Beispiel dieser wahren Rhetorik betrachtet werden kann.

2 Forschungsstand

Auffälligerweise im Vergleich zu den Reden im *Phaidros*, im *Symposion*, im *Menexenos* und in der *Apologie* fehlen bislang Versuche fast vollständig, auch die grosse Rede des *Timaios* auf die Erfüllung der Kriterien der wahren Rhetorik hin zu untersuchen.[6]

Nach Hadot ist die Rede des *Timaios* ein „échantillon de cette rhétorique philosophique", indem sie die Seele im All situiert und somit ein meteorologisches Thema, wie es im *Phaidros* gefordert werde, enthält, und er erklärt den *eikōs logos* mit den Vorgaben der Schriftkritik.[7] Auch wenn beide Argumente kaum zutreffend sind, bleibt seine Schlussfolgerung dennoch richtig.

Nach Mesch ist im *Timaios* ebenfalls die wahre Rhetorik erfordert (und umgesetzt), da das behandelte Thema (Abbilder von Ideen und nicht Ideen selbst) im besten Fall diese Art von Rhetorik ermöglicht, weil die eigentlich höher stehende Dialektik „an eine Grenze in der dialektischen Thematisierbarkeit von Gegenständen stösst" und damit nicht verwendet werden könne. Er erklärt ausserdem die ungewöhnliche Länge und die Bildhaftigkeit der Rede als „Sonderfall einer gegenstandsadäquaten Rhetorik".[8] Die Frage, ob diese Rhetorik auch adressatenadäquat sei, wird von ihm jedoch nur in Ansätzen beantwortet.

---

5 Unter dem Begriff „sophistische Rhetorik" ist im Folgenden die gesamte nichtplatonische Rhetorik zusammengefasst (also nicht nur die Ansichten von Protagoras und Gorgias, sondern auch von Korax, Teisias, usw.).

6 Vgl. *e.g.* Colloud-Streit, *Fünf platonische Mythen im Verhältnis zu ihren Textumfeldern*, zum *Phaidros*, Thompson, „The Symposion: a neglected Source for Plato's Ideas on Rhetoric", zum *Symposion*, Eucken, „Die Doppeldeutigkeit des platonischen *Menexenos*", zum *Menexenos*, Colaiaco, *Socrates against Athens*, zur *Apologie*. Kritisch sind beispielsweise Werner, „Rhetoric and philosophy in Plato's *Phaedrus*", zum *Phaidros* und Guthrie, *A History of Greek Philosophy III–V*, zum *Menexenos*.

7 Hadot, „Physique et poésie dans le *Timée* de Platon", 127.

8 Mesch, „Die Bildlichkeit der platonischen Kosmologie", 203.

Racionero sieht in der Rede des Timaios ebenfalls ein „exercise of legitimate rhetoric", wobei er in seiner Begründung ausschliesslich vom Kriterium der Wahrheit und ihrer (durch den Gegenstand der Rede bedingten) nur teilweise möglichen Kommunikation ausgeht.[9]

Sowohl Johansen als auch Ashbaugh zeigen aufgrund des Vergleichs einer Rede mit einem Lebewesen aus dem *Phaidros* (*Phdr.* 264c), dass Timaios' Rede diese Vorgabe an die Struktur weitgehend erfüllt.[10] Brague nimmt die *Phaidros*-Stelle sogar zum Anlass (aus meiner Sicht wenig überzeugend), die einzelnen Teile der Rede mit menschlichen Körperteilen zu vergleichen.[11]

In ihrem nur sehr marginal der Rhetorik gewidmeten Aufsatz sprechen auch Lampert/Planeaux (leider ohne Verweis auf den *Phaidros*) davon: „*Timaeus-Critias* is an example of that alliance of philosophy and rhetoric, the theory of which is presented in the *Republic*."[12] Gleiches gilt auch für Nevsky, welcher den *Timaios* an die *Politeia* anschliessen lässt und ihn für „un échantillon de la bonne manière de parler « de la nature de l'univers »" hält.[13]

Die vorhandene Forschung bescheinigt der Rede des Timaios also die Erfüllung einzelner Kriterien der wahren Rhetorik, doch basieren diese Resultate teilweise auf falschen Annahmen oder wenig überzeugenden Übertragungen und widerspiegeln nur einen Teil der im *Phaidros* oder anderswo formulierten Forderungen, so dass sich bloss ein unvollständiges Bild ergibt. Ziel meiner Untersuchung ist es, diese lückenhaften Resultate durch einen möglichst systematischen und umfassenden Ansatz zu verifizieren und zu vervollständigen.

3   Kriterien der wahren Rhetorik

Auf der Basis hauptsächlich des *Phaidros*, der sich von allen Dialogen am intensivsten mit den technischen Einzelheiten der Rhetorik auseinandersetzt, sollen im Folgenden die wichtigsten Kriterien der wahren Rhetorik dargestellt werden.[14]

---

9   Racionero, „*Logos*, myth and probable discourse in Plato's *Timaeus*", 58.
10   Johansen, *Plato's Natural Philosophy: A Study of the Timaeus-Critias*, Ashbaugh, *Plato's Theory of Explanation*, vgl. unten Anm. 32.
11   Brague, „The Body of the Speech". So kann u.a. die Identifikation des Kopfs der Rede mit ihrem Anfang kaum richtig sein, vgl. *Tim.* 69b1.
12   Lampert und Planeaux, „Who's Who in Plato's *Timaeus-Critias* and Why", 121.
13   Nevsky, *Voir le monde comme une image*, 310.
14   Auch der *Gorgias* enthält neben seiner Kritik an der sophistischen Rhetorik Ansätze einer wahren Rhetorik (*Gorg.* 503a ff.), die sich nicht von derjenigen des *Phaidros* unterscheidet. Auf das Primat des Inhalts vor der Form weisen auch das *Symposion* (198b ff.), die *Apologie* (17a ff.) und der *Menexenos* (234c f.) hin.

Die Grundidee von Sokrates' Rhetorikentwurf im *Phaidros* besteht darin, dass die Rhetorik (als *rhētorikē technē*[15]) die Bedingungen einer *technē* erfüllen muss,[16] d.h.

a) sie muss über Kenntnis ihres Gegenstands verfügen (→ *alētheia* statt *eikos*),
b) sie muss ihre Effekte wissenschaftlich erklären können (→ Psychologie),
c) sie muss auf das Beste ausgerichtet sein (→ Ethik),
d) sie muss lehrbar sein (→ Schriftkritik).

3.1 Kenntnis der Wahrheit (*Fachwissen* und *Ideenwissen*)

Der Redner muss grundsätzlich die Wahrheit dessen kennen, worüber er spricht. In der Regel ist dabei auch ethisches Wissen (für die Ausrichtung auf das Gute ohnehin) notwendig, also automatisch ein Ideenwissen.[17] So fragt Sokrates rhetorisch:

Ἆρ' οὖν οὐχ ὑπάρχειν δεῖ τοῖς εὖ γε καὶ καλῶς ῥηθησομένοις τὴν τοῦ λέγοντος διάνοιαν εἰδυῖαν τὸ ἀληθὲς ὧν ἂν ἐρεῖν πέρι μέλλῃ;

(Sokrates:) Aber muss nicht zumindest für das, was gut und schön gesagt werden soll, der Verstand des Sprechers *die Wahrheit von dem wissen*, worüber er sprechen will?*

Phdr. 259e

3.2 Methode zur Erkenntnis der Wahrheit: Dialektik

Die Erkenntnis der Wahrheit erfolgt über die Methode der Dialektik. Diese lässt sich hauptsächlich durch zwei Verfahren beschreiben:

1) *Hypothesisverfahren* (*Phd.* 100a ff., *Rep.* 510b ff., *Men.* 86e ff.): Man geht von einer Hypothese aus und entwickelt daraus die Konsequenzen (nach unten), dann geht man über die Hypothese hinaus und sucht sich eine weitere, übergeordnete Hypothese, bis man zur *anypothetos archē*

---

15 Zum Begriff *rhētorikē* vgl. Schiappa, „Did Plato coin Rhêtorikê?", und (zurecht kritisch) Pernot, *La rhétorique dans l'antiquité*, 38 ff. Die Rhetorik wird im *Gorgias* in deutlichem Anklang an sophistische Definitionen als πειθοῦς δημιουργός (*Gorg.* 454e) umschrieben. Im *Phaidros* ist sie als ψυχαγωγία διὰ λόγων (261a) definiert, wodurch die zentrale Rolle der Psychologie unterstrichen wird.

16 Vgl. Balansard, *Technè dans les Dialogues de Platon*, Brickhouse und Smith, *Plato's Socrates*, Heinimann, „Eine vorplatonische Theorie der τέχνη".

17 Anders Heitsch, *Platon, Phaidros, Übersetzung und Kommentar*, vgl. aber *Phdr.* 260a1 ff. (τὰ τῷ ὄντι δίκαια und τὰ ὄντως ἀγαθὰ καὶ καλά) sowie *Phdr.* 260c6, 263a9, 272d5, 273e2, 278a3 f.; die Psychologie ist ohne Ideenwissen undenkbar, ebenso die wahre Rhetorik ohne Philosophie (*Phdr.* 261a4 f.).

(*Rep.* 510b7) gelangt; je nachdem muss die ursprüngliche Hypothese angepasst oder ganz aufgegeben werden, wenn sie zu Widersprüchen führt.[18]

2) *Dihairesisverfahren*, wie es im *Phaidros* explizit beschrieben ist, um Genus und Spezies eines Begriffs umfassend verstehen zu können:[19]

Εἰς *μίαν* τε *ἰδέαν* συνορῶντα ἄγειν τὰ πολλαχῇ διεσπαρμένα, ἵνα ἕκαστον ὁριζόμενος δῆλον ποιῇ περὶ οὗ ἂν ἀεὶ διδάσκειν ἐθέλῃ [...] Τὸ πάλιν κατ' *εἴδη* δύνασθαι διατέμνειν κατ' ἄρθρα ᾗ πέφυκεν.

(Sokrates:) Das überall Verstreute *durch den Gesamtblick in ein Genus* zurückzuführen, damit man jedes, worüber man jeweils lehren möchte, klar macht, indem man es definiert [...] Umgekehrt in der Lage zu sein, es in *Spezies zu unterteilen* gemäss der natürlichen Gliederung.

Phdr. 265d f.

Das dialektische Verfahren (als Denkprozess) muss in der Rede selbst nicht abgebildet werden, sondern geht dieser üblicherweise voran, wie es auch aus Sokrates' Reden im *Phaidros* klar wird.

3.3 Struktur

Nach Sokrates sind die Erkenntnisse der sophistischen Rhetorik auch für die wahre Rhetorik durchaus nützlich (*Phdr.* 269b7 f. τὰ πρὸ τῆς τέχνης ἀναγκαῖα μαθήματα). Dazu gehören insbesondere die Vorschriften zur Strukturierung von Reden, und seine eigenen Reden im *Phaidros* zeichnen sich in diesem Bereich ganz ausgesprochen aus. Er sieht hauptsächlich drei Kriterien: a) die Rede als Lebewesen, b) ihre Logik und c) die Notwendigkeit des Definierens.

3.3.1 Lebewesen (Vollständigkeit, Wohlproportioniertheit)

Erstens vergleicht er eine Rede mit einem Lebewesen, wobei es ihm dabei um ihre Vollständigkeit und Wohlproportioniertheit geht.

Δεῖν πάντα λόγον ὥσπερ ζῷον συνεστάναι σῶμά τι ἔχοντα αὐτὸν αὑτοῦ, ὥστε μήτε ἀκέφαλον εἶναι μήτε ἄπουν, ἀλλὰ μέσα τε ἔχειν καὶ ἄκρα, πρέποντα ἀλλήλοις καὶ τῷ ὅλῳ γεγραμμένα.

---

[18] Vgl. u.a. Byrd, „Dialectic and Plato's Method of Hypothesis".
[19] Vgl. u.a. Sayre, *Metaphysics and Method in Plato's Statesman*, und Stenzel, *Studien zur Entwicklung der platonischen Dialektik von Sokrates zu Aristoteles*.

(Sokrates:) Es ist notwendig, jede Rede wie ein *Lebewesen* aufzubauen, welches einen eigenen Körper hat, so dass es weder *kopf-* noch *fusslos* ist, sondern *mittlere* und *äussere* Teile hat, die in der Gestaltung zueinander und zum Ganzen *passen*.

    Phdr. 264c

3.3.2 „Logik" (Argumentation, sinnvolle Gedankenfolge)

Zweitens sollte eine Rede auch „logisch" aufgebaut sein, d.h. eine sinnvolle, argumentativ nachvollziehbare Gedankenfolge aufweisen.[20] Lysias' Rede im *Phaidros* hat nach Sokrates gerade dieses Kriterium nicht erfüllt:

Σὺ δ' ἔχεις τινὰ ἀνάγκην λογογραφικὴν ᾗ ταῦτα ἐκεῖνος οὕτως ἐφεξῆς παρ' ἄλληλα ἔθηκεν;

(Sokrates:) Hast du aber einen ‚*logographischen Zwang*', nach dem jener <Lysias> diese <ersten Zeilen der Rede> so in dieser Reihenfolge angeordnet hat?

    Phdr. 265b

3.3.3 Definition

Drittens erhält jede Rede ihre inhaltliche Stimmigkeit und Widerspruchsfreiheit, wenn zu Beginn die zentralen (und umstrittenen) Begriffe definiert werden. Dies wird von Sokrates in beiden Reden (im Gegensatz zu Lysias) umgesetzt, wobei die Forderung selbst in der ersten Rede zunächst auch theoretisch reflektiert wird.

Περὶ ἔρωτος οἷόν τ' ἔστι καὶ ἣν ἔχει δύναμιν, ὁμολογίᾳ θέμενοι ὅρον, εἰς τοῦτο ἀποβλέποντες καὶ ἀναφέροντες τὴν σκέψιν ποιώμεθα.

(Sokrates:) Indem wir in Übereinstimmung über den Eros *festlegen*, wie er ist und welche Kraft er hat, indem wir jeweils darauf blicken und uns darauf beziehen, wollen wir die Untersuchung führen.

    Phdr. 237c

Τὰ νυνδὴ περὶ Ἔρωτος – ὃ ἔστιν ὁρισθέν – εἴτ' εὖ εἴτε κακῶς ἐλέχθη, τὸ γοῦν σαφὲς καὶ τὸ αὐτὸ αὑτῷ ὁμολογούμενον διὰ ταῦτα ἔσχεν εἰπεῖν ὁ λόγος.

---

20   Heitsch, *Platon, Phaidros*, übersetzt mit „Kompositionsprinzip".

(Sokrates:) In Bezug auf das, was soeben über Eros – wie er *definiert worden ist* – sei es gut, sei es schlecht gesagt worden ist, konnte die Rede deswegen <wegen der Definition> wenigstens das Klare und mit sich selbst Übereinstimmende sagen.
> Phdr. 265d

3.3.4 Länge

Im *Phaidros* äussert sich Sokrates nur am Rand zur Länge einer Rede (*Phdr.* 267b, 269a, 272a). Immerhin zeigen seine eigenen Beispiele, dass eine Rede nicht zwingend sehr kurz sein muss. Die oben erwähnten Vorwürfe an seine Gesprächspartner im *Gorgias* und im *Protagoras* sind daher unbedingt in ihrem Kontext zu lesen: Nicht lange Reden an sich sind problematisch, sondern lange Reden in einem dialektischen Gespräch mit dem Zweck, durch die Länge von dem mangelnden Inhalt abzulenken und das Gespräch zu verunmöglichen. Die Länge der Rede ist, wie dies aus dem *Gorgias* selbst unmissverständlich hervorgeht, abhängig vom Inhalt und insbesondere auch vom Adressaten. So muss Sokrates gegenüber Polos, den er kurz vorher gebeten hat, sich ebenfalls wie Gorgias möglichst kurz zu halten, auch einmal zu einer längeren Antwort greifen, um seine Sicht verständlich zu machen.

> Ἴσως μὲν οὖν ἄτοπον πεποίηκα, ὅτι σε οὐκ ἐῶν μακροὺς λόγους λέγειν αὐτὸς συχνὸν λόγον ἀποτέτακα. Ἄξιον μὲν οὖν ἐμοὶ συγγνώμην ἔχειν ἐστίν· λέγοντος γάρ μου βραχέα οὐκ ἐμάνθανες, οὐδὲ χρῆσθαι τῇ ἀποκρίσει ἥν σοι ἀπεκρινάμην οὐδὲν οἷός τ' ἦσθα, ἀλλ' ἐδέου διηγήσεως. Ἐὰν μὲν οὖν καὶ ἐγὼ σοῦ ἀποκρινομένου μὴ ἔχω ὅτι χρήσωμαι, ἀπότεινε καὶ σὺ λόγον, ἐὰν δὲ ἔχω, ἔα με χρῆσθαι.

(Sokrates:) Vielleicht bin ich nun zwar unpassend vorgegangen, weil ich dich keine *langen Reden* halten liess, aber selbst meine Rede *verlängert* habe. Es ist nun freilich angemessen, mir Verständnis entgegenzubringen: denn als ich mich *kurz* hielt, hast du mich nicht verstanden, und *du warst nicht in der Lage*, mit der Antwort, die ich dir gegeben habe, etwas anzufangen, sondern du *benötigtest* noch eine zusätzliche Ausführung. Wenn nun freilich auch ich mit deiner Antwort nichts anzufangen weiss, *verlängere* auch du deine Rede, andernfalls lass es bleiben.
> Gorg. 465e f.

3.4 *Adressatenbezogenheit (Psychologie)*

Die sophistische Rhetorik sah ihre Wirkung insbesondere in der Erzeugung von *pathē*, und ihren Vertretern wurden teilweise magische Fähigkeiten zugeschrieben.[21] Sokrates anerkennt diese Leistung, aber er fordert eine profunde Kenntnis der Seele des Adressaten, um in Analogie zur Medizin eine kunstgemässe Rhetorik zu ermöglichen.

Der Redner muss demnach die Seelen der Adressaten mit einem dialektischen Verfahren (*Phdr.* 270c ff.) typologisieren und ebenso die verschiedenen Reden.[22] Anschliessend kann er die passenden Redetypen den Seelentypen zuordnen und ihre Effekte wissenschaftlich erklären (*Phdr.* 271b3 ff. ὑφ' οἵων λόγων δι' ἣν αἰτίαν ἐξ ἀνάγκης ἡ μὲν <ψυχὴ> πείθεται, ἡ δὲ ἀπειθεῖ).

> Ἐπειδὴ λόγου δύναμις τυγχάνει ψυχαγωγία οὖσα, τὸν μέλλοντα ῥητορικὸν ἔσεσθαι ἀνάγκη εἰδέναι ψυχὴ ὅσα εἴδη ἔχει. Ἔστιν οὖν τόσα καὶ τόσα, καὶ τοῖα καὶ τοῖα, ὅθεν οἱ μὲν τοιοίδε, οἱ δὲ τοιοίδε γίγνονται· τούτων δὲ δὴ οὕτω διῃρημένων, λόγων αὖ τόσα καὶ τόσα ἔστιν εἴδη, τοιόνδε ἕκαστον. Οἱ μὲν οὖν τοιοίδε ὑπὸ τῶν τοιῶνδε λόγων διὰ τήνδε τὴν αἰτίαν ἐς τὰ τοιάδε εὐπειθεῖς, οἱ δὲ τοιοίδε διὰ τάδε δυσπειθεῖς· [...] ᾗ προσοιστέον τούσδε ὧδε τοὺς λόγους ἐπὶ τὴν τῶνδε πειθώ, ταῦτα δ' ἤδη πάντα ἔχοντι, προσλαβόντι καιροὺς τοῦ πότε λεκτέον καὶ ἐπισχετέον, βραχυλογίας τε αὖ καὶ ἐλεινολογίας καὶ δεινώσεως ἑκάστων τε ὅσα ἂν εἴδη μάθῃ λόγων, τούτων τὴν εὐκαιρίαν τε καὶ ἀκαιρίαν διαγνόντι, καλῶς τε καὶ τελέως ἐστὶν ἡ τέχνη ἀπειργασμένη, πρότερον δ' οὔ.

(Sokrates:) Da die Kraft der Rede eine Seelenleitung ist, so muß derjenige, der ein Redner werden will, notwendig wissen, wie viele Arten die *Seele* hat. Deren gibt es also so und so viele und so und so beschaffene, daher auch die Menschen einige so, andere so beschaffen sind. Nachdem aber nun dieses eingeteilt worden ist, gibt es andererseits auch so und so viele Arten von *Reden*, und jede so oder so beschaffen. Die so beschaffenen Menschen sind nun durch die so beschaffenen Reden aus der so beschaffenen *Ursache* zu den so beschaffenen Zwecken leicht zu bereden, – die so beschaffenen aber sind aus diesen Gründen schwer zu bereden. [...] <jene Natur nämlich>, bei welcher gerade diese Reden auf diese Art zur Überzeugung über diese Gegenstände angewendet werden müssen, – wenn er also dieses alles

---

21 Vgl. *Phdr.* 267c f. (zu Thrasymachos), Gorgias, *Hel.* 8 sowie Platon, *Ion*; zur Magie *Menex.* 235a2 und *Prot.* 328d4. Zur Wirkung auf Sokrates vgl. *Menex.* 235a ff., *Symp.* 198b f., *Phdr.* 234d, *Apol.* 17a. Umgekehrt wirkte auch Sokrates selbst in gleicher Weise auf seine Zuhörer, vgl. *Symp.* 215c1 und *Men.* 80a2 ff.

22 In *Phdr.* 277c spricht er von „einfachen" (*haplous*, schlicht, „wissenschaftlich", z.B. der Unsterblichkeitsbeweis *Phdr.* 245c ff.) bzw. „bunten" (*poikilous*, ausgeschmückt, metaphorisch, z.B. der Mythos vom Seelengespann *Phdr.* 246a ff.) Reden und Seelen. Sein Gesprächspartner Phaidros besitzt mit hoher Sicherheit eine „bunte" Seele, vgl. Colloud-Streit, *Fünf platonische Mythen,* 150, und Yunis, *Plato: Phaedrus.*

schon inne hat und damit nun noch die *Erkenntnis der Zeit*, wann geredet und wann inne gehalten werden müsse, verbindet, wenn er ferner für das *Kurzreden* und *die Sprache des Mitleids* und *der Steigerung*, überhaupt für alle Redearten, die er etwa gelernt hat, die rechte Zeit und die Unzeit zu unterscheiden weiß, dann erst ist seine Kunst in schönem und vollkommenem Maße ausgebildet, eher aber nicht.*

Phdr. 271d ff.

Letztendlich kann eine solche wissenschaftlich begründete Rhetorik angesichts der schier unermesslichen Vielfalt der verschiedenen Seelentypen nur auf einen einzigen Adressaten hin ihre volle Wirkung entfalten.[23] Gegenüber vielen Adressaten muss sie kapitulieren; daher sieht Sokrates die philosophische Rhetorik hauptsächlich im Gespräch zwischen Lehrer und Schüler, wie es exemplarisch im *Phaidros* vorgeführt wird.[24]

3.5 Gottgefälligkeit

Da die wahre Rhetorik an sich die Philosophie voraussetzt (durch das Ideenwissen, die Psychologie und die dialektische Methode), lässt sie sich nur mit grossem (auch zeitlichem) Aufwand erlernen. Den Vorwurf dieses ungünstigen Kosten-Nutzenverhältnisses kontert Sokrates damit, dass er das Ziel der Rhetorik darin sieht, den Göttern und nicht den Menschen zu Gefallen zu sprechen.

Ἣν (πραγματείαν) οὐχ ἕνεκα τοῦ λέγειν καὶ πράττειν πρὸς ἀνθρώπους δεῖ διαπονεῖσθαι τὸν σώφρονα, ἀλλὰ τοῦ θεοῖς κεχαρισμένα μὲν λέγειν δύνασθαι, κεχαρισμένως δὲ πράττειν τὸ πᾶν εἰς δύναμιν. Οὐ γὰρ δὴ ἄρα, ὦ Τεισία, φασὶν οἱ σοφώτεροι ἡμῶν, ὁμοδούλοις δεῖ χαρίζεσθαι μελετᾶν τὸν νοῦν ἔχοντα, ὅτι μὴ πάρεργον, ἀλλὰ δεσπόταις ἀγαθοῖς τε καὶ ἐξ ἀγαθῶν.

(Sokrates:) Dieser Übung darf sich aber nun der Besonnene nicht um des Redens und Handelns mit Menschen willen unterziehen, sondern *um den Göttern Gefälliges* reden und in allem nach Vermögen ihnen *gefällig* handeln zu können. Denn ja nicht darf, o Teisias, – so sagen die, welche weiser als wir sind, – wer Vernunft hat, sich bestreben, seinen Mitknechten sich gefällig zu zeigen, außer in Nebendingen, sondern seinen guten und von Guten kommenden Gebietern.*

Phdr. 273e f.

---

23 Weniger skeptisch gegenüber der Wirkung auf ein grösseres Publikum ist z.B. Yunis, *Taming Democracy*.
24 Das Scheitern der philosophischen Rhetorik vor der Masse wird z.B. im *Gorgias* (486a ff. und 521c ff.), im *Theaitetos* (172c ff.) und natürlich in der *Apologie* thematisiert.

Auch hier ist der *Phaidros* ein perfekt passendes Beispiel, da er von Beginn an durch das Göttliche geprägt ist und faktisch ein Enkomion auf einen Gott, den Eros, enthält.[25]

3.6 Distanz zur Schrift, Spiel vs. Ernst, Aussparungsstellen

Der *Phaidros* endet mit der bekannten Schriftkritik (*Phdr.* 274b ff.). Diese ist insbesondere auch eine Kritik an der sophistischen Rhetorik, welche das Buch als Möglichkeit zur Vermittlung ihres Wissens stark propagierte und nutzte.[26] Als Konsequenzen aus der Schriftkritik ergeben sich für den wahren Redner, dass er

a) den Stellenwert der Schrift für gering hält:

> Εἰ μὲν εἰδὼς ᾗ τὸ ἀληθὲς ἔχει συνέθηκε ταῦτα, καὶ ἔχων βοηθεῖν, εἰς ἔλεγχον ἰὼν περὶ ὧν ἔγραψε, καὶ λέγων αὐτὸς δυνατὸς τὰ γεγραμμένα φαῦλα ἀποδεῖξαι <darf man den Autor als „Philosoph" bezeichnen>.
>
> (Sokrates:) Wenn er dies im Wissen, wie sich das Wahre verhält, verfasst hat und ihm helfen kann, indem er sich der kritischen Auseinandersetzung über das, was er geschrieben hat, stellt, und beim Sprechen selbst in der Lage ist, *das Geschriebene als minderwertig* zu erweisen, <dann darf der betreffende Autor als „Philosoph" bezeichnet werden>.
>
> *Phdr.* 278c

b) der Schrift nur Spielerisches anvertraut, während das Ernste (= philosophisch Relevante) nur mündlich tradiert werden kann (*Phdr.* 276d f., 277e f.).

Platon selbst hat die Problematik der schriftlichen Überlieferung eingesehen und seine Prinzipienlehre in den Dialogen ausdrücklich ausgespart.[27]

4 Die grosse Rede des Timaios als Beispiel der wahren Rhetorik

Im Folgenden soll gezeigt werden, dass die Rede des Timaios diese Kriterien weitgehend erfüllt.

---

25 Vgl. Görgemanns, *Beiträge zur Interpretation von Platons Nomoi*, 63 ff., und Heitsch, „Dialektik und Philosophie in Platons ›Phaidros‹".
26 O'Sullivan, „Written and Spoken in the First Sophistic", 119: „the Sophists and the book as their favoured means of communication".
27 Vgl. Szlezák, *Platon und die Schriftlichkeit der Philosophie*.

4.1 Kenntnis der Wahrheit (*Fachwissen* und *Ideenwissen*)

Grundsätzlich könnte man die Tatsache, dass im *Timaios* nicht Sokrates spricht, als Anlass sehen, Platon distanziere sich hier stärker von den Aussagen des Protagonisten.[28] Allerdings ist Timaios' Rede in vielem derart genuin platonisch, dass eine solche Unterscheidung kaum glaubwürdig erscheint.[29] Dass sich Platon für Timaios als Redner entschied, hängt wohl eher damit zusammen, dass Sokrates auf dem Gebiet der Kosmologie eben kein ausgewiesener Experte war. Über Timaios wissen wir nur das, was uns Platon zu ihm überliefert:[30]

> Τίμαιός τε γὰρ ὅδε, εὐνομωτάτης ὢν πόλεως τῆς ἐν Ἰταλίᾳ Λοκρίδος, οὐσίᾳ καὶ γένει οὐδενὸς ὕστερος ὢν τῶν ἐκεῖ, τὰς μεγίστας μὲν ἀρχάς τε καὶ τιμὰς τῶν ἐν τῇ πόλει μετακεχείρισται, φιλοσοφίας δ' αὖ κατ' ἐμὴν δόξαν ἐπ' ἄκρον ἁπάσης ἐλήλυθεν.

(Sokrates:) Denn Timaios hier ist aus dem italischen Lokris gebürtig, welches sich der vortrefflichsten Verfassung erfreut, steht keinem von seinen Landsleuten an Vermögen und Herkunft nach und hat dabei einerseits die höchsten Ämter und Ehrenstellen im Staate bekleidet, andererseits in allem, was nur *wissenschaftliches Streben* heißt, nach meinem Dafürhalten *das Höchste* erreicht.

Tim. 20a

Timaios' Voraussetzungen sind also optimal, und er rückt ganz in die Nähe des Philosophenherrschers der *Politeia*.[31] Sokrates billigt ihm höchstes philosophisches Wissen zu („wissenschaftliches Streben" von Susemihl ist viel zu schwach), und gemäss Kritias kann er als Fachexperte für Astronomie gelten.

> ἅτε ὄντα ἀστρονομικώτατον ἡμῶν καὶ περὶ φύσεως τοῦ παντὸς εἰδέναι μάλιστα ἔργον πεποιημένον.

---

28 So Bryan, *Likeness and Likelihood in the Presocratics and Plato*, Lampert und Planeaux, „Who's Who in Plato's *Timaeus-Critias* and Why", Rowe, *Plato and the Art of Philosophical Writing*, und Schoos, „Timaeus' Banquet".

29 So Carone, *Plato's Cosmology and its Ethical Dimension*, Morrow, „Plato's Theory of the Primary Bodies in the *Timaeus* and the Later Doctrine of Forms", und Robinson, „The World as Art-Object: Science and the Real in Plato's *Timaeus*".

30 Vgl. Marg, *Timaeus Locrus. De Natura Mundi et Animae*, 83: „Nichts nötigt dazu, in der Titelperson von Platons Dialog eine historische Person zu sehen." Ähnlich skeptisch auch Morrow, „Plato's Theory of the Primary Bodies", und Nails, *The People of Plato*, s.v. Timaios.

31 So Erler, *Die Philosophie der Antike 2/2: Platon*, Schofield, „The disappearance of the philosopher king", und Szlezák, „Über die Art und Weise der Erörterung der Prinzipien im *Timaios*". Kritisch Rowe, *Philosophical Writing*, und Schoos, „Timaeus' Banquet".

(Kritias:) weil er sich unter uns am *meisten auf die Sternkunde versteht* und es sich *am meisten* zur Aufgabe gemacht hat, über die Natur des Alls zur *Erkenntnis zu gelangen.*

Tim. 27a

Es spricht also nichts dagegen, dass er die Wahrheit kennt (sofern dies einem Menschen möglich ist), und aus dem Proömium seiner Rede geht klar hervor, dass er auch über Ideenwissen verfügen muss, ganz abgesehen davon, dass er in der Fiktion des Dialogs am Vortag einer Diskussion in der Art der *Politeia* beigewohnt hat.

Nichtsdestotrotz sind ihm die Grenzen menschlicher Erkenntnis bewusst, wenn er in Bezug auf die *gignomena* stets nur das „Wahrscheinliche" (*eikos*) seiner Darstellung betont und allein dem Gott die Kenntnis der Wahrheit zubilligt.

τὸ μὲν ἀληθὲς ὡς εἴρηται, θεοῦ συμφήσαντος τότ' ἂν οὕτως μόνως διισχυριζοίμεθα· τό γε μὴν εἰκὸς ἡμῖν εἰρῆσθαι, καὶ νῦν καὶ ἔτι μᾶλλον ἀνασκοποῦσι διακινδυνευτέον τὸ φάναι καὶ πεφάσθω.

<Das die Seele Betreffende nun> der *Wahrheit* gemäß angegeben zu haben, das dürften wir wohl nur dann, wenn *Gott* selbst uns seine Zustimmung dazu gäbe, versichern; daß jedoch wenigstens das *Wahrscheinliche* hierüber von uns vorgebracht worden, das dürfen wir sowohl schon jetzt, als auch bei noch näherer Betrachtung zu behaupten wagen und wollen es hiermit behauptet haben.

Tim. 72d

4.2 Methode zur Erkenntnis der Wahrheit: Dialektik

Dass Timaios über philosophisches Wissen verfügt, ergibt sich auch daraus, dass er offensichtlich die dialektische Methode kennt und einsetzt, und zwar sowohl das Hypothesisverfahren als auch das Dihairesisverfahren. Auf ersteres weisen eine Reihe von Stellen in der Rede selbst hin (48e6 ὑποτεθέν, 53d5 ὑποτιθέμεθα, 61d ὑποθετέον δὴ πρότερον θάτερα, τὰ δ' ὑποτεθέντα ἐπάνιμεν αὖθις, 63b1 ὑποθεμένοις), und Proklos erwähnt dies ausdrücklich in seinem Timaioskommentar.

ἔοικεν ὁ Πλάτων ὥσπερ οἱ γεωμέτραι πρὸ τῶν ἀποδείξεων ὅρους προλαμβάνειν καὶ ὑποθέσεις

Es scheint Platon wie die Mathematiker vor den Beweisen Definitionen und *Hypothesen* vorwegzunehmen.

Procl., *In Tim.* I, 236

Auf letzteres weisen die zahlreichen Kategorisierungen und Differenzierungen in der Rede hin, von denen hier nur die erste erwähnt werden soll.

πρῶτον διαιρετέον τάδε· τί τὸ ὂν ἀεί, γένεσιν δὲ οὐκ ἔχον, καὶ τί τὸ γιγνόμενον μὲν ἀεί, ὂν δὲ οὐδέποτε.

Man muß nun nach meiner Meinung zuerst folgendes *unterscheiden* und feststellen: wie haben wir uns das immer Seiende, welches kein Werden zuläßt, und wie das immer Werdende zu denken, welches niemals zum Sein gelangt?

Tim. 27d5

Auch in der Literatur wird in der Regel die Ansicht vertreten, dass Timaios die Dialektik einsetze.[32]

4.3 Struktur

4.3.1 Lebewesen (Vollständigkeit, Wohlproportioniertheit)

Timaios unterteilt seine Rede in ein Proömium (*Tim.* 27c–29d), einen umfangreichen Hauptteil (*Tim.* 29d–92c) und einen kurzen Epilog (*Tim.* 92c – *Criti.* 106b). Der Hauptteil selbst gliedert sich in drei grosse Abschnitte à 17, 20 und 23 Seiten in der Oxfordausgabe, die man ihrerseits in weitere Unterabschnitte zerlegen kann. Als Grundlage für seine Ausführungen verwendet er die Abfolge Kosmogonie–Theogonie–Anthropogonie, die er je durch das Walten des *nous*, der *anankē* und beider Kräfte erklärt.

Die Rede deckt ihren Gegenstand offensichtlich vollständig ab:

Καὶ δὴ καὶ τὰ νῦν ἡμῖν ἐξ ἀρχῆς παραγγελθέντα διεξελθεῖν περὶ τοῦ παντὸς μέχρι γενέσεως ἀνθρωπίνης σχεδὸν ἔοικε τέλος ἔχειν. (es folgt noch die Entstehung der anderen Lebewesen aus dem Menschen)

Und nunmehr scheint denn auch die uns jetzt gesteckte Aufgabe, das Weltall von seinen Anfängen aus bis zur Entstehung der Menschen zu verfolgen, so *ziemlich* ihr Ziel erreicht zu haben.

Tim. 90e

---

32 Brisson, *Le Même et l'Autre dans la structure ontologique du Timée de Platon. Un commentaire systématique du Timée de Platon*, 390 mit einer schematischen Darstellung, Runia, „The Language of Excellence in Plato's *Timaeus* and Later Platonism", 22: „Platonic dialectic", Ashbaugh, *Plato's Theory of Explanation*, 3: „a series of divisions and collections". Kritisch z.B. Mesch, „Die Bildlichkeit".

und ihre Teile sind wie bei einem Lebewesen wohlproportioniert und aufeinander abgestimmt:

τελευτὴν τε κεφαλὴν ἁρμόττουσαν τοῖς πρόσθεν

<unserer Dichtung> einen dem Vorhergehenden *entsprechenden* Schluß hinzuzufügen
Tim. 69b

wie dies auch in der Forschung immer wieder betont wird.[33]

Dass Timaios seine Rede gleichsam dreimal wieder neu beginnen muss, hat zu kontroversen Einschätzungen geführt.[34] Aus meiner Sicht ist dieses mehrfache neue Einsetzen v.a. auf die Adressatenbezogenheit der Rede zurückzuführen. Er wollte nämlich zunächst das Thema präsentieren, das den Zuhörern am geläufigsten war und auf den meisten Vorkenntnissen aufbaute: Die teleologische Erklärung von der Entstehung des Kosmos als Abbild. Erst nachher ging er auf die komplexeren Einzelheiten der Grundelemente und des menschlichen Körpers ein, welche hohe mathematische und medizinische Anforderungen ans Publikum stellen und bei einer Thematisierung gleich zu Beginn die Gefahr in sich geborgen hätten, dass die Zuhörer überfordert gewesen wären und daher der Rede nicht mehr hätten folgen können und wollen.

4.3.2   „Logik" (Argumentation, sinnvolle Gedankenfolge)
Indem Timaios seine Kosmologie als Kosmogonie gestaltet, folgt er einem narrativen Prinzip und kann so von Beginn an eine „Logik" in seine Rede einbringen.[35] Diese besticht zudem durch zahlreiche Aufzählungen, Differenzierungen und

---

33   Ashbaugh, *Plato's Theory of Explanation*, 73: „the *eikōs logos* is constructed in the semblance of a living thing", Johansen, *Plato's Natural Philosophy*, 171: „In the *Timaeus* this idea [von der Rede als Lebewesen] is applied with particular pertinence since the subject matter of Timaeus' speech is itself an animal".
34   Vgl. *e.g.* Morgan, *Myth and Philosophy from the Presocratics to Plato*, 274: „there is no sense that the narrative is an organic whole" und umgekehrt Osborne, „Space, Time, Shape, and Direction: Creative Discourse in the *Timaeus*", 193 f.: „the orderly arrangement of Timaeus' description matches the orderly arrangement of the world itself" (siehe auch die vorangegangene Anmerkung).
35   Die „falsche" Reihenfolge bei der Schaffung des Weltkörpers und der Weltseele (*Tim.* 34b f.) kann ebenso auf die Adressatenbezogenheit zurückgeführt werden: Timaios beginnt in voller Absicht mit dem Teil, der für seine Zuhörer aufgrund ihres Vorwissens und durch die Argumentationsstruktur verständlicher ist, und führt erst nachher die mathematisch komplexe Mischung der Weltseele ein.

Kategorisierungen, Binnenverweise und kurze Zusammenfassungen, und ihre Aussagen werden in der Regel bewiesen.

4.3.3 Definition

Timaios definiert jeweils zu Beginn die entscheidenden Begriffe – *on* und *gignomenon* (28a), *chōra* (49a, 51a), *dēmiourgos* (28a, 29a, 29e), *chronos* (37d), die vier Grundelemente (51b) – und der Unterbruch nach dem Proömium (29d) ist gerade darauf zurückzuführen, dass er dem Publikum die Gelegenheit geben wollte, zu seinen Grundaussagen und insbesondere zu seinen Definitionen Stellung zu nehmen. *Exempli gratia* sei hier auf die Definition des Kosmos hingewiesen, der sowohl von der Begrifflichkeit her (*ouranos, kosmos, pan*) erklärt wird als auch als *gignomenon* und *eikōn* seine spezifischen Eigenschaften erhält (28b ff.).

4.3.4 Länge

Da die Rede des *Timaios* kein dialektisches Gespräch unterbricht und verunmöglicht, stellt sie für Sokrates nicht grundsätzlich ein Problem dar. Denn sie ist sowohl inhaltsadäquat, wie dies in der Forschung immer wieder konstatiert wird,[36] als auch adressatengerecht, da die beiden anderen Zuhörer neben Sokrates einem ungleich längeren und sicher nicht weniger anspruchsvolleren Dialog in Form einer *Politeia* offenbar ohne Schwierigkeiten folgen konnten, wie aus dem Einleitungsgespräch des *Timaios* hervorgeht. Zudem ist zu berücksichtigen, dass die Rede sogar kürzer ausgefallen ist, als theoretisch nötig gewesen wäre, da Timaios gewisse Teile weglassen kann:

> Τὰ δ' ἄλλα οἷ δὴ καὶ δι' ἃς αἰτίας ἱδρύσατο, εἴ τις ἐπεξίοι πάσας, ὁ λόγος πάρεργος ὢν πλέον ἂν ἔργον ὧν ἕνεκα λέγεται παράσχοι. Ταῦτα μὲν οὖν ἴσως τάχ' ἂν κατὰ σχολὴν ὕστερον τῆς ἀξίας τύχοι διηγήσεως· (vgl. auch *Tim.* 54b διότι δέ, λόγος πλείων; Verzicht auf Erklärung, weshalb er sich gerade für die beiden rechtwinkligen Dreiecke entscheidet)

> Was aber die übrigen anlangt, so würde, wenn man von allen angeben sollte, wohin und aus welchen Gründen er sie dahin versetzte, diese Auseinandersetzung, die doch nur eine *beiläufige* wäre, umständlicher sein als die Erörterung selber, welche uns hieraufgeführt hat. Vielleicht wird denn auch dieser Gegenstand *späterhin* bei größerer Muße eine Darlegung finden, wie er sie verdient.
> *Tim.* 38d f.

---

36   90e5 *emmetroteros*. Vgl. Johansen, *Plato's Natural Philosophy,* und Mesch, „Die Bildlichkeit".

διὰ βραχέων ἐπιμνηστέον, ὃ μή τις ἀνάγκη μηκύνειν (verkürzte Darstellung der Entstehung von Frauen und Tieren)

<die Entstehung von Frauen und Tieren> ist nur noch *kurz* zu erwähnen, es sei denn, daß die Sache hier und da ein *Mehreres fordert*.
Tim. 90e

4.4 Adressatenbezogenheit

Wir haben bereits im Zusammenhang mit der Struktur und der Länge gesehen, dass die Rede offensichtlich adressatenbezogen ist.

Auch wenn das Publikum aus drei (statt, wie im Idealfall gefordert, einer) Personen besteht, so verfügen die Zuhörer doch über eine enge Seelenverwandtschaft und repräsentieren eine absolut hochkarätige Gesprächsrunde. So sagt Sokrates selbst über Kritias und Hermokrates:[37]

Κριτίαν δέ που πάντες οἱ τῇδε ἴσμεν οὐδενὸς ἰδιώτην ὄντα ὧν λέγομεν. Τῆς δὲ Ἑρμοκράτους αὖ περὶ φύσεως καὶ τροφῆς, πρὸς ἅπαντα ταῦτ' εἶναι ἱκανὴν πολλῶν μαρτυρούντων πιστευτέον

Von dem Kritias aber wissen wir Athener es ja alle, daß ihm *nichts* von den Dingen, um welche es hier sich handelt, *fremd* ist, und ebenso darf man es von der Naturanlage wie der Bildung des Hermokrates glauben, daß sie ihnen *allen gewachsen* sei, da dies von so vielen Seiten bezeugt wird.
Tim. 20a

Man kann wohl zurecht mit Erler sagen: „Als Besonderheit gegenüber anderen Dialogen ist festzuhalten, dass Sokrates' Gesprächspartner im ‚Timaios' als besonders qualifiziert, kundig in der Wissenschaft (*Tim.* 53c) und ihm geradezu gleichrangig vorgestellt werden",[38] und man kann ihnen mit Bestimmtheit eine hohe Kompetenz zugestehen, aber sie sind kaum in allen Fällen als eigentliche Philosophenherrscher im Sinn der *Politeia* zu sehen; ihre unterschiedliche Charakterisierung weist zudem auf eine gewisse Binnendifferenzierung hin.

Die Adressatenbezogenheit kann als gute und plausible Erklärung für die oben erwähnten strukturellen „Defizite" der Rede (d.h. den zweimaligen Neubeginn) verwendet werden, indem Timaios seine Zuhörer dort abholt, wo sie stehen (nämlich bei der *Politeia*, d.h. auf einem philosophisch sehr hohen Niveau):

---

[37] Zu Timaios vgl. oben D.1.
[38] Erler, *Platon*, 263 f.

	Thema	Notwendige Vorkenntnisse
1)	Proömium	Philosophie
2)	Weltkörper	basiert auf 1) und minimalen Kenntnissen der Physik (Existenz von vier Grundelementen)
3)	Weltseele	Mathematik und Astronomie (Kenntnisse werden vertieft)
4)	Elemente	Mathematik und Physik (Kenntnisse werden vertieft)
5)	Mensch	Medizin (Kenntnisse werden vertieft)

Zudem lässt sich durch die Ausrichtung auf das Publikum der zurückhaltende Einsatz von Stilmitteln der sophistischen Rhetorik (so insbesondere der weitgehende Verzicht auf den Parallelismus und das Parison bzw. Isokolon, während umgekehrt z.B. das Polyptoton bei Timaios viel häufiger auftritt) erklären: Sie sind gar nicht notwendig, um überzeugend zu wirken. Ebenso ist darin eine Begründung für die Metapher der Kosmogonie und des Demiurgen zu sehen: Beides ermöglicht nämlich die Darstellung auf der Basis der philosophischen Vorkenntnisse der Zuhörer.

4.5 Gottgefälligkeit

Ähnlich wie den *Phaidros* prägt auch den *Timaios* das Göttliche ungemein. Er findet fiktiv während eines Götterfests statt (26e τῇ παρούσῃ τῆς θεοῦ θυσίᾳ), und er ist faktisch eine Lobrede auf den Demiurgen und den von ihm geschaffenen göttlichen und von Göttern beherrschten Kosmos. Timaios wendet sich gleich zweimal an die Götter (27c f. s.o. und beim zweiten Proömium in 48d):

> Θεὸν δὴ καὶ νῦν ἐπ' ἀρχῇ τῶν λεγομένων σωτῆρα ἐξ ἀτόπου καὶ ἀήθους διηγήσεως πρὸς τὸ τῶν εἰκότων δόγμα διασῴζειν ἡμᾶς ἐπικαλεσάμενοι πάλιν ἀρχώμεθα λέγειν.

> *Gott* also wollen wir auch jetzt bei diesem neuen Beginne unserer Auseinandersetzung *anrufen*, daß er uns *glücklich* durch diese fremdartige und ungewöhnliche Darstellungsweise hindurchführen und uns zur wahrscheinlichen Ansicht verhelfen wolle, und dann wirklich von neuem beginnen!
> *Tim.* 48d f.

und insbesondere bittet er nach seiner Rede im *Kritias* um die wohlwollende Aufnahme durch den Gott:

> Τῷ δὲ πρὶν μὲν πάλαι ποτ' ἔργῳ, νῦν δὲ λόγοις ἄρτι θεῷ γεγονότι προσεύχομαι, τῶν ῥηθέντων ὅσα μὲν ἐρρήθη μετρίως, σωτηρίαν ἡμῖν αὐτὸν αὐτῶν

διδόναι, παρὰ μέλος δὲ εἴ τι περὶ αὐτῶν ἄκοντες εἴπομεν, δίκην τὴν πρέπουσαν ἐπιτιθέναι.

Nun *bete* ich aber zu dem soeben in meiner Rede entstandenen *Gott*, uns selbst über das Gesagte, sofern es korrekt gesprochen war, *unterstützende Zustimmung* zu geben, wenn wir jedoch etwas darüber unabsichtlich falsch gesagt haben, uns die passende Strafe aufzuerlegen.

Criti. 106a f.

Auch in ihrer ethischen Ausrichtung ist die Rede ganz sicher gottgefällig.

4.6   *Distanz zur Schrift*

Als Rede erfüllt Timaios' Darstellung natürlich die Konsequenzen der Schriftkritik *per se*, und dies kann als ein Grund für die Wahl einer Rede statt eines schriftlichen Traktats angesehen werden.

4.6.1   Spiel vs. Ernst

Darüber hinaus ist die im *Phaidros* erwähnte Differenzierung zwischen Ernst (der Philosophie) und Spiel (allem anderen) auch Timaios geläufig, wenn er sagt:

ἣν ὅταν τις ἀναπαύσεως ἕνεκα τοὺς περὶ τῶν ὄντων ἀεὶ καταθέμενος λόγους, τοὺς γενέσεως πέρι διαθεώμενος εἰκότας ἀμεταμέλητον ἡδονὴν κτᾶται, μέτριον ἂν ἐν τῷ βίῳ παιδιὰν καὶ φρόνιμον ποιοῖτο.

und wenn man einmal zum Zwecke der *Erholung* die Untersuchungen über das ewig Seiende zur Seite legt und auf die über das Werden, welche nur Wahrscheinlichkeit gewähren, sein Augenmerk richtet und sich so einen *Genuß, dem keine Reue folgt*, bereitet, so hat man damit für sein Leben eine *unterhaltende Beschäftigung* gewonnen, wie sie *angemessen* und verständig ist.

Tim. 59c f.

4.6.2   Aussparungsstellen

Zudem verhindert Platon durch gezielte Aussparungsstellen, dass selbst in der schriftlichen Version der Rede ein Wissen über die Prinzipienlehre dem problematischen Instrument der Schrift anvertraut wird. So verzichtet er auf eine exakte Darstellung des Demiurgen (28c), der *archē* aller Dinge (48c) und der *archē* der Grundelemente (53d).[39]

---

39   Vgl. Szlezák, *Platon und die Schriftlichkeit.*

τὸν μὲν οὖν ποιητὴν καὶ πατέρα τοῦδε τοῦ παντὸς εὑρεῖν τε ἔργον καὶ εὑρόντα εἰς πάντας ἀδύνατον λέγειν

Den Schöpfer und Vater dieses Alls nun zu finden ist freilich schwierig, und wenn man ihn gefunden hat, ist es *unmöglich*, sich für alle verständlich über ihn auszusprechen.

Tim. 28c

χαλεπὸν εἶναι κατὰ τὸν παρόντα τρόπον τῆς διεξόδου δηλῶσαι τὰ δοκοῦντα

<weil> es zu *schwer* ist, nach dem ihr zugrunde gelegten Verfahren meine Ansicht hierüber kund zu tun

Tim. 48c

ἀρχὰς ἄνωθεν θεὸς *οἶδεν* καὶ *ἀνδρῶν, ὃς ἂν ἐκείνῳ φίλος ᾖ*

die noch ursprünglicheren Urbestandteile aber *kennt* nur *Gott und von den Menschen* etwa der, den er *lieb* hat

Tim. 53d

4.7 eikōs logos *und* eikōs mythos

In der Einleitung habe ich bereits auf die Relativierung des Wissens hingewiesen, welche Timaios durch die Einführung des *eikōs logos* vornimmt, indem er eine völlig exakte und widerspruchsfreie Darstellung der *gignomena* verneint (*Tim.* 29c). Hier sollen noch ein paar Gedanken zum *eikōs logos* bzw. *mythos* sowie zum *logos–mythos*-Gegensatz folgen, der in der Forschung immer wieder Anlass zu Diskussionen gegeben hat.[40]

Man kann unschwer erkennen, dass *eikōs logos* im Singular stets ein einzelnes, konkretes, bereits erbrachtes, in der Regel logisch (oder mathematisch) nachvollziehbares Argument bezeichnet (*Tim.* 30b7, 53d5 f., 55d5, 56a1, 56b4, 90e8; 57d6 thematisiert allgemein ein solches Argumentieren); im Plural werden *eikotes logoi* ausschliesslich in methodologischem Kontext als Argumente verwendet (29c2, 29c8, 48d2). Der *eikōs mythos* steht im Singular für die ganze Darstellung (29d2, 68d2) oder im Plural generell für jede Art solcher Reden (59c6), die hinwiederum aus *eikotes logoi* aufgebaut ist.

---

40 Vgl. u.a. Brisson, „Why is the *Timaeus* called an *eikôs muthos* and an *eikôs logos*?", Bryan, *Likeness and Likelihood*, Burnyeat, „ΕΙΚΩΣ ΜΥΘΟΣ", Gloy, *Studien zur Platonischen Naturphilosophie im Timaios*, und Johansen, *Plato's Natural Philosophy*.

Eine Rede als *eikōs mythos* hebt gleichsam doppelt ihre Defizienz hervor, indem sie einerseits „nur" *eikōs* ist (d.h. nicht völlig widerspruchsfrei und exakt ist bzw. nur Argumente mit einer solchen Einschränkung enthält, vgl. 29c) und andererseits „nur" ein *mythos* (d.h. eine nicht verifizierbare Geschichte mit göttlichem Beiwerk). Und gleichzeitig ist vor dem Hintergrund von Kritias' Auffassung, wie sie sowohl im Einleitungsgespräch des *Timaios* (*Tim.* 22c, 23b, 26c ff.) als auch im Einleitungsgespräch des *Kritias* (*Criti.* 106c ff.) vorkommt, der *eikōs mythos* nur aus historischer oder poetologischer[41] Sicht dem angeblichen *logos* unterlegen. Epistemologisch steht der „Mythos" des Timaios Sokrates' philosophischer Erörterung über den idealen Staat offensichtlich näher als die reine narrative Darstellung des Kritias, bei welcher ein Bezug zu den *onta* überhaupt fehlt – und deren fehlender Wahrheitsgehalt dem Leser ebenso klar ist.

Mythos und *logos* werden so gesehen tatsächlich austauschbar, wie es in der Forschung teilweise postuliert wird,[42] aber eben nicht als Begriffe an sich und mithin nicht als Zeichen einer unpräzisen Definition durch Timaios, sondern als Ausdruck der unterschiedlichen Perspektive: Von aussen her, aus der Sicht von (fiktiv Sokrates' und real Platons) Zeitgenossen ist die Darstellung ein Mythos, von innen her jedoch ein Logos beziehungsweise genauer angesichts der von Timaios vertretenen Einschränkungen, die durch das Subjekt des Redners und das Objekt der *gignomena* gegeben sind, fast ein Logos.

Das von Timaios benutzte *eikos* stimmt im Übrigen nicht mit dem *eikos* der sophistischen Rhetorik überein, das sich durch drei Kriterien fassen lässt:
(1) was den Zuhörern wahrscheinlich oder plausibel erscheint (*Phdr.* 260a2, 273b1)
(2) was wichtiger ist als die Wahrheit (*Phdr.* 260a3 f., 272d8 f., 267a6 f.)
(3) was teilweise anstelle der Wahrheit zu verwenden ist (*Phdr.* 272e2 f.)

(3) gilt sicher nicht – man denke nur an das abschliessende Gebet im *Kritias* (*Criti.* 106a f.) –, ebenso (2). Denn Timaios erstrebt an sich die Wahrheit, die aber im Bereich der *gignomena* zumal für einen Menschen nicht vollumfänglich erreichbar ist. Und auch (1) trifft nicht zu: Timaios erzählt eben nicht das, was seine Zuhörer erwarten, sondern was der – teilweise überraschenden oder ungewohnten (*Tim.* 48d5: ἀτόπου καὶ ἀήθους) – Wahrheit möglichst nahe kommt. Zudem lässt Timaios seine Zuhörer nie im Glauben, dass er die uneingeschränkte Wahrheit sagt, sondern kommuniziert gerade an den

---

41 Vgl. Erler, „Ideal und Geschichte. Die Rahmengespräche des *Timaios* und *Kritias* und Aristoteles' *Poetik*".
42 So e.g. Gloy, *Studien zur Platonischen Naturphilosophie im Timaios*, und Guthrie, *History of Greek Philosophy*.

Stellen, die etwas apodiktisch erscheinen könnten, mit grosser Transparenz die Unvollkommenheit seiner Darstellung.

Die vorangegangenen Ausführungen haben deutlich zum Ausdruck gebracht, dass Timaios in seiner Rede die Kriterien der philosophischen Rhetorik, wie sie hauptsächlich im *Phaidros* definiert werden, so gut wie möglich einhält. Seine Rede steht in dieser Hinsicht praktisch auf der gleichen Stufe wie die zweite Rede des Sokrates im *Phaidros*, die ebenfalls als ein Beispiel der wahren Rhetorik angesehen werden kann.

5 Erklärung der Eigentümlichkeiten

Damit lassen sich jetzt auch die in der Einleitung aufgeworfenen Fragen oder Auffälligkeiten des *Timaios* erklären. Das Einleitungsgespräch ist notwendig, um das Kriterium der Adressatenbezogenheit zu erfüllen: Die Rede ist nicht an ein beliebiges Publikum gerichtet, sondern explizit auf Sokrates, Kritias und Hermokrates mit ihren spezifischen Voraussetzungen zugeschnitten. Dessen muss sich umso mehr auch ein potenzieller Leser des Dialogs bewusst sein.

Der Götteranruf ist in der Tat teilweise der Tradition geschuldet (als Verweis auf die mythischen Kosmogonien von Platons Vorgängern, so insbesondere auf Hesiod), doch wird er von Timaios hauptsächlich um des Inhalts willen verwendet, da nur die Götter die Wahrheit der Darstellung verbürgen können.[43]

Das scheinbar unschlüssige Hin- und Herschwanken zwischen *mythos* und *logos* lässt sich als absolut geschicktes Verfahren des Timaios interpretieren, seine aus zeitgenössischer Sicht durchaus mythische Rede nicht als wissenschaftlich oder philosophisch minderwertig zu markieren. Auf Kritias' Kategorisierung von Sokrates Staatsutopie als *mythos plastheis* (*Tim.* 26e4) antwortet Timaios, indem er seine eigene Kosmogonie als *mythos eikōs* (*Tim.* 29d2) bezeichnet und damit geradezu eine neue Gattung definiert.

Die mündliche Darstellungsform basiert auf den Grundlagen der Schriftkritik, die ein situationsbezogenes Gespräch der unveränderlichen Fassung eines Textes vorzieht. Dass die Rede von Platon dann doch als Schrift publiziert worden ist, widerspricht diesen Vorgaben nicht, da sie den Kernbereich der Philosophie, die (ungeschriebene) Prinzipienlehre, fast vollständig ausblendet.

---

43   Auch im *Phaidros* kommt ja ein Musenanruf vor – notabene zu Beginn der sonst eher nüchtern-argumentativen ersten Rede (*Phdr.* 237a).

Sokrates' Interesse für naturphilosophische Themen im *Timaios* steht nicht im Gegensatz zum üblichen Bild aus den anderen Dialogen. Denn Timaios vertritt genau die teleologische Variante der Kosmologie, die sich Sokrates auch von Anaxagoras erhofft hätte.[44] Dazu kommt, dass sie auf Platons Unterscheidung zwischen *onta* und *gignomena* basiert und unsere Welt nicht in Konkurrenz zur Ideenwelt erklärt, sondern als Ergänzung mit der notwendigen Relativierung der Erkenntnisse.

Wenn Timaios dazu immer wieder auf den Begriff des *eikos* zurückkommt, verwendet er zwar ein Schlagwort der sophistischen Rhetorik, aber in einer völlig verschiedenen Funktion und vor allem so transparent, dass die Zuhörer dadurch nicht getäuscht und mutwillig von der Wahrheit weggeführt werden.

Die ungewöhnliche Länge der Rede widerspricht Sokrates' Ansichten im *Gorgias* und *Protagoras* nicht, da sie eben nicht ein dialektisches Gespräch unterbricht oder beeinträchtigt. Sie ist stattdessen durch den Inhalt bedingt, und sie entspricht den Aufnahmefähigkeiten ihrer Adressaten.

Vgl.	Eigentümlichkeit	Begründung
Allgemein	Einbettung der Rede in einen Dialog, Unterbruch	Adressatenbezogenheit
	Götteranruf	Gottgefälligkeit
	Mythos und *logos*	Aussen- vs. Innensicht
	Mündlichkeit statt Schriftlichkeit	Schriftkritik
Platon	Inhalt (naturphilosophische Erklärung der Welt)	Teleologie, *onta – gignomena*
	Prinzip des *eikos*	Epistemologie
	Länge	Sach- und Adressatenadäquatheit

Soweit sich also Platons Forderungen an eine philosophische Rhetorik aufgrund der teilweise offenen Aussagen im *Phaidros* überhaupt verifizieren lassen, sind sie in der grossen Rede des Timaios konsequent zur Anwendung gebracht worden. Besonders die Forderung, der Redner müsse die Wahrheit über seinen Gegenstand kennen, das Kriterium der passenden Strukturierung, die Erkenntnisse im Bereich einer wissenschaftlichen Psychologie und die Resultate der Schriftkritik hat Platon in seinem grossen kosmologischen Werk

---

44 Vgl. Neschke-Hentschke, *Le Timée de Platon, contributions à l'histoire de sa réception*, XV. Zur teleologischen Welterklärung im *Phaidon* selbst vgl. Sedley, „Teleology and Myth in the *Phaedo*".

folgerichtig in die Praxis umgesetzt und damit die gewaltige Wirkung des *Timaios* mit grosser Wahrscheinlichkeit überhaupt erst ermöglicht.

Zitierte Literatur

Ashbaugh, Anne F. *Plato's Theory of Explanation*. New York: SUNY Press, 1988.
Balansard, Anne. *Technè dans les Dialogues de Platon*. Sankt Augustin: Academia Verlag, 2001.
Brague, Rémi. „The Body of the Speech". In *Platonic Investigations*. Herausgegeben von Dominic O'Meara. Washington: Catholic University of America Press, 1985, 53–83.
Brickhouse, Thomas C. und Nicholas D. Smith. *Plato's Socrates*. New York: Oxford University Press, 1994.
Brisson, Luc. *Le Même et l'Autre dans la structure ontologique du Timée de Platon. Un commentaire systématique du Timée de Platon*. Zweite Auflage. Sankt Augustin: Academia Verlag, 1994.
Brisson, Luc. „Why is the *Timaeus* called an *eikôs muthos* and an *eikôs logos*?". In *Plato and Myth*. Herausgegeben von Catherine Collobert, Pierre Destrée und Francisco Gonzalez. Leiden: Brill, 2012, 369–391.
Bryan, Jenny. *Likeness and Likelihood in the Presocratics and Plato*. Cambridge: Cambridge University Press, 2012.
Burnyeat, Myles. „ΕΙΚΩΣ ΜΥΘΟΣ". *Rhizai* 2/2 (2005): 143–166.
Byrd, Miriam N. „Dialectic and Plato's Method of Hypothesis". *Apeiron* 40 (2007): 141–158.
Carone, Gabriela Roxana. *Plato's Cosmology and its Ethical Dimension*. Cambridge: Cambridge University Press, 2005.
Colaiaco, James. *Socrates against Athens*. New York: Routledge, 2001.
Colloud-Streit, Marlis. *Fünf platonische Mythen im Verhältnis zu ihren Textumfeldern*. Fribourg: Academic Press, 2005.
Erler, Michael. „Ideal und Geschichte. Die Rahmengespräche des *Timaios* und Kritias und Aristoteles' *Poetik*". In *Interpreting the* Timaeus – Critias. *Proceedings of the IV Symposium Platonicum*. Herausgegeben von Thomas Calvo und Luc Brisson. Sankt Augustin: Academia Verlag, 1997, 83–98.
Erler, Michael. *Die Philosophie der Antike 2/2: Platon*. Basel: Schwabe Verlag, 2007.
Eucken, Christoph. „Die Doppeldeutigkeit des platonischen *Menexenos*". *Hyperboreus* 9 (2003): 44–55.
Gloy, Karen. *Studien zur Platonischen Naturphilosophie im* Timaios. Würzburg: Königshausen u. Neumann, 1986.
Görgemanns, Herwig. *Beiträge zur Interpretation von Platons* Nomoi. München: C. H. Beck, 1960.

Guthrie, William K. C. *A History of Greek Philosophy III–V*. Cambridge: Cambridge University Press, 1969–1978.

Hadot, Pierre. „Physique et poésie dans le *Timée* de Platon". *RThPh* 115 (1983): 113–133.

Hartmann, Lucius. *Die grosse Rede des Timaios – ein Beispiel wahrer Rhetorik*. Basel: Schwabe Verlag, 2017.

Heinimann, Felix. „Eine vorplatonische Theorie der τέχνη". *Museum Helveticum* 18 (1961): 105–130.

Heitsch, Ernst. *Platon, Phaidros, Übersetzung und Kommentar*. Zweite Auflage. Göttingen: Vandenhoeck & Ruprecht, 1997.

Heitsch, Ernst. „Dialektik und Philosophie in Platons ‚Phaidros'". *Hermes* 125 (1997): 131–152.

Johansen, Thomas. *Plato's Natural Philosophy: A Study of the* Timaeus-Critias. Cambridge: Cambridge University Press, 2004.

Lampert, Laurence und Christopher Planeaux. „Who's Who in Plato's *Timaeus-Critias* and Why". *The Review of Metaphysics* 52 (1998): 87–125.

Marg, Walter, ed. *Timaeus Locrus. De Natura Mundi et Animae*. Leiden: Brill, 1972.

Mesch, Walter. „Die Bildlichkeit der platonischen Kosmologie". In *Platon als Mythologe*. Herausgegeben von Markus Janka und Christian Schäfer. Darmstadt: WBG Academic, 2002, 194–213.

Morgan, Kathryn A. *Myth and Philosophy from the Presocratics to Plato*. Cambridge: Cambridge University Press, 2000.

Morrow, Glenn R. „Plato's Theory of the Primary Bodies in the *Timaeus* and the Later Doctrine of Forms", *Archiv für Geschichte der Philosophie* 50 (1968): 12–28.

Nails, Debra. *The People of Plato*. Indianapolis: Hackett, 2002.

Neschke-Hentschke, Ada, ed. *Le* Timée *de Platon, contributions à l'histoire de sa réception*. Louvain: Peeters, 2000.

Nevsky, Alexandre. *Voir le monde comme une image*. Bern: Peter Lang, 2011.

Osborne, Catherine. „Space, Time, Shape, and Direction: Creative Discourse in the *Timaeus*". In *Form and Argument in Late Plato*. Herausgegeben von Christopher Gill. Oxford: Oxford University Press, 1996, 179–211.

O'Sullivan, Neil. „Written and Spoken in the First Sophistic". In *Voice into Text*. Herausgegeben von Ian Worthington. Leiden: Brill, 1996, 115–127.

Pernot, Laurent. *La rhétorique dans l'antiquité*. Paris: Le Livre de Poche, 2000.

Racionero, Quentin. „*Logos*, myth and probable discourse in Plato's *Timaeus*". *Elenchos* 19 (1998): 29–60.

Robinson, Thomas M., „The World as Art-Object: Science and the Real in Plato's *Timaeus*". *Illinois Classical Studies* 18 (1993): 99–111.

Rowe, Christopher. *Plato and the Art of Philosophical Writing*. Cambridge: Cambridge University Press, 2007.

Runia, David Theunis. „The Language of Excellence in Plato's *Timaeus* and Later Platonism". In *Platonism in Late Antiquity*. Herausgegeben von Stephen Gersh. Notre Dame: University of Notre Dame Press, 1992, 11–37.

Sayre, Kenneth M. *Metaphysics and Method in Plato's Statesman*. Cambridge: Cambridge University Press, 2006.

Schiappa, Edward. „Did Plato coin Rhêtorikê?". *American Journal of Philology* 111 (1990), 457–470.

Schofield, Malcolm. „The disappearance of the philosopher king". In *Boston Area Colloquium in Ancient Philosophy 13*. Herausgegeben von John J. Cleary und Gary M. Gurtler, Leiden: Brill, 1999, 213–254.

Schoos, Daniel J. „Timaeus' Banquet". *Ancient Philosophy* 19 (1999): 97–107.

Sedley, David. „Teleology and Myth in the *Phaedo*". In *Boston Area Colloquium in Ancient Philosophy 5*. Herausgegeben von John J. Cleary and Daniel C. Shartin, Lanham: University Press of America, 1991, 359–383.

Stenzel, Julius. *Studien zur Entwicklung der platonischen Dialektik von Sokrates zu Aristoteles*. Zweite Auflage. Leipzig: B. G. Teubner, 1931.

Szlezák, Thomas A. *Platon und die Schriftlichkeit der Philosophie*. Berlin, 1985.

Szlezák, Thomas A. „Über die Art und Weise der Erörterung der Prinzipien im *Timaios*". In *Interpreting the* Timaios – Critias*, Proceedings of the IV Symposium Platonicum*. Herausgegeben von Thomas Calvo und Luc Brisson. Sankt Augustin: Academia Verlag, 1997, 195–203.

Tarán, Leonardo. „The Creation Myth in Plato's *Timaeus*". In *Essays in Ancient Greek Philosophy*. Herausgegeben von John Peter Anton und George Kustas. New York: SUNY Press, 1971, 372–407.

Thompson, Wayne N. „The Symposion: a neglected Source for Plato's Ideas on Rhetoric". In *Plato: True and Sophistic Rhetoric*. Herausgegeben von Keith Erickson. Amsterdam: Brill 1979, 325–338.

Werner, Daniel. „Rhetoric and philosophy in Plato's *Phaedrus*". *Greece & Rome* 57 (2010): 21–46.

Yunis, Harvey. *Taming Democracy*. Ithaca: Cornell University Press, 1996.

Yunis, Harvey, ed. *Plato: Phaedrus*. Cambridge: Cambridge University Press, 2011.

Panteles zōion e *pantelōs on*: Vita, anima e movimento intelligibile nel *Timeo* (e nel *Sofista*)

Francesco Fronterotta

Abstract

In this article, I try to propose some reflections about the nature and status of the intelligible in the *Timaeus*, particularly with respect to its features of a *properly being* and above all *vital* reality. The attribution of "life" and "vitality" to the intelligible certainly has an analogical character, that is, it depends on the consideration of the sensible: since the cosmos is a sensible living being and is a copy of an intelligible model, then the intelligible model must be configured as an intelligible living being. Now, to be "living", for a sensible reality, means to have a soul that animates a body, that is a soul which is embodied; but this seems to apply only in the case of the sensible. What does it mean, then, and what does it entail, to be "living" for an intelligible reality? Some interpretative hypotheses on this point are examined here and a possible overall explanation is suggested.

Keywords

Plato – *Timaeus* – intelligible (being) – life – soul – intellect

Per tentare di svolgere qualche considerazione intorno alla natura e allo statuto dell'intellegibile nel *Timeo*[1], particolarmente rispetto ai suoi tratti di realtà propriamente essente e vitale, è necessario prendere le mosse dalla ben nota distinzione, posta in 27d–28b, fra « ciò che sempre è, senza avere generazione » (τὸ ὂν ἀεί, γένεσιν δὲ οὐκ ἔχον) e « ciò che sempre diviene, senza mai essere » (τὸ γιγνόμενον μὲν ἀεί, ὂν δὲ οὐδέποτε): ciò che è sempre, ed è estraneo al divenire, « si coglie con il pensiero e se ne può rendere conto razionalmente » (νοήσει μετὰ λόγου); ciò che invece sempre diviene, e non partecipa dell'essere,

---

[1] Per una presentazione introduttiva che fornisce le coordinate d'insieme che presiedono all'esposizione di Timeo, e per l'indicazione della bibliografia pertinente, sia lecito rinviare alla mia *Introduzione* a Fronterotta, ed., *Platone, Timeo*, 23–35, cui farò nuovamente riferimento in seguito.

è « oggetto dell'opinione che deriva dalla sensazione di cui non si può rendere conto razionalmente » (δόξῃ μετ'αἰσθήσεως ἀλόγου). Una simile distinzione si basa sul fatto che, mentre ciò che è davvero, mai divenendo, resta immobile e immutabile (ἀεὶ κατὰ ταὐτὰ ὄν) e può perciò costituire l'oggetto di una conoscenza vera e a sua volta immutabile, ciò che diviene, invece, mai essendo davvero, si genera e si corrompe (γιγνόμενον καὶ ἀπολλύμενον) continuamente e può costituire soltanto l'oggetto di una conoscenza incerta, a sua volta mutevole e corruttibile, l'opinione[2].

Fra gli ambiti dell'essere e del divenire sussiste inoltre una duplice relazione causale, perché l'intera sfera di ciò che diviene, in quanto è caratterizzata da generazione e corruzione, suppone l'intervento di una causa a partire da cui appunto si verifichi la generazione (πᾶν δὲ αὖ τὸ γιγνόμενον ὑπ'αἰτίου τίνος [...] γίγνεσθαι) – una causa efficiente, quindi, giacché è « impossibile, per qualunque cosa, avere generazione senza una causa » (παντὶ [...] ἀδύνατον χωρὶς αἰτίου γένεσιν σχεῖν), i cui tratti propriamente produttivi inducono ad associarla a una funzione artigianale e demiurgica – e l'esistenza di un modello in conformità al quale la realtà generata sia costituita nella sua forma e nelle sue proprietà (τοιούτῳ [...] τινὶ παραδείγματι, τὴν ἰδέαν καὶ δύναμιν αὐτοῦ) – una causa paradigmatica, dunque, che, se coincide con l'essere immobile e immutabile (τὸ κατὰ ταὐτὰ ἔχον), conduce alla riproduzione, a partire da se stessa, di copie o immagini *belle*, nella misura in cui conservano traccia della perfezione del modello; mentre, se tale causa paradigmatica coincidesse con un'altra realtà generata, le copie o immagini riprodotte a partire da questa non potrebbero che rispecchiare l'imperfezione del modello nella loro estraneità alla bellezza[3]. È chiaro come causa efficiente e causa paradigmatica – il demiurgo e il modello, *ho*

---

2 Si tratta del caratteristico principio, onnipresente nei dialoghi platonici, che stabilisce la corrispondenza fra l'ambito epistemico delle diverse forme e facoltà della conoscenza e l'ambito ontologico dei diversi oggetti che esse assumono come proprio contenuto, in virtù della quale natura e grado di verità della conoscenza dipendono dallo statuto dei suoi oggetti. Devo rinviare, per una formulazione generale della questione e per una discussione della relativa bibliografia, a Fronterotta, ΜΕΘΕΞΙΣ. *La teoria delle idee e la partecipazione delle cose empiriche. Dai dialoghi giovanili al* Parmenide, specie 62–79; e all'acuta disamina di Leszl, « Ragioni per postulare idee ».

3 Sulla natura di tale relazione causale e sulle diverse proposte esegetiche intorno alla natura della causalità, formale, paradigmatica o propriamente efficiente, delle idee intelligibili rispetto alle cose sensibili, rinvio a una serie di lavori recenti che hanno significativamente rinnovato il panorama degli studi platonici: Sedley, « Platonic Causes »; Natali, « La forma platonica è una causa formale ? »; Ferrari, « Questioni eidetiche »; Fronterotta, « Chiusura causale della fisica e razionalità del tutto : alcune opzioni esegetiche sull'efficienza causale delle idee platoniche »; e, con particolare riferimento al *Timeo*, Fronterotta, « Modello, copia, ricettacolo : monismo, dualismo o triade di principi nel *Timeo*? ».

dēmiourgos e *to paradeigma* – siano strettamente connesse, dal momento che l'azione produttiva del demiurgo, che innesca il processo della generazione fra le realtà in divenire, si basa e dipende da un modello, appunto, da riprodurre nelle sue copie o immagini; come pure la funzione paradigmatica del modello, perché possa realizzarsi nella riproduzione delle sue copie o immagini, esige l'intervento "operativo" di un agente, senza il quale rimarrebbe inerte da un punto di vista produttivo, appunto come un modello che attenda di essere riprodotto. Dei diversi aspetti che il semplice richiamo di questo passo evoca desidero porne in rilievo soltanto tre, in forma puramente generale: (1) nessuna generazione è possibile se non in seguito a, e in conseguenza di, un'azione causale; (2) ogni generazione consiste per necessità nella riproduzione di un modello; (3) il modello si configura come una causa paradigmatica, e non efficiente, della generazione, perché la causa efficiente della generazione, benché indubbiamente connessa al modello, ne è altrettanto evidentemente dissociata, se viene posta l'alternativa relativa al genere di modello, eterno o generato, assunto e riprodotto nell'atto generativo vero e proprio[4].

Questo schema ontologico, applicato all'esame del cosmo (28b-29b), della sua natura e della sua struttura, porta a riconoscere che il nostro mondo, in quanto è di natura sensibile e perciò soggetto al divenire e alla trasformazione, fa parte delle realtà caratterizzate da generazione e corruzione (τὰ δ'αἰσθητά [...] γιγνόμενα καὶ γεννητά), in modo che, in virtù di quanto spiegato in precedenza, deve possedere un principio e una causa della generazione (ἀπ'ἀρχῆς τινος ἀρξάμενος [...] ὑπ'αἰτίου τινὸς γενέσθαι); d'altra parte, se così non fosse, il cosmo si rivelerebbe esso stesso, in quanto privo di generazione e corruzione, eterno e finirebbe per coincidere allora con il modello intelligibile, sicché il riconoscimento che vi è un ambito di realtà in divenire impone la postulazione di un ambito di realtà eterne come suo modello: rimane controverso, ma non intendo toccare qui questo punto, se l'ammissione del carattere diveniente del mondo implichi che esso ha avuto un inizio e un'origine nel tempo, e sia stato dunque effettivamente generato, o semplicemente che è di natura sensibile, e sia dunque affetto nel suo complesso ed eternamente da generazione e

---

4 In favore dell'interpretazione opposta, di un'identificazione della causa paradigmatica rappresentata dal modello intelligibile e della causa efficiente associata al demiurgo, si è espresso Ferrari, « Causa paradigmatica e causa efficiente: il ruolo delle idee nel *Timeo* », e « Der entmythologisierte Demiurg », riprendendo e ampiamente sviluppando alcuni spunti suggeriti, fra gli altri, da Perl, « The Demiurge and the Forms. A Return to the Ancient Interpretation of Plato's *Timaeus* ». Ho discusso, e in certa misura criticato, questa proposta esegetica nell'articolo « Questioni eidetiche in Platone: il sensibile e il demiurgo, l'essere e il bene », 421-424.

corruzione rispetto alle cose in esso contenute⁵. Ed è in base a tali premesse che Timeo richiama nuovamente, come «costruttore e padre» (ποιητὴν καὶ πατέρα) e come «artigiano» (τεκταινόμενος) del cosmo, ossia come sua causa produttiva o efficiente, il demiurgo; e come modello in conformità al quale si realizza l'attività produttiva di quest'ultimo (πρὸς πότερον τῶν παραδειγμάτων [...] αὐτὸν ἀπηργάζετο), ossia come causa paradigmatica del cosmo in divenire, quella realtà «che rimane sempre identica e immutabile [...] eterna» (τὸ κατὰ ταὐτὰ καὶ ὡσαύτως ἔχον [...] τὸ ἀίδιον) – che si tratti senza dubbio di un modello appartenente all'ambito di «ciò che sempre è, senza avere generazione» è reso certo dalla semplice constatazione della bellezza del cosmo che, come già sappiamo, rinvia di necessità alla perfezione di un paradigma eterno a partire dal quale è stato riprodotto, e dall'assunto indiscusso della bontà del demiurgo, qualificato come «la migliore delle cause» (ὁ δ'ἄριστος τῶν αἰτίων), vale a dire, presumibilmente, la più compiutamente efficace⁶. Se ne conclude così che il cosmo non è altro che un'immagine generata di un modello eterno – immagine e modello costituendo due generi da tenere fra loro opportunamente distinti (περί τε εἰκόνος καὶ περὶ τοῦ παραδείγματος αὐτῆς διοριστέον) – la prima di natura sensibile, il secondo che «si coglie con il ragionamento e con il pensiero» (τὸ λόγῳ καὶ φρονήσει περιληπτόν) ed è perciò di natura intelligibile.

A tale scansione Timeo non esita a ricondurre anche l'ambito dei *logoi*: come fra le cose che sono e fra i modi di conoscenza che a esse si rivolgono, anche fra i discorsi si distinguono infatti quelli «stabili e solidi» (μονίμους καὶ ἀμεταπτώτους), quando riguardano un contenuto a loro volta «stabile, saldo ed evidente al pensiero» (τοῦ [...] μονίμου καὶ βεβαίου καὶ μετὰ νοῦ καταφανοῦς), cioè la realtà intelligibile che è sempre, e quelli soltanto «verosimili» o «probabili» (εἰκότας), quando si riferiscono invece a un contenuto «che imita il modello e che non è che un'immagine» (τοῦ πρὸς ἐκεῖνο ἀπεικασθέντος, ὄντος δὲ εἰκόνος), quindi alla realtà sensibile in divenire che, in quanto copia o imitazione della prima, è solo simile, ma non identica, a essa. Donde la ben nota affermazione della "congenericità" dei *logoi* e dei loro contenuti (τοὺς λόγους,

---

5 Non esamino dunque qui la delicatissima questione dell'inizio nel tempo della vicenda cosmica o della sua eternità, come risposta alla domanda esplicitamente posta da Timeo (28b) «se [il mondo] sia sempre stato, senza avere né principio né generazione, oppure se sia stato generato a partire da un principio». Si veda in proposito il mio articolo «Ἀρχὴ τοῦ κόσμου and ἀρχὴ τοῦ λόγου. A New Hypothesis on the Beginning of the World in Plato's *Timaeus*» con gli opportuni riferimenti bibliografici.

6 Pure da parte rimane in questa sede la questione della "bellezza" del cosmo generato e della "bontà" del demiurgo che lo ha prodotto, che fissa i termini della prospettiva rigorosamente teleologica sottesa alla cosmologia del *Timeo*. Cfr. ancora Fronterotta, ed., *Platone, Timeo*, 85–88.

ὧνπέρ εἰσιν ἐξηγηταί, τούτων αὐτῶν καὶ συγγενεῖς ὄντας), e la conseguente indicazione di una corrispondenza fra essere e verità delle cose che sono e dei discorsi pienamente scientifici che ne parlano e fra divenire e semplice verosimiglianza delle cose soggette a generazione e corruzione e dei discorsi solo opinativi a esse relativi (29b–d)[7].

Più avanti, il dialogo torna a più riprese, per precisarla e articolarla ulteriormente, su questa generale scansione onto-cosmologica. In 48e–49a, Timeo precisa che, in aggiunta ai *duo eidē* individuati in precedenza, « l'uno posto come genere del modello, intelligibile e sempre identico a se stesso » (ἓν μὲν ὡς παραδείγματος εἶδος ὑποτεθέν, νοητὸν καὶ ἀεὶ κατὰ ταὐτὰ ὄν), « il secondo come imitazione del modello, soggetto a generazione e visibile » (μίμημα δὲ παραδείγματος δεύτερον, γένεσιν ἔχον καὶ ὁρατόν), occorre stabilirne adesso un terzo, che prima non era apparso necessario e che risulta « difficile e oscuro » (χαλεπὸν καὶ ἀμυδρόν) all'indagine: la sua proprietà (δύναμις) e la sua natura (φύσις) sembrano consistere essenzialmente nel ruolo che a tale genere spetta di « ricettacolo e nutrice, per così dire, di ogni generazione » (πάσης εἶναι γενέσεως ὑποδοχὴν αὐτὴν οἷον τιθήνην). Senza che venga per il momento fornita nessuna ulteriore delucidazione, pare però plausibile intendere questa duplice denominazione del terzo genere nel senso che esso *accoglie*, come "ricettacolo", e *alimenta*, come "nutrice", ogni processo produttivo, cioè precisamente ogni processo che, a partire dal primo genere, il modello intelligibile, conduce alla realizzazione del secondo genere, che consta delle imitazioni, appunto soggette al divenire, alla generazione e alla corruzione, del modello intelligibile; in tal senso, il terzo genere sembra prestare un fondamento "spaziale" o "locale" e a un tempo "materiale" o "sostanziale" alla generazione del sensibile a imitazione dell'intelligibile[8]. Poco oltre, in 50c–d, questo schema triadico risulta confermato, perché si indicano ancora tre generi da tenere a mente (χρὴ γένη διανοηθῆναι τριττά): « ciò che viene all'essere » (τὸ μὲν γιγνόμενον), che corrisponde evidentemente al secondo genere del passo precedente, alla

---

[7] Un articolato esame dei diversi livelli di "verità" e "verosimiglianza" del discorso di Timeo è stato condotto da Donini, « Il *Timeo*: unità del dialogo, verosimiglianza del discorso », specie 37–50.

[8] Dell'ampissima serie di studi relativi alla natura e alla funzione onto-cosmologiche della *chōra*, di cui è impossibile trattare qui, ricordo soltanto alcuni indispensabili punti di riferimento recenti, che danno conto anche del dibattito critico pertinente: si vedano Algra, *Concepts of Space in Greek Thought*, 74–120; Miller, *The Third Kind in Plato's* Timaeus; e i più agili lavori di Ferrari, « La chora nel *Timeo* di Platone. Riflessioni su "materia" e "spazio" nell'ontologia del mondo fenomenico », e di Brisson, « La matière chez Platon et dans la tradition platonicienne ». Ho a mia volta esaminato e discusso i tratti "spazio-materiali" della *chōra* appena evocati nell'articolo « Luogo, spazio e sostrato "spazio-materiale" nel *Timeo* di Platone e nei commenti al *Timeo* ».

realtà sensibile in divenire soggetta a generazione e corruzione, paragonato a una « natura intermedia » fra gli altri due generi (τὴν δὲ μεταξὺ τούτων φύσιν) e come « a un figlio » (ἐκγόνῳ) di quelli; « ciò in cui viene all'essere [*scil.*, ciò che viene all'essere] » (τὸ δ'ἐν ᾧ γίγνεται [*scil.*, τὸ γιγνόμενον]), che evoca il terzo genere, in quanto "spazio" o "luogo" della generazione del secondo genere, ossia il suo « ricettacolo » cui pure si addice di assomigliare « a una madre » (προσεικάσαι ... τὸ μὲν μητρί), così richiamandone nuovamente la funzione "materiale" o "sostanziale"; e « ciò a somiglianza di cui viene all'essere ciò che viene all'essere » (τὸ δ'ὅθεν ἀφομοιούμενον φύεται τὸ γιγνόμενον), che coincide senza dubbio con il primo genere, il « modello » intelligibile a imitazione del quale è generato il secondo genere, che funge per esso da « padre » (τὸ δ'ὅθεν πατρί). Ancora, in 51e–52c, dopo aver rievocato la distinzione tracciata fin da 27d–28b fra realtà intelligibili e sensibili, le prime, le idee, oggetto stabile e immutabile del pensiero, le seconde, le cose che percepiamo tramite i sensi, contenuto variabile e mutevole dell'opinione, presentate come *duo genē* fra loro alternativi, Timeo ribadisce la sua posizione, articolandone i dettagli: bisogna ammettere un primo genere, che è « sempre identico, ingenerato e incorruttibile » (τὸ κατὰ ταὐτὰ [...] ἔχον, ἀγέννητον καὶ ἀνώλεθρον), che si pone separatamente da qualunque altra cosa, che è invisibile e impercettibile, ma si coglie con il pensiero (ἀόρατον [...] ἀναίσθητον [...] ὃ δὴ νόησις εἴληχεν ἐπισκοπεῖν); vi è di seguito un secondo genere, che « ha lo stesso nome ed è simile al primo » (τὸ δὲ ὁμώνυμον ὅμοιόν τε ἐκείνῳ), che è « sensibile, generato e sempre in movimento » (αἰσθητόν, γεννητόν, πεφορημένον ἀεί), soggetto perciò a generazione e corruzione in un certo luogo (γιγνόμενόν τε ἔν τινι τόπῳ καὶ πάλιν ἐκεῖθεν ἀπολλύμενον) e contenuto dell'opinione che si accompagna alla percezione (δόξῃ μετ'αἰσθήσεως περιληπτόν); e vi è infine un terzo genere, cui è attribuita qui la denominazione di *chōra*, « che è sempre e non ammette corruzione » (ὄν [...] ἀεί, φθορὰν οὐ προσδεχόμενον) e il cui modo di conoscenza, in qualche misura intermedio fra ragionamento e percezione sensibile e a un tempo estraneo a entrambi, risulta apparentato al sogno e alla sua debole credibilità, e che, ciononostante, fornisce un luogo o una sede (ἕδραν δὲ παρέχον) per la generazione di ogni cosa (ὅσα ἔχει γένεσιν πᾶσιν). Timeo ripete infine per l'ultima volta, in 52d, la sua triade di principi o generi delle cose che sono (τρία τριχῇ), l'essere o ciò che è (ὄν), la *chōra* e il divenire o ciò che è soggetto alla generazione (γένεσις), che precedono la costituzione del mondo, posti in un rapporto di collaborazione in base al quale la *chōra*, come « nutrice della generazione » (γενέσεως τιθήνην), è per ciò stesso naturalmente disposta ad accogliere forme e figure (μορφὰς δεχομένην) che ne modificano la configurazione e l'aspetto, dapprima secondo un andamento conflittuale e disordinato, in seguito, verosimilmente per l'intervento della divinità demiurgica, a imitazione delle realtà intelligibili, cioè del modello eterno, dando luogo così alla generazione del cosmo, appunto in virtù dell'interazione fra il modello e la *chōra* operata dall'attività ordinatrice della divinità demiurgica (53a–b).

Attenendomi ai miei scopi attuali, lascerò del tutto da parte la temibile questione delle effettive modalità della generazione del cosmo sensibile e, di conseguenza, dell'interpretazione, pure assai controversa, della figura e del ruolo operativo del demiurgo, come anche, d'altro canto, l'altrettanto spinoso problema dello statuto ontologico e della natura funzionale della *chōra*[9]; trarrò invece dalla sintetica ricognizione delle successive prese di posizione di Timeo appena tratteggiata le indicazioni che mi appaiono pertinenti in relazione al tema annunciato della descrizione dei tratti costitutivi del modello intelligibile come realtà propriamente essente e vitale. Abbiamo appreso infatti (fin da 27d–28a, ma cfr. pure 48e–49a e 51b–52a) che le idee intelligibili, che compongono nella loro pluralità e totalità il modello eterno, si pongono senza dubbio come principi appartenenti all'essere che è sempre, esente da generazione e divenire (τὸ ὂν ἀεί, γένεσιν δὲ οὐκ ἔχον), oggetto di pensiero e contenuto di ragionamento (νοήσει μετὰ λόγου), che rimane immobile e immutabile (ἀεὶ κατὰ ταὐτὰ ὄν); di esse il demiurgo si serve come esemplari a partire da cui produrre il mondo sensibile (28b–29a), sicché, appunto in quanto modelli, si trovano paragonate a un "padre" che, esercitando una causalità paradigmatica sul materiale rappresentato dall'elemento materno, definisce la forma del figlio e contribuisce in tale misura alla sua generazione (50d)[10], per essere ancora concepite in seguito alla stregua di schemi formali e numerici di cui la divinità fa uso nella sua opera di ordinamento cosmico (53b); le idee sono dotate infine (51b–c) di piena autonomia e auto-sufficienza ontologica perché tutte in sé e per sé (αὐτὰ καθ'αὑτὰ ὄντα ἕκαστα) e in possesso, ciascuna da sé, del principio del proprio essere (αὐτὸ ἐφ' ἑαυτοῦ). Non è difficile comprendere, a simili condizioni, per quale ragione l'intelligibile nel suo complesso occupi il rango ontologico più elevato in questa gerarchia del reale, configurandosi così

---

9 Rinvio rispettivamente, per questi aspetti, a Brisson, *Le même et l'autre dans la structure ontologique du* Timée *de Platon*, 55–101, che fornisce tuttora un eccellente punto di partenza storico e filosofico per l'esame della figura del demiurgo del *Timeo*, e ai lavori citati nella nota precedente.

10 Vale la pena notare, pur senza poterne approfondire qui le eventuali implicazioni, che la metafora del "padre", che nei passi citati del *Timeo* allude indubbiamente a una forma di causalità paradigmatica, cioè all'esercizio della funzione di un modello cui il figlio assomiglia riproducendone i tratti nell'elemento materiale e ricettivo materno rappresentato dalla *chōra*, è invece utilizzata altrove nei dialoghi platonici (come del resto nel *corpus* aristotelico) come esemplificazione di una forma di causalità propriamente efficiente e produttiva (cfr. per esempio *Hipp. Ma.* 297b–c), tale per cui il "padre" simboleggia il principio attivo della generazione del figlio.

a pieno titolo, in quanto appunto propriamente essente, come modello eterno della generazione del cosmo sensibile.

Ora, tornando alla sezione del dialogo da cui ho preso le mosse, la causa (efficiente) della generazione del cosmo (δι'ἥντινα αἰτίαν γένεσιν καὶ τὸ πᾶν τόδε ὁ συνιστὰς συνέστησεν) è fatta coincidere, in 29e, con la bontà della divinità demiurgica che, appunto in quanto buona, cioè priva di invidia (ἀγαθὸς ἦν, ἀγαθῷ δὲ οὐδεὶς ... ἐγγίγνεται φθόνος)[11], attua la produzione del sensibile in conformità alla propria bontà, vale a dire aspirando a rendere il proprio prodotto "buono" e dunque, per quanto possibile, simile a sé (πάντα ὅτι μάλιστα ἐβουλήθη γενέσθαι παραπλήσια ἑαυτῷ [...] βουληθεὶς γὰρ ὁ θεὸς ἀγαθὰ μὲν πάντα). Questo assunto si traduce immediatamente in tre linee-guida dell'azione produttiva del demiurgo, che consiste (1) nell'attribuzione di un ordine al movimento disordinato che appartiene allo stato pre-cosmico, « considerando che questo è in tutto migliore di quello » (εἰς τάξιν αὐτὸ ἤγαγεν ἐκ τῆς ἀταξίας, ἡγησάμενος ἐκεῖνο τούτου πάντως ἄμεινον, 30a); (2) nel conferimento di un'anima dotata di intelletto al corpo del cosmo (νοῦν μὲν ἐν ψυχῇ, ψυχὴν δ' ἐν σώματι συνιστάς), sulla base dell'argomento che « dalle cose che sono per loro natura visibili » (ἐκ τῶν κατὰ φύσιν ὁρατῶν) è possibile generare un essere migliore rispetto a uno peggiore a condizione di assegnargli l'intelletto (οὐδὲν ἀνόητον τοῦ νοῦν ἔχοντος ὅλον ὅλου κάλλιον ἔσεσθαί ποτε ἔργον) e che, d'altra parte, è impossibile che qualcosa possieda l'intelletto senza un'anima e in un'anima (νοῦν δ' αὖ χωρὶς ψυχῆς ἀδύνατον παραγενέσθαι τῳ, 30b); (3) nell'assunzione, come modello della generazione del cosmo, non di una specie vivente particolare (τῶν ... ἐν μέρους εἴδει πεφυκότων), perché « nulla che assomigli a un essere incompleto potrebbe mai essere bello » (ἀτελεῖ γὰρ ἐοικὸς οὐδέν ποτ' ἂν γένοιτο καλόν), bensì di « ciò di cui fanno parte gli altri viventi, singolarmente o secondo la specie, a questo, fra tutti i viventi, noi poniamo che il mondo sia del tutto simile » (οὗ δ' ἔστιν τἆλλα ζῷα καθ' ἓν καὶ κατὰ γένη μόρια, τούτῳ πάντων ὁμοιότατον αὐτὸν εἶναι τιθῶμεν, 30c). Lasciando da parte il primo di questi criteri operativi, che ha carattere piuttosto generale, è interessante osservare come il secondo di essi implichi che la questione della presenza dell'anima e dunque dell'animazione vitale

---

11 Il termine greco *phthonos*, letteralmente "invidia" o "gelosia", designa, per esempio, l'atteggiamento della divinità nei confronti dell'uomo che oltrepassa, a qualunque titolo, i limiti della propria natura, per avvicinarsi alla condizione divina. In questo caso, la divinità diviene "invidiosa" o "gelosa" dell'uomo e procede alla sua punizione, facendolo cadere in errore o ingannandolo in qualche modo, per esempio accecando i suoi occhi e la sua mente. È da tale punto di vista che il demiurgo, non essendo per nulla "invidioso" o "geloso", non intende privare il cosmo prodotto dalla sua azione generativa di nessuna delle caratteristiche che possano renderlo "buono", cioè, per quanto possibile, simile a sé. Si veda in proposito Brisson, « La notion de phtónos chez Platon ».

riguarda esclusivamente le realtà sensibili dotate di corpo: è in relazione alle «cose che sono per loro natura visibili», infatti, che ha senso chiedersi quale sia l'apporto che al loro statuto viene dall'attribuzione del *nous* e dell'anima, se il *nous* non può sussistere, per definizione, dissociato da quella; ed è appunto «in virtù di questo ragionamento» (διὰ τὸν λογισμὸν τόνδε) che il demiurgo procede alla costituzione del cosmo ponendo il *nous* nell'anima e l'anima nel corpo – si tratta evidentemente qui dell'anima e del corpo del mondo – tale duplice innesto, dell'intelletto nell'anima e dell'anima nel corpo, che conduce a concepire il cosmo generato come «un vivente dotato di anima e di intelletto» (ζῷον ἔμψυχον ἔννουν τε), dovendosi intendere come a un tempo originario e strutturale, vale a dire come assolutamente necessario e universalmente vero: se l'associazione dell'intelletto all'anima e dell'anima al corpo è parte del disegno demiurgico, comunque lo si interpreti, ciò comporta senza alcun dubbio che nessun intelletto può sussistere indipendentemente da un'anima né nessun'anima indipendentemente da un corpo, cioè al di fuori dell'ambito delle cose sensibili ossia, ancora, nell'intelligibile. E del resto, se all'anima spetta di "animare" un corpo e se all'intelletto compete di rendere migliore un essere che potrebbe, in sua assenza, essere peggiore, quale contributo offrirebbero l'anima e l'intelletto in un ambito rispettivamente *già* perfetto e compiuto e privo di corpo, come è di per sé l'intelligibile?

Ciò non impedisce che, pur rinunciando a ogni riferimento all'anima e al corpo, venga ammessa una forma di "vitalità" dell'intelligibile, come risulta chiaramente dall'assunzione del terzo criterio operativo dell'azione produttiva demiurgica, se il modello eterno cui essa si ispira consiste nella totalità dei viventi e si configura quindi esso stesso come quello, fra i viventi, che tutti li comprende. Infatti, è proprio a questo punto che il tratto "vitale" dell'intelligibile si trova esplicitato: innanzitutto (30c), il modello è detto includere «tutti i viventi intelligibili» (τὰ νοητὰ ζῷα πάντα) *proprio come* il cosmo sensibile contiene «noi e tutti gli altri esseri viventi visibili» (ἡμᾶς ὅσα τε ἄλλα θρέμματα ... ὁρατά); tale analogia, o comparazione di uguaglianza, fra l'intelligibile e il sensibile è subito spiegata (30d), giacché Timeo precisa che la divinità ha prodotto «un vivente unico, visibile, che comprende in sé tutti i viventi che gli sono per natura congeneri» (ζῷον ἓν ὁρατόν, πάνθ᾽ ὅσα αὐτοῦ κατὰ φύσιν συγγενῆ ζῷα ἐντὸς ἔχον ἑαυτοῦ), *perché* il cosmo sensibile «assomigliasse quanto più possibile al più bello e al più perfetto in tutto fra gli esseri intelligibili» (τῷ γὰρ τῶν νοουμένων καλλίστῳ καὶ κατὰ πάντα τελέῳ μάλιστα αὐτὸν [...] ὁμοιῶσαι): non è lecito né consigliabile concepire questa analogia in forma ascendente (ossia attribuendo al termine superiore caratteristiche che appartengono al termine inferiore e che da questo dunque gli deriverebbero), in modo che, *se* il cosmo sensibile è generato come un vivente in quanto dotato di anima e intelletto, *allora anche* il suo modello intelligibile deve essere rappresentato come un vivente in quanto a sua volta dotato di anima e intelletto; bensì, evidentemente, in forma discendente (ossia attribuendo al termine inferiore caratteristiche che appartengono al termine superiore e che da questo dunque gli derivano), riconoscendo perciò che, *se* il cosmo sensibile, generato come un vivente in quanto dotato di anima e intelletto, è una copia del modello intelligibile, *allora* il suo modello intelligibile deve essere rappresentato come un vivente in quanto a sua volta dotato di uno statuto e di una condizione "vitali", a qualche titolo superiore e in qualche senso eminente, che, al livello del sensibile, si manifestano nella forma e nei modi della "vita" sensibile, vale a dire nella presenza di un'anima dotata di intelletto innestata in un corpo che anima. Si giunge così al coerente compimento della rappresentazione dell'intelligibile come "vivente" (31a–b): se infatti, argomenta Timeo nel corso di una breve dimostrazione dell'unicità del cosmo[12], « ciò che contiene tutti quanti i viventi intelligibili » (τὸ γὰρ περιέχον πάντα ὁπόσα νοητὰ ζῷα) deve essere unico e primo, anche il cosmo sensibile sarà uno solo, appunto in virtù della relazione di somiglianza, stabilita dal demiurgo, al « vivente perfetto » (τῷ παντελεῖ ζῴῳ). Questa solenne dichiarazione, che implica l'esplicita denominazione di *panteles zōion* per qualificare l'intelligibile, appare rieccheggiata più volte nel seguito del dialogo e nuovamente menzionata in 37d, ancora in riferimento all'obiettivo del demiurgo di rendere il cosmo sensibile quanto più possibile simile al suo modello, « che si trova a essere un eterno vivente » (αὐτὸ τυγχάνει ζῷον ἀίδιον ὄν); poi, forse, in 39e, quando viene evocata la capacità dell'intelletto di cogliere le specie che si trovano in « ciò che è propriamente il vivente » (ὃ ἔστιν ζῷον), una formula che designa abitualmente, nel lessico platonico, proprio la realtà delle idee[13].

Quanto si può trarre da questi passi, attenendosi a una lettura rigorosa quanto prudente ed evitando brutali sovra-interpretazioni, è in primo luogo il carattere certamente analogico dell'attribuzione della "vita" e della "vitalità" all'intelligibile a partire dalla considerazione del sensibile: *poiché* il cosmo è un vivente sensibile ed è copia di un modello, *allora* il modello deve configurarsi come un vivente intelligibile. Ora, essere "vivente", per una realtà sensibile, significa disporre di un'anima che anima un corpo in cui è innestata, ma ciò pare valere appunto soltanto, come abbiamo visto poco sopra, nel caso del sensibile; cosa significa quindi, e cosa comporta, essere "vivente" per una realtà intelligibile? Non certo il possesso di un'anima, o di un intelletto (che

---

12 Cfr. soltanto su questo argomento Parry, « The unique world of the *Timaeus* »; e Patterson, « The unique worlds of the *Timaeus* ».
13 Si veda in proposito Ferrari, « L'anima dell'essere. *Sofista*, 248 E–249 A e *Timeo*, 30 C–31 A », 608, n. 13.

non può sussistere se non in un'anima), perché, anche al di là di quanto già argomentato sulla base dei passi esaminati del *Timeo* (rispetto all'esigenza che l'anima e l'intelletto siano introdotti *nel sensibile*, precisamente per renderlo il più possibile simile alla perfezione del modello, che è invece privo di corpo sensibile e di per sé già perfetto), l'anima è in generale concepita da Platone, per esprimersi in modo molto sommario, secondo due tratti ontologici fondamentali. Essa ha innanzitutto natura e struttura intermedie fra il sensibile e l'intelligibile, sì da risultare composta tanto da elementi sensibili quanto da elementi intelligibili o da un *mix* di entrambi[14], non lasciandosi così ricondurre interamente né all'ambito sensibile né all'ambito intelligibile, ma piuttosto rivelandosi in grado di esercitare, in virtù della sua funzione motrice, il governo del mondo sensibile e dei corpi, che a sua volta dipende dalla retta conoscenza dell'intelligibile che la sua funzione noetica le garantisce[15]. Quindi, e di conseguenza, l'anima intrattiene con l'intelligibile una relazione che non è evidentemente di identità, ma, come i dialoghi platonici spesso ripetono, di "congenericità" (συγγένεια)[16], una forma di "parentela" e di parziale "comunanza", che le permette di accedere all'intelligibile e di giungere alla contemplazione delle idee[17], il che ne attesta al di fuori di ogni dubbio la diversità da esse, giacché, se così non fosse e l'anima si rivelasse identica alle idee, non avrebbe senso porre il problema del suo accesso all'intelligibile né delle condizioni della sua contemplazione.

Ma torniamo così alla stessa conclusione già raggiunta in precedenza: se è privo di anima, non è certo in quanto "animato" che l'intelligibile può essere considerato un "vivente", perfetto o eterno; bisognerà dunque individuare per esso una condizione suscettibile di essere qualificata come "vitale", pur in assenza dell'anima, in quanto modello della condizione "vitale" che, nel sensibile, dipende invece dalla presenza dell'anima. Prima di compiere questo passo ulteriore, possiamo però constatare intanto che una simile conclusione porta a escludere una prima interpretazione, pure autorevolmente difesa, del *panteles zōion* del *Timeo* come propriamente dotato di un'anima o caratterizzato come un intelletto[18]. Non resta dunque che tentare di percorrere

---

14   Cfr. *Tim.* 34c–36d.
15   Cfr. *Tim.* 36d–37c.
16   Cfr. per esempio *Men.* 81c–d, *Phd.* 79b–d, *Rep.* x 611d–e.
17   Cfr. ancora *Rep.* x 611d–e e *Tim.* 42b; ma si veda pure il celebre mito di *Phdr.* 248a–c.
18   Posizione difesa, benché con sfumature diverse, da Krämer, *Der Ursprung der Geistmetaphysik. Untersuchungen zur Geschichte des Platonismus zwischen Platon und Plotin*, 194–201, e da Halfwassen, « Der Demiurg: seine Stellung in der Philosophie Platons und seine Deutung im antiken Platonismus », che tendono a concepire il *panteles zōion* del *Timeo*, in stretta relazione con il *pantelōs on* del passo del *Sofista* che passerò subito

un'altra via che consenta cioè di comprendere altrimenti, vale a dire indipendentemente dall'implicazione di un'anima e di un intelletto, questa "vitalità" dell'intellegibile[19].

Ora, se il *Timeo* non sembra offrire spunti in tale direzione, un passo particolarmente noto e controverso del *Sofista* appare invece piuttosto promettente. Si tratta di *Soph*. 248e–249a, che si colloca verso la conclusione della celebre *gigantomachia* fra i "nati dalla terra" e gli "amici delle idee", i primi che escludono dall'essere tutto ciò che non sia "corpo", i secondi che invece identificano ciò che è con certe "idee" immobili e immutabili: come possibile mediazione fra le due posizioni viene introdotta qui una nuova e diversa definizione dell'essere come δύναμις εἴτ᾽ εἰς τὸ ποιεῖν ... εἴτ᾽ εἰς τὸ παθεῖν, che, ammessa senza troppe resistenze dai "materialisti", incontra invece la strenua opposizione degli "idealisti", consapevoli del fatto che, se accogliessero tale definizione dell'essere, si troverebbero pure costretti a riconoscere che le idee, realtà veramente essenti, risultano affette da un qualche genere di passione o azione (πάθημα ἢ ποίημα) e, di conseguenza, soggette a una forma di movimento (κίνησις), il che è impossibile secondo la loro dottrina, che impone che il movimento sia confinato all'ambito del divenire[20]. Si noti soltanto, fin d'ora, che il nodo intorno al quale ruota il confronto con gli "idealisti" consiste precisamente, e *unicamente*, nell'inclusione (cui li si vuole costringere) o nell'esclusione (cui essi si attengono accanitamente) della *kinēsis*, o di una sua qualche forma, nell'essere (248e); e non è certo un caso che l'esito di questo confronto, con la definitiva confutazione degli "idealisti" che esso comporta, preveda appunto, ancora una volta, l'unica ed esplicita ammissione loro estorta della *kinēsis*, o di una sua qualche forma, nell'essere (249b–d). Riproduco dunque il passo che segue e sul quale occorre adesso soffermarsi.

---

    a esaminare, nella forma dell'identità organica di pensiero ed essere, vale a dire, secondo la celebre dottrina neoplatonica delle ipostasi, come essere "pensante" e "pensato" a un tempo; cfr. anche, in tale direzione e con particolare riferimento al *Sofista*, le vigorose osservazioni di Gerson, « The "Holy Solemnity" of Forms and the Platonic Interpretation of Sophist ».

19 Così pure, giustamente, Ferrari, « L'anima dell'essere », 608.

20 Per quanto riguarda la traduzione e la comprensione di questa sezione del *Sofista*, che solleva notevoli problemi interpretativi, fin dalla ricostruzione delle diverse tappe della sua sequenza argomentativa, rinvio all'introduzione e alle note *ad locum* in Fronterotta, ed., *Platone, Sofista*, 75–89 e 370–379; ho invece particolarmente approfondito la natura e le implicazioni della definizione dell'essere come *dynamis* di agire e patire nei miei successivi studi « L'être et la participation de l'autre. Une nouvelle ontologie dans le *Sophiste* », e « La notion de ΔΥΝΑΜΙΣ dans le Sophiste de Platon: ΚΟΙΝΩΝΙΑ entre les formes et ΜΕΘΕΞΙΣ du sensible à l'intelligible ».

Τί δὲ πρὸς Διός; ὡς ἀληθῶς κίνησιν καὶ ζωὴν καὶ ψυχὴν καὶ φρόνησιν ἦ ῥᾳδίως πεισθησόμεθα τῷ παντελῶς ὄντι μὴ παρεῖναι, μηδὲ ζῆν αὐτὸ μηδὲ φρονεῖν, ἀλλὰ σεμνὸν καὶ ἅγιον, νοῦν οὐκ ἔχον, ἀκίνητον ἑστὸς εἶναι;

Ma allora, per Zeus? Ci lasceremo convincere senza colpo ferire che movimento, vita, anima e intelligenza davvero non siano presenti nella totalità dell'essere pieno, e che l'essere né viva né pensi, ma, venerabile e santo, se ne stia, privo d'intelletto, immobile e fermo?

Conviene limitare l'esame di questo passo, estremamente complesso e discusso, all'aspetto decisivo per i miei scopi attuali, vale a dire, come è ovvio, l'inclusione di « movimento, vita, anima e intelligenza » (κίνησιν καὶ ζωὴν καὶ ψυχὴν καὶ φρόνησιν) nel *pantelōs on*[21]: in cosa consiste esattamente tale "inclusione"? E che relazione ha, se ne ha una, con la "vitalità" attribuita all'intelligibile nel *Timeo*? Per rispondere a queste domande, bisogna innanzitutto prendere posizione sul significato del sintagma *pantelōs on*. È infatti possibile intendere l'avverbio *pantelōs* in senso *estensivo*, cioè con riferimento all'"insieme" o alla "totalità" dell'essere e delle cose che sono, a designare così un ambito ontologico tanto esteso da comprendere allora sia il mondo sensibile sia la sfera intelligibile: in tal caso, l'inclusione di movimento, vita, anima e intelligenza nell'"insieme" o nella "totalità" dell'essere non si rivelerebbe affatto problematica, perché si potrebbe arguire, coerentemente con la posizione difesa dagli "idealisti", che

---

21 Fra gli aspetti più controversi, è decisivo per la comprensione del passo il significato da attribuire alla caratterizzazione del *pantelōs on* come « venerabile e santo » (σεμνὸν καὶ ἅγιον), che si può intendere in almeno due modi diversi: (1) in senso concessivo, come tenderei a preferire (« [...] che l'essere né viva né pensi, ma, *pur essendo* venerabile e santo, se ne stia, privo d'intelletto, immobile e fermo [...] »), oppure (2) in senso causale (« [...] che l'essere né viva né pensi, ma, *in quanto* venerabile e santo, se ne stia, privo d'intelletto, immobile e fermo [...] »). Nel primo caso, la "venerabilità" e la "santità" dell'essere dipenderebbero dalla sua "motilità" e "vitalità", sicché risulterebbe contraddittorio ammettere che esso « se ne stia [...] immobile e fermo », se è davvero « venerabile e santo » e dunque necessariamente "mobile"; nel secondo caso, invece, la "venerabilità" e la "santità" dell'essere sarebbero connesse alla sua "immobilità", sicché risulterebbe impossibile accettare che esso « venerabile e santo, se ne stia [...] immobile e fermo », perché occorre invece riconoscergli "motilità" e "vitalità". Questa scelta non è indifferente né, evidentemente, per la comprensione dell'argomento platonico né per la storia delle sue interpretazioni, da Aristotele a Plotino: si vedano ora in proposito Abbate, « Die dynamische und lebendige Natur des intelligiblen Seins bei Platon und in der neuplatonischen Überlieferung », Morel, « L'argomento della "venerabilità dell'essere" e la sua fortuna (Aristotele e Plotino, eredi di Platone, *Sofista*, 248e–249a) », e Fronterotta, « Movimento, vita, anima e intelligenza: la σεμνότης del παντελῶς ὄν nel *Sofista* platonico. Nota a margine di P.-M. Morel, *L'argomento della 'venerabilità dell'essere' e la sua fortuna* ».

movimento, vita, anima e intelligenza sono, sì, compresi nell'"insieme" o nella "totalità" delle cose che sono, ma confinati esclusivamente in quella parte del *pantelōs on* che coincide con la sua sezione sensibile, salvaguardando in tal modo l'assoluta immobilità della sua sezione intellegibile[22]. Vi è però da osservare, contro questa lettura, che il *pantelōs on*, pur rinviando a un ambito di realtà effettivamente plurale e comprensivo, non sembra tuttavia poter includere anche il mondo sensibile, e ciò per più ragioni. In primo luogo, il sintagma *to pantelōs on* deve essere certamente posto in contrapposizione a *to mēdamōs on*, evocato in 237b: ora, poiché quest'ultimo si riferisce senza alcun dubbio al non essere assoluto, pare plausibile dedurne che il suo contrario, appunto *to pantelōs on*, indichi un ambito di realtà realmente e pienamente essente. Inoltre, in 249b, si afferma risolutamente che, se non si comprendesse il movimento fra le cose che sono, nel *pantelōs on*, e tutto fosse immobile (come vogliono gli "idealisti"), non si darebbe *nous* « per nessuno, di nessuna cosa e in nessun modo »: ma *nous* è un termine che richiama abitualmente la vera conoscenza dell'essere in senso proprio, così distinguendosi da quella forma epistemica intermedia che coincide con l'opinione, rivolta esclusivamente alle cose sensibili. Infine, in 249c–d, si giunge alla conclusione che il "filosofo" deve ammettere « che entrambi gli ambiti, sia delle cose immobili sia di quelle in movimento, sono l'essere e il tutto »: ma, poco oltre (254a–b), il filosofo è descritto come colui il quale, nei suoi ragionamenti, si attiene sempre all'essere (τῇ τοῦ ὄντος ἀεὶ διὰ λογισμῶν προσκείμενος ἰδέᾳ), una "regione" difficile da scorgere per la sua luminosità (διὰ τὸ λαμπρὸν αὖ τῆς χώρας), perché gli occhi dell'anima dei più sono incapaci di resistere alla vista della divinità (τὰ γὰρ τῆς τῶν πολλῶν ψυχῆς ὄμματα καρτερεῖν πρὸς τὸ θεῖον ἀφορῶντα ἀδύνατα), dal che si può trarre che l'oggetto della contemplazione del filosofo, che consiste nell'essere totale e comprensivo delle cose immobili come di quelle in movimento, altro non è che l'ambito ontologico più elevato, ossia appunto l'intellegibile soltanto.

Tutto ciò suggerisce pertanto di adottare una traduzione e un'interpretazione *intensive* del sintagma *pantelōs on*, da rendere dunque con "ciò che è realmente o pienamente" e da intendere in esclusivo riferimento all'intellegibile, tornando allora al problema di illustrare natura e modi dell'inclusione di movimento, vita, anima e intelligenza nell'essere in senso proprio, nell'intellegibile[23]. Sarei

---

22   Questa è l'interpretazione tradizionale del sintagma *pantelōs on* suggerita per esempio da Cornford, *Plato's Theory of Knowledge*, 245, e difesa oggi da Brisson, « La définition de l'être par la puissance. Un commentaire de Sophiste 247B–249D ».

23   Adottano una traduzione e un'interpretazione intensive del sintagma *pantelōs on*, pur traendone poi conseguenze diverse, Gerson, « The 'Holy Solemnity' of Forms », 292, n. 3; Centrone, *Platone, Sofista*, xxxv–xxxix; Ferrari, « L'anima dell'essere », 602–604; e Morel, « L'argomento della "venerabilità dell'essere" ». Pur nel quadro di un'interpretazione

tuttavia propenso a integrare questa opzione *intensiva*, che, per le ragioni appena esposte, considero più convincente, con una sfumatura *estensiva* che porti a riconoscere che il *pantelōs on*, senz'altro coincidente con l'intelligibile in senso stretto, implica però a un tempo una struttura plurale e organica, non certo tale da includere in sé il mondo sensibile, ma compatibile con un'articolazione dell'essere reale e pieno appunto in una pluralità organica di intelligibili: il significato complessivo del passo esaminato, del resto, non è tanto (o soltanto) quello di mostrare *quanto sono* movimento, vita, anima e intelligenza, bensì di collocarli nell'*insieme* o nella *totalità delle cose che sono realmente e pienamente*, il che è confermato oltre ogni dubbio dal fatto che l'inclusione di movimento, vita, anima e intelligenza nel *pantelōs on* è resa con il verbo *pareinai*, "essere presente" o "trovarsi compreso in", che esprime perciò la presenza di qualcosa in un luogo o, in questo contesto, in un ambito determinato di realtà, e non solo un grado maggiore o minore di intensione ontologica[24]. Comunque sia di ciò, come intendere a questo punto la "presenza" di movimento, vita, anima e intelligenza nel *pantelōs on* e quali implicazioni attribuirle? Ora, come ho chiarito in precedenza, vi sono a mio avviso decisivi argomenti, nei dialoghi platonici, che si oppongono alla possibilità di assegnare un'anima e un intelletto all'intelligibile, che si tratti del *panteles zōion* del *Timeo* o del *pantelōs on* del *Sofista*[25], sicché conviene riprendere la questione a partire dal primo dei termini della sequenza costruita nel passo del *Sofista*, vale a dire dal movimento.

Già a questo livello infatti, e prima ancora di interrogarsi intorno all'anima e all'intelletto, emerge una difficoltà, giacché dall'introduzione del movimento nel *pantelōs on* parrebbe dover conseguire che questo ne sia affetto, contraddicendo così uno degli assunti più classici della concezione platonica dell'intelligibile come di per sé immobile e immutabile[26]. Non credo però, con buona parte dei commentatori[27], che un simile esito sia inevitabile né,

intensiva del sintagma *pantelōs on*, si oppone tuttavia alla conclusione che l'argomento conduca a includere in esso movimento, vita, anima e intelligenza, Karfik, « Gott als *Nous*. Der Gottesbegriff Platons ».

24 In questa stessa direzione mi pare argomentare Abbate, « Die dynamische und lebendige Natur des intelligiblen Seins », 228.
25 Questa è invece, come già ricordato, la tesi di Gerson, « The 'Holy Solemnity' of Forms ».
26 Che le idee intelligibili finiscano, in ragione di questo argomento, per rivelarsi soggette al movimento, se non integralmente o in modo essenziale, almeno nella misura in cui vengono conosciute, e perciò mosse, dall'intelletto, è la conclusione di Moravcsik, « Being and meaning in the *Sophist* », 40, e di Bluck, *Plato's* Sophist. *A Commentary*, 96–100.
27 Fra quanti hanno negato recisamente la possibilità di ascrivere a Platone un mutamento di prospettiva così radicale nella propria concezione dell'intelligibile, che attribuirebbe alle idee e all'essere tratti di mobilità e di mutamento, vanno ricordati soprattutto Cornford, *Plato's Theory of Knowledge*, 244–248, Cherniss, *The Riddle of the Early*

d'altro canto, suggerito dal testo: tendo a pensare piuttosto che l'introduzione del movimento nel *pantelōs on* e la relazione così stabilita fra il movimento e l'intellegibile, due acquisizioni teoriche che si ricavano indubbiamente da questo passo del *Sofista*, si lascino spiegare senza compromettere la tesi dell'immobilità e dell'immutabilità dell'essere, ma semplicemente tenendo conto della differenza ontologica che sussiste fra il mondo sensibile e l'ambito intellegibile. Così come nel caso di qualunque proprietà sensibile rispetto all'idea intellegibile corrispondente si constata che la prima manifesta concretamente ed effettivamente i tratti di cui è la proprietà, mentre la seconda non esprime che l'essenza o la forma di quella proprietà – la molteplicità, per esempio, si manifesta sul piano sensibile sotto l'aspetto di una concreta ed effettiva pluralità di enti, laddove, sul piano intellegibile, essa si pone come essenza o forma della molteplicità senza essere per questo più di una, se è vero che l'idea della molteplicità è in sé appunto una e non molteplice – analogamente, per quanto riguarda il movimento, si potrà sostenere che, a differenza della sua "versione" sensibile, la *kinēsis* dell'intellegibile e nell'intellegibile non consiste in un concreto mutamento di luogo o di aspetto né tantomeno in un'effettiva alterazione, ma soltanto in una condizione a qualche titolo *dinamica* che sia compatibile con i requisiti ontologici dell'immobilità e dell'immutabilità che devono appartenere per definizione all'intellegibile. Per capire di quale condizione precisamente si tratti, e in cosa consista il suo *dinamismo*, si può forse prestare attenzione agli altri tre termini della sequenza presentata nel passo del *Sofista*, ossia "vita", "anima" e "intelligenza", da intendere a questo punto

---

Academy, 81, e Vlastos, « An Ambiguity in the *Sophist* », Appendix 1: *On the Interpretation of* Sph. *248d4–e4*, 309–317. A sostegno di questa posizione si può ricordare che *Euthyphr.* 11a, ammettendo « la possibilità di πάθη relativi all'οὐσία che non modificano la natura di ciò che è affetto » (cfr. Centrone, « ΠΑΘΟΣ e ΟΥΣΙΑ nei primi dialoghi di Platone », 151, n. 45), permetterebbe di sostenere che le idee costituiscono l'oggetto della conoscenza, e in tal senso subiscano un *pathos*, senza che ciò imponga loro necessariamente di essere mosse. Una tesi diversa sostiene De Rijk, *Plato's* Sophist. *A Philosophical Commentary*, 105–109, che capovolge la prospettiva di lettura: non si tratta in effetti di chiedersi se le idee si muovano, ma di riconoscere che il movimento è assunto, accanto alle idee e fra le idee, nell'intellegibile. Ciò non toglie, tuttavia, che ci si interroghi sulle conseguenze di questo passo: una volta introdotto il movimento nell'intellegibile, ne seguirà che le idee si muovano? A tale ragionevole questione, De Rijk risponde suggerendo una distinzione in base alla quale, come enti separati e trascendenti, le idee rimangono del tutto pure e immobili, mentre invece, in quanto soggette alla partecipazione da parte dei sensibili, entrano in questa misura in contatto con le realtà in divenire, subendo un'affezione che le pone in movimento. Personalmente, ritengo implausibile una simile distinzione, se non altro perché qui nessun accenno è rivolto al problema della partecipazione delle cose in divenire alle idee intellegibili né la realtà sensibile *tout court* sembra in nessun modo chiamata in causa.

piuttosto come esplicativi del primo, del movimento, che non come altrettanti caratteri supplementari da aggiungere nel *pantelōs on*.

Che ciò sia possibile, e anzi probabile, si ricava fra l'altro da quanto già osservato in relazione alla pressoché esclusiva centralità della *kinēsis* nel corso dell'esame e della confutazione della posizione degli "idealisti": la proposta di una nuova definizione dell'essere come *dynamis* di agire e patire (247d–e) ha proprio il fine di costringere gli "idealisti" ad ammettere che l'essere non è completamente immobile e inerte e, per questa ragione, è da essi respinta (248e); e anche la conclusione dell'esame comporta sostanzialmente l'unico risultato di accogliere il movimento nell'essere e, per conseguenza, di abbandonare la posizione degli "idealisti", facendo cadere così, implicitamente, la loro opposizione alla definizione dell'essere come *dynamis* di agire e patire (249b–d). Ritengo inoltre che il testo stesso del nostro passo, in 248e–249a, si lasci interpretare in questo senso, solo che si legga la sequenza κίνησιν καὶ ζωὴν καὶ ψυχὴν καὶ φρόνησιν con valore epesegetico, quindi ponendo la *kinēsis* e la sua inclusione nel *pantelōs on* quale fulcro della dimostrazione e i termini *zōē*, *psychē* e *phronēsis* come sue specificazioni, appunto per precisare il tipo di movimento di cui si stabilisce l'inclusione nell'essere[28]. Il passo potrebbe allora essere parafrasato come segue: "Ci lasceremo convincere senza colpo ferire che il movimento, *cioè* quel movimento *vitale* che è dello stesso genere di quello prodotto dall'attività dell'*anima* e che corrisponde alla funzione noetica dell'*intelletto*, davvero non sia presente nella totalità dell'essere pieno, e che l'essere non possieda tratti *vitali* né *intellettuali*, ma, venerabile e santo, se ne stia, privo di carattere *noetico*, immobile e fermo?" In tal caso, come si vede, ci troveremmo di fronte a una risposta coerente alla questione sollevata poco sopra: a differenza del movimento sensibile, che implica un concreto mutamento di luogo o un'effettiva alterazione di stato, la *kinēsis* dell'intelligibile e nell'intelligibile coincide con un dinamismo che può essere detto "vitale" in quanto omogeneo a quello prodotto dall'anima, e dunque sottoposto a un rigoroso criterio di ordine e regolarità che non suppone alcun movimento nello spazio, e che si svolge in termini esclusivamente noetici o intellettuali, e quindi indipendentemente da ogni connessione con la materia e i corpi e dal mutamento a essi intrinseco. Si tratterebbe insomma di riconoscere al *pantelōs on* un movimento "vitale" *analogo* a quello dell'anima, ma che non implica la presenza dell'anima, e un carattere "dinamico" *analogo* a quello dell'intelletto, ma che non implica la presenza dell'intelletto, senza che, in altre parole, questa

---

28 Sull'intima connessione fra "movimento", "vita" e "anima" (e "intelligenza"), che rappresenta una costante nella riflessione di Platone, si veda ancora Fronterotta, ed., *Platone, Timeo*, 72–74.

duplice analogia conduca all'estrema e ai miei occhi insostenibile conclusione che il *pantelōs on* sia effettivamente "animato" e "pensi".

Di una simile prospettiva esegetica mi spingerei infine a tratteggiare l'esito ultimo, formulando l'ipotesi, che andrebbe certo più adeguatamente fondata, ma di cui non posso dare conto qui estesamente, secondo la quale il movimento "vitale" del *pantelōs on* evocato in questo passo e fatto oggetto di analisi altro non riveli che il concreto sviluppo della definizione dell'essere come *dynamis* di agire e patire, che, richiamata nel seguito del dialogo nella forma di una *dynamis koinōnias* (in 251e; oppure *dynamis epikoinōnias* in 252d), si traduce allora nella capacità, di cui gli intelligibili dispongono e in cui consistono propriamente il loro essere e la loro definizione, di stabilire reciproci rapporti di "comunicazione" o "partecipazione"[29]. La *kinēsis* dell'essere, assimilata a un tratto psichico o noetico, andrebbe a questo punto concepita come l'insieme di movimenti, prodotti o subiti, che pongono gli intelligibili in reciproca *koinōnia* – "comunicare" equivalendo a un'azione, e pertanto a un movimento prodotto che discende da una *dynamis* di agire, ed "essere comunicato" equivalendo a una passione, e pertanto a un movimento subito che discende da una *dynamis* di patire –, la "vitalità" del *pantelōs on* manifestandosi quindi senza residui nella sua dimensione dinamico-relazionale interna[30].

Mi pare che questa interpretazione, pur basata su elementi che sono in parte inevitabilmente congetturali, si presenti come la più coerente (o la meno incoerente) per una comprensione non aporetica del passo esaminato del *Sofista* e del suo contesto argomentativo, ma anche, derivativamente, per una spiegazione efficace dell'altrimenti oscura rappresentazione dell'intelligibile come un *panteles zōon* nel *Timeo*, rendendo conto in entrambi i casi della natura dinamica e della struttura organica dell'essere nella sua funzione di modello della realtà sensibile plurale e diveniente[31].

---

29   Per l'interpretazione della definizione dell'essere come *dynamis* di agire e patire (249b–d) e i suoi successivi sviluppi, nel *Sofista*, come *dynamis koinōnias* e dunque come chiave di volta per la comprensione della sezione ontologica del dialogo dedicata alla *koinōnia tōn genōn*, rinvio nuovamente ai miei studi « L'être et la participation de l'autre », e « La notion de ΔΥΝΑΜΙΣ ».

30   A una conclusione appena meno esplicita di quella da me tratteggiata giungono Centrone (ed.), *Platone, Sofista*, xxxix, e, più prudentemente, Morel, « L'argomento della "venerabilità dell'essere" ». Non mi è chiaro invece se Abbate, « Die dynamische und lebendige Natur », accolga anch'egli un'interpretazione soltanto dinamico-relazionale della "vitalità" dell'intelligibile o se invece intenda attribuire a quest'ultimo una dimensione propriamente psichica e noetica, come parrebbe suggerito dal suo richiamo alla lettura plotiniana del passo del *Sofista*.

31   Diversamente intende Ferrari, *L'anima dell'essere*, 608–613, che, ricollegandosi alla sua interpretazione della figura e della funzione del demiurgo (cfr. *supra*, n. 4), considera la

Works Cited

Abbate, Michele. « Die dynamische und lebendige Natur des intelligiblen Seins bei Platon und in der neuplatonischen Überlieferung ». In *Selbstbewegung und Lebendigkeit. Die Seele in Platons Spätwerk*. A cura di Michele Abbate, Julia Pfefferkorn e Antonino Spinelli. Berlin: De Gruyter, 2016, 227–242.

Algra, Keimpe. *Concepts of Space in Greek Thought*. Leiden: Brill, 1995.

Bluck, R. S. *Plato's* Sophist. *A Commentary*. Manchester: Manchester University Press, 1975.

Brisson, Luc. *Le Même et l'Autre dans la structure ontologique du* Timée *de Platon*. Terza edizione. Sankt Augustin: Academia Verlag, 1998.

Brisson, Luc. « La notion de phtónos chez Platon ». Ora in *Lectures de Platon*. Vrin, Paris 2000, 219–234.

Brisson, Luc. « La définition de l'être par la puissance. Un commentaire de *Sophiste* 247B–249D » In ΔΥΝΑΜΙΣ. *Autour de la puissance chez Aristote*. A cura di Michel Crubellier, Annick Jaulin, David Lefebvre, e Pierre-Marie Morel. Louvain-La-Neuve: Peeters, 2008, 173–186.

Brisson, Luc. « La matière chez Platon et dans la tradition platonicienne ». In Materia, XIII Colloquio Internazionale, *Roma, 7–9 gennaio 2010*. A cura di Delfina Giovannozzi e Marco Veneziani. Firenze: Olschki, 2011, 1–40.

Centrone, Bruno. « ΠΑΘΟΣ e ΟΥΣΙΑ nei primi dialoghi di Platone », *Elenchos* 16 (1995): 131–152.

Centrone, Bruno, ed. *Platone, Sofista*. Torino: Einaudi, 2008.

Cherniss, H. F. *The Riddle of the Early Academy*. Princeton: Princeton University Press, 1945.

Cornford, Francis. *Plato's Theory of Knowledge. The* Theaetetus *and the* Sophist *of Plato*. Translated with a running commentary. London: Routledge & Kegan Paul, 1935.

De Rijk, L. M. *Plato's* Sophist. *A Philosophical Commentary*. Amsterdam: North-Holland Publishing Company, 1986.

Donini, Pier Luigi. « Il *Timeo*: unità del dialogo, verosimiglianza del discorso ». *Elenchos* 9 (1988): 5–52.

"vitalità" del *panteles zōon* del *Timeo* come l'espressione della sua funzione causale efficiente nei confronti del cosmo sensibile, per estendere retrospettivamente questa lettura al *pantelōs on* del *Sofista*, cui non può però che attribuire un'azione causale *interna* all'intelligibile stesso (non troppo dissimile da quella da me prefigurata sopra). Anche al di là delle mie perplessità sulla prima parte di questa opzione esegetica (cfr. ancora *supra*, n. 4), ritengo poco plausibile che la "vitalità" del *panteles zōon* e del *pantelōs on* si esplichi in forme, modi e contesti tanto distanti da apparire irriducibili a una comprensione unitaria e omogenea.

Ferrari, Franco. « Questioni eidetiche ». *Elenchos* 24 (2003): 93–113.

Ferrari, Franco. « Causa paradigmatica e causa efficiente: il ruolo delle idee nel *Timeo* ». In *Plato physicus. Cosmologia e antropologia nel* Timeo. A cura di Carlo Natali e Stefano Maso. Amsterdam: Hakkert, 2003, 83–96.

Ferrari, Franco. « La *chora* nel *Timeo* di Platone. Riflessioni su "materia" e "spazio" nell'ontologia del mondo fenomenico ». *Quaestio* 7 (2007): 3–23.

Ferrari, Franco. « Der entmythologisierte Demiurg ». In *Platon und das Göttliche*. A cura di Dietmar Koch, Irmegard Männlein-Robert e Niels Weidtmann. Tübingen: Attempto Verlag, 2010, 62–81.

Ferrari, Franco. « L'anima dell'essere. *Sofista*, 248 E-249 A e *Timeo*, 30 C-31 A ». In *Logon didonai. La filosofia come esercizio del rendere ragione. Studi in onore di Giovanni Casertano*. A cura di Lidia Palumbo. Napoli: Loffredo, 2012, 601–613.

Fronterotta, Francesco. « L'être et la participation de l'autre. Une nouvelle ontologie dans le *Sophiste* ». *Les Etudes Philosophiques* (1995/3): 311–353.

Fronterotta, Francesco. ΜΕΘΕΞΙΣ. *La teoria delle idee e la partecipazione delle cose empiriche. Dai dialoghi giovanili al* Parmenide. Pisa: Edizioni della Scuola Normale Superiore, 2001.

Fronterotta, Francesco. « Questioni eidetiche in Platone: il sensibile e il demiurgo, l'essere e il bene ». In *Giornale critico della filosofia italiana* LXXXV (2006): 412–436.

Fronterotta, Francesco, ed. *Platone, Sofista*. Milano: Rizzoli, 2007.

Fronterotta, Francesco. « La notion de ΔΥΝΑΜΙΣ dans le *Sophiste* de Platon: ΚΟΙΝΩΝΙΑ entre les formes et ΜΕΘΕΞΙΣ du sensible à l'intelligible ». In ΔΥΝΑΜΙΣ. *Autour de la puissance chez Aristote*. A cura di Michel Crubellier, Annick Jaulin, David Lefebvre, e Pierre-Marie Morel. Louvain-La-Neuve: Peeters, 2008, 187–224.

Fronterotta, Francesco. « Chiusura causale della fisica e razionalità del tutto: alcune opzioni esegetiche sull'efficienza causale delle idee platoniche ». *Plato. The Internet Journal of the International Plato Society* (8): 2008, http://gramata.univ-paris1.fr/Plato/.

Fronterotta, Francesco. « Ἀρχὴ τοῦ κόσμου and ἀρχὴ τοῦ λόγου. A New Hypothesis on the Beginning of the World in Plato's *Timaeus* ». In *Philosophy and Dialogue. Studies on Plato's Dialogues*. A cura di Antoni Bosch-Veciana and Josep Monserrat-Molas. Barcelona: Barcelonesa d'Edicions, 2010, 141–155.

Fronterotta, Francesco, ed. *Platone, Timeo*. Terza edizione. Milano: Rizzoli, 2011.

Fronterotta, Francesco. « Luogo, spazio e sostrato "spazio-materiale" nel *Timeo* di Platone e nei commenti al *Timeo* ». In *Locus-Spatium. XIV Colloquio Internazionale, Roma, 3–5 gennaio 2013*. A cura di Delfina Giovannozzi e Marco Veneziani. Firenze: Olschki, 2014, 7–42.

Fronterotta, Francesco. « Modello, copia, ricettacolo: monismo, dualismo o triade di principi nel *Timeo*? » Méthexis, XXVII (2014): 95–118.

Fronterotta, Francesco. « Movimento, vita, anima e intelligenza: la σεμνότης del παντελῶς ὄν nel *Sofista* platonico. Nota a margine di P.-M. Morel, L'argomento della 'venerabilità dell'essere' e la sua fortuna ». *Antiquorum Philosophia* 12 (2018): 27–36.

Gerson, Lloyd. « The "Holy Solemnity" of Forms and the Platonic Interpretation of *Sophist* ». *Ancient Philosophy* 26 (2006): 291–304.

Halfwassen, Jens. « Der Demiurg: seine Stellung in der Philosophie Platons und seine Deutung im antiken Platonismus ». In *Le* Timée *de Platon. Contribution à l'histoire de sa réception. Platos* Timaios. *Beiträge zu seiner Rezeptionsgeschicht*. A cura di Ada Neschke-Hentschke. Louvain: Peeters, 2000, 39–62.

Karfík, Filip. « Gott als Nous. Der Gottesbegriff Platons ». In *Platon und das Göttliche*. A cura di Dietmar Koch, Irmegard Männlein-Robert e Niels Weidtmann. Tübingen: Attempto Verlag, 2010, 82–97.

Krämer, Hans-Joachim. *Der Ursprung der Geistmetaphysik. Untersuchungen zur Geschichte des Platonismus zwischen Platon und Plotin*. Seconda edizione. Amsterdam: Grüner, 1967.

Leszl, Walter. « Ragioni per postulare idee ». In *Eidos-Idea. Platone, Aristotele e la tradizione platonica*. A cura di Francesco Fronterotta e Walter Leszl. Sankt Augustin: Academia Verlag, 2005, 37–74.

Miller, Dana. *The Third Kind in Plato's* Timaeus. Göttingen: Vandenhoeck & Ruprecht, 2003.

Moravcsik, J. M. E. « Being and meaning in the *Sophist* ». *Acta Philosophica Fennica* 14 (1962): 23–78.

Morel, Pierre-Marie. « L'argomento della "venerabilità dell'essere" e la sua fortuna (Aristotele e Plotino, eredi di Platone, *Sofista*, 248e-249a) ». *Antiquorum Philosophia* 12 (2018): 11–26.

Natali, Carlo. « La forma platonica è una causa formale? » In *Platon und Aristoteles – sub ratione veritatis. Festschrift für* W. Wieland zum 70. *Geburtstag*. A cura di Gregor Damschen, Rainer Enskat e Alejandro Vigo. Göttingen: Vandenhoeck & Ruprecht, 2003, 158–173.

Parry, R. D. « The unique world of the *Timaeus* ». *Journal of the History of Philosophy* 17 (1979): 1–10.

Patterson, R. A. « The unique worlds of the *Timaeus* ». *Phoenix*, 35 (1981): 105–119.

Perl, Eric. « The Demiurge and the Forms. A Return to the Ancient Interpretation of Plato's *Timaeus* ». *Ancient Philosophy* 18 (1998): 81–92.

Sedley, David. « Platonic Causes ». *Phronesis* 43 (1998): 114–132.

Vlastos, Gregory. « An Ambiguity in the *Sophist* ». In *Platonic Studies*. Princeton: Princeton University Press, 1973, 270–317.

How to Make a Soul in the *Timaeus*

Luc Brisson

Abstract

In the *Timaeus*, various kinds of soul are mentioned: the soul of the world, of the gods, of mankind (and of animals), and even the soul of plants. All these other kinds have as their principle the soul of the world fashioned by the Demiurge. The immortal soul of the gods—including the world soul and the stars—is fastened to a body which is indestructible, not in itself, but because the Demiurge does not want to undo his work. The human soul is fashioned by the Demiurge out of the same mixture as the world soul and the souls of the gods, but less pure. Subsequently, the Demiurge's assistants go on to implant into a mortal body this immortal soul, which is the principle of all psychic and physical motions. A human soul is immortal in its totality, even if at death the previous experiences of its spirit (*thymos*) and of its desire (*epithymia*) are forgotten; only the excellence of its intellectual life is taken into account in the process of reincarnation.

Keywords

Plato – *Timaeus* – soul – world – celestial bodies – gods – mankind – plants

In the *Timaeus*, various kinds of soul are mentioned: the soul of the world, of the gods, of mankind (and of animals), and even the soul of plants. All these other kinds have as their principle the soul of the world fashioned by the Demiurge.[1]

1 The Soul of the World

The world soul, ensuring the permanence of the order established by the Demiurge within the world, displays the following characteristics, whenever it comes to exert absolute power (*Tim.* 34b10–35a1): it is an intermediate reality, which resembles a series of overlapping circles (the most "noble" of plane

---

1 See Karfík, *Die Beseelung des Kosmos: Untersuchungen zur Kosmologie, Seelenlehre und Theologie in Platons* Phaidon *und* Timaios.

figures, for it exhibits the greatest symmetry), which are interrelated mathematically with one another, and explains all motions in the world, whether psychic or physical.

1.1 Composition

In the *Timaeus*, the description of the making of the world soul is limited to illustrating two things: on the one hand, its ontological dependence on the intelligible, and on the other, its status as an intermediary reality between the intelligible Forms and the world of sensible particulars. The higher genera of Plato's ontology are used as components: Being, the Same, and the Different, as evoked in the *Sophist* (254d–259b). This is what Timaeus seems to mean when he describes the two mixtures (Figure 1) carried out by the Demiurge to fashion the world soul:

> The composition from which he made the soul and the way in which he made it were as follows. In between the Being that is indivisible and always changeless, and the one that is divisible and comes to be in the corporeal realm, he mixed a third, intermediate form of being derived from the other two. Similarly, he made a mixture of the Same, and then one of the Different, in between their indivisible and their corporeal, divisible counterparts. And he took the three mixtures and mixed them together to make a uniform mixture, forcing the Different, which was hard to mix, into conformity with the Same. Now when he had mixed these two together with Being, and from the three had made a single mixture, he re-divided the whole mixture into as many parts as his task required, each part remaining a mixture of the Same, the Different, and of Being.
>
> 35a1–b1[2]

First Mixture	Second Mixture	Result
Indivisible Being		
Divisible Being	Intermediate Being	
Indivisible Same		
Divisible Same	Intermediate Same	Word Soul
Indivisible Different		
Divisible Different	Intermediate Different	

FIGURE 1

---

2 The construction of *Tim.* 35a1–b1 is based on Proclus' construction. The English translations are from Cooper, *Plato: Complete Works*, sometimes modified.

As an intermediate entity, soul represents the origin of all orderly motion in the sensible world (see *Phaedrus* 245c9), the circular movements of the heavenly bodies, and from them the rectilinear movements of sublunary realities (*Laws* X 893b–895a); and as such it maintains some order in the sensible world.

1.2 *Motor Function*

In order to account for the permanence and the regularity of the movement of the celestial bodies, Plato formulates two postulates: 1) The movements of the heavenly bodies follow a circular trajectory, so that their motion is permanent; 2) These motions obey laws defined by three types of mathematical relations known at the time, so that their movement is regular, despite appearances to the contrary.

1.2.1 Circularity

After carrying out the basic mixture that serves to fashion the world soul, the Demiurge laminates this mass like a blacksmith, in order to transform it into a plate, into which he introduces several divisions. He begins by cutting it lengthwise, in order to obtain two bands, which he calls the band of the "Same" and the band of the "Different" (although each of these bands is still constituted by a mixture of Being, Same, and Different). The Demiurge continues his work, this time cutting the band of the "Different" into seven pieces, following a geometrical progression of base 2 and 3: 1, 2, 3, 4, 8, 9, 27.

That is, **1, 2, 3, 4** (2×2), **9** (3×3), **8** (2×2×2), **27** (3×3×3). (Figure 2)

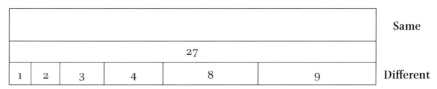

FIGURE 2

This initial mechanical operation does not suffice. It has enabled the construction of two bands, the second of which is cut into seven pieces, but these two bands must be curved, in order to provide the circles along which the heavenly bodies will move.

Two other operations are necessary: one to account for the ecliptic, and the other to produce circles. These operations are steps toward fashioning the circles along which the celestial bodies will move, their permanence being ensured by the circle's perfect symmetry in two-dimensional space:

> Next, he sliced this entire compound in two along its length, joined the two halves together center to center like a *chi* (see Figure 3), and bent

HOW TO MAKE A SOUL IN THE TIMAEUS 73

them back in a circle, attaching each half to itself end to end and to the ends of the other half at the point opposite to the one where they had been joined together (see Figure 4).

36b5–c2

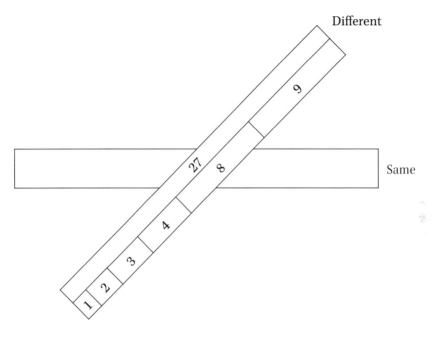

FIGURE 3

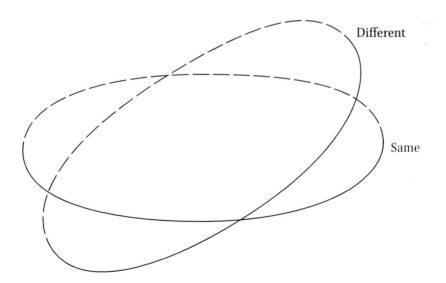

FIGURE 4

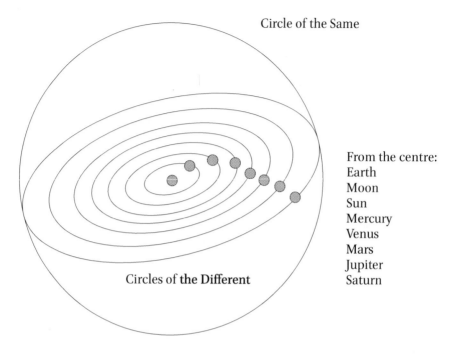

FIGURE 5

The radii of these circles, on the circumference of which the celestial bodies move, will therefore also obey a geometrical progression, starting out from the earth. Thus, the *Timaeus* presents the constitution of the world soul as if it were the construction of an armillary sphere, that is, a globe made up of rings or circles, representing the movement of the heavens and the stars (mentioned at *Tim.* 40d2–3). We must bear this image in mind in order to understand what follows. The technical operations subsequently carried out by the Demiurge account metaphorically for the distinction observed between the fixed stars and the planets: Saturn, Jupiter, Mars, Venus, Mercury, Sun and Moon, with Earth in the middle (see Figure 5).

1.2.2   Harmony
By bringing in mathematical relations (geometrical, arithmetical, and harmonic), which are also used in music, at the level of the world soul (see Figure 6), Plato is merely trying to account for the regularities that had been observed since earliest antiquity in the heavenly bodies.

The introduction of means that engender musical intervals into the world soul seems disconcerting at first glance, but it pertains to analogical reasoning. Plato seems to have extrapolated from the discovery of musical harmony, thus making harmonics serve astronomy (Figure 7).

Geometric mean $\dfrac{a}{x} = \dfrac{x}{b}$ or $x^2 = ab$ or $x = \sqrt{ab}$

Harmonic mean $\dfrac{(x-a)}{a} = \dfrac{(b-x)}{b}$ or $\dfrac{(x-a)}{(b-x)} = \dfrac{a}{b}$ or $x = \dfrac{2ab}{(a+b)}$

Arithmetic mean $(x-a) = (b-x)$ or $x = \dfrac{(a+b)}{2}$

FIGURE 6

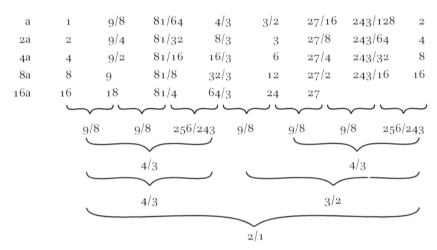

FIGURE 7

By applying the same mathematical proportions to material objects, in this case strings of different lengths, one can produce sounds, always the same ones, that constitute a harmony which, for its part, has nothing material about it. In other words, with the help of mathematical proportions, which pertain exclusively to reason, one can explain musical sounds, and even produce them in the sensible world. Why, then, would the same not be true in astronomy, especially since the motions of the heavenly bodies, in their regularity and permanence, have astonished human beings, since earliest antiquity, to the point that they were assimilated to gods: material, to be sure, but gods nevertheless.

That said, in the *Timaeus* (38c–39e), Plato proposes an astronomical system of astonishing simplicity. This astronomical explanation brings only the following two elements into play: the circular movement of the celestial bodies, a hypothesis which was accepted until Kepler (the law of orbits, formulated in 1609), and three types of mathematical relations—geometrical, arithmetical, and harmonic. The extraordinary complexity of the movements which seem to affect the celestial bodies is thus reduced to two elements of a mathematical nature: circles and means.

1.3 Cognitive Function

However, the circles of the Same and the Different do not merely have a motor function; they also have a cognitive function, as is natural in a living being such as the world:

> Because the soul is a mixture of the Same, the Different and Being, because it was divided up and bound together in various proportions, and because it circles round upon itself, then, whenever it comes into contact with something whose being is scatterable or else with something whose being is indivisible, it is stirred throughout its whole self. It then declares what exactly that thing is the same as or what it is different from, and in what respect and in what manner, as well as when, it turns out that they are the same or different and are characterized as such. This applies both to the things that come to be, and to those that are always changeless. And when this contact gives rise to an account that is equally true whether it is about what is different or about what is the same, and is borne along without utterance or sound within the self-moving thing, then, whenever the account concerns anything that is perceptible, the circle of the Different goes straight and proclaims it throughout its whole soul. This is how firm and true opinions and beliefs sure and certain come about. Whenever, on the other hand, the account concerns any object of reasoning and the circle of the Same runs well and reveals it, the necessary result is understanding and science. And if anyone should ever call that in which these two arise, not soul but something else, what he says will be anything but true.
>
> 37a2–c5

The cognitive abilities of the world soul are associated with the physical motions of its circles; the mention of "without utterance or sound" contains a criticism of the Pythagoreans.[3] Through the circle of the Different, the soul of the world is informed of what takes place within it, whereas through the circle of the Same, it grasps the intelligible, and can thus make the sensible conform to it. A question then arises: how can the world soul know the sensible without sense organs?[4] No answer is given to this question, but it is probably this lack of organs that explains why, by means of the circle of the Different, "opinions and beliefs, firm and true, are formed." This could never be said of human

---

3 Brisson, "Platon, Pythagore et les Pythagoriciens."
4 *Tim.* 33b–d.

opinion,[5] which is no more than likely. The definition of truth is the one presented in the *Sophist*.[6]

2 The Human Soul

In his address to the gods he has just fashioned, the Demiurge explains why, even they are not immortal nor indissoluble, they will not be dissolved or die.[7] He then goes on to say that if the world is to be perfect, mortal creatures of three kinds have to be brought into being (41b7–c2): those that live in the air, on earth and in water (91d–92b). Their bodies will be dissolved, even if they are moved by an immortal soul migrating from one body to another (human or animal).

2.1 *Made by the Demiurge*

The human soul is fashioned by the Demiurge out of the same mixture as the world soul and the souls of the gods. The immortal soul of the gods—including the world soul and the stars—is fastened to a body[8] which is indestructible, not in itself, but because the Demiurge does not want to undo his handiwork:

> When he had finished this speech,[9] he turned again to the mixing bowl he had used before, the one in which he had blended and mixed the soul of the world. He began to pour into it what remained of the previous ingredients and to mix them in somewhat the same way, though these were no longer invariably and constantly pure, but of a second and third grade of purity. And when he had compounded it all, he divided the mixture into a number of souls equal to the number of the stars and assigned each soul to a star.
>
> 41d4–e1

Having sown these souls into the celestial bodies,[10] which is a sign of the importance of astrology in this context, the Demiurge hands them to the newly

---

5   Lafrance, *La théorie platonicienne de la* doxa.
6   *Soph.* 262d–264c.
7   Brisson, Luc, "Le corps des dieux."
8   "[…] a god is an immortal living being which has a body and a soul, and that there are bound together by nature for all time." (*Phaedr.* 246d1–2).
9   To the gods.
10   That is why Karfík, *Beseelung*, 114–117, thinks the newly born gods could be the celestial bodies. Cf. Karfík, "What the Mortal Parts of the Soul Really are."

born gods, and asks them to fashion living beings (humans and animals) by weaving together in them what is mortal to what is immortal.

2.2 Weaving Immortal to Mortal

Subsequently, the Demiurge's assistants go on to implant into a mortal body this immortal soul, which is the principle of all psychic and physical motion.

> So, once the souls were of necessity (*ex anankēs*) implanted in bodies, and these bodies had things coming to them and leaving them,[11] there must necessarily be first sensation (*aisthēsis*) the same for all, arising naturally from violent sensations, and second desire (*erōs*) blended with pleasure and pain, and beside these fear and spiritedness (*thymos*), plus whatever goes with having these affections, as well as all their natural opposites. And if they could master these affections (*pathēmata*), their lives would be just, whereas if they were mastered by them, they would be unjust.
>
> 42a3–b2

Because it is implanted in a body, the soul has to deal with corporeal affections that have an impact on the immortal soul. This is why affections should be mastered, a further proof that ethics cannot be dissociated from knowledge. This passage anticipates the following one which is more explicit:

> They[12] imitated the Demiurge: having taken the immortal principle that is the soul (*archēn psychēs athanaton*),[13] they proceeded next to turn[14] for it a mortal body and to give it the entire body as its vehicle. And within the body they housed (*prosōikodomoun*)[15] another kind of soul (*allo te eidos psychēs*) as well, the mortal kind (*to thnēton*), which contains within it those dreadful but necessary affections (*pathēmata*), first of all, pleasure (*hēdonēn*) evil's most powerful lure; then pains (*lypas*),[16] that make us run away from what is good, besides these, boldness (*tharros*) also and fear (*phobon*), foolish counselors both; then also the spirit of anger (*thymon*)

---

11   Bodies are always changing. More precisely, see *Tim.* 44a1–c4 cited *infra*.
12   The Demiurge's assistants.
13   This, it seems to me, is how we must translate *archēn psychēs athanaton*, considering that the genitive *psychēs* is a subjective genitive: "the immortal principle which is the soul." This translation is in agreement with what we read in the *Phaedrus* (245c5), where *psychē pasa athanatos* can be read: "The soul in its totality is immortal."
14   The verb *perietorneusan* refers to the potter's technique.
15   My translation of *prosōikodomoun* which, referring to the architect's technique, is not frequent in Ancient Greek.
16   Pleasure and pain are sensation, see *Tim.* 64a2–65b3.

hard to assuage, and expectation (*elpida*) easily led astray. These affections (*pathēmata*) they mixed (*sunkerasamenoi*) with unreasoning sense perception (*aisthēsei alogōi*) and all-venturing desire (*epicheirētēi pantos erōti*), and so, as was necessary, they composed the mortal type of soul.
69c5–d6

This passage is not easy to translate and to interpret. In order to understand it, one should take the central myth of the *Phaedrus* (245c–246b) into account. In this myth, soul appears as a totality, even if it is described as being by nature a composite power (*symphytē dynamis*). Plato does not give a description of the structure of the soul; he limits himself to comparing the soul to a chariot drawn by two horses that are led by a charioteer. If one refers to other dialogues, the charioteer can be identified with intellect (*nous*), and the two horses with spirit (*thymos*) and desire (*epithymia*). Intellection (*noēsis*) is the highest faculty of the soul, and Intellect (*nous*) has the Forms as its objects. Hence, the soul is a totality consisting of three parts, that are not pieces, but functional activities.

As such, soul is a totality. Several arguments tend in this direction: 1) As we have seen, the world soul and the human soul result from the same mixture. 2) In the central myth of the *Phaedrus*, the soul of the gods contains these three parts: intellect (*nous*), spirit (*thymos*) and desire (*epithymia*).[17] But because their body is indestructible, they do not need to activate these parts, which are not pieces but resources; human beings must do so, because they need to protect their body and provide it with subsistence. 3) Everywhere else in Plato, the soul exhibits a unity that implies the association of these three parts. 4) The process of retribution through *metensōmatōsis* implies that the soul, which moves from one body to another, remains the same.[18]

2.2.1 Housing the Soul in a Body

Having received the soul, which is immortal, the assistants of the Demiurge do not fashion a new kind of soul, but must weave the immortal soul they have received with the mortal body it moves. They must first establish relations between external bodies and the human body.

2.2.1.1 *The Mortal Part of the Soul*

The gods made by the Demiurge are getting their job done, namely to weave what is mortal to what is immortal.

---

[17] "The gods have horses and charioteers that are themselves all good and come from good stock besides, while everyone has a mixture." (*Phaedr.* 246a7–b3).

[18] Brisson, "Le corps animal comme signe de la valeur d'une âme chez Platon."

2.2.1.1.1 The Components of the Mortal Part of the Soul

They link affections, sensation and desire, which are corporeal processes, to the soul fashioned by the Demiurge.

a. The mortal type of the soul is the place where *pathēmata* are to be found. The *pathēmata* are not characteristics or qualities, for example "hot" or "cold," which reside in an object independently of its effect upon a sensible percipient. This claim founders on Plato's repeated qualification[19] that the *pathēmata* have to do with the human body, whether with the human body taken as a whole, or at least with what is specified as "flesh" or with "individual parts" of the body.[20] Moreover, the *pathēmata* are not themselves quite the same as the *sensibilia* of the *Theaetetus* (156a3–157c2, 182a3 sq.), qualities of "white" which exist only when, and for as long as they are being perceived.

b. The *pathēmata* are simply the effects, as movements, which one body has upon another one and which, if the body affected is sufficiently receptive, will be transmitted, through the blood,[21] to the *phronimon* (64b2–6)[22] and will thereby be recognized as sensations[23] leading to intellection.[24]

---

19 *Tim.* 61c3–68d7.

20 *Tim.* 61d7, 62a6–7, 62b6–7, 64a2–3, 64a4–5, 65c2–3, 66d1–2, 67a7–c3, 67c4–68d7, 67e6–68b1.

21 According to Karfík, "Mortal Parts," 205, n.45, it should be blood. I do not agree, even if the suggestion is very interesting. Blood is red because fire is predominant in it (*Tim.* 80e1–4). But one finds fire everywhere in the body, just not as forwarding information.

22 Two arguments may provide evidence to support our interpretation. A textual argument: it appears that Plato uses the word *phronimon* to allude to the rational part of the soul, as in the *Republic* (VI 530c1, IX 586d7, X 604e2) and in the *Laws* (VIII 837c7, X 897b8). And a technical argument: if the *pathēmata* were not able to reach the rational part of the soul, how could the circuits of the immortal soul in the head suffer violent motions when assailed by sensations (*Tim.* 43a6–44c7)?

23 On sense perception, see Brisson, "Plato's Theory of Sense Perception in the *Timaeus*. How it Works and What it Means."

24 Such an interpretation of the meaning of *phronimon* is not usual, because it brings forward what is considered as Plato's metaphysical (or mythological) epistemology. In fact, even if this passage does not explicitly allude to *anamnēsis*, that is the remembrance of the Forms seen by the soul before its incarnation, one need no longer think that it remains the most probable solution. Why not? Because when the *pathēmata* have reached the rational part of the soul and have reported the quality of the agent, we are able not only to say "I feel hot," but by a transference of terms we also say that "the fire is called hot"; and by a further transference of terms we say that "the fire heats and melts metal." The persistence of this feature in the *Timaeus* proves that it is not accidental. Denis O'Brien has counted 29 occurrences in the *Timaeus*: 58d2, d3, e7, 59a6–8, b5, c5, d5–6, e5, 60a1, a2–3, a4, b2–3, b5, d2, 62a4–5, b5–6, 63a6, c4, d3, 31, 66a1–2, b, c7, 67a1–3, e2, e5, 68a2, a6–b1, b4–5, cf. O'Brien, *Theories of Weight in the Ancient World: Four Essays on*

To refer to the *pathēmata* involves reference to sensation, and reference to sensation involves referring to flesh and things associated with flesh and to the mortal parts of the soul. But the reverse is also true: an account of the mortal soul, and of flesh and things associated with flesh requires an account of sensation and therefore an account of *pathēmata*.

c. Moreover, the *pathēmata* can be triggered by *erōs*:

> And this [the birth of women] explains why at that time the gods fashioned the desire for sexual union (*synousias erōta*), by constructing one living being (*zōion*) in us as well as an ensouled being (*empsychon*) in women.[25] This is how they made them in each case.
>
> There is [in a man] a conduit by which fluids exit from the body, where it receives the liquid that has passed between the lungs down into the kidneys and on into the bladder and expels it under pressure of air. From this conduit, they[26] bored a connecting one into the compacted marrow[27] that runs from the head along the neck through the spine. This is in fact the marrow that we have previously called "sperm."[28] Now because it has soul breathed by it,[29] this marrow instilled a life-giving desire for emission right at the place of breathing, and so produced the love of procreation. This is why of course, the male genitals are unruly and self-willed, like an animal that will not be subject to reason[30] and, goaded by the sting[31] of its passionate desires, seeks to overpower everything else.[32]

Democritus, Plato and Aristotle, vol. 2: *Plato: Weight and Sensation. The Two Theories of the "Timaeus"*, 147–149.

25   See also *Tim.* 91c1–2. The sexual organs are described as living beings, because they seem to move independently of our own will. But it is one and the same human soul which is involved in the sexual organs.

26   The Demiurge's assistants.

27   See *Tim.*73b1–c6.

28   See *supra Tim.*74a4, 86c3–d5.

29   The formula *labōn anapnoēn* is similar to *anapnoēn labousa* in *Phaedrus* 251e4. This passage in Aristotle seems to be relevant: "The same objection lies against the view expressed in the 'Orphic' poems: there it is said that the soul comes in from the whole when breathing takes place, being borne in upon the winds (τὴν ψυχὴν ἐκ τοῦ ὅλου εἰσιέναι ἀναπνεόντων, φερομένην ὑπὸ τῶν ἀνέμων)." (*De anima*, I 5, 410b28–30 = Kern, fr. 27 = 421 F Bernabé). We must acknowledge that this connection poses a number of problems, since it assimilates the soul, which is incorporeal to a material entity.

30   As is made by "all-venturing desire" (*epicheirētēi pantos erōti, Tim.*69d4).

31   For the metaphor of the sting, see *Phaedr.* 240d1, *Rep.* IX 577e2, and *Laws* VI 782e3.

32   These references to sensation and *erōs*, make this sentence clear: "These affections (*pathēmata*) they mixed with unreasoning sense perception (*aisthēsei alogōi*) and

The very same causes operate in women. A woman's womb or uterus,[33] as it is called, is a living being (*zōion*) within her with a desire for childbearing. Now when this remains unfruitful for an unseasonably long period of time, it is extremely frustrated and travels everywhere up and down her body. It blocks up her respiration passages, and by not allowing her to breathe it throws her into extreme emergencies, and visits all sorts of other illnesses upon her until finally the desire that is the passionate desire[34] bring the man and the woman together, and, like plucking the fruit from a tree,[35] they sow the seed into the ploughed fields of her womb, living beings too small to be visible and still without form. And when they have again given them distinct form, they nourish these living beings so that they can mature inside the womb. Afterwards, they bring them to birth, introducing them into the light of the day.

91a1–d5

In the formula *hē epithymia kai ho erōs*, the *kai* is epexegetic. Here, as at *Timaeus* 42a3–b2, these words refer to the desire for food and sexual intercourse, which are problematic. The influx of food at birth, but also afterwards, disturbs the process of knowledge, which has consequences on an ethical level.[36] And when the sperm in the marrow is overabundant, a man becomes mad and vicious.[37]

Thus we get the three parts of the soul: intellect (*nous* or the *phronimon*), the spirit (*thymos*) and desire (*epithymia*) like in the *Phaedrus*. The mortal parts of the soul are not an autonomous entity, separated from an immortal part, but the center of a communication network between the soul in its totality which is immortal and the mortal body it moves, and which is under the influence of desire, and in contact with external objects through sense perception. In other words, the assistants of the Demiurge establish an interface up between soul and body.

2.2.1.1.2   The Soul in a Body

The younger gods fasten the different kinds (*genē*) of soul into one and the same corporeal tissue, the marrow. The soul as such is sown in the brain, whose

---

all-venturing lust (*epicheirētēi pantos erōti*), and so, as was necessary, they composed the mortal type of soul." (69d4–5)

33 In Ancient Greek: *mētrai te kai hysterai*. The word *hystera* "what is at the bottom" is like *aidoia* a euphemism refering to the sexual organs.
34 *Erōs* and *epithymia* seem to be equivalent.
35 See *Timaeus* 86c3–d5.
36 *Tim.* 44a1–c4.
37 *Tim.* 86c3–e3.

extension is the spinal marrow and finally the sperm. As a safeguard against external aggression, the brain is enclosed in the skull, which is spherical like the body of the world, and the spinal marrow in the vertebrae, which are elongated, both being made of bone. Thus, the immortal principle that is soul is anchored in the same tissue, marrow, protected by bones.

The divine (*to theion*)[38] element, that is, the intellect (*nous* or *phronimon*), is established in the head, separated from the rest of the body by means of the neck which is compared to an isthmus. The mortal part (*to thnēton*) which is dual, is located in the thorax; and the diaphragm introduces a new division, between the heart, where spirit (*thymos*) which is better (*ameinon*) is situated, and the region of the liver, where one finds desire (*epithymia*) which is worse (*cheiron*) as in the *Phaedrus*.[39]

Spirit occupies an intermediary position between intellect and desire, transmitting the intellect's orders to desire, and information on the dangers incurred by desire to the intellect. Desire, for its part, deals with the needs relative to nutrition and reproduction: "What in the soul has appetites (*epithymētikon*) for food and drink and whatever else it feels a need for, given the body's nature [...]"[40] (*Timaeus* 70d7–8). This bodily location may, as in the *Republic*, be placed in relation to the functional tripartition of the city, but I will not discuss this point here.

But, even if it is anchored in the marrow, one and the same tissue, the three parts—that is activities—of the soul are located in three different places in the body. The head seems to be the seat of the *phronimon* or the *nous*, and the heart the seat of the *thymos*, while the *epithymia* is situated in the lower abdomen: the neck keeps apart the mortal and the immortal parts of the soul, and the midriff the *thymos* and *epithymia*.

These kinds are not isolated, because there is a constant connection between them. The divine part, intellect is separated, from the other kinds only by an isthmus, the neck; spirit in the area of the heart, is nearer to the head and under the direct influence of the intellect, because it is obedient to the orders coming from it;[41] that said, the intellect has to use, as a go-between, the liver which plays the role of a screen to prevent the *epithymia* misbehaving.[42]

---

38   In the *Timaeus* (41c7, 69d6, 72d4, 73c7, 90a8, c4, 8), *theion* refers obviously to the intellect. And because that part of the soul is also referred to as *athanaton*, just like the soul as a whole, confusion arises.
39   *Phaedr.* 246b1–4.
40   Probably sex (see *supra*).
41   *Tim.* 70b3–4.
42   *Tim.* 71a3–72b5. See Luc Brisson, "Du bon usage du dérèglement."

2.2.2 Weaving the Mortal to the Immortal

The soul framed by the Demiurge is implanted in a body by his assistants. Because the soul is implanted in a body, it must take into account corporeal affections that have an impact on the soul.

2.2.2.1 *The Phronimon or the Nous*

Having received the immortal principle of the soul from the Demiurge, his assistants encase it inside the head, which is spherical as an image of the world's body, and then house (*prosōikodomoun*) within the body the mortal kind of the soul.[43] The main activity of the human soul whose constitution is very similar to the world soul is cognition.

2.2.2.1.1 Geometrical and Mathematical Structure

The immortal principle that is the human soul contains the same two circles as the world soul, which possess the same mathematical structure. This can be seen by reading this description of the soul's disturbances at the moment of birth:

> They (sensations) cooperated with the continually flowing channel to stir and violently shake the orbits of the soul. They completely bound that of the Same by flowing against it in the opposite direction, and held it fast just as it was beginning to go its way. And they further shook the orbit of the Different right through, with the result that they twisted every which way the three intervals of the double and the three of the triple, as well as the middle terms of the ratios of 3:2, 4:3, and 9:8 that connect them. These agitations did not undo them, however, because they cannot be completely undone except by the one who had bound them together [...] and though they remained in motion, they moved without rhyme or reason, sometimes in the opposite direction, sometime sideways and sometimes upside down.
>
> 43c7–e8

As in the case of the world soul, the revolution of these circles is linked to a cognitive ability. By the circle of the Different, the human soul is informed of what takes place within and around it in the sensible world, whereas by the circle of the Same, it grasps the intelligible.

---

[43] References to the "mortal parts of the soul" in the *Timaeus*: 61c7–8, 69c7–8, 69e4, 73d3.

2.2.2.1.2 Cognitive Ability

But human cognitive ability, which, as in the case of the world soul, is associated with the proper functioning of these circles, is disturbed at birth by the influx of food and sensations. It is this very thing—and others like it—that have such a dramatic effect upon the revolutions of the soul.[44]

> Whenever they encounter something outside of them characterizable as same or different, they will speak of it as "the same as" something, or as "different from" something else when the truth is just the opposite, so proving themselves to be misled and unintelligent. Also, at this stage souls do not have a ruling orbit taking the lead. And so when certain sensations come in from outside and attack them, they sweep the soul's entire vessel along with them. It is then that these revolutions, however much in control they seem to be, are actually under their control. All these disturbances are no doubt the reason why even today and not only at the beginning, whenever a soul is bound within a mortal body, it at first lacks intelligence. But as the stream that brings growth and nourishment diminishes and the soul's orbits regain their composure, resume their proper courses and establish themselves more and more with the passage of time, their revolutions are set straight, to conform to the configuration each of the circles takes in its natural course. They then correctly identify what is the same and what is different, and render intelligent the persons who possess them. And to be sure, if such a person also gets proper nurture to supplement his education, he'll turn out perfectly whole and healthy, and will have escaped the most grievous of illnesses. But if he neglects this, he'll limp his way through life and return to Hades uninitiated,[45] that is unintelligent.
>
> 44a1–c4

This passage is highly interesting, for it shows the influence exerted by the body on the soul; it also shows that these troubles are a consequence of interference between movements, the revolutions of the soul, and the other movements[46] coming from the external objects. But these troubles in the revolutions of the soul leave traces the skull[47] and even explain why the heads of quadrupeds

---

44 Those of the Same and the Different.
45 For a parallel, see *Gorg.* 493b3–7. The vocabulary of the Mysteries is often used in Plato to describe the philosophical experience (*Symp.* 210a ff. and *Phaedr.* 250c)
46 *Laws* x 893b–895a.
47 *Tim.* 76a6–b1. See also, Sedley, "'Becoming like God' in the *Timaeus* and Aristotle."

are elongated.[48] The influx of food and sensation at birth, but also afterwards, disturbs the acquisition of knowledge, which has consequences on an ethical level. Since the true and the good are deeply intertwined in Plato, the current way of life of a given human being will have consequences for the soul's *post-mortem* destiny.

2.3 What Does "Mortal" Mean?

If we consider the soul's incarnation within a human body, what can we infer from this doctrine?[49] When the soul is in a body, it remains in contact, through one of its activities, viz. the intellect (*nous*), with the intelligible, which in fact allows the quality of the soul in question to be defined. Yet this soul also has activities that must enable it to take care of the body to which it is attached. It must ensure the survival of this body through the ingestion of food and drink, and ensure its reproduction (thanks to *epithymia*). It must also defend this body against aggression coming from without, or even from within (thanks to *thymos*). This is why spirit and desire are required. Yet what happens when this soul is separated from its body? Its higher activity remains what it is, and it retains the memory of its object, the intelligible, simply because this object is immutable. However, this contemplative activity is qualified by the fact that when the soul was within a body, it paid more or less attention to the sensible, hence the application of a retributive system. One can from this see why ethics is linked to knowledge.

By contrast, when the soul is detached from the body of which it had taken care, the activities it had in this area cease, and it loses the memory of the objects and events associated with these activities. It is in this sense that one can, it seems to me, declare the functions represented by spirit (*thymos*) and desire (*epithymia*) to be "mortal." Insofar as they are the activities of a soul, these functions share this soul's immortality. And the fact that they subsist in the gods, without being exercised, is a good indication, in my view, of the fact that we must consider the soul to be naturally composite. *Qua* capacities of acting and undergoing, however, these functions cease to be exercised as a result of the soul's separation from its body, and since no memory of what they have done in the past subsists, they can be qualified as "mortal." From this perspective, the "death" that affects these functions of the human soul represented by spirit and desire may be defined as forgetting the management of the body, consecutive upon the soul's separation from this body.

---

48   *Tim.* 91e8–92a1.
49   See Brisson, "The mortal parts of the soul, or death forgetting the body."

After a specific period of time, the soul in question rejoins a body. Its lower functions then adapt themselves to this new body and remain in relation with it until they are separated from it. This soul's identity or individuality is thus attached to this series of particular existences. This identity or individuality persists for a certain stretch of time, but not for eternity, since it is linked to the history of a soul for a cycle of ten periods of one thousand years.[50] At the end of this cycle, we can imagine that this soul loses its identity before it starts once again its ascent toward the intelligible with the gods, and that it acquires, for a new period, a new individuality which will then be called into question once again. In other words, it is soul in its totality that is immortal, not an individual soul.

2.4 *Metensōmatōsis*

These specifications are necessary in order to understand the description of the *post-mortem* destiny of those souls that are not souls of gods, during one of the ten periods of the cycles they must undertake periodically, according to Plato's doctrine of metempsychosis (or reincarnation).

During the first period following the death of the physical organism,[51] the soul is separated from all mortal bodies, whereas during the nine others,[52] it passes from body to body as a function of the moral value of its previous existence, which is determined by the quality of the exercise of its reason.

Like those of human beings, whether men or women, the souls of animals, even of shellfish, are endowed with a rational part, and this is true even though animals are what they are because they make little or no use of their intellect. In any case, nothing prevents an animal, whatever it may be, from climbing back up the ladder to become a human being. This way of looking at things implies an absolute respect for life, not only within human society, but also in the animal kingdom. How, in this case, can the survival of human beings, who need to feed themselves, be ensured, without automatically making cannibals of them? By giving them as food a kind of living being that is not endowed with intellect: vegetables.

After mentioning the four types of living beings that populate the universe, the gods, associated with fire; human beings, both men and women; the birds that inhabit the air; the animals that walk or crawl on the earth; and the aquatic beasts, Timaeus, in a particularly difficult passage, briefly mentions the origin of vegetables, which he associates with the third, or desiring kind of soul.

---

50 In Ancient Greek, we read *chilias*, which means a thousand or a very large number.
51 *Phaedr.* 245d–248c.
52 *Phaedr.* 248c–e.

3 The Soul of Plants

It should be noted, moreover, that the Demiurge's assistants, who are his offspring, do not fashion the soul, but receive it from the Demiurge to weave it with the body. Things are different with the soul of the plants,[53] which results from a mixture made by the Demiurge's assistants:

> So all the parts, all the limbs[54] of the mortal living thing[55] came to constitute a natural whole.[56] Of necessity, however, it came about that he lived his life surrounded by fire and air, which cause him to waste away and[57] be depleted, and so to perish. The gods,[58] therefore, devised something to protect him. They caused another nature to grow, one congenial to our human nature, though mixed with other features and other sensations,[59] so as to be a different living thing.[60] These are now cultivated trees, plants and seeds, taught by the art of agriculture to be domesticated for our use. But at first the only kinds there were wild ones, older than our cultivated kinds. We may call these plants "living things" on the grounds that anything that partakes of life has an incontestable right to be called a "living thing."[61] And in fact, what we are talking about now partakes of the third type of soul, the type that our account has situated between the midriff and the navel.[62] This type is totally devoid of opinion, reasoning or understanding, though it does share in sensation, pleasant or painful, and desires.[63] For throughout its existence

---

53 On plants, see Repici, *Uomini capovolti: le piante nel pensiero dei Greci.*
54 Note the play on words: *merē melē.*
55 It is the possible destruction of its body that distinguishes the other living beings from gods.
56 An allusion to the constitution of the human body, which has just been described (*Tim.*73b–76e).
57 If one accepts the *te.*
58 The assistants of the Demiurge, see *Tim.* 69c5.
59 Than those of man. Only touch is taken into account, and more particularly pleasure and pain. On the translation of *aisthēsesin*, see Jouanna, "La théorie de la sensation, de la pensée et de l'âme dans le traité hippocratique *Du régime*: ses rapports avec Empédocle et le *Timée* de Platon," and, in response, Brisson, "Le *Timée* de Platon et le traité hippocratique *Du régime*, sur le mécanisme de la sensation."
60 The accusative *physin* seems to be the direct object complement of both *phyteuousin* and *kerannyntes.*
61 Plants are thus animated by a soul, which should be the soul of the Earth. I agree with Karfík "Mortal Parts," 215 on this point.
62 In a human being.
63 See Brisson, "Sense Perception."

it is completely passive, and its formation has not entrusted it with a natural ability to discern and reflect upon any of its own characteristics, by revolving within and about itself,[64] repelling movement from without and exercising its own inherent movement. Hence it is alive, to be sure, and unmistakably a living thing, but it stays put, standing fixed, and rooted, since it lacks self-motion.

76e7–77c5

To help human beings to survive, the assistants of the Demiurge will fashion plants, which are a new type of living being, endowed with a body and a soul. What is the nature of this soul? It is the result of a mixture, like the soul of the world (35a1–b1) and the souls of human beings and animals (41d4–7). Yet this mixture is no longer carried out by the Demiurge, but by his assistants who combine the third type of soul with other features and other sensations.

The plant is a living being, insofar as it is endowed with spontaneous motion, whose principle can only be a soul.[65] However, this spontaneous motion features two essential differences with regard to the motion of animals: 1) The soul in question feels only sensations of pleasure and pain associated with appetites, which makes it akin to the third part of the human soul. It is completely bereft of any form of intelligence and opinion, which means that the affections on their body coming from external things do not reach the rational part of the soul. 2) In addition, it lacks any local motion. We can therefore understand how the plant, as a living being, is both similar to and different from human beings and animals. But it is impossible to know where this inferior species of soul comes from and how it is related to the world soul and to the human soul. The assistants of the Demiurge, as it seems, grow " a nature congenial to our human nature, though mixed with other features and other sensations."

This new species of living being is plants, which are at the service of mankind. When cultivated, they are to serve as our food, thus eliminating any need for us to intervene in the process of transmigration set in place by the gods. Insofar as the living being that will result from the implantation of this soul in a body is to serve as food for mankind, this soul must be akin to the soul of human beings, by virtue of the fact that only like can be known by or act upon like.[66]

If a human being were to eat a living being endowed with an intellect, even if that living being no longer made use of that higher ability, he would be

---

64 The verbs *trephō* is equivalent to the Latin verb *versari*: to reside in, be limited to.
65 This soul could the soul of the earth, see Karfík, "Mortal Parts," 215.
66 Brisson, "La réminiscence dans le *Ménon* (81c5–d5)."

committing an act of cannibalism. This is no longer the case for plants, which possess a soul, but lack an intellect. As a result, the following problem is solved: how can man eat without being a cannibal? The decomposition of plants within the human body enables the constitution of blood, which nourishes all the other tissues. The plants thus enable the human body, which unlike the body of the world may be destroyed by the external aggressions of fire and air, to reconstitute itself without consuming living beings endowed with an intellect. In short, Plato "invents" plants[67] to be able to maintain his scale of living beings.

In conclusion, the systematic association of the human soul with a body that illustrates its quality leads us to consider the world of living beings as a vast system of signs, and to wonder about the place and role of mankind in this whole. The human soul is immortal as a soul, but not as an individual, because it loses its personality at the end of each cycle. That said, a human soul is immortal in its totality, even if at death the previous experiences of its spirit (*thymos*) and of its desire (*epithymia*) are forgotten; only the excellence of its intellectual life is taken into account in the process of reincarnation.

Works Cited

Brisson, Luc. "Du bon usage du dérèglement." In *Divination et rationalité, Recherches anthropologiques*. Edited by Remo Guidieri. Paris: Seuil, 1974, 220–248.

Brisson, Luc. "Plato's Theory of Sense Perception in the *Timaeus*. How it Works and What it Means." *Proceedings of the Colloquium in Ancient Philosophy* 13. Edited by John Cleary and Gary Gurtler. Lanham: University Press of America, 1999, 147–176.

Brisson, Luc. "Le corps animal comme signe de la valeur d'une âme chez Platon." In *L'Animal dans l'Antiquité*. Edited by Barbara Cassin, Jean-Louis Labarrière and Gilbert Romeyer Dherbey. Paris: Vrin, 1997, 227–245.

Brisson, Luc. "Le corps des dieux." In *Les dieux de Platon. Actes du Colloque international organisé à l'Université de Caen Basse-Normandie, les 24, 25 et 26 janvier 2002*. Edited by Jérôme Laurent. Caen: Presses Universitaires de Caen, 2003, 11–23.

Brisson, Luc. "Platon, Pythagore et les Pythagoriciens." In *Platon, source des Présocratiques. Exploration*. Edited by Monique Dixsaut and Aldo Brancacci. Paris: Vrin, 2003, 21–46.

Brisson, Luc. "La réminiscence dans le *Ménon* (81c5–d5)." *Gorgias-Menon: Selected Papers from the Seventh Symposium Platonicum*. Edited by Michael Erler and Luc Brisson. Sankt Augustin: Academia Verlag, 2007, 199–203.

---

67   Note the admirable image: man himself is considered as a plant, and his head, in which the intellect which makes him akin to the divinity is located, is its root.

Brisson, Luc. "The mortal parts of the soul, or death forgetting the body." In *Inner Life and Soul: Psyche in Plato*. Edited by Maurizio, Migliori, Linda Napolitano Valditara and Arianna Fermani. Sankt Augustin: Academia Verlag, 2011, 63–70.

Brisson, Luc. "Le *Timée* de Platon et le traité hippocratique Du régime, sur le mécanisme de la sensation." *Études Platoniciennes* 10 (2013). Open access.

Cooper, John M. and David S. Hutchinson, eds. *Plato: Complete Works*. Indianapolis: Hackett Publishing Company, 1997.

Jouanna, Jacques. "La théorie de la sensation, de la pensée et de l'âme dans le traité hippocratique *Du régime*: ses rapports avec Empédocle et le *Timée* de Platon." *Aion* (filol) 29 (2007): 8–38.

Karfík, Filip. *Die Beseelung des Kosmos: Untersuchungen zur Kosmologie, Seelenlehre und Theologie in Platons* Phaidon *und* Timaios. Munich: Saur, 2004.

Karfík, Filip. "What the Mortal Parts of the Soul Really are." *Rhizai* 11, 2 (2005): 197–217.

Lafrance, Yvon. *La théorie platonicienne de la* doxa. Paris: Les Belles Lettres, 1981. Reprint 2015.

O'Brien, Denis. *Theories of Weight in the Ancient World: Four Essays on Democritus, Plato and Aristotle*, vol. 2: *Plato: Weight and Sensation. The Two Theories of the* "Timaeus". Leiden: Brill, 1984.

Repici, Luciana. *Uomini capovolti: le piante nel pensiero dei Greci*. Roma: Laterza, 2000.

Sedley, David. "'Becoming like God' in the *Timaeus* and Aristotle." In *Proceedings of the Symposium Platonicum* 4. Edited by Tomas Calvo and Luc Brisson. Sankt Augustin: Academia Verlag, 1997, 263–374.

Planets and Time: A Timaean Puzzle

Karel Thein

Abstract

In the *Timaeus*, the issue of planets is revelatory of the twofold subject of the plausible account of how our universe acquired its present shape. If Timaeus speaks about the nature of the Whole *and* about human nature, the creation of the planets is where these two parts of his account meet and intersect. To clarify this suggestion, the chapter starts with the creation of time and with its role in Timaeus' account (some more metaphysical remarks on the nature of time are relegated to the Postscript). The second part of the chapter turns to the planets as a pivotal moment where Timaeus passes from the immortal to the mortal species. This passage will play an important role in explaining why Timaeus uses various temporal idioms without offering a unified theory of time.

Keywords

Plato – *Timaeus* – planets – time

In the overall framework of Timaeus' plausible account of how our universe acquired its present shape, the issue of planets is revelatory of the twofold nature of Timaeus' task: Timaeus is invited to speak about the nature of the Whole *and* about human nature. The planets, I will suggest, are precisely where these two parts of the story meet and intersect.

Before focusing on this intersection, in other words on planets and human beings, I need to start with Timaeus' rather entangled narrative of how—and especially *why*—the planets were created in the first place. By the same token, this first part of my contribution cannot avoid the issue that is at the heart of this narrative, namely the creation of time. I will limit myself to the role of the planets and time within Timaeus' cosmic story and leave aside a more metaphysical inquiry into time, which goes necessarily beyond the text of our dialogue. A taste of such an inquiry is given in the "Postscript," which offers some further remarks on how Timaeus speaks about time and what are *some* possible implications of his story for a more abstract treatment of it. In the second part of my contribution, I will turn to the planets as a pivotal moment where Timaeus' story passes from the immortal to the mortal living species.

The first part of my contribution starts naturally with line 37c6, where we meet the Demiurge who pauses to take a look at his creation so far. This is actually the only time in the story that we observe him doing so, and this unusual dramatic device has a reason: while contemplating the world consisting of a soul and a body put together, the Demiurge conceives an idea, which he will realize in the guise of planets, including the structure of their motions that we call "time." In order to properly evaluate this invention, we first need to assume the posture of the demiurge so as to see what exactly it is that he contemplates at this point of the story.

On the flatly descriptive level, we can observe the world's body and its soul woven intricately together in a way which implies that the soul is itself a tridimensional structure that both encompasses and permeates the world as a physical compound. Obviously, the soul is not visible as such, and the verb Timaeus employs, *noein*, signals that we grasp much more than the observable facts. What we understand is not only that the universe moves, but that its motion is internally animated. To which the Demiurge reacts as follows:

> Now when the father who had begotten the universe observed it set in motion and alive (κινηθὲν αὐτὸ καὶ ζῶν ἐνόησεν), a thing that had come to be as a shrine for the everlasting gods (τῶν ἀιδίων θεῶν γεγονὸς ἄγαλμα), he was well pleased, and in his delight he thought of making it more like its model still (ἠγάσθη τε καὶ εὐφρανθεὶς ἔτι δὴ μᾶλλον ὅμοιον πρὸς τὸ παράδειγμα ἐπενόησεν ἀπεργάσασθαι).
> 37c6–d1[1]

Two things happen here: first, we have the thoughtful contemplation whose joyful character is emphasized by the verbs *agazō* and *euphrainō*, but also by the description of the object in question as *tōn aidiōn theōn agalma*, a kind of charming sanctuary, a wonderful invitation for gods to be at home in the universe—here we may notice a certain temporal oscillation of the narrative which conflates what already is and what is yet to come.[2] For now, we are more interested in the second moment: the state of joyful contemplation (verb *noein*) which mixes intellectual alertness with the father's affection for his offspring. This state inspires a new idea, which will carry the project still further forward (verb *epinoein*). In other words, looking at what is already wonderful,

---

[1] Here as elsewhere the translation I use is Zeyl, *Plato: Timaeus*.
[2] On *agalma* as joy-provoking image see Kerényi, "Agalma, eikon, eidolon." Cf. Cohen, "Etymology of Greek *agalma, agallô, agallomai*." *Agallomai* means to exult, to rejoice greatly; it designates the rapture of those who find themselves face to face with the divine.

the Demiurge thinks about how to make it even more so. First, I will quote this train of Demiurgic thought in Zeyl's translation which reflects probably the most common interpretation of the text:

> So, as the model was itself an everlasting Living Thing (ζῷον ἀίδιον ὄν), he set himself to bringing this universe to completion in such a way that it, too, would have that character to the extent that was possible. Now it was the Living Thing's nature to be eternal (αἰώνιος), but it isn't possible to attach [the eternal nature] fully to anything that is begotten. And so he began to think (ἐπενόει) of making a moving image of eternity (εἰκὼ κινητόν τινα αἰῶνος ποιῆσαι): at the same time (ἅμα) as he brought order to the heavens, he would make an eternal image (αἰώνιον εἰκόνα), moving according to number (κατ' ἀριθμὸν ἰοῦσαν), of eternity remaining in unity (μένοντος αἰῶνος ἐν ἑνί). This image (τοῦτον), of course, is what we now call "time."
> 37d1–7

At first sight, this reasoning is more than a little bit strange: if it is eternity and unity as such that are to be passed on, insofar as possible, to the universe, then the introduction of time is not only of little help, but it would actually seem to make the difference even bigger since it would enable us to count, thanks to the distinctly observable motions, an increasing number of different states. This probably means that the effect intended by the Demiurge is not one of an undifferentiated eternality, but consists rather in conferring to the world a still higher degree of nobility which is not entirely unlike the value of what is *aiōnios* or *aidios*—in other words, the value proper to living beings alone. Here it should be noted these two expressions (of which the first, *aiōnios*, may well be Plato's coinage) seem to be interchangeable; or, at least, the text of the dialogue offers no clue as to their possible difference. To which a *caveat* must be added: the quoted passage contains a number of lexical problems and rather peculiar constructions, and things will not get better in the next lines. I will leave aside most of the textual issues, including the disconcerting presence of various tenses,[3] and focus only on what is crucial for our understanding of what exactly it is that we "now call time." And because this understanding can only be gained if we clarify the *function* of time, we can start by emphasizing

---

[3] On the textual problems in this part of the *Timaeus* see Brague, "Pour en finir avec 'le temps, image mobile de l'éternité' (Platon, *Timée*, 37d)."

the double use of *aidios*, which applies not only to what simply is eternal, but also to what came to be but will not perish.[4]

Hence the peculiar expression "eternal image" (*aiōnion eikōn*) and the much-discussed question of what exactly this image is and how it differs from what it is an image of. As for the first part of this question, Zeyl's translation offers an apparently clear answer: the image in question is time, which implies that the masculine accusative *touton* in the last quoted sentence refers to the feminine noun *eikōn* in the previous sentence.[5] The philosophical sense we obtain from this reading follows in the steps of Philo of Alexandria who was the first, as far as we know, to take the text to speak about time as the "the imitation of eternity" (*mimēma aiōnos*).[6] However, there are two other candidates for the meaning of *touton* at 37d7, and they are both masculine nouns. The first of them is the accusative *ouranon* at 37e6, which seems syntactically rather disconnected from *touton*, and would yield a more direct identification of time with the motion of the whole universe than both the whole sentence and its wider context suggest. The second is the accusative *arithmon*, which seems quite naturally placed to be referred back by the *touton* in the next clause.[7] I find the choice of *arithmos* as the referent of *touton* very appealing, and not only for syntactical reasons. I believe that it does not at all contradict the

---

4 It is beyond the scope of my contribution to address the debates about Plato and the introduction of "eternity" into philosophical discourse. My own view concerning the *Timaeus* is that, simply put, this dialogue deals less with the metaphysics of eternity *versus* time than with the premise of an everlasting divine life whose perfection is neither augmented nor diminished by duration—such a life still echoes in Boethius' definition of eternity as divine life, which is also an exegesis of the *Timaeus*: "it is one thing to progress like the world in Plato's theory through everlasting life, and another thing to have embraced the whole of everlasting life in one simultaneous present" (*Consolation*, V vi.9–11; translated by V. E. Watts, London, Penguin, 1969). So even if eternity has no externally measurable duration, there is still some sort of duration *in* eternity insofar as what is eternal is *alive*, hence somehow active (here I agree with Stump and Kretzmann, "Eternity," and Leftow, *Time and Eternity*). In any case, the positing of two very different kinds of unceasing life is necessarily distinct from the discussions which concern the (atemporal) status of Platonic Forms. On these discussions, including a perceptive criticism of some earlier interpretations, see Mason, "Why Does Plato Believe in a Timeless Eternity?"
5 This is grammatically sound. For different options of how to construe the whole quite entangled sentence see Brague, *"Pour en finir"*, 66, and Johns, "On the translation of *Timaeus* 38b6–c3."
6 Philon, *Quis rerum divinarum heres sit* (34) 165 (= III 38.15 Cohn-Wendland).
7 Some modern translations seem to reproduce the ambivalence of the original. See e.g. Cornford's rendering: "But he took thought to make, as it were, a moving likeness of eternity; and, at the same time that he ordered the Heaven, he made, of eternity that abides in unity, an everlasting likeness moving according to number—that to which we have given the name Time." What does "that" refer to? To "likeness" or to "number"?

traditional reading, which makes time into the image of eternity; but it enables us to refine this reading and to give it much more flesh by bringing into focus the particular cosmic structures which serve to introduce time into the divinely produced universe.

The first statement in favor of my attempt is simply the explicit characterization of time offered already at 37d5–6: *chronos* is a number, *arithmos*, "according to which" the eternal, yet produced, image (whatever it is) moves (cf. *kat' arithmon iousan*). This is the second favorable statement: it would seem that, here as elsewhere in Plato, to be a *produced* image (with the exception of *speech* as image) means being something which is visibly and materially part of the sensible world—but neither time nor number, if considered on the purely abstract level, are of such a nature. What they require to fit the present context of *making things* is a support which can actually move, "according to number," in the three-dimensional world. And it is the creation of such a support, or the completion of such a creation, that Timaeus will go on to describe in the guise of the making of planets. As Timaeus will state later on, "time really is [or, as Archer-Hind has it, "arises from"] the wanderings of these bodies." (39d1–2)

The planets, therefore, are what connects lines 37d1–7 with what follows in the next four to five Stephanus pages. My aim is therefore to demonstrate that these pages only confirm that time *as such*, taken abstractly, is not the image in question, although time, defined as number, is *embedded* in what the image in question—namely the celestial bodies—*does* or, more exactly, in how that image *moves*. Here I assume that, throughout the *Timaeus*, the motion described by the verb *kinein* implies physicality: only bodies are properly *kinoumena*.[8] And if so, then the best candidate for the role of the *moving yet eternal image* are the planets *together with* the structure of their various motions including the relation between this structure and the sphere of the fixed stars. Time as number—a mathematical structure—is not identical to this image, but it enables the planets themselves, as living beings whose motions express the appropriate number, to maintain the ordered *regularity* of their motion. This, as we will see further on, is an important aspect of the created image: not only it is visible, and therefore corporeal, but this "eternal image," once created, can be self-governing only in virtue of its being *alive*. This dimension of the argument should not be forgotten: there is little doubt that *aiōnios*, like *aiōn*, strongly implies an everlasting *life* and could hardly be predicated of either something only abstract or something entirely inanimate. Taking into account

---

8   Correlatively, I doubt that the souls as described by Timaeus, including the world soul and the souls of the stars, are simply "incorporeal" (while having spatial properties) without further qualifications. For more on this issue see Thein, "Soul and incorporeality in Plato."

this last feature of the argument (which, in contrast to its commentators, is far from distinguishing between various modalities of everlastingness, but has its eye on the everlasting glory of what is either simply divine or divinely *fabricated*), I propose a modified translation of 37d1-7 with a freer rendering of *aiōnios* and *aiōn*, and a differently construed last sentence:

> So, as the model was itself an eternal Living Thing, he set himself to bringing this universe to completion in such a way that it, too, would have that character to the extent that was possible. Now it was the Living Thing's nature to be eternally alive, but it isn't possible to attach [the eternal life] fully to what is begotten. And so it occurred to him to make a moving image of the eternal life; at the same time as he brought order to the universe, he would make an eternally living image of the eternal life that remains in unity: [the image] moving according to that number (*touton*) which we call "time."[9]

Once Timaeus turns to the planets as such, the proposed reading will receive further and quite explicit support. First, however, we are offered a supplementary explanation concerning the issue of time and tenses (37d1–38b5). Right from the first sentence of this supplement, the presence of planets is presupposed insofar as the talk about days and nights, months and years would make little sense without them:

> For before the heavens came to be (πρὶν οὐρανὸν γενέσθαι), there were no days or nights, no months or years. But now, at the same time (ἅμα) as he framed the heavens, he devised their coming to be.
> 37e1–3

Here "heavens" refer to the state of the universe at the moment of the planets' making which is as yet to be accounted for: when Timaeus will be done with the more formal issues, the planets will enable the Demiurge to project a new kind of time literally into the world. In the two quoted sentences we also notice that Timaeus gets around the dilemma of "how could there have been some 'before and after' if there was still no time." He does not

---

9 My version of the last sentence concurs with Wilberding, "Eternity in Ancient Philosophy": "But he took thought to make a kind of moving image of eternity (αἰών), and simultaneous with his ordering of the heavens he created of eternity that abides in unity (μένοντος αἰῶνος ἐν ἑνί) an eternal (αἰώνιος) image moving according to number, and this number is what we have labeled 'time.'"

repeat that the planets, as the next stage of creation, will only be produced after the world soul and the world's basic body, but prefers to point out that there were no days, no nights, no months, and no years πρὶν οὐρανὸν γενέσθαι, which is a general expression specified, in the next sentence, by ἅμα which can mean "at the same time," but also "together with." Both meanings take off the edge of sequentiality, and so does the parallel expression used by Timaeus at 38b6, μετ' οὐρανοῦ γέγονεν, which is said with reference to time. Here Timaeus seems to imply a certain simultaneity of the heavens and time despite the fact that his *description* of how the Demiurge produces the heavens in its present shape proceeds in three neatly distinct steps, where three very different procedures are employed: first, the world's body is inscribed within the structure of the world soul; then, the planets are added; finally, the fixed stars are fashioned as the likeness of the first of the species that compose the intelligible model of the universe. Sequential or not, these are fundamentally different operations.

The cosmic structure which results from all these operations (of which the second and the third one are still to be described in some detail) forms an implicit background for the next part of the explanation where Timaeus introduces two basic dimensions of time, one which is generically akin to time as number and hence structure, and another one which follows from the changes of particular bodies "within" this structure, including the processes of generation and corruption. This explanation is clearly an aside to the main storyline; it is designed so as to highlight the inescapable duality implied in our conception of time and, by consequence, in our ways of speaking about it:

> These [sc. days, nights, months, and years] all are parts of time (μέρη χρόνου), and *was* and *will be* are forms of time that have come to be (χρόνου γεγονότα εἴδη). Such notions we unthinkingly but incorrectly apply to everlasting being (ἐπὶ τὴν ἀΐδιον οὐσίαν). For we say that it *was* and *is* and *will be*, but according to the true account only *is* is appropriately said of it. *Was* and *will be* are properly said about the becoming that passes in time, for these two are motions. But that which is always changeless and motionless cannot become either older or younger in the course of time (διὰ χρόνου)—it neither ever became so, nor is it now such that it has become so, nor will it ever be so in the future. And all in all, none of the characteristics that becoming has bestowed upon the things that are borne about in the realm of perception are appropriate to it. These, rather, are forms of time that have come to be—time that imitates eternity and circles according to number (ἀλλὰ χρόνου ταῦτα αἰῶνα μιμουμένου

καὶ κατ' ἀριθμὸν κυκλουμένου γέγονεν εἴδη). And what is more, we also say things like these: that what has come to be *is* what has come to be, that what is coming to be *is* what is coming to be, and also that what will come to be *is* what will come to be, and that what is not *is* what is not. None of these expressions of ours is accurate. But I don't suppose this is a good time right now to be too meticulous about these matters.

37e3–38b5

The initial division is clear: there are "parts of time" that belong to (and express *for us*) its numerical structure. There are also "forms of time," namely the past and the future, which are connected to generation and corruption or, more generally, to the changes of material states of affairs. It is to the forms of time that Timaeus turns at some length, mostly in order to clarify our misuses of the linguistic idioms concerning time and tenses. This oft-commented upon clarification, which concerns less the issue of the planets than the metaphysical theory of time, I will leave for the "Postscript" to my contribution (see below; it is worth keeping in mind that Timaeus says more about how we *speak about* time than about time as such). Here I only wish to emphasize the basic distinction between the parts of time and the forms of time, a distinction which follows from the fact that only the forms of time, but not the parts of time, are connected to the flow of time or to "time's arrow" in the sense of things coming one after another in the unidirectional "before" and "after." In contrast, there will once again be a day after a night, and after this November there will once again be November next year. This, in and of itself, does *not* imply the irreducible difference of the *content* of what happens this November and the next November: it is me, not November that will grow older. November is, *per se*, entirely indifferent to what was, is, and will be. That it is so is imperative in order for us to have time as *arithmos*, not in the sense of counting, endlessly, months and years *one after another*, but in the sense of there being a structure which enables us to differentiate between the temporal units which are days and months and years.

This much being clear, the translation quoted above still contains a sentence which would seem to threaten my suggestion that the proper image of eternity or eternal life (*aiōn*) is not time in the abstract, but planets as ensouled celestial bodies whose motions express time and make it intelligible for us. The sentence in question is rather tangled and follows from a general summarizing claim that the characteristics or features caused in the sensible things by generation do not belong to what is always changeless and motionless. To which Timaeus adds that "*tauta* are instead forms of time (χρόνου εἴδη) imitating *aiōn* and circling according to number." It is obvious that *tauta* are the characteristics of generated and perishable things, which have a past and a future different from their present state. The quoted sentence is therefore a general statement, which is not a direct part of the narrative sequence of events: at this point of the story, no such generated and changing (yet particular) things are in existence.

Moreover, the sentence fits badly its present context as well since the evoked *activity* of imitating the eternal life should belong, at best, to the *parts* of time (time as structure), not to its *forms* (time as time's arrow).[10] We should stress "activity" here since activity is what the verb *mimeisthai* implies. This is its first occurrence in Timaeus' speech but, throughout the dialogue, this verb usually describes an activity of a living being, whether this activity is exercised in its mind or its body.[11] That the *forms* of time (in contrast to the *parts* of time connected to the planets) could be active in this way appears quite implausible. In the same vein, the mention of a *cyclical* revolution suits much better the constantly revolving parts of time than the past, present and future tenses. All these things considered, it seems that the quoted sentence presents us with a rather relaxed inclusive statement and, as such, it prepares the almost immediately following (and even more general) summary at 38b6–c3. Before continuing to this summary, Timaeus himself concludes his digression on the parts and the forms of time by admitting that he will not try to be entirely rigorous in applying his own temporal distinctions. At this point, the distinction between the two views on time ("parts of time" *versus* "before and after") seems to already have receded into the background. This does not, of course, mean that this important and logical distinction loses something of its philosophical value. Nothing in the dialogue contradicts the basic assumption that time is not reducible to "the forms of time" (or the "before and after") since these are *logically* contingent on motion and change (starting perhaps with the elemental motion on which they would not be apparent *phenomenally*; but this is only relevant for the question of whether there is a directional time at the level of the elemental transformations—this question eludes our present context and will only be mentioned in the "Postscript," note 19).

---

10 I therefore do not think that Timaeus alludes here to the as yet uncreated chain of generations of perishable animals. On such a chain see, in contrast, *Symposium* 207d; it is reforged in Aristotle, *De anima* II 4, 415a26–b7.

11 Timaeus uses *mimeisthai* three times about the lesser gods imitating the Demiurge while creating mortal bodies, and then about our intellectual imitation of the regular celestial motions (46c7–47c4). At 81b1–2 it is used to describe how the blood particles in our bodies "of necessity imitate the universe's motion" (τὴν τοῦ παντὸς ἀναγκάζεται μιμεῖσθαι φοράν). On our bodily parts as "an imitation of the structure of the universe" see also 88c7–d1. This "imitation" follows of course from divine intention that governs the making of our bodies.

The already mentioned more general summary following on it confirms the independent role of "the parts of time" by first sketching an analogy between the eternal life of the model and the life of the universe, and then by finally passing—almost in the same breath—to the fabrication of planets as a means of making this analogy not only notional, but real:

> Time, then, came to be together with the universe (μετ' οὐρανοῦ) so that just as they were begotten together (ἅμα), they might also be undone together (ἅμα), should there ever be an undoing of them. And it came to be after the model of that which is sempiternal (τῆς διαιωνίας φύσεως), so that it might be as much like its model as possible. For the model is something that has being for all eternity (πάντα αἰῶνά ἐστιν ὄν), while it, on the other hand, has been, is, and shall be for all time (διὰ τέλους τὸν ἅπαντα χρόνον γεγονώς τε καὶ ὢν καὶ ἐσόμενος). Such was the reason, then, such the god's design for the coming to be of time (πρὸς χρόνου γένεσιν), that he brought into being the Sun, the Moon and five other stars, for the begetting of time. These are called "wanderers," and they came to be in order to set limits to and stand guard over the numbers of time (εἰς διορισμὸν καὶ φυλακὴν ἀριθμῶν χρόνου).
> 38b6–c6

We certainly do not need seven planets in order to make time pass from the future to the past; by contrast, we need them in order to express time as number in an organized and, in all its complexity, beautiful way. By the same token, time as number does *not* explain what we call the flow of time (even the world soul, once produced, simply starts to live its unceasing and intelligent life "for all time" [πρὸς τὸν σύμπαντα χρόνον], 36e4–5).[12] But once the planets are there, the universe becomes analogical to its model in virtue of being a well-structured unity which perseveres through "all time" (διὰ τὸν ἅπαντα χρόνον), past, present and future alike.[13]

Here we should take a step back, just like the Demiurge did a moment ago, and take a panoramic look at where we are. First, it should be said that, *until the invention of planets*, the universe—or what will soon become a complex world—is not really measured by the degree of direct resemblance to its eternal model.

---

12   Cf. Goldin, "A Plato and the Arrow of Time," 133–134. And see the "Postscript" below.
13   A full-blown version of the resulting analogy appears in Calcidius' commentary, ch. CV: the *mundus sensibilis* relates to the parts of time in the same way as the *mundus intelligibilis* relates to eternity. See Bakhouche, ed., *Calcidius: Commentaire au* Timée *de Platon*, 338, and Magee, ed., *Calcidius, On Plato's* Timaeus, 297.

This is because the model does not contain the blueprint of the world's body (although it arguably contains the geometrical blueprints of the elements), and it does not seem to encompass a soul which would be a blueprint for the world soul. The latter, much like the structure of the world's body, is produced by the Demiurge in his effort to make the world as good as possible. In this respect, we must not forget that the primary motivation of the good Demiurge is to make the world *like himself* (see 29e–30a). Hence the choice of the perfect model, but also a certain double bind since "to make the world in my image" and "to make the world resemble an unchanging intelligible model" is not entirely the same thing. Those ancient interpreters who solved this tension by transplanting the model right into the mind of the Demiurge therefore proceeded logically, but they made a huge step beyond the letter of the dialogue which leaves the model metaphysically quite indeterminate except for a few general and mostly negative characteristics (absence of generation, absence of all change). It lacks all determinate properties that could directly guide an effort at its imitation. The expression *noēta zōia* (31a5), which describes what the model contains, is not a solution to this difficulty since it is hopelessly ambivalent: it can describe an entirely unknown and metaphysically original form of life, but it can just as well be the label for an intelligible Form of what the known life forms are like (this is the ambivalence between "the model is a living being" and "the model is *of* living beings").

In this situation, the decision to create the planets is *both* contingent upon the already established structure of the world soul (it makes use of the divisions within the circle of the Different) *and* largely independent of Timaeus' introductory and quite general description of the likeness between a generated entity and its eternal model. Even the world soul's structure is independent in the same sense: although it acquires a life of its own, it is first and foremost a means to guarantee the stability of the resulting overall likeness. The Demiurge will continue to be creative and resourceful concerning various ways of establishing the complex likeness in question: for instance, to take the most obvious case, the idea of producing the likenesses of the last two intelligible living beings by letting humans *degenerate* into them is not exactly how we usually imagine the relation between things and Platonic forms.

Having summarized the genetic coordination of heavens and time, Timaeus proceeds to describe the more technical aspects of how the planets came into being and of how they move according to their assigned numbers. This part of his discourse about planets was one already most discussed by the Ancients who—just like present-day commentators—try to make sense of the more technical or astronomical aspects of what Timaeus ventures about the "dancing motions" of the planets and "their juxtapositions and back-circling" (40c).

I have nothing original to say on this count,[14] and I am also not able to determine how exactly the planetary trajectories relate to the rotation of the corresponding circles of the world soul.[15] So I will instead point out two simpler things.

First, planets are living creatures composed of a body and a soul, and it is apparently in virtue of their soul's activity that they do not deviate from their pre-determined orbits. This follows from their guardian role, specified as "co-operation in producing time" for which their bodies were "bound by bonds of soul": it is the latter that had "learned (ἔμαθεν) their assigned tasks" (38e5–6). Hence the notion of planets as "instruments of time" (42d5) or "instruments of *times*" (41e5). This equivocation follows from the fact that each planet's motion must have its own numerical pattern whose expression is "what we call time."[16] Timaeus confirms this clearly at 39d1–2: "time really is the wanderings of these bodies, which are both bewilderingly numerous (πλήθει μὲν ἀμηχάνῳ χρωμέ-νας) and astonishingly variegated (πεποικιλμένας δὲ θαυμαστῶς)." This rather unusual praise of visible complexity and variety anticipates upon Timaeus' final summary of why the planets are good for the universe: the purpose of their making "was to make this living thing [*sc.* this universe] as like as possible to that perfect and intelligible Living Thing, by way of imitating its eternal nature" (39d8–e2).

In other words, the planets, precisely in virtue of increasing the organized complexity of the universe, make the latter *more* like its model which consists of the intelligible living things. What the Demiurge achieves by construing the planets is the *indirect* imitation of the life present in the model's noetic composition: the model contains exactly four intelligible species of living being; the planets have no such noetic blueprints but are the newly conceived life-forms whose motions exhibit regular complexity. This is strikingly different from what immediately follows in Timaeus' story, which is the creation of the fixed stars as the first step in completing the likeness of this universe to its model by a *direct* imitation of the exactly four species contained in the model.

---

14 On this issue, I tend to concur with Bowen, "Simplicius and the Early History of Greek Planetary Theory," 158, on *Timaeus* 38c7–d6 and the image of planets as runners: "All the image requires is a sense of the overall eastward direction of the race, and this itself may have been inferred from the fact that the planets rise later and later in relation to the fixed stars over the course of time. In any case, the image is no warrant for talk of planetary stations and retrogradations."

15 Nor, as far as I can tell, is anybody else; were they exactly the same, there would be no need for the planets to possess their own calculating souls: to firmly fix their bodies would be enough. On this usually overlooked problem see Mason, "The *Nous* Doctrine in Plato's Thought," 216–217.

16 See Brague, "Pour en finir," 62–63. For Proclus, this plurality is unified in the higher, intellectual time.

Of these four species, which are implicitly attuned to the four elements, fixed stars, composed mainly of fire, are the first. Their creation thus marks a new stage in the whole story: *until now*, the Demiurge was creating the setting for the four species that will correspond to the equally four intelligible living beings. At the same time, this setting is not a neutral container and its function is not only to be beautiful and ordered in its motions. This order has its own value and its complex unity *already* does imitate, albeit indirectly, the intelligible character of the model, although it does *not yet* directly imitate the four intelligible living beings.[17] Importantly—and this is the second thing I wish to point out—planets will play a role even in the completion of this new and direct imitation.

In this respect, the planets play a pivotal role in Timaeus' story in that they prepare the shift from the immortal visible species (fixed stars) to the mortal ones. The construction of the planets starts to make further sense once human beings are created as observers of cosmic complexity. At that moment, planets acquire a second, and then a third function which relate to human practical well-being and human intellectual progress respectively.

Concerning human well-being, Timaeus leaves no doubt that, on his account, there is a teleological connection between planets and the good things in human life. In order to better measure the slowness and quickness of *all* celestial motions, the Demiurge lights up the sun which helps all those who can be taught to "participate in number" (39b5–c1). At 47a–b, it is confirmed that both planets and fixed stars are, together with the gift of sight, mankind's helpers in acquiring "the art of number" and "the notion of time." Apparently, this is not why the celestial bodies were created in the first place; but it is how the Demiurge deliberately *uses* them beyond their first purpose. And he will make further, more cunning use of the celestial bodies in orchestrating the conditions for the coming to be of the lower animal species, more exactly of those generated species that will be described as "lower" compared to other created species even if *all* created species are equal as likenesses of their respective intelligible models, and are therefore equally necessary for the universe to be complete (see 41b–c).

It is at this point of the story that planetary motions will themselves become a model or a paradigm. This role will be part of their quite complicated—and not entirely clarified—relation to the immortal part of human soul fashioned by the Demiurge. The latter is said to have produced human intellects in the

---

17   For a succinct summary of this level of imitation (where complex construction takes place of simplicity) see Sattler, "A time for learning and for counting—Egyptians, Greeks and empirical processes in Plato's *Timaeus*," 253.

same number as he had just produced the fixed stars, and then placed one intellect on each star in order to parade them all around the universe—and showing them the complex dance of the planets—while revealing to them the laws of their incarnation and announcing to them that "he would sow each of the souls into that instrument of time suitable to it" (εἰς τὰ προσήκοντα ἑκάσταις ἕκαστα ὄργανα χρόνων, 41e5). This "suitability" is left unexplained, but it should imply that there are human beings on all the planets, and that the intellects, once detached from bodies, return from these planets to those fixed stars where they were placed before their first reincarnation on the planets. All in all, there is a lot of soul-travelling in between the circles of the Same and the Different.

These travels, however, belong to the souls' *preordained* place in the universe and this place is entirely different from the souls' *epistemic* relation to the planets and the fixed stars: the incarnate intellects should construe such a relation, by their own effort, in the guise of a homology between their own original structure and, apparently, the global structure of celestial motions. This last point follows from Timaeus' statement that to subdue irrational mass of our bodies means to handle ourselves in "conformity with the revolution of the Same and uniform" within us (42d1–2), a statement to be read together with the often quoted claim that more or less closes the first part of Timaeus' speech:

> the god invented sight and gave it to us so that we might observe the orbits of the intellect in the heavens (τὰς ἐν οὐρανῷ τοῦ νοῦ κατιδόντες περιόδους) while applying them (χρησαίμεθα) to the revolutions of our own understanding (ἐπὶ τὰς περιφορὰς τὰς τῆς παρ' ἡμῖν διανοήσεως). For there is a kinship between them, even though our revolutions are disturbed, whereas the universal orbits are undisturbed. So once we have come to know them and to share in the ability to make correct calculations according to nature, we should stabilize the straying revolutions in ourselves (τὰς ἐν ἡμῖν πεπλανημένας καταστησαίμεθα) by imitating the revolutions of the god which are completely unstraying (μιμούμενοι τὰς τοῦ θεοῦ πάντως ἀπλανεῖς οὔσας).
> 47b6–c4

This, just like the preceding lines about, again, days and nights and the art of number, is less about the revolution of the Same than about the complex orbits of the planets (Timaeus speaks about "orbits" in the plural). Still, since the "god" mentioned at 47c4 is clearly the universe, Timaeus brings all celestial bodies together again, regardless of their different origin. Here, as elsewhere,

Timaeus sticks to his premise of a complete structural homology of the world soul on the one hand and the human intellect on the other hand (cf. 44d3–5 on "the two divine orbits"—θείας περιόδους δύο—packed into "a ball-shaped body" which is our head; see also 90c6–d5).

Now the question is what to make, philosophically, of this homology, wherein the planets play a role which is *epistemologically* more complex than the role of the fixed stars in the circle of the Same. Apparently, it is the planets that give humans the initial nudge to search for the regularity beyond the constantly changing phenomenal variety for which the fixed stars offer a slow-moving background canvas—and the richness of this variety presents us with puzzles left unsolved by both Timaeus and the ancient commentators on his speech. This only underscores the difference between the two kinds of celestial beings and their relation to human beings. The fixed stars truly *are* like us in being the created likeness of the intelligible living model: they are like us from the perspective of similarly created artefacts. The planets, in contrast, only *seem* to be like us in virtue of their *apparent* disorder which, however, should remind us of something which is different from—and better than—our own disorganized state caused by the shock of our seemingly contingent birth.

To sum up, Timaeus describes the planets from two strikingly different angles: first as a brilliant invention of a true creator, but thereafter as a key element in the providential arrangement of the visible universe in view of the good terrestrial life. It is easy to find this second perspective congenial to Aristotelian teleology (at least as seen by commentators such as Alexander; cf. Simplicius *In Aristotelis de cael.* 421.7–33). But it is equally important to acknowledge the first perspective as a rare instance where Plato positively evaluates the phenomenal variety or *poikilia* and praises invention as such. In other dialogues, the latter is usually reserved for politics as a realm of second best options (the *Republic*, the *Laws*, and certainly the *Statesman* could all furnish us with examples). At the same time, something similar happens here too: the Demiurge deliberates while coping with various constraints and, in this respect, the *Timaeus* exhibits obvious connections to practical philosophy. This is why I gladly subscribe to the conclusions of Myles Burnyeat's article on *eikōs mythos*.[18] But I also believe that the resulting universe is perhaps more of a patchwork than Burnyeat's reading implies and that it is difficult to see Timaeus' speech as a mirror of the discourse that establishes the best city in the *Republic*. This is because the latter may actually have *less* to do with practical philosophy while the *Timaeus* may retain a stronger connection to natural science than Burnyeat suggests. Timaeus' speech needs to account for what is

---

18   Burnyeat, "Εἰκὼς μῦθος." Cf. Betegh, "What Makes a Myth Εἰκώς?"

experientially there, including planets that seem hard to tackle without bringing in some reference to a human presence in the universe. About the planets, Timaeus would then speak "plausibly" in much the same sense as Aristotle does in *De caelo* II 12, when he imagines their different orbits analogically to human activities. Both accounts are plausible in giving sense to a puzzling diversity, yet neither has the means to undo the puzzle by referring to an independent observational verification.

1 Postscript: Timaeus' Speech and Time

Timaeus unhesitatingly evokes the flow of time even before the celestial time is there (or, in any case, as independent on the celestial time): see 36e4–5 on the life of the world soul as continuing, unceasingly, "for all time" (πρὸς τὸν σύμπαντα χρόνον). Here I wish to offer a few remarks on the implication of this "all time" as expressing the flow of time; I will raise this issue concerning *both* the world soul together with the created universe, *and* the latter's unchanging, everlasting model.

Timaeus' "all time" seems to be essentially tenseless even if:

(1) It allows for the distinction between "before" and "after" (see 37a–c on the world soul as pronouncing what it experiences in a clearly sequential manner: this soul's states cannot be simply interchangeable in respect of the direction of time, if only because Timaeus describes them in propositional terms, i.e. as a veridical internal speech about the composite states of affairs).

(2) It is time's flow—rather than "time as number"—that gets divided into the past, the present, and the future, with corresponding verbal tenses.

The expression *pros ton sympanta chronon* is therefore synonymous with *dia ton hapanta chronon* which is predicated, at 38c2, of the universe, together with the explanation that the latter "has been, is, and shall be for all time" (διὰ τέλους τὸν ἅπαντα χρόνον γεγονώς τε καὶ ὢν καὶ ἐσόμενος, 38c2–3). It is therefore legitimate to speak about the duration *of* the universe *in* time, whether it is predicated of the world soul or of the universe as such. Note that this does not answer the question of whether there is time in the sense of either duration or the flow of time in respect of what "is always changeless and motionless." Regarding the latter, Timaeus says that it "cannot become either older or younger in the course of time (διὰ χρόνου)" (38a3–4). But does he mean that time may flow among eternal things but without them ageing (as they have no date of birth), or does he mean that, among eternal things, time does not flow at all? This ambiguity is left unexplained.

By contrast, Timaeus clearly explains, at 38c3–6, that time as the number expressed by the planets was created precisely as an instrument that enables us to date events. Time as number therefore serves to impose some structure upon the flow of "all time"; it is *not*, however, *constitutive* of the latter. Moreover, time as number cannot explain the language of the tenses analyzed by Timaeus, no matter how loosely, at 38a8–b5. Briefly put, time as number (imposed upon the flow of time) and the tensed language used about time are *not* mutually explanatory. One of the results is that we do not know where time's directionality, which we observe on bodies and their behavior, and also in our soul, comes from. In this respect, there would seem to be a lot more to say than Timaeus actually says about the relation between time, the directionality of time, and soul.[19]

The situation where time as number and the tensed language are not conceptually unified but simply express different perspectives assumed by Timaeus in his speech, is similar to the problem of how to translate the sequential idiom of "before" / "after" into the past, the present and the future tenses: this is the problem associated nowadays with McTaggart.

McTaggart's article "The Unreality of Time" (*Mind* n. s. 17, 1908, 457–74) deals with two ways of conceptualizing time (which he finds incompatible):

A-series: employs past, present, and future as implying the *changing* status of the states of affairs (so that the future states will become present and then past).

B-series: an ordered and *unchangeable* sequence of the states of affairs (what is "before" relatively to some "after" will always remain so and vice-versa).

Timaeus' way of speaking would confirm the impossibility of an exact translation between these two idioms; moreover, neither is an exact expression of "time as number" nor lets itself be translated into the latter's structure.[20]

This limitation concerns the time *of* the world and *in* the world. There is, however, yet another problem, related to the above-mentioned ambiguity concerning the time's flow outside the universe: the problem of the present as a

---

19   Indeed, Timaeus speaks about the flow of "all time" or about "all eternity" only there where some thinking soul is present. Perhaps Timaeus comes close to the assumption, pondered by Aristotle, that time requires soul. This, then, would take the mutual transformations of elements (and thus the receptacle) out of time—or, at least, out of any directional time. Whether it is truly so would depend on a detailed analysis of Timaean account of the genesis of the four elements. For a suggestive analysis of this sort (without a thematic focus on time) see Broadie, *Nature and Divinity in Plato's* Timaeus, 173–242.

20   This is indirectly supported by the fact that the later Neoplatonic discussions of time, which bring in the *Parmenides*, focus on the issue of temporal series including the (divisive) status of the present and proceed quite independently of the structure of planetary motions.

tense, and also as the "eternal present." On Timaeus' account, there are things about which only "is" can be legitimately predicated and this tense should only be used about what (metaphysically) "is" in the eternal present.

Timaeus therefore uses "is" in a way which takes it away from the temporal A-series, but still without implying that "is" should only refer to a truly timeless present. This is because he describes the unchanging Forms outside the universe as "intelligible *living* beings." Speaking of these as a "paradigm which has an eternal nature" (τὸ παράδειγμα τῆς διαιωνίας φύσεως, 38b8), Timaeus comes indeed close to indicating some ongoing process. The peculiar adjective *diaiōnios* (38b8 and 39e2) can be understood as "through all *aiōn*": it designates the same kind of ongoing activity which is implied in the description of *aiōn* as staying/remaining (*menontos*) in unity (37d6).

There seems therefore to be an "eternal present" only in the sense of a specific temporality proper to something which *actively* sustains itself without any local motion or change.

Hence probably Iamblichus' idea that the unified and unmeasured *aiōn* is a measure (*metron*) for the noetic realm (*In Tim.* fr. 64): the latter, while motionless, cannot lack some sort of activity (*aiōn* as not timelessness but an ongoing uninterrupted activity; this connects to fr. 62 and the rejection of the Aristotelian connection between time and motion).[21]

In a similar vein, Proclus can claim that time in the sense of an unmeasured unity ("monadic" time) is better and more divine than soul (see *In Tim.* III 3.29–4.6; III 27.18–21), and is the same everywhere (III 57.15–27); Iamblichus and Proclus elaborate upon Timaeus' way of speaking about *aiōn* as itself *diaiōnios* or stretching in its own time.

This way of speaking might seem to resemble what McTaggart introduces as the C-series, of which he says that "it is not temporal, for it involves no change, but only an order," this order itself being not changeable (462). But the celestial time as number could correspond to this C-series even better: indeed, for McTaggart, only C-series in conjunction with change describable in terms of "before" and "after" generates the B-series in the sense of *both* regular *and* temporal pattern.

In Timaeus' speech, this conjunction is realized through the making of planets and the numerical prescription of their orbits. But, again, there is no "number" that could connect this cosmic clock to the eternal now. Moreover, on

---

21 Cf. Simplicius, *Corollaries on Place and Time* 789.16–18: "Is time the number of the earlier and later in motion rather than in rest? For likewise in the latter there is the earlier and later." See already Theophrastus' objection to Aristotle's account of the spheres: rest would seem to be a better way of imitating eternity than motion (*Metaphysics* 5a23–28).

both McTaggart's and Timaeus' account, this is still not enough to explain the unchanging *direction* of the temporal flow ("time's arrow"), which thus appears to be an independent constant.

To sum up: Timaeus offers no instructions for how to map various temporal idioms on each other; an independent ontology (the Neoplatonic one, the Hegelian one, etc.) will be needed to posit, more or less artificially, the transitions between various senses of "time."[22]

Works Cited

Bakhouche, Béatrice, ed. *Calcidius: Commentaire au* Timée *de Platon*. Vol. 1. Paris: Vrin, 2011.

Betegh, Gábor. "What Makes a Myth Εἰκώς?" In *One Book, the Whole Universe: Plato's* Timaeus *Today*. Edited by Richard D. Mohr and Barbara Sattler. Las Vegas: Parmenides Publishing, 213–226.

Bowen, Alan C. "Simplicius and the Early History of Greek Planetary Theory." *Perspectives on Science* 10 (2002): 155–167.

Brague, Rémi. "Pour en finir avec 'le temps, image mobile de l'éternité' (Platon, *Timée*, 37d)." In *Du temps chez Platon et Aristote*. Paris: PUF, 1982, 11–71.

Broadie, Sarah. *Nature and Divinity in Plato's* Timaeus. Cambridge: Cambridge University Press, 2012.

Burnyeat, Myles. "Εἰκὼς μῦθος." *Rhizai* 2 (2005): 143–165.

Cohen, Gerald L. "Etymology of Greek agalma, agallô, agallomai." *Proceedings of the 2nd Annual Meeting of the Berkeley Linguistics Society* (1976): 100–104.

Goldin, Owen. "Plato and the Arrow of Time." *Ancient Philosophy* 18 (1998): 125–143.

Johns, Jeff. "On the translation of *Timaeus* 38b6–c3." *Études platoniciennes* 11 (2014): §13 (accessible online at http://etudesplatoniciennes.revues.org/599).

Kerényi, Karl. "Agalma, eikon, eidolon." *Archivio di Filosofia* 1–2 (1962): 161–171.

Leftow, Brian. *Time and Eternity*. Ithaca: Cornell University Press, 1991.

Magee, John, ed. *Calcidius, On Plato's* Timaeus. Cambridge, MA: Harvard University Press, 2016.

Mason, Andrew S. "Why Does Plato Believe in a Timeless Eternity?" In *New Essays on Plato: Language and Thought in Fourth-Century Greek Philosophy*. Edited by Fritz-Gregor Herrmann. Swansea: The Classical Press of Wales, 2006, 177–188.

Mason, Andrew S. "The Nous Doctrine in Plato's Thought." *Apeiron* 46 (2014): 201–228.

---

22   The work was supported by the European Regional Development Fund-Project "Creativity and Adaptability as Conditions of the Success of Europe in an Interrelated World" (No. CZ.02.1.01/0.0/0.0/16_019/0000734).

Sattler, Barbara. "A time for learning and for counting—Egyptians, Greeks and empirical processes in Plato's *Timaeus*." In *One Book, the Whole Universe: Plato's* Timaeus *Today*. Edited by Richard D. Mohr and Barbara M. Sattler. Las Vegas: Parmenides Publishing, 2010, 249–266.

Stump, Eleonore and Norman Kretzmann. "Eternity." *The Journal of Philosophy* 78 (1981): 429–458.

Thein, Karel. "Soul and Incorporeality in Plato." *Eirene. Studia Graeca et Latina* 54 (2018): 53–95.

Wilberding, James. "Eternity in Ancient Philosophy." In *Eternity*. Edited by Yitzhak Y. Melamed. Oxford: Oxford University Press, 2016.

Zeyl, Donald J. *Plato: Timaeus*. Indianapolis: Hackett, 2000.

The Day, the Month, and the Year: What Plato Expects from Astronomy

István M. Bodnár

Abstract

The *Timaeus* apparently assigns a different task to astronomy than that in the educational programme set out in the *Republic*. There is no word about the reorientation required in the *Republic* that astronomers should ascend to a post-observational study of "the real decorations [of the heavens]—the real movements that these move by true quickness and true slowness in true number and in all true figures in relation to each other, carrying along the things contained in them, which can be grasped by reason and thought, and not by sight." (*Republic* 529d) Nevertheless, I argue that—albeit with vastly different theoretical presuppositions about perceptible entities—the *Timaeus* takes into consideration some of the strictures of the *Republic*. Similar to the way the reform of astronomy required in the *Republic*, only such observational astronomy can pass muster in the *Timaeus* whose major aim is to reduce the regularities of the motions of the different celestial objects to components that are connected to the fundamental motions of the World Soul. This enterprise can be claimed—within the confines of this likely story—to integrate in its fully developed form every important intellectual pursuit there is.

Keywords

Plato – *Timaeus* – observational astronomy – educational programme – celestial periods – component motions – intellect – unity of science

If we compare the account of astronomy in the educational programme of the *Republic* and in the *Timaeus*, we see that in the *Timaeus* astronomy has taken on a central role it was not yet assigned in the *Republic*. That much should be small wonder: if you are harangued by someone who is a most accomplished astronomer, and has made the greatest effort to know about the nature of the universe (27a),[1]

---

[1] The formulation of *Timaeus* 27a might be taken to suggest that this is true only in comparison to the other people present at the discussion (ἀστρονομικώτατον ἡμῶν καὶ περὶ φύσεως τοῦ παντὸς εἰδέναι μάλιστα ἔργον πεποιημένον). I do not think, though, that this is the intended

you surely should expect a very favourable, or indeed, a biased task assignment with respect to astronomy.

Call this the *deflationary* reading. Here I will argue that there is more to the new task assignment in the *Timaeus* than a mere marketing ploy on behalf of someone whose views are not endorsed by Plato. Indeed, why would Plato canvass these views, unless he intends to give them at least a favourable hearing, to the extent a likely story deserves? But once the views about the role of astronomy expressed by Timaeus are admitted to bear on Plato's own thought, an assessment of the differences between the *Timaeus* and the *Republic* is in order.

This comparison should address two different, but intricately related issues. One, the revision of the *place* of astronomy in a framework of intellectual enlightenment, the other the *content* of astronomy. Both of these problems should be subsumed under the broader question of the *status* of these different frameworks of intellectual enlightenment. This last issue I will not address in detail. Nevertheless, on occasion, I will have to remark that the different assessments of astronomy are maintained in two different modalities: one in the straightforward exposition of the philosophically grounded pedagogical reform of the *Republic*, the other as part of the likely story of the *Timaeus*.

1

First, the *Republic*. A full discussion of the role of the mathematical disciplines in the educational programme of the *Republic* would exceed the limits of a paper. Here I can give only very brief assertions, with just the bare minimum of a sketch of the argumentation for my proposals. For a comparison with the *Timaeus* at least three major issues should be broached. First, presumptions about the status of celestial entities, which bear upon what can, and what cannot, be achieved by astronomy. Second, the reform of astronomy Socrates proposes in the face of these limitations. And finally, third, the place of astronomy within the curriculum.

Celestial entities are, on Socrates' telling, in principle of the same kind as everyday objects around us, even if their behaviour follows very regular patterns.

---

point of Critias' remark: Timaeus is an accomplished astronomer in his own right and the comparison is made in order to explain why Timaeus—and not someone else from among those present—will be speaking in the main part of the dialogue. This hypothesis is also borne out by Socrates' characterisation of Timaeus at the beginning of the dialogue, that "he has come to occupy positions of supreme authority and honor in his city [and] has, in my judgment, mastered the entire field of philosophy" (20a—translations from the *Timaeus*, unless otherwise indicated, are from Zeyl's translation in Cooper, ed. *Plato: Complete Works*).

> But as for the ratio of night to day, of days to a month, of a month to a year, or of the motions of the stars to any of them or to each other, don't you think [the real astronomer will] consider it strange to believe that they're always the same and never deviate anywhere at all or to try in any sort of way to grasp the truth about them, since they're connected to body and visible?
>
> 530a–b[2]

This is in full agreement with Socrates' earlier injunction that "we should use the decoration in the sky as models (*paradeigmasi*) in the study" of the real objects of astronomy (529d, Grube-Reeve translation, slightly modified). These are:

> the real decorations—the real movements that these move by true quickness and true slowness in true number and in all true figures in relation to each other, and they carry along the things contained in them which can be grasped by reason and thought, and not by sight.
>
> 529d, my translation

This last phrase, to the effect that these true motions (or the true decorations performing these true motions) carry along the things contained in them, is crucial, because it makes clear that even though there is an ontological divide between the true objects of astronomy and what is observable in the heavens, the true objects of astronomy have a similar structure to the objects observable in the heavens and their visible motions. This is indeed why the latter can be used as models on the basis of which the truly insightful and informative astronomical "problems" (530b) can be formulated, and then solved, even when in the course of this investigations we can "leave the things in the sky alone" (530b).[3]

This means, then, a thorough revamping of astronomy as Plato's contemporaries knew it. In the first, interrupted introduction of astronomy, Glaucon submitted that astronomy provides knowledge of seasons, months and years (527d), indispensable for agriculture and for military purposes alike. This position is, however, rebuffed by Socrates, who insists that the mathematical

---

[2] Translations from the *Republic*, unless otherwise indicated, are from the Grube's translation revised by Reeve in Cooper, ed., *Plato: Complete Works*.

[3] This characterisation is paralleled by the way Socrates chastises the harmonic theory of the Pythagoreans, who "seek out the numbers that are to be found in these audible consonances, but they do not make the ascent to problems." (531c) For further discussion of Plato's criticism of Pythagorean harmonic theory, see Huffman, *Archytas of Tarentum: Pythagorean, Philosopher and Mathematician King*, 423–425.

studies should not be oriented towards practical ends. Instead they should lead the soul to grasp reality, that is, they should further the philosophical, or dialectical cognition which follows the mathematical part of the curriculum (527d). Then, again, as I have quoted above, Socrates submits that "as for the ratio of night to day, of days to a month, of a month to a year, of the motions of the stars to any of them, or to each other [...]" it is strange "to try in any sort of way to grasp the truth" about the perceptible heavenly bodies, or about the perceptible periods of these bodies (530a). If the usual astronomical method of observation and geometrical modelling cannot provide certainty about these motions, the task must be reformulated as one of grasping those real, not-perceptible movements which true astronomy aims at uncovering and understanding. But grasping these real movements will not mean that through them we will be able to account for the residual irregularity of the motions of these celestial entities. Such irregularity is inherent in their bodily nature.

Socrates does not give an example of what the inquiry into these non-perceptible movements should be like. Nevertheless, the context—astronomy is introduced after stereometry—strongly suggests that we should expect a geometrical analysis of complex motions into component revolutions. But even if the contents of this astronomy remain underspecified, the place of astronomy is clearly set out in this educational programme. The would-be guardians start with arithmetic. This is then followed by geometry—two-dimensional geometry, that is. Then, Socrates remarks that the lack of a developed stereometry should be remedied, and only after this can astronomy be tackled. After astronomy, harmonics completes the curriculum. Astronomy holds a central place in this programme—it comes after stereometry, but it also relies on arithmetic, because it investigates:

> the real movements, which they [the true decorations] move by true quickness and true slowness *in true number* and in all true figures in relation to each other.
>
> 529d, my emphasis

The next step, harmonics, a mathematical investigation of the audible feature of motion, does not immediately follow arithmetic. In contrast to astronomy, the investigation of motions for which the eyes were framed, harmonics is the investigation of motion for which the ears were framed.[4] These sciences are,

---

4 Here I follow Shorey's translation of *pepēgen* and *pagēnai* of 530d (Shorey, *The Republic*, 189). In note *d*, Shorey convincingly compares the use of this verb here to the use at 605a. Another consideration in favour of this understanding of the verb is that on this interpretation the

accordingly, sort of sister sciences (*adelphai tines*), as Socrates asserts, referring approvingly to the Pythagoreans. If this relationship is closer than those between all the other mathematical sciences, this might motivate us to place them together.[5]

We do not know, however, why these sister disciplines are given in the order astronomy–harmonics, and there is not much point in speculating about this order. We should, nevertheless, note that the order of the two sister sciences reverses the order arithmetic–geometry, and, even more importantly, astronomy is not presented as the culmination of mathematical education. This is even clearer, if we keep in mind that the list of mathematical disciplines is in an important sense open-ended in the *Republic*. Socrates warns at 530e ff. that the Pythagoreans must be consulted about the characterisation of the five sciences on the curriculum, and asked whether they have any other mathematical disciplines to add. Socrates does not indicate that he would rule out the inclusion of these further Pythagorean candidates in the educational programme.[6] Instead, he insists that the would-be guardians:

---

passage would be in line with Timaeus' assertions about sight, namely that the observation of the heavens is the "supremely beneficial function for which the god gave [the eyes] to us" (τὸ δὲ μέγιστον αὐτῶν εἰς ὠφελίαν ἔργον, δι' ὃ θεὸς αὔθ' ἡμῖν δεδώρηται, 46e–47a), as well as with the assertion about sound and hearing that "[l]ikewise, the same account goes for sound and hearing—these too are the gods' gifts, given for the same purpose and intended to achieve the same result" (φωνῆς τε δὴ καὶ ἀκοῆς πέρι πάλιν ὁ αὐτὸς λόγος, ἐπὶ ταὐτὰ τῶν αὐτῶν ἕνεκα παρὰ θεῶν δεδωρῆσθαι, 47c–e). The other option is to follow the Grube–Reeve translation, then eyes and ears "fasten on" (= "are attentively directed to") these two kinds of motions.

5   The investigation of mathematical studies should aim at bringing out their community (*koinōnia*) and kinship (*syngeneia*), and those respects in which they are akin (ταῦτα ᾗ ἐστὶν ἀλλήλοις οἰκεῖα, 531d). It is an open question whether this allows for different grades of kinship among the different mathematical sciences. Cf. Archytas B1, where all four branches of mathematics—astronomy, geometry, arithmetic and harmonics—are said to be sister sciences (or kindred sciences, the term used is *adelphea*).

6   Here I deviate from Burnyeat's interpretation in Burnyeat, "Plato on why mathematics is good for the soul," 16–19. Note that I concur with Burnyeat's formulation that "[a]ny science that does not lend itself to such redirection [i.e. redirection to the same abstract level as geometry or arithmetic] is to be excluded altogether"(18). I differ, however, in maintaining that Socrates does not pass judgment on whether such a redirection is possible in the case of those sciences which will be established during Plato's lifetime. Accordingly, I do not think that Plato blacklisted mathematical mechanics and optics (cf. Burnyeat, "Mathematics," 16 f.). What he must insist on in their case is the same as what he did in the case of Pythagorean astronomy or harmonics: they do not have to be blacklisted. Instead they can be admitted to the programme after proper reorientation.

Note that beyond the reorientation of astronomy and harmonics there is the further reform of arithmetic and geometry, although in their case this does not extend to changing their standard operational procedures. In the case of astronomy and harmonics the reform is not just one of placing the discipline in a larger epistemological and ontological scheme

should never try to learn anything incomplete of these, anything that doesn't reach the end that everything should reach—the end we mentioned just now in the case of astronomy.

530e

The last requirement, I take it, stipulates that these new candidates for the educational programme should be reformed in the same way astronomy has been: whatever the primary manifestations are that they study, they have to acknowledge that these do not constitute the actual objects of their investigation. Instead they should concentrate on those true—that is, non-perceptible and immutable—realities which form their proper object of study. Indeed, immediately after these admonitions the next discipline on the programme, harmonics, will undergo exactly this same kind of reform at the hands of Socrates.

But if there are further possible candidates lined up for admission to the programme, the relative place of astronomy within this programme is even less secure. The objectives and the results of astronomy remain the same, but astronomy might turn out to have a slightly different contribution to the interdependence of mathematical disciplines depending on what exactly these disciplines turn out to be.

2

In turning to the *Timaeus* we can follow the same checklist we covered in the *Republic*. First, we need to check what presumptions are operative about the status of celestial entities and celestial motions. Next, we will need to discuss whether Timaeus' practices amount to something like a reform of astronomy as prescribed by the *Republic*. And finally, we will turn to the question I raised in my title: what does Plato expect from astronomy in the *Timaeus*?

All of the celestial entities—planets and fixed stars alike—are visible and generated gods (40d).[7] Among these, the case of the planets (the Sun and the Moon included) is complicated, as Timaeus admits at 38d–e and 40c–d. The fixed stars are gods, whose bodies are made mostly out of fire (40a). These follow the motion of the circle of the Same, revolving around the Earth, and have an additional rotation of their own. The important difference from the account

---

(Burnyeat, "Mathematics," 42). In their case a major reassessment and change of the standard aims and procedures of the disciplines are also in order.

7 For further discussion of these corporeal gods see Broadie, "Corporeal Gods, with Reference to Plato and Aristotle," and Betegh's contribution in this volume.

of the *Republic* is that the revolution these entities perform under the causal influence of the circle of the Same does not admit of variations. No matter that these stars are corporeal, perceptible entities, they "stay fixed by revolving without variation in the same place" within these celestial revolutions (40b). Similarly with the planets. Timaeus does not go into details, nevertheless he submits that Venus and Mercury, have the same period as the Sun, but that Mercury and Venus receive a contrary power to that of the Sun. This does not mean that they have a revolution in a contrary sense to that of the Sun. Instead the claim is that "the Sun, the star of Hermes [i.e. Mercury] and the Dawnbearer [i.e. Venus] overtake one another and are overtaken by one another in the same pattern" (38d, Zeyl translation, slightly modified).[8] Timaeus does not specify the details of how this celestial *pas de trois* is accomplished. Nevertheless, it is clear that the fundamental claim, namely that the period of these planets is identical, is valid, and will always remain valid. Similarly, for the other planets:

> the wandering of these bodies [is] bewilderingly numerous as they are and astonishingly variegated[, i]t is none the less possible, however, to discern that the perfect number of time brings to completion the perfect year at that moment when the relative speeds of all eight periods have been completed together [...].
>
> 39c–d

Again, the situation is the same as in the case of Sun, Mercury and Venus: the very complex motions these planets may perform do not rule out in the least that they have constant periods, and that these periods together give rise to an overarching regularity like the Great Year. Again, this presupposes that behind all the variation and complexity some periodicities of planetary motion are, and will always remain, valid.

This claim, that celestial revolutions are endowed with some fundamental constancy makes sense in the context of the *Timaeus* in light of two further considerations. One is that the eternity and constancy of features of celestial objects is intimately related to what the Demiurge solemnly announces about the products of his making. These entities, "as creatures that have come to be, are neither completely immortal nor exempt from being undone. Still [they] will not be undone [...] since [they] have received the guarantee of [the Demiurge's] will" (41b). This guarantee, as the Demiurge hastens to add, "is

---

8 I translate *kata tauta* "in the same pattern." The phrase may express nothing more than that, when any of these three planets overtakes another one among them, the latter must as a next step overtake the former.

greater [...] than those with which [these entities] were bound when [they] came to be." These entities, then, possess some greater, divinely ordained stability than what their constitution, on its own, could ever provide them with.

Moreover, the divine guarantee of the eternity of created corporeal entities also rests on the fact that celestial bodies, and the body of the whole cosmos as such, are under the causal influence—or even: the guidance and care—of soul. In the case of celestial bodies, the soul is directly responsible for the motion of these bodies, that is why Timaeus speaks about setting the fixed stars "in the wisdom of the dominant circle" (40a), whereas the planets are set "into the orbits traced by the revolution of the Different" (38c, Zeyl translation, slightly modified)—the Moon in the first circle, the Sun in the second and so on with respect to the other planets. This means that the motions of the celestial bodies have more regularity than their material constitution would allow for; their motion is dependent on the operation of the World Soul.

All of these psychological and divine warrants, then, allow that—contrary to the claims of the *Republic*—observational astronomy can be pursued in a meaningful way. Note that this may still allow for discrepancies between the supremely, unerringly regular motion of the World Soul,[9] which is evidenced in the sky, and the actual corresponding revolution of a planet. Nevertheless, even in such cases the discrepancies cannot accumulate: if the path of a planet for any reason does not match the revolutions of the World Soul, such a discrepancy cannot be augmented to the point when the planet would be out of sync with whatever overall regularity the revolution of the World Soul has. And come to think of it, this is already a lot to ask by the lights of the *Republic*.[10]

But this observational astronomy, as I shall argue, takes into consideration some of the strictures of the *Republic*. This is possible, because where the *Timaeus* and the *Republic* differ, they do so within the context of their vastly different theoretical presuppositions about the investigation of perceptible

---

9   See 47b–c, speaking about the function of sight "that we might observe the orbits of intelligence in the universe," in the course of which we will realise that these "universal orbits are undisturbed" and as a result we can "imitat[e] the completely unstraying revolutions of the god."

10 Note that the characterisation I have given here about planetary motions has obvious resemblances to the description of planetary motions in the Myth of Er, in Book X of the *Republic*. There the motions of the celestial bodies are induced by the Moirai, each of them providing different component motions—Clotho the diurnal motion of the sky, Atropos provides contrary motions for each of the planets, whereas Lachesis provides additional motions in both directions, deflecting the planets from their course provided by Atropos, and then directing them back again to where they should have been, and beyond (see 617c–d). On the planetary account of *Republic* X see Knorr, "Plato and Eudoxus on the Planetary Motions."

entities. Most importantly, the more positive account of the *Timaeus* is set out within the framing of an account which is introduced as a likely story. So whatever positive assurances Timaeus gives us about the stability of the world and the feasibility of investigating it, this remains embedded in the larger claim that what he sets out is only a likely story. So the change between the two dialogues is not so much one of fundamental convictions, but rather an appreciation of how the fundamental divide between the non-perceptible, immutable realm and the physical realm does nevertheless allow for a meaningful mathematical investigation of some parts of the physical, an investigation which at the same time will appeal to the teleological considerations, reaching into psychology and theology. In a way, then, the *Timaeus* can be looked upon as a dialogue which after the critical attitude of the *Republic* provided the necessary theoretical assurances for a feasible research programme in astronomy.

Not of any old kind of astronomy though. As I have already indicated—and I will come back to it shortly—this astronomy is one which does relate celestial motions to some non-perceptible, non-physical motion similar to the way the reform of astronomy required in the *Republic*. This is intimately connected to a further restriction: those cosmological accounts which deploy theories of retardation are ruled out. This is clear from the characterisation of the planetary periods:

> Some [planets] would move [with their own movement, of the Different] in a larger circle, others in a smaller one, the latter moving more quickly and the former more slowly. Indeed, because of the movement of the Same, the ones that go around most quickly appeared to be overtaken by those going more slowly, even though in fact they were overtaking them.
>
> 39a[11]

It is only in such composite motions as the one Timaeus propounds that it is meaningful to raise problems about the issue of which of the two celestial

---

11 Cf. *Laws* 822a–b: "This belief, my dear fellows, that the moon and sun and other stars 'wander' in any way whatsoever, is incorrect: precisely the opposite is true. Actually, each of them covers the same path, and not many, but always a single one in a circle, although it is true that to all appearances it moves many paths. Further, the quickest body is wrongly supposed to be the slowest, and the opposite [i.e. the slowest—is wrongly supposed] to be the opposite [i.e. the quickest]." (οὐ γάρ ἐστι τοῦτο, ὦ ἄριστοι, τὸ δόγμα ὀρθὸν περὶ σελήνης τε καὶ ἡλίου καὶ τῶν ἄλλων ἄστρων, ὡς ἄρα πλανᾶταί ποτε, πᾶν δὲ τοὐναντίον ἔχει τούτου—τὴν αὐτὴν γὰρ αὐτῶν ὁδὸν ἕκαστον καὶ οὐ πολλὰς ἀλλὰ μίαν ἀεὶ κύκλῳ διεξέρχεται, φαίνεται δὲ πολλὰς φερόμενον—τὸ δὲ τάχιστον αὐτῶν ὂν βραδύτατον οὐκ ὀρθῶς αὖ δοξάζεται, τὸ δ' ἐναντίον ἐναντίως. Saunders' translation in Cooper, ed., *Plato: Complete Works*, slightly modified.)

bodies overtakes the other one. In models of retardation—or in vortex models, as they are usually called—such issues are completely straightforward. Whichever celestial body performs a quicker overall revolution, will be the one that overtakes the celestial body with a slower overall period.[12]

In contrast to such a model, we can be certain that in Plato's case the rejection of the retardation model means that the motion of the apparently slower celestial body must be parsed in terms of at least two component motions—one, which is identical for all of the celestial bodies, and another, in an opposite sense, which is responsible for the differences between the motion of the circle of the fixed stars and those of the different planets, and between the motions of the different planets themselves. I do not think much argumentation is needed to show that this kind of analysis into component motions adheres to the injunctions of the *Republic*, namely that celestial motions should be treated as problems which invite general considerations and solutions. Such a methodological precept should not rule out, even by the lights of the *Republic*, that the astronomer takes his cue from the celestial motions themselves.

This is brought into sharp relief if we compare the strictures of the *Republic* with the account of how the Demiurge kindles light in the circle of the Sun with the aim of:

> bestow[ing] upon all those living things appropriately endowed and taught by the revolution of the Same and the uniform, a share in number.
> 39b–c

Then, as instances of the numbers inculcated by the Same and the uniform under the illuminating light of the Sun, the day, the month and the year are mentioned: periods, that is, whose precise investigation was branded as futile by the *Republic*.

Note, however, that the *Timaeus* passage does not just bypass the strictures of the *Republic*. It immediately conveys a theoretical understanding of these periods, over and above any observational accuracy there may be in their case. Most importantly, as the story of the kindling of the light in the circle of the Sun suggests, all three periods rely fundamentally on the presence of the Sun. Most

---

12   Such vortex theories as Timaeus rejects were widespread: Anaxagoras and Democritus subscribed to some version of such a theory, see e.g. Anaxagoras A 78 = Aëtius II 16.1 (*Doxographi graeci*, 345) Ἀναξαγόρας, Δημόκριτος, Κλεάνθης ἀπ' ἀνατολῶν ἐπὶ δυσμὰς φέρεσθαι πάντας τοὺς ἀστέρας. Details of such a theory nevertheless are lacking in the reports about Anaxagoras and Democritus.

straightforwardly, "a year [comes to be],[13] when the Sun makes a turn of its own circle" (39c, my translation), as Timaeus puts it. Also unmistakable is the role of the Sun in the case of the month: "A month [comes to be] when the Moon having made a turn of its own circle overtakes the Sun" (39c, my translation).

This neat connexion between the basic periods and the motion of the Sun may seem to break down in the case of day and night. Jowett, Archer-Hind, Cornford and Zeyl (and I trust, countless other modern translators) apparently presume that day and night correspond directly to the revolution of the Same, and the only role of the Sun in this case is that it accentuates this revolution by illuminating half of the Earth by its daylight. Of all these many translations it is sufficient to quote the one by Cornford:

> Thus and for these reasons day and night came into being, the period of the single and most intelligent revolution.
> 39c[14]

This, however, would be bad astronomy—as, for instance, was already objected by Taylor: the period of the circle of the Same, the sidereal day, is slightly shorter than the mean solar day. Moreover, it would make what Timaeus says terribly awkward: night and day may well be generated by kindling the light of the Sun on the second orbit, but the revolution of the circle of the Same—or the period of this revolution, as some translators put it—exists irrespective of whether the light of the Sun was kindled. Neither the revolution, nor its period is brought into being by the Demiurge's intervention when he kindled the Sun on an orbit around the Earth.

---

13 I translate the verb *gegonen* in the present tense, because although Timaeus formulates his claim in present perfect, he does not speak about the historical generation of the first day, or first month, or first year. This is clear from the clauses about the month and the year. The conditional clauses are formulated with *epeidan* plus conjunctive and *hopotan* plus conjunctive constructions respectively, expressing the recurrence of the astronomical events which give rise to the periods, of a month and of a year, respectively. Accordingly, the sentence with its perfect tense main verb stresses that these periods have been established through the kindling of the light of the Sun to be recurrent phenomena. (Cf. Cornford, *Plato's Cosmology*, 115, which uses the present tense "comes to be"—supplied from the context—for these latter two clauses, whereas Cornford translates the first, and actually only occurrence of the verb *gegonen* in the past tense as "came into being.")

14 Cornford, *Plato's Cosmology*, 115. See furthermore Jowett, *The Dialogues of Plato*, 458 (cf. also Jowett's paraphrase: "The revolution of the world around the earth, which is accomplished in a single day and night, is described as the most perfect or intelligent." 404), Archer-Hind, *The Timaeus of Plato*, 129, and also Zeyl's translation.

One alternative solution to this conundrum is to bite the bullet and suggest that Timaeus' list of the generation of night and day, of the month and of the year deliberately starts with a curious oversimplification, or—if you wish—with a riddle. Whereas in the case of the month and the year, Timaeus provides the correct account, the first instance, that of day and night, is presented with the problematic identification of the two periods. As for the emergence of "the period of the single and most intelligent revolution" itself, perhaps one way of evading the difficulty could be to suggest that the presence of the light of the Sun dramatically accentuates the change caused by this revolution. Without the sequence of days and nights the revolution would not be noticeable. As an additional consideration for this one could adduce that according to 39e–40b the fixed stars are "set into the thought of the most powerful [circle], following it" (40a, my translation) only after the coming to be of time. Accordingly, at this point the motion of the Same is not yet articulated by these fixed stars.

But it is one thing to imply the prior unnoticeability of "the period of the single and most intelligent revolution," and another to imply its prior absence. Hence it may be preferable to take the sentence in a different construal. Here Timaeus certainly speaks about the generation of night and day, but he need not be understood as speaking about the generation of the revolution of the circle of the Same. Instead, he can call attention to the fact that once the Sun lights up in the sky, night and day come to be,[15] and the revolution of the circle of the Same comes to be night and day. And the change of this revolution into night and day can acknowledge the difference between the length of the revolution itself, which is the sidereal day, and the length of the solar day.[16]

---

15   The coming to be of night and day, of month and of year was already announced earlier: "For there were no days and nights, no months, and no years before the heavens came to be. But now, at the same time as the heavens are organized, he devises their coming to be" (37e, Zeyl's translation, slightly modified).

  Note furthermore that the coming to be of night and day by kindling light in the orbit of the Sun also presupposes the presence of the Earth, the "guardian and maker of night and day" (φύλακα καὶ δημιουργὸν νυκτός τε καὶ ἡμέρας 40c)—there is day in the hemisphere lit by the Sun, whereas in the other hemisphere there is night.

16   Another construal of the clause to the same effect could be to delete the comma before ἡ τῆς μιᾶς καὶ φρονιμωτάτης κυκλήσεως περίοδος and translate "[t]hus and for these reasons the period of the single and most intelligent revolution came to be night and day." This then would be followed up by the two further claims "and it comes to be a month when the Moon having made a turn of its own circle overtakes the Sun, and a year when the Sun makes a turn of its own circle" (39c, my translation). This reading, however, could be problematic on two counts. First of all, readers of the *Timaeus* have been primed by the announcement of 37e to expect the coming to be of days, nights, months and years, and not something coming to be them. Moreover, even though the revolution of the circle

Such an understanding fits smoothly with the context: the immediately following clause—"a month comes to be when the Moon, having completed its own cycle, catches up with the Sun"[17]—describes how the period of the Moon relates to the synodic month. Indeed, the relationship between the two different days is somewhat similar to that between the two different months: in the time that it takes for the orbit of the Moon to make a complete revolution, the Sun has covered almost 1/13 part of its annual orbit. In order to reach alignment, the Moon, after completing its own circuit, will also need to catch up with the much slower Sun. In the case of the day, the circle of the Same and that of the Sun revolve in opposite directions, but the Sun also takes part in the revolution of the Same.[18] Consequently, between e.g. two middays the circle of the Same needs to make more than one revolution, since the circle of the Sun has covered almost 1/366 part of its own orbit in the meantime. The circle of the Same, accordingly, has to cover additional distance, and this takes some additional time—on account of which the solar day, between e.g. two middays, is slightly longer than the sidereal day of a single revolution of the circle of the Same. Or, put differently: once night and day are determined by the presence (and absence) of the light of the Sun, having a slow contrary motion to the revolution of the circle of the Same, the cycle of night and day will not be exactly the original period of the circle of the Same. Instead, just as Timaeus puts it, through the presence of light in the circle of the Sun "night and day come to be, the turning of the single and most intelligent revolution [comes to be night and day]," indicating not only that this revolution will be perceived differently by the presence of light, but also allowing for the slight difference between the two periods—that of that most intelligent revolution, the sidereal day, and that of the period of day and night, the solar day.[19]

It is instructive to contrast this understanding of the passage with Taylor's remarks on 39c2 ff. at this point. In exact opposition to my interpretation above, he bases his understanding of the text on the claim that "the distinction between the mean solar day and the sidereal day [...] was not yet discovered"

---

of the Same can be looked upon as coming to be night and day, it is only a sequence of several such revolutions that can come to be a month, or a year.

17 39c, my translation.
18 In the account of the difference between the synodic and sidereal month we did not need to take into account this additional component, because both Sun and Moon take part in the diurnal revolution of the stars.
19 By speaking about the solar day without further specification I intend to avoid using any more precise indication, like the apparent solar day, or the mean solar day. Timaeus speaks about a single "orbit traced by the revolution of the Different" for each planet, for considerations about the possible discrepancies between these revolutions and the actual path of the planets see p. 119, at n. 10 above.

and draws the immediate conclusion that "[t]he period [i.e. of the complete revolution of the circle of the fixed stars] is therefore taken to be 24 hours, a *nychthēmeron*."[20]

This, as I have suggested above, is already problematic.[21] But it is further compounded by Taylor's claims about the month: "the month is said to run from one conjunction of moon and sun to the next, and at the same time to be the period of one revolution of the moon in its orbit." Most importantly, it is gratuitous to claim that Timaeus would have asserted that these two periods are the same. Instead, what Timaeus says is that "[a] month [comes to be] when the Moon having made a turn of its own circle overtakes the Sun," and this allows for the Moon first completing its own cycle, and then overtaking the Sun only afterwards. All in all, Taylor's closing remark that "As no figures are given, we may perhaps fairly suppose that Timaeus is not distinguishing either of these 'months' from the conventional 'calendar month'" is unwarranted. There are ways of distinguishing the sidereal and the synodic months without

---

20   Taylor, *A Commentary on Plato's* Timaeus, 214.
21   This was first pointed out by Vlastos, *Plato's Universe*, Appendix C, 100:

> There is a problem here which Cornford and most other commentators have ignored. Plato appears to be talking as though the period of the diurnal revolution of the sun—the solar day—were identical with the movement of the Same, while his theory requires it to be a little shorter [...]. Only A. E. Taylor [...] shows awareness of the difficulty, and he cuts the knot by declaring that "the distinction between the mean solar day and the sidereal day [...] was not yet discovered" paying no attention to the fact I have just mentioned: that on the very theory expounded in the *Timaeus* there must be a small, but appreciable, difference between the two units.

Vlastos, nevertheless, keeps the traditional translation, claiming that "Plato is overlooking (and not denying) the difference [between the two periods] in this context" (ibid.). He supports this claim by two considerations. Firstly, that the teleological function of making humans aware of number, is served by the "dramatic alterations of day and night" (101). This is correct—and the clause indeed mentions night and day—but the passage does not require Plato's overlooking the difference, just as there is no need to suppose (as Taylor does, see my critical remarks in the main text above) that the following lines require overlooking the difference between the sidereal and the synodic month. As a second consideration Vlastos remarks that "for practical, calendric, purposes the solar day is inevitably the basic unit of measurement," and Greek astronomers use this unit in their calendar reforms by devising different Great Years (ibid.). Nevertheless when Timaeus introduces his own perfect year that is completed "when the relative speeds of all eight periods have been completed together and, measured by the circle of the Same that moves uniformly, have achieved their consummation" (39d4–7), the reference to the period of the motion of the Same among the eight periods mentioned need not refer to solar days. Indeed, the question – apart from the issue of contention, namely the interpretation of 39c—will be moot: if there is a Great Year of exactly k solar years comprising of altogether exactly n solar days, that period will be exactly $n + k$ sidereal days long, as each year is exactly one day longer measured in sidereal days than it is in solar days.

providing specific values for the length of either of them. Indeed, the way in which Timaeus describes the month may make it clear beyond reasonable doubt that he is speaking about the synodic month, taking it to be longer than the specific period of the circle of the Moon, i.e. the sidereal month.

Accordingly, Timaeus' description indicates that what we encounter in celestial cycles are actually complex phenomena and not just the different periods of the revolution of the circle of the Same, or of the different circles of the Different. This is so in the case of the month, and can well be so in the case of night and day. And even though the period of the orbit traced by the revolution of the Different where the Sun is set is identical to the year, neither is this period given to us in complete isolation. The motion of the Same was given dominance over the motions of the Different (36c7 f.). In order to grasp the motions of the Different one needs to isolate them from the overbearing influence of the motion of the Same. In the case of the Sun, across the year the daily path of the Sun will be somewhat different from day to day. It would be quite an obvious move to attribute the period of days and nights to the motion of the Sun. Timaeus instead stressed that this period is at its root the revolution of the Same (perhaps combined with the motion of the Sun), under the influence of the light of the Sun. When it comes to identifying the period of the orbit of the Sun one needs to grasp the component motions of its complex motion: the overbearing daily component, of the revolution of the Same, and the other revolution with a yearly period. Indeed, reverse-engineering the period of the yearly motion of the Sun, and the possible reverse-engineering of the period of the day and night into the two component motions should run on a parallel track. These are also a major prerequisite for a similar analysis of the motions behind the period of the synodic month.

As a result, Timaeus' astronomy will turn out to be observational astronomy, but its major aim is not just to record the regularities of the motions of the different celestial objects. Instead, the aim of this astronomy is to grasp the fundamental motions of the World Soul which give rise to the periods and regularities that can be detected in these complex motions.

3

This, then, can serve as a cue for us to return to our initial question—what did Plato expect from astronomy in the *Timaeus*? As we have seen, in an important way Timaeus' astronomy is an exercise in reverse-engineering celestial motions onto the workings of the universal soul. At this point we should look at this process of reverse engineering in some more detail. For a start, Timaeus submits that perceiving the astronomical regularities evokes a rudimentary grasp of number (47a–c). Once number is invented and time is understood—I trust in terms I have just set out—the nature of the universe can be investigated, and philosophy can be worked out.

For all of the obvious differences, this line of development has, in various ways, some affinity with the educational curriculum of the *Republic*. Number plays a crucial role in both accounts, even though its origin is characterised differently: according to Timaeus it is astronomical regularities which induce us to count, whereas in the *Republic* just about anything can start us off in the direction of numbers: in the example starting at 523c, Socrates illustrates the problems arithmetic tackles by counting up three fingers.

After this initial triggering of the recognition of number, celestial motions continue to aid further studies—astronomy prominent among them—and lead to a full scale investigation into the nature of the universe. This may be thought to include a somewhat smaller amount of mathematics than what featured on the curriculum of the *Republic*, but that will depend on what is contained in the investigation about nature, and in the whole realm of philosophy. Philosophy here is the greatest gift from the gods to the human race—I take it, it is the summit of intellectual insight, comparable in status to the dialectics of the *Republic*. This does not, however, settle the question of its content yet. Timaeus' remarks could still allow that after the triggering and initializing functions of pre-astronomy and astronomy the two latter phases of the investigation into the nature of the universe, and of philosophy are decoupled from what instigated their occurrence first, and afterwards they constitute separate disciplines in their own right. Nevertheless, the phrasing of 47a–b (speaking about "the realm of philosophy"), and also the passage, where Socrates introduces Timaeus at 20a as someone who has mastered the entire field of philosophy,[22] suggest that the realm of philosophy can stand for a collection of different, but related intellectual pursuits, and these can also encompass the mathematical disciplines.[23]

---

22 *Timaeus* 20a: φιλοσοφίας δ' αὖ κατ' ἐμὴν δόξαν ἐπ' ἄκρον ἀπάσης ἐλήλυθεν· and 47a–b: ἐξ ὧν ἐπορισάμεθα φιλοσοφίας γένος, see also 88c: τόν τε αὖ σῶμα ἐπιμελῶς πλάττοντα τὰς τῆς ψυχῆς ἀνταποδοτέον κινήσεις, μουσικῇ καὶ πάσῃ φιλοσοφίᾳ προσχρώμενον, [...] and 91e: τὸ δ' αὖ πεζὸν καὶ θηριῶδες γέγονεν ἐκ τῶν μηδὲν προσχρωμένων φιλοσοφίᾳ μηδὲ ἀθρούντων τῆς περὶ τὸν οὐρανὸν φύσεως πέρι μηδέν, [...].

23 Cf. also the question Socrates asks from Theodorus at the beginning of the *Theaetetus*: εἴ τινες αὐτόθι περὶ γεωμετρίαν ἤ τινα ἄλλην φιλοσοφίαν εἰσὶ τῶν νέων ἐπιμέλειαν ποιούμενοι (143d).

Hence, what is truly remarkable about the *Timaeus* most probably does not lie in restricting the importance of mathematical knowledge as compared to the *Republic*. Instead, the *Timaeus* account differs markedly from the educational programme of the *Republic* in that it stresses the seamless integration of philosophical insight with mathematical, and within that, with astronomical understanding. The most important factor in this integration is the description how the World Soul, a supreme subject of cognition uses its circles, of the Same and of the Different, in order to grasp in an adequate manner the different objects of cognition. In this model, whatever counted as mathematical or dialectical cognition in the *Republic* will be performed by the circle of the Same (37a–c). Once, however, this supreme *subject* of cognition, which is to some extent accessible to our senses, is admitted in the *Timaeus*, the aim and objective of human cognition can be described in two related ways: one is that we have to complete the entirety of the realm of philosophy (as Timaeus puts it at 47a–b), *and* the other, that we have to grasp and imitate the operations of this huge celestial mind: we have "to observe the orbits of intelligence in the universe and apply them to the revolutions of our own understanding," as a result we will "come to know them and [...] share in the ability to make correct calculations according to nature," this will "stabilize the straying revolutions within ourselves by imitating the completely unstraying revolutions of the god." (47b–c)[24]

To put it otherwise, the process of human development can be described both in terms of the objects of cognition, and in terms of the subject of cognition, and Timaeus' claim is that due to this latter type of description astronomy, or one might even say, an astronomically backed psychological theory, is a crucially important asset to mend our own souls, damaged on delivery (47a–c and 90b–d). Accordingly, the right kind of astronomy is not just another mathematical discipline among many, but it is the foremost discipline to understand and imitate the operations of the World Soul. Hence it will be intimately connected to and, indeed, in its fully developed form it will in a sense integrate every important intellectual pursuit there is.

This would be a huge claim, or even an incredible one about any science, even discounting the possibility that Timaeus might be overselling his likely

---

[24] Note, that this is true only about astronomy practiced in the appropriate way. Indeed, the stakes can be menacingly high in this respect: people engaged in astronomy that is not pursued in the right way—"innocent but simpleminded men, who studied the heavenly bodies but in their naiveté believed that the most reliable proofs concerning them could be based upon visual observation"—will be deprived of their humanity on rebirth and will have to lead their next life as birds of the sky (91d–e).

story about the creation of the cosmos. But there is a more charitable way of setting out these large claims of the *Timaeus*. They may be taken as propounding that the knowledge we gain about the world cannot be neatly parcelled out into separate disciplines. When someone is out to understand the operations of the celestial mind, that should not just be astronomy: it should include a full grasp of how this world came about, what sort of paradigm the Demiurge used, what sort of considerations he had, and further, a full grasp of the connexions between the paradigm and whatever other paradigms there are included in it. Add furthermore all the things the World Soul may be thinking about—an imitation of these revolutions may very well require that to the extent it is humanly possible, we should entertain the same thoughts as the World Soul. Both of these considerations, then, suggest that on the *Timaeus'* likely story, the understanding we should seek about celestial revolutions should not stop at the mathematical level of investigation.[25]

Works Cited

Archer-Hind, R. D. *The* Timaeus *of Plato*. London: Macmillan and Co., 1888.

Broadie, Sarah. "Corporeal Gods, with Reference to Plato and Aristotle." In *ΣΩMA: Körperkonzepte und körperliche Existenz in der antiken Philosophie und Literatur*. Edited by Thomas Buchheim, David Meissner and Nora Wachsmann. Hamburg: Felix Meiner Verlag, 2016.

Burnyeat, Myles. "Plato on why mathematics is good for the soul." *Proceedings of the British Academy* 103 (2000): 1–81.

Cooper, John and David S. Hutchinson, eds. *Plato: Complete Works*. Indianapolis: Hackett, 1997.

Cornford, Francis. *Plato's Cosmology: The* Timaeus *of Plato*. London: Routledge, 1935.

Huffman, Carl. *Archytas of Tarentum: Pythagorean, Philosopher and Mathematician King*. Cambridge: Cambridge University Press, 2005.

Jowett, Benjamin. *The Dialogues of Plato*. Vol. III. 3rd ed. Oxford: Clarendon Press, 1892.

Knorr, Wilbur R. "Plato and Eudoxus on the Planetary Motions." *Journal for the History of Astronomy* 21 (1990): 313–329.

---

[25] I am grateful to the participants of the Prague meeting for questions and critical remarks. I was also greatly helped by written comments from Gábor Betegh, and also by his forthcoming paper "Cosmic and Human Cognition in the *Timaeus*." The final revision of the paper was supported by a sabbatical leave from Eötvös University, a faculty fellowship at the Institute for Advanced Study of Central European University, and by the project OTKA K-112253.

Shorey, Paul. *Plato: The Republic*. With an English translation, vol. ii. London: William Heinemann – Cambridge, Mass.: Harvard University Press, 1935.

Taylor, A. E. *A Commentary on Plato's* Timaeus. Oxford: Clarendon Press, 1928.

Vlastos, Gregory. *Plato's Universe*, Seattle: University of Washington Press, 1975. Reprinted with a new introduction by Luc Brisson. Las Vegas: Parmenides Publishers, 2005.

Bodies and Space in the *Timaeus*

Ondřej Krása

Abstract

Bodies are shown to be related to something else from the very beginning of Timaeus' speech. The original twofold distinction between being and becoming is later on expanded by the addition of a third kind. In this paper, I try to shed some light on the relationship between bodies and the third kind. In the passage dealing with the three kinds (48a–53b) relationship between bodies and the third kind has three prominent facets. First, bodies are "in" the third kind as in a receptacle or container. Second, bodies are modifications of the third kind and therefore parts of the third kind are bodies themselves. Third, bodies are modifications of the third kind that do not prevent other modifications from taking place. At the end of the section 48a–53b, the third kind is identified with space, and starting from line 53b bodies are shown to have a geometrical nature. From this perspective, we can see how the first two facets of the relationship of bodies to the third kind are materialized: a geometrical figure is both in space and it is a modification of space. However, Timaeus' third characterization of this relationship cannot be explained from this perspective. This inconsistency is due to the different connotations of bodies in both passages. In the passage dealing with the three kinds, bodies are shown to be an utterly dependent image of the eternal paradigm in the receptacle. In the passage dealing with geometrical nature of bodies, body is shown to be an independent and self-sufficient geometrical structure. Neither of these connotations should be rejected, and it is clear that Plato wants us to think about body as an image of eternal being, whose specific independence has a geometrical nature.

Keywords

Plato – *Timaeus* – body – space – geometry

Becoming is shown to be related to something else from the very beginning of Timaeus' speech. The original twofold distinction between being and becoming is subsequently expanded by the addition of a third kind. In this paper, I will try to shed some light on the relationship between corporeal becoming and the third kind.[1]

I will try to show that in the passage dealing with the three kinds (48a–53b) this relationship has three prominent facets.[2] First, becoming is "in" the third kind as in a receptacle or container. Second, becoming is a modification of the third kind and therefore parts of the third kind are becoming itself. Third, becoming is a modification of the third kind that does not prevent other modifications from taking place.

At the end of the section 48a–53b, the third kind is identified with space, and starting from line 53b corporeal becoming is shown to have a geometrical nature. From this perspective, we can see how the first two facets of the relationship of becoming to the third kind are materialized: a geometrical figure is both in space and it is a modification of space.

However, Timaeus' third characterization of this relationship—becoming is a modification of the third kind that does not prevent any other modifications from taking place—cannot be explained from this perspective. This inconsistency is due to the different connotations of becoming in both passages. In the passage dealing with the three kinds, becoming is shown to be an utterly dependent image of the eternal paradigm in the receptacle. In the passage dealing with geometrical nature of bodies, becoming is shown to be an independent and self-sufficient geometrical structure. Neither of these connotations should be rejected, and it is clear that Plato wants us to think about corporeal becoming as an image of eternal being, whose specific independence has a geometrical nature.

---

[1] Timaeus uses many words to describe the middle kind, e.g. *to gignomenon* (*Tim.* 27d6), *genesis* (*Tim.* 49a6), *sōma* (*Tim.* 50b6). Although the question of the relationship of the soul to the third kind is very important and has not been very much debated, I will deal with corporeal becoming only.

[2] There is at least one more facet of this relationship, namely the moving/being moved relation of becoming to the third kind in the passage dealing with pre-cosmic becoming (*Tim.* 52d2–53b7, cf. 57c2–6, 88d1–89a1). Whether the movement of the receptacle is something different from the movement of pre-cosmic becoming is dependent on the answer to the question whether there is a difference between pre-cosmic becoming and the receptacle. I am inclined to think that even pre-cosmic becoming is nothing other than a modification of the receptacle and therefore one cannot distinguish between the movement of receptacle and the movement of pre-cosmic becoming. For the identity of becoming and the receptacle, see the section 1.2 "Shapeless but Modified" below.

1 The Threefold Relationship

In this section I will go through the relevant passages from the section 48a–51b and I will identify three facets of the relationship of becoming to the third kind.

1.1 *A Difficulty with the Elemental Bodies*
In section 31b4–32c4, fire, earth, water and air were introduced as the primary constituents of the world which has come to be. In the section starting from 48a, one of the first statements connected with the new beginning of the inquiry is that these elemental bodies are certainly not the principles and elements of everything. The reason for our previous misconception of the elemental bodies is said to be the fact that we have not shown their origin (*genesis*).[3]

Before Timaeus answers the question "What is then the origin of the elemental bodies?" he outlines the nature of the third kind. It is the receptacle (*hypodochē*) and nurse (*tithēnē*) of all becoming (*pasa genesis*).[4] We will see how both characterizations are elaborated in the following sections—becoming is said to be in the third kind as in a container or receptacle, but there is also a more constitutive relationship between the third kind and becoming that is adumbrated by the designation "nurse."

1.1.1 The Dependency of the Elemental Bodies
At 49b7–c7, Timaeus says that the elemental bodies and similar physical entities seem to transmit their origin (*genesis*) to one another.[5] We think that we see the thing we call water condensing and becoming (*gignomenon*) earth, or dissolving and becoming air, with the process continuing such that ignited air becomes fire, condensed fire turns back into air, and so on …[6]

This passage puts the emphasis on the interdependency of each elemental body on the others—air is dissolved water, fire is ignited air, etc. But if we look more closely at what exactly it is that becomes one or the other elemental body, we can also identify the other principle which is going to play a key role in the following section of the dialogue. Timaeus starts his description by speaking about what we call water (*ho hydōr ōnomakamen*) which solidifies

---
3   *Tim.* 48b5–c2.
4   *Tim.* 49a4–6.
5   Beside water, earth, air and fire, Timaeus mentions stones, wind, clouds and fog.
6   Earth has a distinctive position in this "circular becoming": earth is created out of water, but it gives rise to anything. Elements are not only created out of other elements, they also give rise to other elements. This distinctive position of earth adumbrates the role of the earth in the geometrical account of the bodies, see *Tim.* 54b5 ff.

and becomes earth, and becomes air, when the very same thing (*tauton touto*) dissolves and disperses. Although he refers in the majority of the cases to the elemental bodies themselves, which are transforming into other elemental bodies (e.g. *synkautheis aēr*), this mention of the "very same thing" being water, earth and air at different times is an adumbration of very important topic.

The origin of each elemental body is not simple, because air is not only air, but also the other element which has been changed into air. But, on the other hand, it is also the very same thing which was water and is now air. Elemental bodies are therefore not only interdependent on each other, which is the main emphasis of the current passage, but there is also an invariable principle going through all the changes of one elemental body into the other. An elemental body comes into being not only through the transformation of other elemental bodies, but also through the modification—e.g. condensation, dissolution, or ignition—of the very same thing which was modified differently prior to becoming the new elemental body. Each elemental body depends not only on another elemental body, e.g. air on water, it depends also on something permanent.

1.1.2 This and Such

The dependency of becoming on something permanent is further elaborated in the immediately following passage 49c7–50a4, which further discusses the instability of becoming. These lines are notoriously difficult even to translate. There are two main ways of translating them, with many minor variants and corresponding interpretations. According to the traditional translation we should not call e.g. fire, which is an example of all that is becoming (*gignomenon*),[7] by the name "this" (*touto*) but rather by the name "such" (*to toiouton*). According to the alternative translation we should not call that which is becoming by the name "fire," but we should call by the name "fire" only that which is on each occasion "such" (*to toiouton hekastote*).[8]

---

7 In this passage Timaeus is talking about everything that has origin—see ὅσονπερ ἂν ἔχῃ γένεσις (*Tim.* 49e7).

8 The alternative reading was established by Cherniss, "A Much Misread Passage of the *Timaeus* (*Timaeus* 49c7–50b5)." The traditional reading was defended against Cherniss by Gulley, "The Interpretation of Plato: *Timaeus* 49d–e." There have been numerous articles dealing with this problem since then. The proponents of the alternative reading after Cherniss are e.g. Lee, "On Plato's *Timaeus* 49d4–e7," and Silverman, "Timaean Particulars." The proponents of the traditional reading besides Gulley are e.g. Zeyl, "Plato and Talk of a World in Flux: *Timaeus* 49a6–50b5," and Gill, "Matter and Flux in Plato's *Timaeus* 49d–e."

The most difficult problem with the traditional reading is that Timaeus seems to say both that becoming is very unstable and fleeting[9] and that it is "suchness" in all cases and that it is always moving around while being similar.[10] Timaeus seems to attribute to becoming both instability and stability without stressing the transition or the meaning of this transition in any way.

The alternative reading is problematic primarily because of the new ontological realm it introduces. This new realm, which comprises the true object of reference of words like "fire," is characterized in terms of "self-identical characteristics."[11] They are always the same, unlike the realm of becoming, but they move around unlike Forms. Although there is sometimes ambiguity about what is entering the receptacle,[12] in his ontological divisions Timaeus never mentions this realm even though he divides ontological realms just a couple of lines above our passage,[13] as well as a couple of lines below it.[14]

From a systematic point of view, the traditional reading is preferable. Unlike in the alternative reading, its main theses are in accord with the rest of Timaeus' speech and with the passage 48a–53b particularly.[15] Difficulties with the traditional reading can be mitigated by interpreting stability of the visible fire as a stable resemblance to Forms. Fire always resembles the Form of fire and as a "suchness" moves around while being similar.[16]

---

9   *Tim.* 49e2–4.
10 *Tim.* 49e4–7.
11 See e.g. Algra, *Concepts of Space in Greek Thought*, 102.
12 E.g. *Tim.* 50c2–6.
13 *Tim.* 48e2–49a6.
14 *Tim.* 50c7–d2. Similar argument against alternative reading are proposed by Gulley, "*Timaeus* 49d–e," 64, and Charles H. Kahn, "Flux and Forms in the *Timaeus*," 123–125. Cf. *Phaed.* 102d5 ff. where Socrates speaks about forms (*ideai, eidē*) in sensible things, these forms are destructible. In the theory of geometrical atomism developed later in the *Timaeus*, there is one new ontological realm: triangles that never vanish. However, these triangles are not elements but are constituents of the elemental bodies and therefore they cannot be what the alternative reading calls self-identical characteristics. They are not e.g. "fire," but they are constitutive of fire, see Section 2 "Geometrical Figures and Space" below.
15 Besides being preferable from a systematic point of view, I think the traditional reading fits better into the immediate context of this passage. It answers the question raised at *Tim.* 49a7–b7 and 49c7–d4: What should we call e.g. the fire that appears to us? We should call fire "such" and never "this." It is also in accord with Timaeus' summary of his account in *Tim.* 51b2–6.
16 There is textual support for this reading of ἀεὶ περιφερόμενον ὅμοιον (*Tim.* 49e5) in the passage *Tim.* 52a4–7 where becoming is said to be always moving and similar to the Forms. The phrase τὸ διὰ παντὸς τοιοῦτον (*Tim.* 49e6–7) has no relevant counterpart outside of this passage.

What can be deduced from the traditional translation of our passage? Becoming is not stable (*monimon*), but escapes (*pheugei*). Therefore we should not designate it by names indicating some measure of stability, but only by names that are more appropriate to its nature—i.e. we should not call it "this" but only "such." There is, however, another object of reference for the word "this." It is that in which becoming always becomes and appears, and from which it vanishes again. If we want to understand, for instance, what this visible fire in front of us is, we have to understand it as a "suchness" that is in something. Phenomenal fire has no nature of its own; it is nothing other than similarity to the Form of fire that appears in something else. Visible fire is to be understood from the perspective of two kinds of stability: the stability of the Form of fire and the stability of the receptacle in which it appears. Phenomenal fire depends on the one hand on a permanent "this," because fire always becomes in something, and, on the other hand, it is "suchness," because it resembles the Form of fire.

We have seen in the previous section (49b7–c7 the circular becoming of elements) that each phenomenal fire comes into being not only through the changing of other element into the form of fire, but also through the changing of something permanent that is modified into fire, but that was previously modified into air. In the passage about fire as "suchness" (49c7–50a4), Timaeus speaks about permanent "thisness" in which something similar to the Form of fire appears. Both passages deal with the problem of naming something visible: How can one call something "fire," for instance, if this very thing was air before and will be air again? We should call it the "suchness" of some "thisness." Phenomenal fire that is changing into another element is constituted by the relation between the enduring Form of fire and the enduring receptacle. The enduring Form and the enduring receptacle provide us with the grounds for calling the thing in front of us "this fire."

This reading of 49c–50a is supported by the example of gold that is supposed to clarify this issue.[17] If someone points at gold, which is ceaselessly reshaped from one form into another, and asks what it is, the most certain answer would be "gold." But we should also be happy, if we can call it, with some certainty, a "suchness," e.g. a "triangle." The triangular form is the form in the gold. Gold is the stable element, it is the "thisness." The triangular form is one of the always changing "suchnesses" of the gold, i.e. of the "thisness."

1.2 *Shapeless but Modified*

The relationship of becoming to the third kind is further elaborated in the passage 50b5–51b6. In this passage Timaeus describes the relationship between

---

17   *Tim.* 50a4–b5.

BODIES AND SPACE IN THE TIMAEUS   137

becoming and the third kind in both of the directions we have already identified—he underlines both that becoming is in the third kind as in the receptacle and therefore that it is in a way separate from it and that becoming is always the same thing which is modified in different ways. Let us look at these descriptions more closely.

In the first part of this passage (50b5–e5), Timaeus starts by saying that the third kind always receives all bodies, i.e. becoming,[18] but that it never takes on the shape (*morphē*)[19] of any of the things which enter it and therefore it never departs from its character (*dynamis*). According to this description bodies are something different from the third kind which receives them and the characters of bodies and the third kind are also different—bodies have shapes which the third kind does not have and by entering into the third kind bodies do not change its character. The third kind is devoid of all the forms (*ektos pantōn eidōn*) of the things which enter it—the third kind receives bodies but it is never affected by them. This account is akin to the description of the receptacle which receives all becoming in itself—the third kind is in fact called "in which" also in this passage.[20] This receptacle is different from the things which enter it, such that it does not take upon itself the shapes or forms of the things which are in it.

But, Timaeus continues, saying that the nature upon which all the impressions are made (*ekmageion*) is modified (*diaschēmatizomenon*) by the things that enter it and appears different at different times (*phainetai allote alloion*). According to this description, the third kind—quite surprisingly given the previous characterization—receives shape (*schēma*) from the things which enter it and it itself appears different.[21] This description reminds us of a permanent thing which undergoes different modifications—becoming is some modification of the third kind.

---

18   "All bodies": *ta panta sōmata Tim.* 50b6, "becoming": *to gignomenon Tim.* 50c7–d1.
19   Timaeus uses many different words to express what the third kind does not receive: *morphē* (*Tim.* 50c1, see also *Tim.* 50d7: *amorphon*), *idea* (*Tim.* 50d7), *ti tōn epeisiontōn* (*Tim.* 50e1–2), *opsis* (*Tim.* 50e3), *eidos* (*Tim.* 50e4). I do not think there is any substantial difference between these terms in our passage.
20   *Tim.* 50d6.
21   Are bodies something different from the modified third kind which only *appears* different at different times or are they the same? For difference, see Silverman, "Timaean Particulars," 93. The receptacle is said to *appear* to be something in three passages (*Tim.* 50c2–4, 51b4–6, 52d4–e1), but each time it is also modified. Since becoming is itself that which appears different at different times according to Timaeus' previous statements (*Tim.* 49c7–d1) we may be tempted to think that the third kind, which appears different, is identical with becoming. This alternative is confirmed when Timaeus says that the third kind likens itself (*aphomoioi, Tim.* 50e3), because in the very same passage becoming is itself called likeness (*aphomoioumenon*) of the Forms (*Tim.* 50d1, see also *Tim.* 51a2).

What is, then, the relationship between these descriptions—becoming as something which does not affect the third kind in which it is and becoming as modification of the third kind?[22] In the sentence beginning at 50c2, we are told that the second description is an explanation of the first one: the third kind does not take on any shape, since (*gar*) it is modified by receiving all impressions and therefore appears to be different at different times. The key to understanding this train of thought is to understand what it means to be the perfect receiver of all impressions (*ekmageion panti*). Timaeus explains this at 50d4–e4: that in which imprints (*ektypōmata*) are situated has to be completely shapeless in order to liken itself perfectly to whatever form it receives. If it had any form, it would exhibit not only the shape of the thing which is imprinted on it, but also its own appearance, and therefore it would not be a perfect receiver.

I interpret the apparent contradiction between these two characteristics of the relationship of becoming to the third kind in this way: the third kind is modified by the things which enter it, but it never really accepts the shapes of these things, because it is never modified in a way that would hinder other modifications from taking place. The third kind is modified, but the way it is modified never prevents it from being the perfect receiver: it is always capable of taking on any shape without qualification or resistance. This, I propose, is the meaning of Timaeus' statement that the third kind is modified but never accepts any shape.

Two similes exemplify the situation (50e5–51a1).[23] First, the liquid which is the base for the scented ointments has to be made devoid of all possible

---

[22] This double characterisation of the relationship between becoming and the third kind (sometimes referred to as the "receptacle paradox," Gregory, *Plato's Philosophy of Science*, 192–193, 211, 214–216) gave rise to the question whether the receptacle is "space" or "matter." Some interpreters think it is space only, e.g. Baeumker, *Das Problem der Materie in der griechischen Philosophie: Eine historisch-kritische Untersuchung*, 177–187, and Taylor, *A Commentary on Plato's Timaeus*, 312. Some think it is rather matter, e.g. Sachs, *Die fünf platonischen Körper: Zur Geschichte der Mathematik und der Elementenlehre Platons und der Pythagoreer*, 223–233. Still others think Timaeus uses both descriptions, e.g. Aristotle, *Phys.* 209b11–17; Algra, *Concepts of Space*, 72–73, 76 ff.; Gregory, "Aristotle and Some of His Commentators on the *Timaeus*' Receptacle," 35; Miller, *The Third Kind in Plato's* Timaeus, 7, 17. For a more detailed classification of possible interpretations see Miller, *The Third Kind*, 19–32. The third kind has to be thought about from the perspective of its explicit identification with χώρα and from the geometrical nature of corporeal becoming, see section 2 "Geometrical Figures and Space."

[23] *Tim.* 50b5–51b6 contains one more simile; Timaeus likens the third kind to a mother, becoming to an offspring and being to a father (*Tim.* 50d2–4, the third kind is called mother once again in *Tim.* 51a4–5; outside of our passage the Demiurge, and not being, is called father—e.g. *Tim.* 28c3, 41a7). We cannot infer much from this simile, because it is not

scents at the start in order to be able to accept the intended fragrance perfectly. Second, the soft substance upon which impressions are made has to be devoid of all shapes at the start in order to accept whatever shape is intended. These two similes show that whatever is to properly imitate a characteristic, has to be without that characteristic. These similes work with two successive states—the before and the after. Before the liquid accepts fragrance it must be devoid of all fragrance and before the soft substance accepts shape it must be devoid of all shape. However, the third kind is different in this respect. The third kind is not only ready to accept any shape before it accepts a particular shape, but it is prepared to accept any shape even after it has already accepted a shape—it always accepts a shape, but it never hinders any other shape from appearing.[24]

Is it possible to be modified and not to hinder any other modification from taking place? Timaeus' examples are not of this kind. If the base for the scented ointments accepts a fragrance, it hinders other fragrances from being the only ones in the base: the first fragrance changes the odourless nature of the base. If a soft substance accepts, for instance, a triangular shape it will not accept, for instance, a square shape without any hindrance. It has to be remoulded with some effort.

Although Timaeus does not use the simile of the mirror in this context, it is probably the one which could best explain this strange relationship of becoming to the third kind.[25] Mirror images are always in something, namely in a mirror, and are based on relationship between originals and observers mediated

worked out in any further detail. This simile is definitely part of the overall strategy of the passage—it is immediately followed by the explanation of what it is to be the perfect receiver and the second occurrence of the designation "mother" is accompanied by the receptacle. I think Cornford is right in pointing out that the notion of mother, father, and offspring Timaeus has in mind is that of mother as a mere host of the child whose father is the only cause of its generation, Cornford, *Plato's Cosmology*, 187. This simile thus underlines the notion of becoming as being just "in" the third kind without affecting it in any way. It is thus one part of the twofold characterization of the third kind spoken of above.

24 δέχεταί τε γὰρ ἀεὶ τὰ πάντα, καὶ μορφὴν οὐδεμίαν ποτὲ οὐδενὶ τῶν εἰσιόντων ὁμοίαν εἴληφεν οὐδαμῇ οὐδαμῶς (*Tim*. 50b8–c2, my emphasis).

25 Timaeus mentions mirrors in different contexts in *Tim*. 46a2–c6 and 71a7–e2. Lee uses the mirror simile as a key to understanding Timaeus' metaphysics of becoming, see Lee, "On the Metaphysics of the Image in Plato's *Timaeus*," especially 352–360. There are many differences between a mirror and the receptacle: the model, the mirror and the image are things of the same kind (spatio-temporal things), whereas the Forms, the receptacle and becoming are not on the same ontological level; most mirrors do not represent originals without distortions (e.g. inversions of the image on the horizontal axis), while the receptacle is the best thing, in which copies can arise; in order for there to be an image in a mirror, there has to be someone who observes it, while in the pre-cosmic becoming, on the

by the parts of the mirror. The part of the mirror which now reflects the tree for me offers no resistance whatsoever to reflecting any other original to any other observer. The mirror always remains ready to reflect whatever shape it receives—in this way the mirror is itself without any shape although it already reflects a particular shape.

Is this the way Timaeus considers the relationship of becoming to the third kind? I will deal with this question later, after I have examined the nature of corporeal entities.

At the end of the passage 50b5–51b6 (51a1–b6), Timaeus confirms the double nature of this relationship: In its nature (*physis*) the third kind is a receptacle (*hypodochē*) which is shapeless (*amorphon*) and it is improper to call it by the name of any shape, but it accepts shapes in its parts and as a whole, and is modified (e.g. *pepyrōmenon, hygranthen*) and therefore its parts are most correctly called by whatever shape they accept.[26]

2 Geometrical Figures and Space

In the analysis of various passages from *Timaeus* 48a to 51b, I tried to show that there are three interconnected facets of the relationship between becoming and the third kind: first, becoming is in the third kind as in a container; second, becoming is a modification of the third kind; third, becoming is a modification of the third kind that does not change the character of the third kind so that it never prevents other modifications from taking place.

In this section, I will try to show that looking at this threefold relationship from the perspective of the identification of the third kind with space and from the perspective of the geometrical nature of corporeal entities can explain some but not all of the obscurities in this relationship.

After Timaeus provides proof of the existence of the kind of being in itself,[27] he continues to discuss the three kinds in the passages 51e6–52d1 and 52d2–53a7.

---

other hand, there is no one to perceive it. For a discussion of further differences between receptacle and mirror see Kung, "Why the Receptacle is not a Mirror," 167–178.

26 In the last sentence of our present passage Timaeus treats as equivalent the phrase "fiery part" (*to pepyrōmenon meros*) and "accepts imitations" of, for example, fire (*mimēmata dechomai, Tim.* 51b4–6). The verb "accept" (*dechomai*) is very common in describing what the third kind does with regard to becoming.

27 *Tim.* 51b6–e6.

In the first passage Timaeus characterizes becoming as that which becomes in some place and vanishes out of it again.[28] We have already met a rather similar characteristic in the previous passages, where Timaeus told us that there is something in which all things come to be and appear and out of which they again vanish.[29] Now Timaeus establishes what it is in which all becoming becomes: all becoming becomes in some place (*en tini topōi*). Thus the third kind is space (*chōra*) providing a location (*hedra*) for all becoming.[30] Becoming has to be somewhere, i.e. it has to be in some place and occupy some space (*chōra*).[31] The third kind provides the place, or space, or situation or whatever name we will use, for becoming, which is in it, because the third kind is space itself.[32]

Section 52d2–53a7 deals with the situation before the heaven came into being. In this final passage of the dialogue, which is dealing explicitly with the three kinds, the third kind is confirmed to be space and the relationship of becoming to the third kind is described predominantly in a way that suggests that becoming is a modification of the third kind: the third kind was made watery and ignited and received the shapes (*morphas*) of earth and air before the heavens came into being.

Is identification of the third kind with space of any help with regard to the threefold relationship of becoming to the third kind? In order to answer this question, we must move forward to the passage where Timaeus shows what the nature of corporeal entities is.[33]

Fire, earth, water, and air are bodies. Each body which has plane faces is composed of triangles of two sorts, the first being right-angled isosceles triangles, the second being right-angled triangles with a hypotenuse double the length of the shorter side (by being doubled this triangle forms an equilateral triangle).[34] From these two types of triangles two larger plane figures are formed: the equilateral triangle is formed by putting together six right-angled scalene triangle and the square is formed by putting together four right-angled

---

28 *Tim.* 52a6–7.
29 *Tim.* 49e7–50a1, see also 50d6.
30 *Tim.* 52a8–b1.
31 *Tim.* 52b3–5.
32 In many contexts in the *Timaeus*, *chōra*, *topos*, and *hedra* are used interchangeably, see Johansen, *Plato's Natural Philosophy*, 127–128. For the not very clear distinctions among these terms in antiquity, see Algra, *Concepts of Space*, 31–38.
33 Some interpreters think that one should not connect these passages, Cornford, *Plato's Cosmology*, 182–183, Gregory, "Commentators on the *Timaeus*' Receptacle," 35, Gregory, *Plato's Philosophy of Science*, 212 and 221–222.
34 Aristotle criticizes Plato for not carrying out his analysis of solids further than into plane faces. See Aristotle, *De gen. et corr.* 315b30–32.

isosceles triangles. Out of these plane figures four regular solids are formed: four equilateral triangles form a four-sided pyramid, eight of these form an octahedron and twenty of these form an icosahedron; meanwhile, six squares form a cube. Each of these regular solids is assigned to a particular elemental body: the four-sided pyramid to fire, the octahedron to air, the icosahedron to water, and the cube to earth.[35] This account of the structure of the elemental bodies is referred to as geometrical atomism.[36]

Timaeus does not speak explicitly about the three kinds in the passage dealing with geometrical figures and it has been the subject of much criticism that Plato does not use the concept of the third kind in this passage.[37] Although Timaeus does not mention the terms "third kind," "nurse," or "receptacle," he uses the terms "space," "place" and "seat" many times.[38] The predominant usage of "space," "place" or "seat" (*chōra, topos, hedra*) identifies "where" some

---

35   *Tim.* 53c6–56b6. For further discussion of the composite geometrical nature of elements see Cornford, *Plato's Cosmology*, 230–239.

36   See e.g. Gregory, *Plato's Philosophy of Science*, 187–240. Labelling this account "geometrical atomism" should not lead us astray—in this passage Timaeus' universe is not as reductive as the label might suggest. Even though the various processes of coming to be of elemental bodies (*Tim.* 56c7–57b7), their various types of characteristics (*Tim.* 58c5–61c2) and the various sensations we have of them (*Tim.* 61c3–68d7) are explained by way of the dissolution of regular solids into more basic plane figures and their regrouping into another regular solid and by way of the shapes, sizes, and groupings of these solids, there is lot more in universe than just shapes, sizes, and groupings of geometrical figures. For instance, there are characteristics of geometrical bodies, which are closely related to their shapes, like mobility and pliability, stability, sharpness, and lightness (*Tim.* 55e1–56c7). Timaeus' description of change is where principles that are not convertible into shapes, sizes, and groupings of geometrical figures start to play an eminent role. Change occurs only when there is diversity—in the realm of geometrical figures, there is no change among the same figures. The direction of the change is determined by the strength of the diverse parts involved in it. The stronger part makes the weaker assimilate into its own form—strength and weakness being related to, but not identical with, the amount of respective parts (*Tim.* 56e2–57b7). Besides the diversity of parts, locomotion is caused by the movement of the receptacle (*Tim.* 57b7–c6). The reason why the movement of different elements never stops is the compression caused by the circular movement of the universe for which the world soul is responsible (58a2–c4). In order to make Timaeus' account credible, answering the question why the triangles compose in exactly this way, is also needed, see Aristotle, *De caelo* 299b23–31.

37   See Aristotle, *De gen. et corr.* 329a13–24; Lee, "The Image in Plato's *Timaeus*," 349–352; Gadamer, "Idee und Wirklichkeit in Platons Timaeus," 259.

38   The only two usages of the names of the third kind after the passage Tim. 48a–53b is *dechomenēs* at *Tim.* 57c3 and *trophon kai tihēnēn tou pantos* at *Tim.* 88d6—but in these lines there is no specific connection with the geometrical nature of corporeal entities.

corporeal entity is. There is e.g. a seat of fire[39] and a place of fire.[40] The second usage which is also widespread is "to where/from where" some corporeal entity is moving. Everything is e.g. changing places (*chōra*),[41] everything is moving to its own place (*topos*).[42] The third usage is linked to the general structure of the universe. There is no empty space,[43] no two opposite places "up" and "down" in the universe,[44] but only relative places of "up" and "down" only.[45] There is also the central place of the universe[46] and there are places for the masses of each elemental body.[47]

The first and the second type of usage of space/place/seat is akin to the "that in which" relation of becoming to the third kind. Becoming is in the third kind as in a receptacle or a container—geometrical figures are in space: they are in a place and they are moving from one place to another one.

Although the second type of relationship between becoming and the third kind, namely becoming as a modification of the third kind, is never mentioned in this passage, I think we can deduce it based on the geometrical nature of becoming. Corporeal entities have a geometrical nature. Geometrical figures consist of plane figures arranged so as to form the boundaries of solid figures— "figure is the limit of a solid."[48]

In the *Timaeus*, there is nothing filling in the boundaries of the figure other than space itself. Not only is no mention of any specific filling made in the *Timaeus*, but, more importantly, no filling can logically be present. Timaeus' account of the change of one elemental body into another one works only if we take into account the limits of the solid figures and not the specific filling of solid figures: e.g. by dividing one unit of water, one unit of fire, and two units of air can arise.[49] This is possible because the number of boundary triangles of one unit of water (icosahedron) equals the number of boundary triangles of one unit of fire (pyramid) plus two units of air (octahedron). But the volume of one icosahedron does not equal the volume of one pyramid plus

---

39 *Tim.* 59a3.
40 *Tim.* 63b2–3.
41 *Tim.* 57c1.
42 *Tim.* 58b8.
43 *Tim.* 58a7. For the denial of any void see also *Tim.* 79c1, 80c3; but cf. *Tim.* 58a7–b8, 60e5, 61a5, 61b1, 61b4 for allowing some void; for discussion of this issue see Archer-Hind, *The Timaeus of Plato*, 210.
44 *Tim.* 62c5–8.
45 *Tim.* 63d2–4.
46 *Tim.* 62d6–8.
47 *Tim.* 63d4–6.
48 στερεοῦ πέρας σχῆμα εἶναι, *Men.* 76a7.
49 *Tim.* 56d6–e1.

two octahedrons and therefore Timaeus' account of transformations of the elements works only with the triangular boundaries of solid figures and not with respect to its filling. What makes water water is not a specific filling in the icosahedron but only the arrangement of its boundary triangles in a specific way. What is relevant to the solid figure is its shape alone.[50]

If this is the nature of corporeal entities, we can consider corporeal entities to be a modification of space. Geometrical figures are limitations of space, they are parts of space shaped in a certain way by boundary triangles—there is nothing more in geometrical figures than space shaped in a certain way.[51]

Timaeus says that becoming is in the third kind, it is modification of it, but becoming never affects the third kind. We have seen that the motivation behind this last characteristic is that the third kind has to be always ready to accept any modification.

I have tried to show that some kinds of images meet this description—images reflected in the mirror do not hinder other images from modifying the mirror in different ways.[52] Why is this so? Images in the mirror do not hinder other images from appearing because the relationships among these images are only apparent. There is no direct relationship between one mirror image and another mirror image, every relationship is in fact a relationship between the originals and the observers. Because there are no direct relationships between reflections in the mirror, these reflections cannot hinder other reflections from taking place.

However, geometrical figures are not only dependent on the originals, they also have relationships with each other. Geometrical figures, for instance, move to the place where similar figures are, cut other figures into their constituent

---

50 For similar arguments see Baeumker, *Das Problem der Materie*, 172–175 and Vlastos, *Plato's Universe*, 89–90. Why are geometrical figures solid if no filling is present? The basic triangles and the four geometrical figures have shapes which are beautiful and best (*Tim.* 53b1–7, 54a1–b2). These characteristics are probably the reason why geometrical figures are solid for a certain period of time: in order for there to be a constantly moving mixture of elements, geometrical figures must preserve their shape for a certain time and then change into another element (*Tim.* 58a2–c4). The stability of the basic triangles is necessary for the creation of the elements from the destruction of other elements. The impenetrability of geometrical figures is due to their beautiful shapes which enable them to be part of the best and most beautiful world. A similar interpretation, together with serious objections, is provided by Gregory, *Plato's Philosophy of Science*, 237–238.

51 For similar interpretation see Zeller, *Die Philosophie der Griechen in ihrer geschichtlichen Entwicklung : Teil II, Abt. 1 : Sokrates und die Sokratiker, Plato und die alte Akademie*, 736. For systematic problems with this interpretation, see Gregory, *Plato's Philosophy of Science*, 224–225. Cf. "Two straight lines do not enclose space" Καὶ δύο εὐθεῖαι χωρίον οὐ περιέχουσιν (Euclid, *Elements*, κε, 9).

52 See the section 1.2 "Shapeless but Modified" above.

plane faces, and push each other out of the way. These relationships are not only apparent. Although these relationships are based on the relationships between the originals (otherwise there would not be any difference between fire and air, for example), the relationships between geometrical figures themselves do not mirror the relationships among originals. The reason why, for example, fire cuts water into its constituent pieces is not the relationship between Form of fire and Form of water. The reason why this process occurs is that a specific pyramid encounters specific icosahedron in space and the former is stronger than the latter.

3   The Autonomy of the Image

Although identification of the third kind with space and geometrical nature of corporeal becoming sheds some light on the complex relationship between becoming and the third kind, there is still substantial difference between this relationship and relationship between geometrical figures and space. Geometrical figures are both in space and are a modification of space. Because the third kind is explicitly identified with space and corporeal becoming has a geometrical nature, we can see how becoming is both in space and how it is modification of space. However, geometrical figures are not the kind of modification that does not hinder other modification from taking place.

Timaeus does not seem to be bothered with this discrepancy. Why does he not explain physical becoming more radically as a mere reflection of the originals and instead attributes a certain self-sufficiency to relationships among corporeal entities?

Timaeus tries to do justice to our experience with corporeal entities: fire burns[53] and earth is hard.[54] Solids are impenetrable and therefore can directly affect each other. But why did the Demiurge create the world in this way? Why was the world created with specific relationships among corporeal entities that do not reflect the relationships between originals only? The Demiurge created the world as self-sufficient (*autarkēs*)[55] and self-sufficiency is one of the ways in which the world resembles its model, which is "by itself."[56] The self-sufficiency of the world takes many forms.[57] The self-sufficiency

---

53   *Tim.* 61d5 ff.
54   *Tim.* 62b6 ff.
55   *Tim.* 33d1–3, 68e3–4.
56   *Tim.* 51b6–52a4.
57   See e.g. *Tim.* 42e5–6.

of the corporeal entity consists in preserving its shape and thus in identity with itself. This self-sufficiency resembles the self-sufficiency of the model, because that which is "by itself" neither receives anything else into itself nor enters into anything else.[58] Corporeal entities do not enter into each other for some time, they are impenetrable. Impenetrability is a way in which corporeal becoming resembles being in itself.

Why does Timaeus describe the third kind as that which is shapeless first and becoming as stable geometrical form of the space later on? Are we right in interpreting becoming as a modification of the third kind that does not prevent other modifications, given that Timaeus thinks about a physical entity as something that prevents other things from entering the same place?

These tensions in Timaeus' account stem from the different perspectives found in our passages. In the passage dealing with elements in terms of images of the eternal beings that are in the receptacle, dependency on becoming is underlined: corporeal becoming has neither its form nor that in which it becomes from itself. Physical entities are not "this," but only "such," that is, they are unstable resemblances of eternal being. On the other hand, geometrical atomism portrays corporeal becoming as stable and independent: neither unchanging basic triangles nor temporarily stable geometrical figures are depicted as images of eternal being and their stability is not presented as an imitation of an eternal model. In the first passage, Timaeus underlines the absolute dependency of becoming on its model and on the receptacle. In the second passage, he underlines stability and self-sufficiency of becoming. These two emphases should not make us abandon one or the other perspective. We should rather take into account both of them and think about corporeal becoming in terms of images of eternal beings in the receptacle that are in a way stable and independent due to their geometrical nature.

In the *Timaeus*, there is no such account of corporeal becoming that bridges this gap. I tried to show above which aspects of the relationship of becoming to the third kind are preserved in the geometrical account of corporeal world. Timaeus identifies the third kind with space and space is essential in the geometrical atomism in two respects which are shared with the role of the third kind towards corporeal becoming. Space is both that in which geometrical figures are and that which is shaped in the form of geometrical figures: geometrical figures are in space and they are modifications of space. The third type of relationship between becoming and the third kind is not preserved in the relationship of geometrical figures to space: geometrical figures are solid and therefore they are not the kind of modification of space that does not hinder

---

58   *Tim.* 51e6–52a4.

other geometrical figures from occupying the same place. The reason for this impenetrability of bodies is not geometrical, because in geometry figures can penetrate each other. The solidity of the figures is not due to the incapacity of space to be a perfect receiver. Rather, it is due to the aim of the Demiurge to create a world that is in some respects independent. The Demiurge creates elements as arrangements of space that are regular and beautiful and therefore that are able to temporarily preserve their shapes in spite of the opposing influence of other elements.[59]

Works Cited

Algra, Keimpe. *Concepts of Space in Greek Thought*. Leiden: Brill, 1995.

Archer-Hind, R. D. *The Timaeus of Plato*. London: Macmillan and Co., 1888.

Baeumker, Clemens. *Das Problem der Materie in der griechischen Philosophie: Eine historisch-kritische Untersuchung*. Münster: Aschendorffsche Verlagsbuchhandlung, 1890.

Cherniss, Harold. "A Much Misread Passage of the *Timaeus* (*Timaeus* 49c7–50b5)." *The American Journal of Philology* 75 (1954): 113–130.

Cornford, Francis M. *Plato's Cosmology: The Timaeus of Plato*. Indianapolis: Hackett Publishing Company, 1935. Reprint 1997.

Gadamer, Hans G. "Idee und Wirklichkeit in Platons *Timaios*." In *Gesammelte Werke, Band 6: Griechische Philosophie* II. Tübingen: Mohr Siebeck, 1985.

Gill, Mary L. "Matter and Flux in Plato's *Timaeus* 49d–e." *Phronesis* 32 (1987): 34–53.

Gregory, Andrew. *Plato's Philosophy of Science*. London: Duckworth, 2000.

Gregory, Andrew. "Aristotle and Some of His Commentators on the *Timaeus*' Receptacle." In *Ancient Approaches to Plato's* Timaeus. Edited by Robert W. Sharples and Anne Sheppard. London: Institute of Classical Studies, 2003.

Gulley, Norman. "The Interpretation of Plato: *Timaeus* 49d–e." *A Journal of Philosophy* 81 (1960): 53–64.

Johansen, Thomas K. *Plato's Natural Philosophy: A Study of the* Timaeus-Critias. Cambridge: Cambridge University Press, 2004.

---

59 I am grateful for many comments, especially those from Štěpán Špinka and Andrew Gregory. This paper was supported within the project of Operational Programme Research, Development and Education (OP VVV/OP RDE), "Centre for Ethics as Study in Human Value," registration No. CZ.02.1.01/0.0/0.0/15_003/0000425, co-financed by the European Regional Development Fund and the state budget of the Czech Republic, and by Charles University in Prague, Faculty of Arts, program "SVV 2014," project "The Cause of the World in *Timaeus*."

Kahn, Charles H. "Flux and Forms in the *Timaeus*." In *Le Style de la pensée: Recueil de textes en hommage à Jacques Brunschwig*. Edited by Monique Canto-Sperber and Pierre Pellegrin. Paris: Les Belles Lettres, 2002, 113–131.

Kung, Joan. "Why the Receptacle is not a Mirror." *Archiv für die Geschichte der Philosophie* 70 (1988): 167–178.

Lee, Edward N. "On the Metaphysics of the Image in Plato's *Timaeus*." *Monist* 50 (1966): 341–368.

Lee, Edward N. "On Plato's *Timaeus* 49d4–e7." *American Journal of Philology* 88 (1967): 1–28.

Miller, Dana. *The Third Kind in Plato's* Timaeus. Göttingen: Vandenhoeck & Ruprecht, 2003.

Sachs, Eva. *Die fünf platonischen Körper: Zur Geschichte der Mathematik und der Elementenlehre Platons und der Pythagoreer*. Berlin: Weidmann, 1917.

Silverman, Allan. "Timaean Particulars." *Classical Quarterly* 42 (1992): 87–113.

Taylor, Alfred E. *A Commentary on Plato's* Timaeus. Oxford: Clarendon Press, 1928.

Vlastos, Gregory. *Plato's Universe*. With a new introduction by Luc Brisson. Las Vegas: Parmenides Publishing, 2005.

Zeller, Eduard. *Die Philosophie der Griechen in ihrer geschichtlichen Entwicklung: Teil II, Abt. 1: Sokrates und die Sokratiker, Plato und die alte Akademie*. Third Edition. Leipzig: Pues's Verlag, 1875.

Zeyl, Donald J. "Plato and Talk of a World in Flux: *Timaeus* 49a6–50b5." *Harvard Studies in Classical Philology* 79 (1975): 125–148.

Does Plato Advance a Bundle Theory in the *Timaeus*?

George Karamanolis

Abstract

In this paper my main aim is to argue that Plato in the *Timaeus* and especially in the section concerning the receptacle advances a theory according to which instances of properties or particular properties contribute to the constitution of material objects, but he does so without compromising his position, found in earlier dialogues, that sensible objects have essences due to immaterial Forms. I will conclude that Plato does not maintain a bundle theory of material objects there and that he is not a bundle theorist. I will try to back up this claim by exploring how Plotinus speaks of the constitution of material objects. Although Plotinus is not directly commenting on the *Timaeus*, he is inspired, I will suggest, mainly by this dialogue in his explanation of material objects. To the extent that this is the case, Plotinus can be seen as offering a confirmation of my interpretation of the ontology in the *Timaeus* that is presented in the section concerning the receptacle.

Keywords

Plato – *Timaeus* – Plotinus – receptacle – properties – bundle theory – Forms – material objects – essence

Introduction*

The main aim of this paper is to argue that Plato in the *Timaeus*, and especially in the section concerning the receptacle, advances a theory, according to which instances of properties or particular properties contribute to the constitution of sensible, material objects, but that he does so without compromising his

---

* The paper has been developed over a period of four years and it has benefited from discussions I have had with many friends. First of all, I would like to acknowledge the input of the critical questions pressed on me when I presented a version of this paper at the conference on the *Timaeus* in Prague. I mention especially those of Gábor Betegh, Chad Jorgenson, Karel Thein, and Filip Karfik. Phil Horky made some interesting comments on an earlier draft and

essentialism, that is, basically the view that sensible objects have their essences due to immaterial Forms.[1] The role of particular properties in the constitution of material objects is the development of a complex ontological theory that occurs in *Timaeus* 49ef., and can be seen as an ontological novelty when compared with earlier dialogues, but also with the first part of the *Timaeus*, namely the account running from 27c to 49e. In the first part of my paper, I will outline this ontological theory and explain how it should be understood and what its implications are. I will argue that Plato does not maintain a bundle theory of material objects there and that he is not a bundle theorist. I will try to back up this claim by exploring how Plotinus speaks of the constitution of material objects. Although Plotinus is not directly commenting on the *Timaeus*, he is inspired, I will suggest, mainly by this dialogue in his explanation of material objects, as both his claims and his vocabulary show. To the extent that this is the case, Plotinus can be seen as offering a certain confirmation of the ontology present in the *Timaeus*, as interpreted here. Plotinus' contribution will be discussed in the second part of my paper.

1 Receptacle, Forms, and Images of Forms

My starting point in this investigation is the fact that in the *Timaeus*, especially in the section concerning the receptacle (49e–50b), Plato distinguishes between Forms, images of Forms, and the receptacle that accommodates the latter. This passage is of course a battlefield of interpretations and is known in scholarship as "a much misread passage."[2] I do not mean of course to take a position on all of the thorny issues raised in this passage. I will mainly set out to investigate what the role of the images of Forms is, that is, what these images themselves are, what their function is, and how they relate to the receptacle.

Angela Ulacco sent me her unpublished paper mentioned in the bibliography. I have also benefited from the critical remarks of Peter Larsen and Vasilis Politis. I would like to thank Anthony Kroytor and Chad Jorgenson for stylistic improvements.

1   My critique concerns especially the understanding of the ontology of the receptacle as a bundle theory, for instance, by Buckels, "Triangles, Tropes, and *ta toiauta*: A Platonic Trope Theory," and "Making Room for Particulars: Plato's Receptacle as Space not Substratum."
2   The literature on the passage is very rich. See Cherniss, "A much misread passage of the *Timaeus* (*Timaeus* 49C7–50B5)," Lee, "On the Metaphysics of the Image in Plato's *Timaeus*," and "On Plato's *Timaeus* 49D4–E7," Mohr, "Image, Space and Flux in Plato's *Timaeus*," Silverman, "Timaean Particulars," and *The Dialectic of Essence*, 246–284, Harte, "The Receptacle and the Primary Bodies: Something or Nothing," Broadie, *Nature and Divinity in Plato's Timaeus*, 183–185, and more recently Buckels, "Making Room," Ulacco, "*Die präkosmische Bewegung in Platons Timaios:* ἴχνη, χώρα *und Ideen*." Concerning the structure of the passage, see especially Lee, "Metaphysics of the Image," 348.

Let us first take a look at the context of the passage. At 48e Timaeus announces a new beginning (*archē*) in his cosmology, one which claims to advance a fuller classification, as he says.³ It becomes immediately clear what kind of classification is meant here: one of ontological classes. Up to this point, Timaeus had operated with a distinction between two ontological classes, namely being and becoming, corresponding to the intelligible entities on the one hand, namely God and the Forms, and the copies (*mimēma*, 48e6) of the Forms on the other, which make up the sensible entities. While being is eternal and unchanging, becoming (i.e. sensible entities) is subject to change. So far, Plato does not deviate from the ontology we are familiar with from the *Republic* and the *Sophist*. As in *Republic* v, he distinguishes being from becoming, intelligible entities from sensible ones, and confirms that the latter are radically different from, and ontologically dependent on, the former.⁴ And as in the *Sophist*, he not only makes a distinction between being and becoming, but also adds intellect to the class of being (*nous*, *Soph.* 249a), a class that includes the immovable beings (*akinēta onta*, 249b5), that is, the intelligible entities which are not subject to change.⁵ For when Timaeus refers to being (*on*) and distinguishes it from becoming (*genesis*) and the receptacle (49a1–2, 52d), he may well include in "being" the demiurgic intellect and the Forms.

The passage I will focus on here (48ef.) introduces a third class of entities (*triton genos*), containing only one member, the receptacle (*chōra*). The receptacle, we are told, is important in the process of coming into being (*genesis*). The idea that Timaeus advances here is that we cannot explain the coming into being of material entities, and thus of the material world as a whole, without introducing such an entity. Unlike previous cosmologists, Plato is not content with a general theory that explains the coming into being of the world as a whole by means of pointing to a certain principle that accounts for its orderly arrangement; rather, he wants to explain in detail how individual physical objects that occur in the world come about. We need, in particular, to understand their material constitution and their properties. And this is what Timaeus sets out to do in this account. In what follows, Timaeus sets out to explain the receptacle, its nature and its function. In this section, though, we also hear of another class of entities, which I have already mentioned. In addition to the Forms, there are also the images of Forms, which of course are distinct from the Forms. Let us examine his line of thinking.

---

3 Ἡ δ' οὖν αὖθις ἀρχὴ περὶ τοῦ παντὸς ἔστω μειζόνως τῆς πρόσθεν διῃρημένη. (*Tim.* 48e2–3).
4 Cf. *Rep.* 478d.
5 For the ontology of the *Sophist* and the question of the role of the Forms in it, see Silverman *Dialectic of Essence*, ch. 5 and 6, and Politis, "The argument for the reality of change and changelessness in Plato's *Sophist* (248e7–249d5)."

It is important to note that in this passage Timaeus does not simply outline a new theory, but rather presents us with a puzzle, an *aporia*, which concerns material elements like fire and water, and the principles that govern their generation; a project, as he says, that nobody had so far undertaken.[6] Let us see what the precise content of this *aporia* is. Here is the relevant section:

> True, however, as this statement is, it needs to be put in clearer language; and that is hard, in particular because to that end it is necessary to raise a previous difficulty about fire and the things that rank with fire (προαπορηθῆναι περὶ πυρὸς καὶ τῶν μετὰ πυρὸς ἀναγκαῖον τούτου χάριν). It is hard to say with respect to any one of these, which we ought to call really water rather than fire or indeed which we should call by any given name rather than by all names together or by each severally, so as to use language in a sound and trustworthy way.
>
> *Tim.* 49a6–b5; trans. Cornford[7]

The inquiry here concerns both fire and things that are necessarily linked to fire or that rank with fire, as Cornford translates, and similarly water and things that contain water. Before we come to investigate what this means, one thing is clear, namely that Plato, unlike earlier cosmologists, does not take the four elements to be primitive and ultimate, so to speak. And this I take to be precisely the gist of the *aporia*, namely that it is not at all clear which element can actually and legitimately be called fire or water.[8] Timaeus rather thinks that these elements are neither primitive nor foundational, but that they are further analyzable into geometrical solids, as it turns out later. When considering fire and the things necessarily connected with fire, or water and things connected with water, it is hard to say with respect to any of these which we should call by this or that name, i.e. the name "fire" or "water." Things that contain fire in some form, such as a hot iron, and similarly watery and airy things, which contain water or air in some form, count as fiery, watery, or airy, insofar they are subject to the same transformations as their corresponding constitutive elements (fire, water, air). Not only can water turn into air, that is, into steam, but similar transformations are necessary features of watery things, as they are capable of

---

6 οὐδεὶς πω αὐτῶν γένεσιν μεμήνυκεν (*Tim.* 48b5–6). On the structure and the content of this *aporia*, see Silverman, *Dialectic of Essence*, 258–260.

7 I am aware of the fact that Cornford's translation like any other is subject to dispute, because any translation of this passage carries with it interpretative implications. Buckels, "Making Room," 303–305 comments on the implications of Cornford's translation.

8 On the content and the aim of this *aporia*, see Silverman, *Dialectic of Essence*, and Johansen, *Plato's Natural Philosophy*, 119.

becoming steamy or icy. In fact such transformations are evidence that these things are watery.[9]

If this is the case, however, then material elements such as fire, water, and air are not ultimately stuffs; they cannot count as basic, so to speak, or ultimate constituents, since they are subject to transformations, that is, material transformations. This is the reason why they will later be explained with reference to their constituent parts, when Timaeus sets out to explain their constitution with reference to geometrical shapes.[10] The crucial (and much debated) point is that water, fire, air, and earth are rather *suches* (*to toiouton*, 49d5), and not this or that (*touto*, 49d6), since they render objects such and such and such, namely watery, fiery, airy, not this or that. To the extent that this is the case, these elements cannot ultimately be taken as principles of some kind; rather, Timaeus suggests, they are the result of principles;[11] and in the geometrical section later on, he will show that they are composites of geometrical solids. Timaeus goes on to tell us in the following passage that:

> Whenever we observe a thing perpetually changing, fire for example, in every case we should speak of fire not as "this" but as "what is such and such", nor of water as "this" but always as "what is such and such"; nor must we speak of anything else as having some stability, among all the things we indicate by the expressions "this" and "that", imagining we are pointing out some definite thing. For they slip away and do not wait to be described as "that" or "this" or by any phrase that presents them as having permanent being.
>
> *Tim.* 49b4–e4

Timaeus clearly argues that we should not call fire and water a this but rather (at least in Cornford's translation) a what-is-such, namely something which is not stable (βεβαιότητα ἔχον, 49d7) but subject to transformations, and for this reason, he suggests, we should avoid attributing to them definite names,

---

9   See Lee, "Metaphysics of the Image," 357–362, Zeyl, *Plato: Timaeus*, lvi–lix, and Buckels, "Making Room," 304.
10 I will not discuss the geometrical section here; Cornford's analysis, *Plato's Cosmology*, 210–239, remains invaluable.
11 The passage has been much debated in scholarship. Cherniss, "Misread Passage," reacted to the traditional interpretation of Cornford and Taylor, arguing that Timaeus refers not to a phenomenon but to a feature, a property, that enters the receptacle. Lee, "*Timaeus* 49D4–E7," argued further in support of Cherniss' interpretation. For my purposes here, it is crucial only to point out that material elements are neither ultimate stuffs nor principles of generation.

such as fire or water. But to return to the subject of the circle of transformation, Timaeus argues that the same is the case not only for the four elements, which had long been considered principles, but for everything that comes to be.[12] As two examples of what comes to be, Timaeus mentions hot and white and their opposites, cold and black (θερμὸν ἢ λευκὸν ἢ καὶ ὁτιοῦν τῶν ἐναντίων, 50a2–3). We are now presented with a range of entities that belong to the same category: fire, water, hot, cold. We have been told that these entities are "a kind of such" rather than a "this," that is, they function as predicates of qualities or properties, such as, for instance, when we say "this wall is white," or "the iron is hot." By saying this, we generally attribute whiteness or heat to something. Yet on the other hand we need to distinguish between what is fiery or watery, that is, between what is predicated by fire or water and can change at some point, and what is always fire or water as such. As has been pointed out, the latter is actually neither a this nor a such, but a this-such, namely, an instance of a specific property that makes something such as it is, and should be translated accordingly.[13] And the question arises: what is the ontological status of these entities?

To begin with, these are neither particular stuffs, nor particular objects, nor universal qualities. Timaeus makes this clear when he speaks of hot and white, referring to them as ὁποιονοῦν τι, θερμὸν ἢ λευκὸν ἢ καὶ ὁτιοῦν τῶν ἐναντίων (50a2–3). The passage reminds us of Aristotle's passage in the *Categories*, where he speaks of particular qualities, ἡ τὶς γραμματική, τὸ τὶ λευκόν (*Cat.* 1a25–27). It may well be the case that Aristotle was originally inspired by this passage from the *Timaeus* when distinguishing between universal and particular qualities in the *Categories*, given the linguistic similarities between the two passages. But whatever the case may be, the crucial point for us here is that Plato speaks of particular properties or of instances of properties, that is of the existence or inherence of property F in a subject (ἐν ὑποκειμένῳ). The inherence of F-ness (whiteness) in a subject makes it F (white), and this instance of whiteness is, as I said, both a this and such. Instances of properties such as the hotness of this glass of water or the whiteness of that wall are also known as tropes. Such entities are marked by the general feature that they exist insofar as they inhere in a subject that they qualify. A particular whiteness or hotness is the whiteness or

---

12   καὶ δὴ καὶ πῦρ τὸ διὰ παντὸς τοιοῦτον, καὶ ἅπαν ὅσονπερ ἂν ἔχῃ γένεσιν (*Tim.* 49e7–8). See Broadie, *Nature and Divinity in Plato's Timaeus*, 186–188.

13   See Cherniss, "Misread Passage," Buckels, "Making Room." This is how tropes are traditionally understood and described; they are neither objects nor properties and they are non-repeatable; they are often described as here-suches; see e.g. Bacon "Tropes," Schaffer "The Individuation of Tropes," 247.

the hotness of a particular object; the existence of white in an object is white as a trope or the trope of white.[14]

Plato, then, introduces an ontological class other than the receptacle in the section about the receptacle, particular properties or tropes,[15] and in so doing foreshadows a distinction that Aristotle will spell out later, namely that between universal and particular properties. The important difference between the two, however, is that for Plato tropes are images of Forms (and on a certain interpretation of Forms, they are also images of universals), while for Aristotle this is clearly not the case. As Plato makes clear, the receptacle receives and accommodates not the Forms themselves but images of Forms, particular qualities or tropes.[16] And the question of why the receptacle does not accommodate Forms themselves naturally arises. Let us examine the passage where Plato clearly states that the receptacle accommodates imitation of beings, that is, imitations or copies of Forms.

> Now the same thing must be said of that nature which receives all bodies. It must be called always the same; for it never departs at all from its own character; since it is always receiving all things, and never in any way whatsoever takes on any character that is like any of the things that enter it; by nature it is there as a matrix for everything, changed and diversified by the things that enter it, and on their account it appears to have different qualities at different times; while the things that pass in and out are to be called copies of the eternal things, impressions taken from them in a strange manner that is hard to express.
> *Tim.* 50b6–c6; Cornford trans.

This passage states that the receptacle hosts images of Forms, that is, instances of qualities or particular qualities. The receptacle functions as a place for the images of Forms precisely because the receptacle itself is absolutely bereft of qualities. We are told that it is *amorphon*, and that this characteristic feature

---

14   The literature on tropes is very rich; see, for instance, Simons, "Particulars in Particular Clothing: Three Trope Theories of Substance," Bacon, "Tropes," Schaffer, "Individuation of Tropes." Plato comes close to the idea of tropes also in the *Theaetetus* 156e, and he clearly rejects the idea (καὶ ἐγένετο οὐ λευκότης αὖ ἀλλὰ λευκόν). On this passage see also below.
15   Buckels, "Trope Theory," and "Making Room," rightly stresses this.
16   So much at least is clear. There are several different interpretative tendencies here; see Cherniss, "Misread Passage," and Lee, "Metaphysics of the Images," which Silverman, *Dialectic of Essence*, 257–265 critically reviews. See also Broadie, *Nature and Divinity in Plato's Timaeus*, 173–242, a rich and important discussion of the passages that concern me here.

of the receptacle is causally connected with its ability to receive the images of Forms.[17] This is actually the essential feature of the receptacle, to receive the images of Forms that give rise to the four elements. The receptacle is, of course, described both as space and as a material substrate; hence, one of the difficulties concerning it is how exactly we should understand it.[18] The first analogy given by Plato compares the receptacle to gold, a material that a sculptor molds as he likes (50a4–b6), while the second analogy compares it with wax, upon which different impressions may be stamped.[19] Both analogies suggest that the receptacle must be quality-less, that is, without its own properties, in order for it to allow the coming into being of different objects. For my purposes, this is all that matters—namely that the receptacle is without properties and therefore suitable for receiving images of Forms.

However, the question of why the receptacle receives images of Forms and not Forms themselves naturally arises. These images of Forms, it turns out, are Forms of geometrical solids, that is, geometrical Forms. When a Form is reflected in the receptacle, an imprint comes about.[20] The receptacle accommodates that imprint, and this is crucial if we want to understand how exactly the receptacle contributes to the process of coming into being (*genesis*). After all, the receptacle has been introduced to explain *genesis* and the question regards the role played by Forms and their images.[21] To be more precise, the question concerns how the coming into being of material entities should be explained now that we have completed our ontology. For we now have Forms, the receptacle, and the images of Forms, i.e. the geometrical Forms, which are accommodated on the receptacle. The coming into being of material entities ought then to be explained with reference to these three classes of entities, which is different from the account presented in the first part of the *Timaeus*, where the Forms played the main causal role in the constitution of the material world. This is the question I shall address in the next section: how exactly does this process takes place?

17   Πλὴν ἄμορφον ὂν ἐκείνων ἁπασῶν τῶν ἰδεῶν ὅσας μέλλοι δέχεσθαί ποθεν. (*Tim.* 50d7–8). See further Miller, *The Third Kind in Plato's* Timaeus.
18   Buckels, "Making Room," argues in favor of the space option, but this is because he wants to commit Plato to bundle theory, which does not require any material substrate.
19   There is a great deal of discussion concerning the status of the receptacle. See Miller, *Third Kind*, Johansen, *Plato's Natural Philosophy*, ch. 6, Broadie, *Nature and Divinity in Plato's Timaeus*, 173–242, and most recently Buckels, "Making Room."
20   Cherniss, "Misread Passage," and Lee, "Metaphysics of the Image," argue, convincingly in my view, for this interpretation.
21   On the possible senses of *genesis*, roughly speaking the pre-cosmic movements and the coming into being of the physical world, see Ulacco, "Die präkosmische Bewegung."

2 The Constitution of Sensible Entities

When Timaeus speaks of the elements as instances of Forms and says that "we must not apply any of these words to this or that quality, hot or cold or any of the opposites, or to any combination of these opposites" (50a), the reader wonders what he is actually referring to when he says "combination." The Greek phrase πάνθ' ὅσα ἐκ τούτων is, in this case, open to interpretation. Cornford[22] suggests that it might refer to the elements themselves, which are composites of several qualities: fire, for instance, is a combination of hot and yellow, according to him. But it may also refer, he continues, to compound bodies, to mixtures of the four primary elements. The latter seems to me to be a much more plausible suggestion; what Timaeus says from now on concerns the entire sensible world.[23] After all, his intention from the start was to explain the *genesis* of the physical world. In what follows, Timaeus speaks of three kinds of entities, the ungenerated and unchangeable, the sensible and changeable, and the receptacle (*Tim.* 52a). The sensible (and changeable) entities cannot be composed only of sensible qualities or conglomerations of them, at least not exclusively, but must also be composed of compound bodies, namely material objects. And the question is how these bodies, these material objects, are constituted.

There are at least two kinds of answers in the existing literature. The traditional one holds that material entities are mainly copies of Forms. Such an answer would be in line with the ontology presented in the *Republic* or the *Phaedo*. For in these works, as mentioned earlier, sensible entities are dependent on Forms, causally and ontologically.[24] In a number of passages in these dialogues, Plato, as we know, speaks of particular things as resembling their Forms[25] and he refers to the Form of F as what is F (ὅ ἐστιν). The couch, for instance, is a copy of what is a couch, namely the Form of couch.[26] But what about the images of Forms introduced in the *Timaeus*? What role do they play

---

22   Cornford, *Plato's Cosmology*, 180.
23   Thus also Silverman, *Dialectic of Essence*, 258: "Although the specific concern of Timaeus' remarks is the four traditional elements, earth, air, fire, and water, his closing words indicate that the lesson applies to the whole of the physical world (50a1–4)."
24   Denyer, "Plato's Theory of Stuffs," belongs to this category; he argues against the view that Forms are universals and in support of the view that they are similar to modern chemical elements; in that paper he does not consider the section on the receptacle in the *Timaeus* but limits himself to the *Phaedo* and the *Republic*.
25   *Phaedo* 74e, adding in the same context that the thing resembling the Form is by comparison deficient (*endeesteron, phauloteron,* 75b).
26   Τί δὲ ὁ κλινοποιός; οὐκ ἄρτι μέντοι ἔλεγες ὅτι οὐ τὸ εἶδος ποιεῖ, ὃ δή φαμεν εἶναι ὃ ἔστι κλίνη, ἀλλὰ κλίνην τινά; (*Rep.* 597a1–2).

in the coming into being of sensible things? We appear now to have two kinds of Forms, the traditional Forms and the geometrical Forms, which make up the material elements and to some extent also the material objects. The alternative, more recent, answer is given by Christopher Buckels: sensible entities are not copies of Forms, as has been traditionally thought, and as Plato himself suggests in earlier dialogues, but rather aggregates of images of Forms, that is, of the geometrical Forms.[27] According to his account, Plato revises his earlier account of the causal role of traditional Forms with regard to the material entities and adopts a different view, according to which everything in the sensible world, including sensible, material objects, is composed of the effects of Forms on the receptacle, that is, a compound of images or of tropes. And in this sense, sensible entities are bundles of properties. This is an interesting alternative.

I find both answers problematic, however. The problem with the first one is that in Plato's account in *Timaeus* 49–50 it is clear that images of Forms, geometrical Forms, have a causal role in the coming into being of sensible entities, since they enter the receptacle and become stable there, and we need to explain that role. Does this mean, though, that sensible entities—compound bodies—are just aggregates of tropes, as Buckels argues?

One central problem for his interpretation is the following: if material entities are merely collections of tropes, that is, bundles of qualities, how can we explain the fact that we do not perceive bundles of qualities but rather objects bearing certain qualities? The perception of objects x and z and the identification of their qualities as qualities of these objects could not be possible if objects x and z were merely bundles of qualities. The bundle theorist would probably say that the x and z objects you perceive are bundles of qualities. This is fine, but we still perceive qualities or properties as properties of a certain kind of thing, of a man or a horse. We speak of that property of a man, to walk, not simply of one property among many others, but as a property peculiar to man. This is at least what Plato does in the *Theaetetus*: he speaks of a man being such or of a certain quality.[28] There must be something in which the properties adhere, and this cannot simply be a material substrate, because, as I have said, we perceive properties as properties of a man or of a horse. There must be something that accounts for a thing's being a man or a horse (and for its properties being of man or horse). And for Plato, I think, the answer is

---

27 Buckels, "Trope Theory." See also Silverman, *Dialectic of Essence*, ch. 7, who eventually rejects this interpretation.

28 ὅταν φῶμεν ἐμὲ τηλικόνδε ὄντα (*Theaet.* 155b7). The bundle theorist can still, however, remain unconvinced and explain perception in terms of bundle theory.

clear, it is the Form of the thing. It is the Forms that make something the kind of thing it is, an x or a z; the Forms account for the essences that things have.

A more distant yet related question to the bundle theory in Plato is this: what is it that renders sensible entities relatively stable? Sensible entities are subject to change but have a certain identity by means of which we perceive them as such, as x or z. Their relative stability cannot be the result of the impact of images of Forms, since, as we have been told in the section on the receptacle, images of Forms are not stable at all but subject to a cycle of transformations. Actually, they account for the cycles of transformations. The receptacle does not provide stability either; rather it is a bearer of properties, enabling the effect of the inherence of properties.[29] The relative stability of sensible objects is unlikely then to derive either from the images of Forms or from the receptacle. The Forms, on the other hand, are stable entities and make something the thing that it is.

My suggestion is that both the traditional Forms, the images of Forms or the geometrical Forms, and the receptacle contribute to the coming into being of material entities. Each makes a distinct contribution. Sensible entities have a certain identity, an essence, and they are recognized as such. Traditional Forms contribute precisely this. They are the essences of sensible entities. But these entities also have several other properties that pertain to their material constitutions. These are accounted for, I suggest, by the images of Forms. The latter are responsible, so to speak, for the properties of the sensible entities, especially the essential properties, those that pertain to a certain kind of entity, such as man or tree. Material entities of a kind have distinct properties pertaining to their material constitution that are appropriate to the kind of thing they are, that is, properties related to the essences they adhere to. It is important to recognize here that the properties pertaining to material constitution are also determined by Forms, namely geometrical Forms or images of Forms; these Forms account on the one hand for the constant elemental or material transformation and on the other for the relative intelligibility of that process. Finally, the receptacle contributes the space and the material substrate where images of Forms are instantiated and properties of material objects are generated.

If this is the case, then Plato builds on, revises, and expands his previous ontology, the ontology of the traditional Forms. In the *Timaeus*, these Forms play, without a doubt, a major role in accounting for the generation of the world, so it would be difficult to imagine that Plato would simply brush them aside when, in the section on the receptacle, he discusses the constitution of

---

29   See Silverman, *Dialectic of Essence*, 271.

sensible entities. After all these Forms are bearers of the Demiurgic intelligence and craft, which make the world orderly and intelligible. Yet it is in the section on the receptacle that Plato develops his ontology further by adding two more ontological classes, namely the receptacle and the images of Forms, which are responsible in different ways for the properties of material objects, that is, objects generated in the receptacle. Plato realizes that entities in the sensible world differ from those in the intelligible world not only by virtue of their materiality, but also by having properties and not just essences.[30] Nowhere did Plato speak explicitly and at length of such properties in his earlier work.[31] We were rather left to believe that both essences and properties of sensible things were caused by the Forms. This now changes. Forms are essences, and images of Forms are qualities or properties pertaining to the specific material constitution of an object, and these properties are constantly subject to change. Sensible objects are, then, I suggest, neither constitutive of Forms alone nor bundles of properties either; rather, they have essences and also bear essence related properties.

We are now confronted with several open questions, one of which is the following: Plato does not speak of the instantiation of Forms in the receptacle, but only of the images of Forms. Besides, how are we to understand the compresence of Forms and images of Forms in material entities? Such a question involves investigating the division of causal labor between the intelligence of the Demiurge and the necessity of the receptacle. Plato does not enlighten us about such questions. He does not clarify how his account of traditional Forms relates to the account of images of Forms or geometrical Forms in the section on the receptacle. There is, however, a source of enlightenment in this regard, and this is Plotinus. Plotinus of course does not comment directly on Plato, but he means to expound Plato, that is to show how Plato's philosophy should be understood. Plato scholars do not usually resort to Plotinus for exegetical purposes. I do not want to plead for a universal answer here to the thorny question of how Plotinus helps us understand Plato. Yet it does seem to me that Plotinus shows us how we should understand Plato's ontology of the *Timaeus*; his remarks are, in my view, very illuminating in this regard. One lesson that Plotinus teaches us, I shall suggest, is that Plato is by no means a bundle or a trope theorist.

---

30   Forms, however, also have properties, being one, being self-identical etc., but I refer to the properties of material objects here. I thank Peter Larsen for drawing my attention to this distinction.

31   Plato, however, does speak of properties in the *Theaetetus*, esp. 154–156, but he does not explain how they come about and how they relate to Forms/essences. See the commentary of Burnyeat, *Plato's Theaetetus*, 15–17.

3   The Constitution of Sensible Entities in Plotinus

My aim in this section is to look at the accounts given by Plotinus of the constitution of sensible entities, in order, first, to show that these support the above interpretation of Plato's ontology, namely that both the traditional Forms and the property instances play a role in the coming into being and the constitution of sensible entities, and, second, to see what Plotinus has to say about their respective causal roles in the constitution of material entities. It is of course true that Plotinus often works out his own distinct positions as an answer to questions asked or positions advanced by Peripatetics and Hellenistic philosophers, but he nevertheless very often reconstructs a position from the various parts of Plato's works that can be considered as a possible position of Plato himself, at least in a dialectical sense. And this I believe is the case with Plotinus' view on the constitution of sensible entities. His vocabulary in several relevant passages points in this direction, at least.

Let me start with an emblematic passage of Plotinus, namely *Enn.* VI 3.8.20 ff., where he claims that sensible objects are conglomerations of qualities and matter.

> For this sensible [substance] (*aisthētē ousia*) is not simply being, but is perceived by sense, being this whole world of ours; since we maintained that its apparent existence (*dokousan hypostasin*) was a congress of perceptibles (*synodos tōn pros aisthēsin*) and the guarantee of their being comes from sense-perception. But if the composition has no limits, one should divide according to the species-forms (*eidē*) of living things, the bodily species (*eidos*) of man, for instance. For this, a species-form of this kind, is a quality of body and is not out of place to divide by qualities.
>
> *Enn.* VI 3.10.14–20; trans. Armstrong

The passage appears to suggest that sensible objects do not qualify as beings, since they are nothing but a conglomeration of qualities, that is, qualities that we perceive with our senses. This passage would appear then to suggest that sensible objects are bundles of qualities. But this would be a superficial reading of the passage and a misunderstanding of Plotinus' view.[32] This is because the conglomeration of which Plotinus speaks, is an ordered one and because he speaks of Forms that make something the kind of thing it is,

---

[32] See the discussion of the passage by Kalligas, "The Structure of Appearances: Plotinus on the Constitution of Sensible Objects." This and related passages are discussed by Chiaradonna, "Plotinus on Sensible Particulars and Individual Essences."

for instance, a man. There must be a principle, then, that accounts for the arrangement of qualities, which is such that it makes up a specific kind of thing. Plotinus tells us, for instance, that every kind of ordering requires the effect of some soul, which is a principle of order (*Enn.* IV 7.2.22–25).[33] And in a number of passages Plotinus makes clear that there is a formative principle, a *logos* or an *eidos*, that accounts for the orderly arrangement of qualities that make up a sensible object the kind of object it is. Quite revealing is the following passage:

> If then this is what a body is, that which is composed of all the qualities plus matter, this is what corporeity (*sōmatotēs*) would be. And if a *logos* is what by its coming [to matter] makes the body, it is clear that the *logos* comprises all the qualities. But this *logos*, assuming that it is not simply a definition which states the nature of the thing, but a formative principle (*logos*) that makes up the thing cannot include matter, must be a principle enveloping matter which by coming into matter makes up the body. And the body must be matter and a formative principle (*logos*) present in it; while the formative principle itself, since it is a form without matter, must be contemplated bare, even if it is itself as inseparable as it can be from matter. For the separable form is different, the one in intellect.
>
> *Enn.* II 7.3.3–14; Armstrong trans.[34]

This passage makes several crucial points. First, Plotinus distinguishes at the end of the passage between the *logos* in the intellect and the *logos* in the object. Second, he tells us that the former is present in the object and inseparable from it, although it can be considered apart from matter in thought, while the latter exists separately in the intellect. Finally, Plotinus suggests that the immanent *logos*, as I shall call it, the *logos* in matter, includes within it all the qualities of the object in question (ἔχει τὰς ποιότητας ἁπάσας) and makes up that body (ποιῶν πρᾶγμα, ἀποτελεῖν τὸ σῶμα). Plotinus distinguishes, then, here between five entities: a) immaterial Form/*logos*, b) immanent Form/*logos*, c) matter, d) qualities, e) the body, that is, the sensible object, the compound of Form and matter. These entities are part of an account of the constitution

---

33   See Kalligas, "Structure of Appearances," 763–765.
34   Εἰ μὲν οὖν τοῦτό ἐστι τὸ σῶμα τὸ ἐκ πασῶν τῶν ποιοτήτων σὺν ὕλῃ, τοῦτο ἂν εἴη ἡ σωματότης. καὶ εἰ λόγος δὲ εἴη ὃς προσελθὼν ποιεῖ τὸ σῶμα, δηλονότι ὁ λόγος ἐμπεριλαβὼν ἔχει τὰς ποιότητας ἁπάσας. δεῖ δὲ τὸν λόγον τοῦτον, εἰ μὴ ἔστιν ἄλλως ὥσπερ ὁρισμὸς δηλωτικὸς τοῦ τί ἐστι τὸ πρᾶγμα, ἀλλὰ λόγος ποιῶν πρᾶγμα, μὴ τὴν ὕλην συμπεριειληφέναι, ἀλλὰ περὶ ὕλην λόγον εἶναι καὶ ἐγγενόμενον ἀποτελεῖν τὸ σῶμα, καὶ εἶναι μὲν τὸ σῶμα ὕλην καὶ λόγον ἐνόντα, αὐτὸν δὲ εἶδος ὄντα ἄνευ ὕλης ψιλὸν θεωρεῖσθαι, κἂν ὅτι μάλιστα ἀχώριστος αὐτὸς ᾖ. ὁ γὰρ χωριστὸς ἄλλος, ὁ ἐν νῷ. (*Enn.* II 7.3.3–14; cf. *Timaeus* 52a).

of sensible objects. According to that account, sensible objects are not merely bundles of qualities; rather, Plotinus claims, it is the immanent *logos* that comprises these qualities, brings them to matter and makes up the sensible object. In this sense, the immanent Form/*logos* functions as the principle which accounts for the orderly arrangement of the qualities of the sensible object in matter.

Plotinus also repeats this theory in other parts of his work. In his treatise *On Matter* (*Enn.* II.4), for instance, we find a particularly interesting passage concerning the constitution of sensible objects.

> The Form comes on it [matter] bringing everything with it. Every Form has volume and everything that goes along with or is caused by the *logos*. Therefore, in every kind the quantity of matter is determined together with Form, that is, it is different in man, different in birds and different again in every species of birds. Is it more astonishing that something else imposes on matter how much it should be than of what quality it should be? And it is not true that only the quality is *logos* while the quantity not, since this is Form and measure and number.
>
> *Enn.* II 4.8.23–30; Armstrong trans.

Here Plotinus again clearly states that the Form is the principle accounting for the orderly arrangement of qualities in matter and thus accounting for the constitution of sensible objects, including animate ones, such as men and birds. It is the Form, Plotinus says here, that brings with it all the necessary qualities but also determines the quantity of matter that is appropriate for each kind and each species of a kind. It is the Form that is the measure of what is coming to be. Once again, the Form is presented as the formative principle of sensible objects that is responsible for the arrangement of all their qualities, including the necessary amount of matter. The immanent Form is clearly different from the qualities that it brings, which are determined and arranged by it. For Plotinus, then, the immanent Form is the formative principle accounting for the identity of a sensible object, for it being the thing it is, and as such only certain qualities can inhere in it.

Plotinus makes clear that the immanent Form determines the identity of a sensible object also in the following passage from *Ennead* VI 3:

> This so-called substance is the compound of many and is not a "something" (*ti*) but a "quale" (*poion*). And the *logos* of fire, for instance, designates rather the "something," while the shape it produces is rather a quale. And the *logos* of man is the being "something," whereas its product in the

bodily nature, being an image of the *logos*, is rather a sort of quale. It is as if, the visible Socrates being a man, his painted picture, being colors and painter's stuff, was called Socrates. In the same way, therefore, since there is a *logos* according to which Socrates is, the perceptible Socrates should not rightly be said to be Socrates, but rather colors and shapes which are imitations (*mimēmata*) of those in the *logos*.

Enn. VI 3.15.26–36; Armstrong trans.[35]

This passage comes from the treatise in which Plotinus allegedly argues that sensible objects are bundles of qualities. Here he carefully qualifies his view.[36] The *logos* accounts for the identity of a thing, the τί, whereas all other qualities that make up its shape endow it with qualities, which are like the colors of a painter. If we take a painting, such as that of a figure, we can distinguish between the concrete figure and its various features, such as its colors. It is the figure that determines the features of the painting, and not the other way round. This is, I think, what Plotinus means when he says that colors and shapes are *mimēmata* of the *logos*; such features do not imitate the *logos*, the forming principle of a painting, but they are determined by the *logos*, and in this sense the *logos* dictates what these features should be. Plotinus' vocabulary here echoes that of *Timaeus* 48e5–6.

Plotinus makes a similar point when he speaks of the nature in *Ennead* III 8. In this treatise Plotinus sets out to show that nature should not be taken as the main causal agent of the sensible world, but as an intermediary one, since in Plotinus' view nature acquires from the soul the *logoi* which then it transmits to matter. Plotinus describes nature both as a form (*eidos*) and as a formative principle (*logos*). Nature, he says, brings with it the *logos* which is unchangeable (*akinētos*, III 8.2.18) and imposes it on matter, which thus becomes informed (*logōtheisa*; III 8.2.25). Plotinus explains this further, arguing that nature brings with it the *logoi* of animals when they are generated. In this short passage Plotinus distinguishes three kinds of *logoi*: a) nature as *logos*,

---

35 κινδυνεύει ἡ λεγομένη αὕτη οὐσία εἶναι τοῦτο τὸ ἐκ πολλῶν, οὐ τὶ ἀλλὰ ποιὸν μᾶλλον. καὶ ὁ μὲν λόγος εἶναι οἷον πυρὸς τὸ "τὶ" σημαίνων μᾶλλον, ἣν δὲ μορφὴν ἐργάζεται, ποιὸν μᾶλλον. καὶ ὁ λόγος ὁ τοῦ ἀνθρώπου τὸ "τὶ" εἶναι, τὸ δ᾽ ἀποτελεσθὲν ἐν σώματος φύσει εἴδωλον ὂν τοῦ λόγου ποιόν τι μᾶλλον εἶναι, οἷον εἰ ἀνθρώπου ὄντος τοῦ Σωκράτους τοῦ ὁρωμένου ἡ εἰκὼν αὐτοῦ ἡ ἐν γραφῇ χρώματα καὶ φάρμακα ὄντα Σωκράτης λέγοιτο. οὕτως οὖν καὶ λόγου ὄντος, καθ᾽ ὃν Σωκράτης, τὸν αἰσθητὸν Σωκράτη <ὀρθῶς λεκτέον οὐ Σωκράτη>, ἀλλὰ χρώματα καὶ σχήματα ἐκείνων τῶν ἐν τῷ λόγῳ μιμήματα εἶναι. (*Enn.* VI 3.15.26–36).

36 For a discussion of this passage, see Kalligas, "Structure of Appearances," 772–773.

b) the *logoi* born from it and carried with it, c) the *logos* in matter, which is dead (*nekros*), as he says, as it cannot generate anything more.[37]

Before I move forward, one possible worry must be addressed here. Plotinus uses the term *logos* in several contexts and with different senses. *Logos* refers to the Form (*eidos*) and also to the qualities that it carries as the result of a certain form or identity, such as weight, shape, or color. It also refers to the qualities that result from its instantiation in matter, the perceptible qualities, the imprints on the receptacle. In the passage from *Ennead* III.8 discussed above, this becomes particularly clear. It is for this reason that this passage is instructive; for we learn from it that Plotinus can use *logos* both for the formative principle and for the qualities that come into being as the result of its application or instantiation in matter. The term *logos*, however, both as formative principle and as quality suggests that we are dealing with a rational structure that can be logically apprehended and communicated by linguistic means.

All of the above passages show clearly, in my view, that Plotinus assigns the role of the formative principle of sensible objects to intelligible Forms, which means that Forms account for imposing and arranging the qualities that feature in a certain sensible object. Such objects are not, then, for Plotinus mere bundles of qualities; in his view, an object results rather from the presence of an intelligible Form in it. And this presence has a causal efficacy that involves the arrangement of qualities in the sensible objects. These qualities arranged by Forms are essential qualities, not accidental qualities, for as we have seen they are the result of the presence of a Form, which makes up the identity of sensible objects. This is made especially clear in the passage from *Ennead* II 4 cited above, where we hear that qualities of different kinds and different species depend on the formative principle, the Form. This Form is, of course, not an essence for Plotinus, since for him essences strictly speaking exist only in the intelligible realm.[38] Yet, the Form is responsible for the identity or the essence of a sensible object, the "this" (*ti*), as he says.

Plotinus, then, accounts for the constitution of the sensible objects by means of intelligible or traditional Forms, qualities deriving from them, matter, and ultimately soul and intellect. Of course, he does not give us a straightforward interpretation of the ontology in the section on the receptacle in the *Timaeus*, but his own explanation of the constitution of material objects shows that he takes the ontology in that part of the *Timaeus* as complementary

---

37   Similar is Plotinus' suggestion in *Enn.* I 8.8.13–16, καὶ τὰ ἐν τῇ ὕλῃ εἴδη οὐ ταὐτά ἐστιν, ἄπερ ἦν, εἰ ἐφ᾽ αὑτῶν ὑπῆρχεν, ἀλλὰ λόγοι ἔνυλοι φθαρέντες ἐν ὕλῃ καὶ τῆς φύσεως τῆς ἐκείνης ἀναπλησθέντες.

38   See *Enn.* II 6.1.6–8 and Karamanolis, "Plotinus on Quality and Immanent Form."

to the traditional Platonic one, which underlines the role of the traditional Forms. For Plotinus material objects are not at all bundles of qualities or tropes. Apparently, he understands Plato as rejecting tropes (in *Timaeus* and in *Theaetetus* 156–157). After all, Plotinus understands the receptacle as matter, where inhere the *logoi*, the qualities, that make an object such and such, namely of a certain material constitution. This view immediately precludes a bundle theory of material objects, because on such a theory particular properties, tropes, are the fundamental entities that make up an object. For a bundle theorist, objects are derived from or made up of tropes.[39] And this is clearly not how Plotinus understands Plato.

There is something else in Plotinus' position that is important as a reading of Plato's ontology in the *Timaeus*. Material objects are subject to change, but their identities remain stable. Neither matter nor the identity of the object changes; what does change are the properties that make it up. The section on the receptacle teaches us that material particulars and more precisely their geometrical configurations are subject to change and transformation. But this is a feature of bodies that Timaeus makes clear from the beginning of his speech, namely that they are always changing.[40] To the extent that a material body is made up of elements which may be analyzed into geometrical Forms, it is subject to change exactly to the extent that is made up of them, since these Forms can be divided and recomposed (*Tim.* 56c–57c).

4 Conclusion

I have tried to show that, in the *Timaeus*, Plato does, in fact, revise and modify his ontology concerning the coming into being of material objects, but that this revision complements rather than replaces his earlier accounts, including the first part of the *Timaeus*, in which intelligible Forms play an essential causal role in the coming into being of material entities. In the section on the receptacle, Plato aims to give an account of the emergence of properties in material objects, an account that was missing from his earlier ontology, which he now deems indispensable, given that he is engaged with explaining the *genesis* of the material world. According to that account, material objects, to the extent that they are material, have certain properties pertaining to their specific material constitution. These properties, he tells us, are the result of the instantiation and the inherence of images of forms or geometrical Forms

---

39 See Schaffer, "Individuation of Tropes," 247–249.
40 *gignomenon, gignomena*, *Tim.* 28a3–4, 28c1.

in the receptacle. To the extent that this is the case, material objects are subject to change, since geometrical Forms are also subject to change. Yet material objects are not merely bundles or aggregates of such properties; rather, they are constituted by the traditional Forms, which now appear to have a richer causal role. They not only account for the identity of a material body, but they also account for the arrangement and order of the geometrical Forms in the receptacle and thus for the properties pertaining to the specific material constitution of a certain object. It is the traditional Forms that guide the setting up of the geometrical Forms to the extent that the latter account for properties pertaining to the material constitution of a body, yet such a body is of a certain kind (man or tree, for instance), and its specific material constitution is determined by its identity, that is, the traditional, essential Form. The human body, for instance, has the constellation of properties dictated by the Form of man, and similar is the case with any other material object, animate or inanimate; the Form is responsible for the properties associated with the specific material constitution that pertains to a certain thing.[41] On that scenario, the role of intelligence remains prior and ontologically superior to that of necessity. This, I suggest, is confirmed by Plotinus' own theory of the constitution of material objects.

Works Cited

Bacon, John. "Tropes." *The Stanford Encyclopedia of Philosophy*. Edited by Edward Zalta. 1997. Revised edition Winter 2011.
Broadie, Sarah. *Nature and Divinity in Plato's* Timaeus, Cambridge 2012.
Buckels, Christopher. "Making Room for Particulars: Plato's Receptacle as Space not Substratum." *Apeiron*, 49 (2016): 303–328.
Buckels, Christopher. "Triangles, Tropes, and ta toiauta: A Platonic Trope Theory." *Plato Journal*, 18 (2018): 9–24.
Burnyeat, Myles. *The* Theaetetus *of Plato*. Translation by M. J. Levett, Indianapolis 1990
Cherniss, Harold. "A much misread passage of the *Timaeus* (*Timaeus* 49C7–50B5)." *The American Journal of Philology* 75 (1954): 113–130.
Cherniss, Harold. "*Timaeus* 38A8–B5." *The Journal of Hellenic Studies* 77 (1957): 17–23.

---

41 It remains unclear whether other properties attend governing Forms, such as the property of being grammatical attending the Form of man. Plato focuses only on the properties pertaining to the material constitution of material objects here. I would like to thank Philip Horky for raising this issue.

Chiaradonna, Riccardo. "Plotinus on Sensible Particulars and Individual Essences". In *Individuality in Late Antiquity*, Edited by Alexis Torrance and Johannes Zachuber, Farnham: Ashgate, 2014, 47–61

Cornford, Francis. *Plato's Cosmology: The* Timaeus *of Plato*. Indianapolis: Hackett, 1957.

Denyer, Nicholas. "Plato's Theory of Stuffs." *Philosophy* 58 (1983): 315–327.

Harte, Verity. "The Receptacle and the Primary Bodies: Something or Nothing." In *One Book, The Whole Universe: Plato's* Timaeus *Today*. Edited by Richard Mohr and Barbara Sattler. Las Vegas: Parmenides Publishing, 2010, 131–140.

Johansen, Thomas. *Plato's Natural Philosophy*. Cambridge: Cambridge University Press, 2004.

Kalligas, Paul. "The Structure of Appearances: Plotinus on the Constitution of Sensible Objects." *The Philosophical Quarterly* 61 (2011): 762–782.

Karamanolis, George. "Plotinus on Quality and Immanent Form." In *Physics and Philosophy of Nature in Greek Neoplatonism*. Edited by Riccardo Chiaradonna. Leiden: Brill, 2009, 79–100.

Lee, Edward N. "On the Metaphysics of the Image in Plato's *Timaeus*." *The Monist* 50 (1966): 341–368.

Lee, Edward N. "On Plato's *Timaeus* 49D4–E7." *The American Journal of Philology* 88 (1967): 1–28.

Miller, Dana. *The Third Kind in Plato's* Timaeus. Göttingen: Vandenhoeck & Ruprecht, 2003.

Mohr, Richard. "Image, Space and Flux in Plato's *Timaeus*." *Phoenix* 34 (1980): 138–152.

Politis, Vasilis. "The argument for the reality of change and changelessness in Plato's *Sophist* (248e7–249d5)." In *New Essays on Plato*. Edited by Fritz-Gregor Hermann. Swansea: Classical Press of Wales, 2006, 149–175.

Schaffer, Jonathan. "The Individuation of Tropes." *Australasian Journal of Philosophy* 79 (2001): 247–257.

Silverman, Allan. "Timaean Particulars." *The Classical Quarterly* 42 (1992): 87–113.

Silverman, Allan. *The Dialectic of Essence*. Princeton: Princeton University Press, 2002.

Simons, Peter. "Particulars in Particular Clothing: Three Trope Theories of Substance." *Philosophy and Phaenomenological Research* 54 (1994): 553–575.

Ulacco, Angela. "Die präkosmische Bewegung in Platons *Timaios*: ἴχνη, χώρα und Ideen." In *Platon und die Physis*. Edited by Dietmar Koch, Irmgard Männlein-Robert and Neils Weidmann. Tübingen: Mohr Sieback, 2019, 185–202.

Zeyl, Donald. "Plato and Talk of a World in Flux: *Timaeus* 49a6–50b5." *Harvard Studies in Classical Philology* 79 (1975): 125–148.

Zeyl, Donald. *Plato: Timaeus*. Indianapolis: Hackett, 2000.

Matter Doesn't Matter: On the Status of Bodies in the *Timaeus* (30a–32b and 53c–61c)

Gerd Van Riel

Abstract

Many, if not most, commentators assume that Plato's ontology comprises a notion of matter, which, in some way or other, is thought to be connected with the receptacle of the *Timaeus*, or with the elementary triangles that make up the four elements. Indeed, after Aristotle's critique, the Platonists have near always been pointing out that Plato did have a valid alternative to Aristotle's conception of matter. Yet a careful analysis of Plato's works reveals that he does not have any concept of "matter", but that in explaining the order of the cosmos, he is referring to the existence of bodies, without, for that matter, further analyzing their material component.

Keywords

Plato – *Timaeus* – matter – receptacle – elementary triangles – body – geometric atomism

It takes little more than a quick look at the tenth book of the *Laws* to understand that Plato is an anti-materialist: he reacts against the natural philosophers (Presocratics and contemporaries) who explain the world and the order of the cosmos as the result of a self-development of the corporeal realm. The whole discussion against the atheists in *Laws* X is intended to make this point. The materialistic adversaries are described as follows:

> *Ath.* The upholder of this doctrine runs the risk of conceiving of fire and water, earth and air as the first things in the universe, and of using the name of "nature" as referring to those things, whereas the soul is derived from them at a later stage. And he does not just "run the risk" of doing so, but in his argument he explicitly asserts this.[1]

---

1   *Laws* X 891c1–5: κινδυνεύει γὰρ ὁ λέγων ταῦτα πῦρ καὶ ὕδωρ καὶ γῆν καὶ ἀέρα πρῶτα ἡγεῖσθαι τῶν πάντων εἶναι, καὶ τὴν φύσιν ὀνομάζειν ταῦτα αὐτά, ψυχὴν δὲ ἐκ τούτων ὕστερον. ἔοικεν δὲ οὐ

And after an analysis of how motion comes to be in the universe, the interlocutors reach the conclusion that soul must be prior to body:

> *Ath.* So our statement was correct, authoritative, entirely truthful and utterly complete, when we said that soul is prior to body, and that body came later and takes second place. Soul is the leader, and body its natural follower.—*Clin.* That is indeed absolutely true.—*Ath.* We have kept in mind, haven't we, our earlier admission that if soul were shown to be older than body, the things belonging to the soul would also be older than the bodily things?—*Clin.* Certainly.—*Ath.* So habits, customs, will, calculation, right opinion, diligence and memory will be produced prior to material length, breadth, depth and strength, as soul is prior to body.—*Clin.* Unavoidably.[2]

Within soul, the intellect takes pride of place as that which sets things in order:

> *Ath.* "If, my fine fellow," we should say [in reply to the question], "the whole course and movement of the heavens and all that is in them have a nature similar to the motion and revolution and calculation of intellect (*nous*), and proceed in a corresponding fashion, then clearly we have to admit that it is the best kind of soul that cares for the entire universe and directs it along the best path."[3]

All of this is then used as an invective against those who deny the existence of the gods. For if the heavens and all that is in them are ruled by soul (which is endowed with intellect), then the gods must certainly exist. I have argued

---

κινδυνεύειν ἀλλὰ ὄντως σημαίνειν ταῦτα ἡμῖν τῷ λόγῳ. Translation taken from Saunders, *Plato: The Laws*. Thoroughly modified.

2 *Laws* x 896b10–d4: ΑΘ. Ὀρθῶς ἄρα καὶ κυρίως ἀληθέστατά τε καὶ τελεώτατα εἰρηκότες ἂν εἶμεν ψυχὴν μὲν προτέραν γεγονέναι σώματος ἡμῖν, σῶμα δὲ δεύτερόν τε καὶ ὕστερον, ψυχῆς ἀρχούσης, ἀρχόμενον κατὰ φύσιν.—ΚΛ. Ἀληθέστατα μὲν οὖν.—ΑΘ. Μεμνήμεθά γε μὴν ὁμολογήσαντες ἐν τοῖς πρόσθεν ὡς, εἰ ψυχὴ φανείη πρεσβυτέρα σώματος οὖσα, καὶ τὰ ψυχῆς τῶν τοῦ σώματος ἔσοιτο πρεσβύτερα.—ΚΛ. Πάνυ μὲν οὖν.—ΑΘ. Τρόποι δὲ καὶ ἤθη καὶ βουλήσεις καὶ λογισμοὶ καὶ δόξαι ἀληθεῖς ἐπιμέλειαί τε καὶ μνῆμαι πρότερα μήκους σωμάτων καὶ πλάτους καὶ βάθους καὶ ῥώμης εἴη γεγονότα ἄν, εἴπερ καὶ ψυχὴ σώματος.—ΚΛ. Ἀνάγκη. Translation taken from Saunders, *Laws*. Thoroughly modified.

3 *Laws* x 897c4–9: ΑΘ. Εἰ μέν, ὦ θαυμάσιε, φῶμεν, ἡ σύμπασα οὐρανοῦ ὁδὸς ἅμα καὶ φορὰ καὶ τῶν ἐν αὐτῷ ὄντων ἁπάντων νοῦ κινήσει καὶ περιφορᾷ καὶ λογισμοῖς ὁμοίαν φύσιν ἔχει καὶ συγγενῶς ἔρχεται, δῆλον ὡς τὴν ἀρίστην ψυχὴν φατέον ἐπιμελεῖσθαι τοῦ κόσμου παντὸς καὶ ἄγειν αὐτὸν τὴν τοιαύτην ὁδὸν ἐκείνην. Translation taken from Saunders, *Laws*. Lightly modified.

elsewhere how this conclusion can be drawn from these premises.[4] For present purposes, however, we should concentrate on Plato's obviously anti-materialistic standpoint. Anti-materialism is, of course, a modern term, but it is worthwhile to raise the question of what it is exactly that Plato is arguing against. In the second text, I admit, I have modified Trevor Saunders' translation, who translated *sōma* on each occasion as "matter." This is incorrect, surely, and it is symptomatic of a reading that—without further ado—imposes onto Plato some basic metaphysical and ontological concepts that we just take for granted. But we must accept the possibility that Plato's philosophical toolkit was less extensive than ours, and look for an unbiased answer to questions such as: What does Plato talk about when he opposes soul to body? What kind of materialism is he arguing against? and—most importantly—does he have a concept of "matter" at all? I believe the answer to the latter question has to be negative, for reasons I will explain.

An age-old view of Platonic philosophy has it that Plato's receptacle is in fact his account of matter. The Middle and Neo-Platonists were eager to prefer Plato's *Timaeus* to Aristotle's *Physics* (and to reject Aristotle's objections against the *Timaeus* expressed in *Physics* IV and in *De caelo*), and argued that the material substrate existed at different levels, the first of which was the recalcitrant receptacle (fully undetermined and formless matter), to be gradually taken up in the Demiurgic design of order. The Aristotelian hylomorphic constellation of matter and form was thus seen as one of the stages, wherein the strictly formless matter had already been subjected to a number of formal determinations. In an Aristotelian vein, the receptacle became the substrate of formation, which differed from Aristotelian prime matter in the sense that the latter was entirely passive and receptive, whereas the difficult and stubborn nature of the receptacle imposed certain burdens and limitations on the imposition of form.[5]

Yet here again, we see later authors adjusting their interpretation of Plato to the philosophical discussions of their days. Many centuries later, it still is not clear if the receptacle has anything to do with matter in Plato's worldview; it might also be referring to his concept of "place" in ways that are not yet fully understood, or to neither matter nor place.[6] And if the receptacle is not matter,

---

4 Cf. Van Riel, *Plato's Gods*, 95–103.
5 See Van Riel, "Proclus on Matter and Physical Necessity," for Proclus; Van Riel, "Damascius on matter," for Damascius.
6 See Miller, *The Third Kind in Plato's* Timaeus, 21–32 for a survey of the different interpretation of *chōra*. See also Horn, Müller and Söder (eds.), *Handbuch*, 223–224, where *chōra* is identified as Aristotelian matter ("es handelt sich hier allenfalls um einen Stoff, der ebenso bestimmungslos ist wie die *prima materia* des Aristoteles"), which, in Plato's case, is also

then one finds it elsewhere, namely, in the elementary triangles that make up the four elements.[7] But maybe we should raise the question in a different way: why would we *have to* look for matter in Plato? Would it make us unhappy if we were to conclude that Plato has nothing to say about matter? Or put in a more relevant way, would it make Plato a lesser philosopher, inferior to Aristotle, if he had no clear view on the role of a material substrate in the cosmos? Does matter really matter?

If we want to answer these questions in a meaningful way, we should turn to Plato's own terms and concepts, and try to understand what the questions were to which they were designed to give a reply. The passages from *Laws* x with which we started (and which belong roughly to the same period of Plato's writings as the *Timaeus*) provide important clues. The main argument of the *Timaeus* sets out to prove that soul is more important than body, and that the cosmos is governed by soul endowed with intellect. If body were to exist on its own, it would be subject to mere chance, and the cosmos would never be a cosmos. What is at stake, then, is a clear-cut explanation of how this intelligent design works, and how it operates on body. This message can well be upheld without elaborating on the material component of body, and it may well be the case that Plato never even felt the need to spell out what this material component was, as it was not important from his point of view.

1 The Perceptibility of the Receptacle

From the very beginning of Timaeus' cosmogony, the thing in which the God is to bring order is referred to as "all that was visible":

> The god wanted everything to be good and nothing to be bad so far as that was possible, and so he took over all that was visible—not at rest but in discordant and disorderly motion—and brought it from a state of disorder to one of order, because he believed that order was in every way better than disorder.[8]

---

space [= W. Mesch]; *ibid.*, 57, on the disorderly movement ("Meist versteht man darunter die Ur-Materie") [= J. Söder].

7   *Tim.* 53c–56c.

8   *Tim.* 30a2–6: βουληθεὶς γὰρ ὁ θεὸς ἀγαθὰ μὲν πάντα, φλαῦρον δὲ μηδὲν εἶναι κατὰ δύναμιν, οὕτω δὴ πᾶν ὅσον ἦν ὁρατὸν παραλαβὼν οὐχ ἡσυχίαν ἄγον ἀλλὰ κινούμενον πλημμελῶς καὶ ἀτάκτως, εἰς τάξιν αὐτὸ ἤγαγεν ἐκ τῆς ἀταξίας, ἡγησάμενος ἐκεῖνο τούτου πάντως ἄμεινον. See also 30b (τὰ κατὰ φύσιν ὁρατά). All translations are taken from Zeyl, *Plato: Timaeus.*

A few lines further on, this qualification of "visible" is explicitly linked to the corporeal nature of things:

> Now that which comes to be must have bodily form, and be both visible and tangible,[9]

adding that nothing could be visible without the presence of fire:

> but nothing could ever become visible apart from fire, nor tangible without something solid, nor solid without earth.[10]

This means, I take it, that the "material" which the Demiurge was moulding was of a bodily nature, even though at first it was disordered and moving in all directions. Now Timaeus' account notoriously leaves room for discussion, as visibility seems to be the effect of the Demiurge's intervention (ordering the substrate into the elements, with fire as the necessary condition for visibility). This is also stated in the conclusion of this passage:

> Hence the god set water and air between fire and earth, and made them as proportionate to one another as was possible, so that what fire is to air, air is to water, and what air is to water, water is to earth. He then bound them together and thus he constructed the visible and tangible universe.[11]

On the other hand, visibility had been there from the beginning, as indicating that which the God found before him when he first started to work. This contradiction vexed commentators of old.[12] As there seems to be no solution to it, any account will be fallible. But it does not seem too outlandish to suppose that the initial visibility of the receptacle may be linked to the presence of the "traces of the forms," mentioned in Timaeus' account of the role of Necessity as a third kind (from 48e onwards). Here again, visibility is introduced as belonging to

---

9   *Tim.* 31b3–4: Σωματοειδὲς δὲ δὴ καὶ ὁρατὸν ἁπτόν τε δεῖ τὸ γενόμενον εἶναι.
10 *Tim.* 31b5–6: χωρισθὲν δὲ πυρὸς οὐδὲν ἄν ποτε ὁρατὸν γένοιτο, οὐδὲ ἁπτὸν ἄνευ τινὸς στερεοῦ, στερεὸν δὲ οὐκ ἄνευ γῆς.
11 *Tim.* 32b3–8: οὕτω δὴ πυρός τε καὶ γῆς ὕδωρ ἀέρα τε ὁ θεὸς ἐν μέσῳ θείς, καὶ πρὸς ἄλληλα καθ' ὅσον ἦν δυνατὸν ἀνὰ τὸν αὐτὸν λόγον ἀπεργασάμενος, ὅτιπερ πῦρ πρὸς ἀέρα, τοῦτο ἀέρα πρὸς ὕδωρ, καὶ ὅτι ἀὴρ πρὸς ὕδωρ, ὕδωρ πρὸς γῆν, συνέδησεν καὶ συνεστήσατο οὐρανὸν ὁρατὸν καὶ ἁπτόν.
12 Proclus, for one, sees visibility as the effect of the Demiurge's intervention, reading πᾶν ὅσον ἦν ὁρατὸν at 30a as an anticipation: *In Tim.* I 383.1–22.

the second kind, i.e. the sensible world ("the second, an imitation of the model, something that possesses becoming and is visible").[13] Yet the discussion of how the four elements are present in the third kind contains some interesting observations: the receptacle is subject to a permanent flux of transformations, whereby earth, water, fire and air are never present as such; the ever-moving qualities of the receptacle do not allow one to "put one's finger" on one specific quality as "this" (τόδε or τοῦτο, 49d–e). The only definite thing we can point at is the substrate in which these transformations take place. In itself, this receptacle is invisible and formless (ἀνόρατον εἶδός τι καὶ ἄμορφον, 51a7). Hence Timaeus' repeated question about how the existence of the four elements is to be conceived—a question which he now reformulates as follows: do fire and the other elements exist in themselves (ἆρα ἔστιν τι πῦρ αὐτὸ ἐφ' ἑαυτοῦ, 51b7–8), i.e. as corresponding to intelligible forms (see 51d4–5)? The receptacle does not seem to bear these elements in their pure form, as it is always shaken, like a winnowing basket, at one moment being fluid, then burning, then taking the shape of air or earth, in an unstable state of ongoing transformations. It is in this context that the "traces of the forms" are discussed:

> Indeed, it is a fact that before this took place the four kinds all lacked proportion and measure, and at the time the ordering of the universe was undertaken, fire, water, earth and air initially possessed certain traces of what they are now. They were indeed in the condition one would expect thoroughly god-forsaken things to be in. So, finding them in this natural condition, the first thing the god then did was to give them their distinctive shapes, using forms and numbers.[14]

I think the status of these "traces" is often misunderstood, as if the qualities they represent were created somehow by the Demiurge. However, the problem is not that the qualities of the four elements were not present before the Demiurgic intervention, but rather that their perpetual flux did not allow there to be fixed entities like the elements. For indeed the presence of the qualities in the receptacle before the Demiurge's intervention does not seem to be in doubt: the receptacle, though quality-less on its own, does undergo the flux of qualities. The problem at issue is the unstable nature of the flux, and the lack

---

13   *Tim.* 48e6–49a1: μίμημα δὲ παραδείγματος δεύτερον, γένεσιν ἔχον καὶ ὁρατόν.
14   *Tim.* 53a7–b5: καὶ τὸ μὲν δὴ πρὸ τούτου πάντα ταῦτ' εἶχεν ἀλόγως καὶ ἀμέτρως· ὅτε δ' ἐπεχειρεῖτο κοσμεῖσθαι τὸ πᾶν, πῦρ πρῶτον καὶ ὕδωρ καὶ γῆν καὶ ἀέρα, ἴχνη μὲν ἔχοντα αὐτῶν ἄττα, παντάπασί γε μὴν διακείμενα ὥσπερ εἰκὸς ἔχειν ἅπαν ὅταν ἀπῇ τινος θεός, οὕτω δὴ τότε πεφυκότα ταῦτα πρῶτον διεσχηματίσατο εἴδεσί τε καὶ ἀριθμοῖς.

of order that would allow one to recognize the presence of fire, water, earth, and air in it, and yes, even the recognition of "motion" in this pre-cosmic state would presuppose the existence of separate entities.[15] All of this is what the Demiurge offers. So, strictly speaking, it is absolutely correct to say that "there was no fire, water, etc. in the receptacle." But the receptacle *was* burning, watery, earthy and airy before the ordering began. I take this to mean that the qualities of the four elements were there, before the Demiurge's intervention; yet they were floating around, and nothing determinate or stable came out of this.[16] The Demiurge set things straight, so as to "give those elements their distinctive shapes, using forms and numbers." Now, at last, fire, etc. can be recognized as such, and as participating in the intelligible forms, whence they also get a stable and permanent nature.

This may, then, be the reason why the "thing" that the Demiurge found before him was called "all that was visible": it would have been a chaotic whirl in which you could identify nothing steady: one moment you would see something that looks like fire, but before you realized this, it would have become something else already. But it could well be described as "visible."

If this is true, then we should say that even in its pre-ordered state, the whirling chaos would be corporeal (as corporeality is explicitly linked to visibility), again with the qualification that the moment you recognize something like a body in it, it will have become different already. Whatever else the receptacle may be, it does not look like it is the "matter" out of which the bodies are composed. It might be the "place" in which bodies occur, but I am more than happy to leave open the question of what this "place" might be. My question here does not concern the status of the receptacle as such, but rather the reverse: if there is matter in the *Timaeus*, would the receptacle then be a good candidate to locate it in? And despite the incongruities Plato leaves open, I think we can conclude that the receptacle is not the material component of the universe (in the sense of "prime matter"), but that it is of a bodily nature, i.e. something in which visible bodies occur under the guise of floating constellations of qualities.

---

15   Cf. Johansen, *Plato's Natural Philosophy: A Study of the* Timaeus–Critias, 96–97.
16   One might even go as far as to assume that these floating qualities may have come together in an "elemental" combination, i.e. that they became fire, or earth, water, or air for a short and unstable moment. That may explain how the receptacle became fiery or "burning": it would, by mere accident, have the aspect of what the Demiurge was to install in an ordered and permanent way as the element of fire.

2 Plato's Geometric Atomism

If we can take for granted that the receptacle is of a corporeal nature (and not material, in the sense of prime matter), we ought to look further down in Timaeus' account to find clues about where Plato might discuss matter. The place to be is then certainly the account of the composition of the elements out of elementary triangles at *Tim.* 53c–61c. This theory has come to be referred to as "Geometric Atomism," meaning that the elementary triangles are the indivisible atoms, the composition of which constitutes the four elements as specific solids, out of which the entire bodily world is made.[17]

Our question should then be, are those triangles Plato's version of "matter"? Do they correspond—*mutatis mutandis*—to Democritus' atoms in that sense, that they are the bulk or mass out of which a body is composed? That is at least what Aristotle suggests in his *De generatione et corruptione*, comparing Plato's planes to Democritus' solids.[18] Aristotle's criticism of Plato's theory is elaborated in his *De caelo*, which is the oldest extant text that confronts Plato with the shortcomings of his alleged theory of matter. At the end of the third book, Aristotle raises a number of objections (amounting to 15 in total, on Simplicius' count) against Plato's theory of the elements.[19] Most of them deal with specific points about specific elements. Some, however, have a more general bearing. The fourth one in particular is important for our present purposes:

> Further, those who would hold these views must needs suppose that generation does not start from a body. For what is generated out of planes cannot be said to have been generated from a body.
> tr. J. L. Stocks[20]

Aristotle here opposes the two-dimensional nature of the planes to the three-dimensional structure of the body, stating that if things are generated from a plane, then the generation of bodies comes from something incorporeal,

---

17 The relation between this part of the dialogue and the discussion of the receptacle is not clear; see, for an evaluation of possible positions, Miller, *Third Kind*, 186–195.

18 See, e.g., Aristotle, *De gen. et corr.* I 2, 315b24–32; also I 8, 325b25–34.

19 For a full presentation of the objections and the Neoplatonic reactions against them, see Mueller, "Aristotelian Objections and post-Aristotelian Responses to Plato's Elemental Theory."

20 Aristotle, *De caelo* III 8, 306a23–26: "Ἔτι δ' ἀνάγκη τοῖς ταῦτα λέγουσιν οὐκ ἐκ σώματος ποιεῖν γένεσιν· ὅταν γὰρ ἐξ ἐπιπέδων γένηται, οὐκ ἐκ σώματος ἔσται γεγονός. All translations taken from Stocks, *On the Heavens*. Cf. *De gen. et corr.* I 2, 316a3–4: "Nothing except solids results from putting planes together" (οὐδὲν γὰρ γίνεται πλὴν στερεὰ συντιθεμένων [*sc.* ἐπιπέδων]).

which is obviously seen as absurd.[21] In the general conclusion of book three, Aristotle summarizes his argument as follows:

> From what has been said it is clear that the difference of the elements does not depend upon their shape.[22]

This conclusion takes up the question in the terms in which it was stated at the beginning of the book, where Aristotle pointed out that:

> a theory which composes every body of planes is, as is seen at glace, in many respects in plain contradiction with mathematics.[23]

He substantiates this claim, among others, by the argument that, in this theory, the parts of the physical solids are not of the same kind as the whole: planes consist of lines and lines of points (III 1, 299a5–10); moreover, according to him, it would be impossible that planes that have no weight would, by their composition, bring forth things that have weight (III 1, 299a 25–b23).

All of these arguments rely on the implicit view that Plato's geometric atomism is a theory of matter, and that, in this theory, Plato would explain the existence of solidity or mass of bodies in an impossible way, by reducing it to the existence of two-dimensional planes. Aristotle clearly understands the planes and solids as intended, but failed material components of bodies.

Aristotle certainly was not the only one to read Plato's atomism as a theory of matter. Present-day adherents of this interpretation include, for instance, Dana Miller. Ancient Platonic commentators of Aristotle, like Philoponus, would also read Plato's atomism in this way, as in the following passage:

> Plato was not so weak at geometry as to think that body could be dissolved into surfaces, rather he was talking of physical surfaces, i.e. corporeal ones, which had depth as well. And clearly things like this also

---

21   The Neoplatonists, Proclus and Simplicius alike, would reply that Plato's solids have depth, and hence, that he wanted them to be corporeal (Simplicius, *In De caelo* 648.19–22, who is relying on Proclus; cf. Mueller, "Objections," 130). That is to say (as we have seen above), they agree with Aristotle's basic premise, that Plato is talking about physical things, or material components, not about mathematical solids.

22   *De caelo* III 8, 307b18–20: Ὅτι μὲν οὖν οὐ τοῖς σχήμασι διαφέρει τὰ στοιχεῖα, φανερὸν ἐκ τῶν εἰρημένων.

23   Aristotle, *De caelo* III 1, 299a1–5: τοῖς δὲ τοῦτον τὸν τρόπον λέγουσι καὶ πάντα τὰ σώματα συνιστᾶσιν ἐξ ἐπιπέδων ὅσα μὲν ἄλλα συμβαίνει λέγειν ὑπεναντία τοῖς μαθήμασιν, ἐπιπολῆς ἰδεῖν.

have matter in them; so in Plato's view the things that come to be are not without matter.[24]

But we should not be too keen to follow Plato's early interpreters as representing the right reading. In fact, it might well be the case that they were reading him on their own terms, i.e. that they were imposing a specific view on Plato, which they then tried to refute or rescue. Aristotle would surely be propagating his own view of matter as the better one, whilst reading into the *Timaeus* a theory of matter that was bound to be insufficient. And Philoponus would enter the grounds on Aristotle's conditions, in an endeavour to show how Plato's theory of matter was stronger than Aristotle had figured. But maybe we have to de-Aristotelianize the interpretation of Plato, and we should not too easily condone the views Aristotle wants to impose on his old tutor.

What I want to argue here, specifically, is that the triangles and their combinations do not in fact constitute a theory of matter. In order to make this claim, we need to have a careful look at how Plato characterizes the triangles. First of all, whatever else they may be, Plato leaves no doubt about these triangles' being two-dimensional, whilst their combination produces bodies having depth (*bathos*):

> First of all, everyone knows, I'm sure, that fire, earth, water and air are bodies. Now everything that has bodily form also has depth. Depth, moreover, is of necessity comprehended within surface, and any surface bounded by straight lines is composed of triangles.[25]

The triangles' two-dimensionality is implied here, not argued for, but it is clear that a body's depth depends on the combination of flat planes. The triangles (subdivided into the isosceles right-angled triangle and the scalene right-angled one) are thus seen as the basic constituents of any body, which allows Timaeus to say that "this" (i.e. the fact that any body can be seen as composed from these two kinds of triangles) is "the originating principle of fire and of the other bodies" (53d4–5). The triangles can therefore be described as

---

24   Philoponus, *In De gen. et corr.* 329a15 ff., p. 210.12–16: εἰδέναι δὲ χρὴ ὅτι οὐχ οὕτως ἀγεωμέτρητος ἦν ὁ Πλάτων, ὡς οἴεσθαι τὸ σῶμα εἰς ἐπίπεδα διαλύεσθαι, ἀλλ' ἐπίπεδα ἔφασκεν ἐκεῖνος φυσικά, δηλονότι σωματικά, τὰ καὶ βάθος ἔχοντα· τὰ δὲ τοιαῦτα δηλονότι ἐν αὑτοῖς καὶ τὴν ὕλην ἔχει θεωρουμένην. ὥστε οὐκ ἄνευ ὕλης κατὰ Πλάτωνα τὰ γινόμενα. Translation taken from Williams, *Philoponus*.

25   *Tim.* 53c4–8: Πρῶτον μὲν δὴ πῦρ καὶ γῆ καὶ ὕδωρ καὶ ἀὴρ ὅτι σώματά ἐστι, δῆλόν που καὶ παντί· τὸ δὲ τοῦ σώματος εἶδος πᾶν καὶ βάθος ἔχει. τὸ δὲ βάθος αὖ πᾶσα ἀνάγκη τὴν ἐπίπεδον περιειληφέναι φύσιν· ἡ δὲ ὀρθὴ τῆς ἐπιπέδου βάσεως ἐκ τριγώνων συνέστηκεν.

the "elementary constituents" or "elements" (*stoicheia*),[26] not to be confused with the "four elements," which are obviously the result of the combinations of these triangles. The combinations of the triangles (i.e. the four elements) are described as visible only when they are numerous enough to be seen:

> Now we must think of all these bodies as being so small that due to their small size none of them, whatever their kind, is visible to us individually. When, however, a large number of them are clustered together, we do see them in bulk.[27]

The aspect of visibility is now refined, as it only occurs when there are enough particles of an element. For our purposes, though, the main point is that, *a fortiori*, the triangles are invisible. They are, moreover, moving around, i.e. they change place, but there is no consensus about the triangles themselves being unchangeable.[28] Plato does refer to the triangles as not always being perfect, and as being susceptible to wear.[29]

In view of the triangles' being "elements," some have upheld that they must be material components, that is, that they have mass or extension.[30] Yet there is no textual evidence at all to build this claim on, and I don't believe anyone still subscribes to it.

If, then, the two-dimensional triangles have no extension, how about the solids that are constituted by their combination? Shouldn't we say that the three-dimensionality is, ultimately, the bulk we were looking for in the constitution of the universe? In a way that would remain to be explained, the putting together of a number of two-dimensional triangles would lead to the existence of extended things, whereby flat surfaces suddenly yield not only depth, but also bulk. And indeed, depth is what Plato refers to in this context, as we have seen (53c). Moreover, as we saw, this is exactly the way in which Aristotle read the *Timaeus*, as making an illegitimate jump from flat planes to things that have bulk.

---

26 E.g., *Tim.* 54d6, 55a8, 55b4, 57c9, 61a7.

27 *Tim.* 56b7–c3: πάντα οὖν δὴ ταῦτα δεῖ διανοεῖσθαι σμικρὰ οὕτως, ὡς καθ' ἓν ἕκαστον μὲν τοῦ γένους ἑκάστου διὰ σμικρότητα οὐδὲν ὁρώμενον ὑφ' ἡμῶν, συναθροισθέντων δὲ πολλῶν τοὺς ὄγκους αὐτῶν ὁρᾶσθαι.

28 *Pro* the changelessness of the triangles: Johansen, *Plato's Natural Philosophy*, 126; *contra*: Miller, *Third Kind*, 171–172.

29 *Tim.* 73b6; 81c6–d1; 82d6–7; 89c1–4; see Opsomer, "In Defence of Geometric Atomism : Explaining Elemental Properties," 151–152.

30 Martin, *Études sur le* Timée *de Platon*, II 2.241 (cf. Miller, *Third Kind*, 176). Also some ancient Platonists upheld this idea (see Simplicius, *In De caelo* 646.21–24; cf. Miller *Third Kind*, 176–177).

But this reading misses the most important point of Plato's account. Nearly everybody, including Aristotle, agrees that Plato's analysis is a *mathematical* one, but very often—as in Aristotle's case—the consequences of this fact are not properly acknowledged. The mathematical analysis of three-dimensionality (Plato's "depth") does not primarily refer to bulk or mass (or "weight", as Aristotle summarizes it) out of which a physical thing is made. To be sure, Plato does use a constructivist language to explain how solids come to be: the key word of the entire discussion of the composition of the four kinds of polyeders (53c–55c) is the verb *synistamai*,[31] alternated with forms of *sympēgnymi*[32] and *synarmottō*.[33] That does not mean, however, that the two-dimensional triangles are some kind of material constituent of stereometric bodies. *Synistamai* can obviously refer to a physical construct,[34] but it is used very commonly in mathematical contexts to refer to the construal of figures and solids.[35] I believe that is the meaning that applies here.

On the other hand, the four elements, which come into existence as combinations of the triangles, are explicitly referred to as bodies (*Tim.* 53c, quoted above). That would suggest that, after all, their corporeal existence as physical things depends on the presence of the triangles. But that does not *have to* be our reading. Plato in fact never discusses the contents of the four elements, he only explains how their specific quality is based on the specific construction of their nature: the tetrahedron (constituting fire), the octahedron (air), the icosahedron (water), and the cube (earth).[36] This means that the quality (and the possibility to transform into another element) is entirely dependent on the *structure* of the solid, not on its materiality. For indeed, the solid bodies, *sterea*, that come out of the combination of the triangles, are set together as mathematical structures, not as physical things, just like present-day mathematicians and geometricians are dealing with (ideal) structures, abstracted from any material existence. And that would not be an anachronistic comparison, for it would also fit with Plato's own view on the existence of mathematical objects: whatever they may be, they are certainly non-physical—and if indeed the triangles

---

31 συνέστηκεν (53c), συστήσεται (54c), συνιστάμενον (54d and 55b), συνίσταται (55a), συστάντων (55a).
32 συμπαγέντων (55a–b), συμπαγέντα (55c).
33 συναρμόσασθαι (53e), συναρμοσθέν (54c).
34 Cf. Miller, *Third Kind*, 172: "[Plato] treats the triangles as though they were bricks used in building a wall."
35 See, among many other examples, Archimedes, *Stomachion* III 71.18; Euclid, *Elem.* III dem. 32.13. Also Ps.-Aristotle, *De lineis insecabilibus* 970a9, and the sophist Antiphon, DK B 13.42.
36 *Tim.* 54d–56a.

and solids are Platonic mathematical objects, they would be intelligible, i.e., in the ontology of the *Timaeus*, they would belong to the first kind, not to the second (the sensible world) and certainly not to the third one (the receptacle). As we have seen before, the existence of physical or sensible things requires the existence of bodies that are solid (i.e. three-dimensional) and visible. The quality of visibility would then, logically, not apply to these two-dimensional triangles. Yet, just as mathematicians do, the two-dimensional triangles are referred to *as if* they were physical objects. That is not just a specific feature of Timaeus' "likely myth": any mathematical language is bound to describe its objects in terms of physical existence. But a mathematical description always remains void of material content—meaning, for instance, that a description of how polyeders are composed of two-dimensional triangles indicates how the surfaces of these solids are constructed; it does not tell us what is inside them. In fact, when looked at from this perspective, the Platonic polyeders look like glass models or, if you wish, skeletons of those volumes, whereby the sides and surfaces have no mass. The solids do cover (mathematicians would say: "span") a certain volume, without for that matter taking into account what is inside the volume. This abstraction of a reference to the physical state of things is constitutive of mathematics, and I believe this is exactly what Plato is doing here.[37] We never find any reference to an underlying mass that is structured by those figures, even though there is some sort of corporeal existence that predates the ordering by the Demiurge. In that sense, the statement that the triangles "construct" the bodies has to be taken in a specifically mathematical sense: they do indeed determine how things are constructed, but they are not the material out of which the world is made. To be sure, Plato does speak of bulk, but not in the sense of material mass. At 56c3 (quoted above), he says that the four elements as bodies can only be seen when a large number of them is clustered together, and we see them in bulk. Yet the *onkos* referred to is not the "bulk" of the material contents of the polyhedra, but the amount of polyhedra needed in order to have a visible element. Again, at 54d1–3 Plato seems to be referring to the solids' contents:

> When numerous small bodies are fragmented into their triangles, these triangles may well combine to make up some single massive body belonging to another kind.[38]

---

37 Cf. Vitrac, "Les mathématiques dans le *Timée* de Platon: le point de vue d'un historien des sciences," 22.

38 *Tim*.54c8–d2: καὶ σμικρὰ ὅταν αὖ πολλὰ κατὰ τὰ τρίγωνα διασπαρῇ, γενόμενος εἷς ἀριθμὸς ἑνὸς ὄγκου μέγα ἀποτελέσειεν ἂν ἄλλο εἶδος ἕν.

But, when taken in a mathematical sense, this *onkos* can refer to the volume that is spanned by the surfaces (as is ubiquitous in Archimedes' *De corporibus fluitantibus*) rather than to the mass that fills it, in which case again the polyhedra do not have to be taken as material atoms.

Opponents of this view, like Cornford and Miller,[39] may argue that this interpretation makes the elemental bodies empty solids, and indeed they may have a point (as in my example of the glass containers or the skeleton). But that should not be a problem. The point I want to make is that these polyhedra do not exist on their own as physical bodies. They are the mathematical structures *of bodies*, all of which can be analyzed into the elemental solids and triangles. What I mean is that, again, Plato conceives of the world as existing in bodies, rather than in a material constituent, and that a geometrical analysis of these bodies into planes, surfaces and their combination disregards a material factor. To Plato, the bodies simply exist, and they form the content that is delineated by the elemental geometrical figures. Timaeus' theory thus does not suggest the existence of what Cornford refers to (and rejects) as "empty boxes"—the boxes are, rather, the abstract structures that are recognized in the construction of bodies.

Finally, I want to argue that this "non-material" reading does not have to deal with a number of difficulties and incongruities that emerge from a "material" reading—without obviously claiming that no problems are left. First of all, the transition from two-dimensional surfaces to three-dimensional bodies does not cause any problems, if they are seen as mathematical figures and solids. There is no need any longer to argue for a "bulk" that fills up the solids. Moreover, the problem of empty space vanishes. The acceptance of empty space is seen as necessary for Plato's geometric atomism to work, as had already been argued by Aristotle (in his sixth argument against Plato's elements: *De caelo* III 8, 306b3–9): the triangles as building blocks must move and be combined within an empty space (as Leucippus and Democritus had maintained). But Plato denies that there would be empty space (e.g. *Tim.* 58a4), even though, as Jan Opsomer indicates, "Plato occasionally refers to emptiness (58b3) and gaps between the particles (58b5, 60e5, 61a5, b1, b4)"—which Opsomer interprets as a reference to "transient interstitial voids."[40] That may well work, but I think one avoids the problem altogether by accepting that Plato's analysis of the triangles and polyhedra does not subdivide the world into particles of bulk, but applies a mathematical standard to understand their order. The borders between the lines and triangles are no material surfaces,

---

39   Cornford, *Plato's Cosmology*, 205; Miller, *Third Kind*, 163–195.
40   Opsomer, "Geometric Atomism," 151.

then, or places at which one atom comes into contact with another, but markers of mathematical structures within continuous bodies. Thirdly, one no longer has to cope with the problem of how the material bulk of the receptacle could exist before the Demiurge's intervention, if material bulk is always triangular and hence ordered by the Demiurge. If one leaves out the reference to material bulk, then it makes perfect sense to describe the order of bodies solely in terms of the structures imposed by the Demiurge.

Finally, a purely mathematical reading also allows one to understand the wearing down of the triangles as referred to above. Here, again, translators who do not recognize the mathematical jargon render the most relevant passage in a mistaken way: *Tim.* 81c–d explains how an organism grows old and decays as a result of the influx of external triangles that break up the internal ones. In Zeyl's translation, this passage runs as follows:

> Now when the triangles that constitute the young living thing's food enter its body from the outside and are enveloped within it, the body's own new triangles cut and prevail over these others, which are older and weaker than they are. The living thing is thus nourished by an abundance of like parts, and so made to grow big. But when the roots of the triangles are slackened as a result of numerous conflicts they have waged against numerous adversaries over a long period of time, they are no longer able to cut up the entering food-triangles into conformity with themselves. They are themselves handily destroyed by the invaders from outside. Every living thing, then, goes into decline when it loses this battle, and it suffers what we call 'old age'. Eventually the interlocking bonds of the triangles around the marrow can no longer hold on, and come apart under stress, and when this happens they let the bonds of the soul go.[41]

This translation may leave the inattentive reader with the idea that, indeed, the triangles are destroyed. However, from the description of the final destruction of the body, it becomes clear that the triangles themselves are not destroyed, but that their combinations are dissolved. In that respect, εὐπετῶς διαιρεῖται at

---

41   *Tim.* 81c2–d7: τὰ δὴ περιλαμβανόμενα ἐν αὐτῇ τρίγωνα ἔξωθεν ἐπεισελθόντα, ἐξ ὧν ἂν ᾖ τά τε σιτία καὶ ποτά, τῶν ἑαυτῆς τριγώνων παλαιότερα ὄντα καὶ ἀσθενέστερα καινοῖς ἐπικρατεῖ τέμνουσα, καὶ μέγα ἀπεργάζεται τὸ ζῷον τρέφουσα ἐκ πολλῶν ὁμοίων. ὅταν δ' ἡ ῥίζα τῶν τριγώνων χαλᾷ διὰ τὸ πολλοὺς ἀγῶνας ἐν πολλῷ χρόνῳ πρὸς πολλὰ ἠγωνίσθαι, τὰ μὲν τῆς τροφῆς εἰσιόντα οὐκέτι δύναται τέμνειν εἰς ὁμοιότητα ἑαυτοῖς, αὐτὰ δὲ ὑπὸ τῶν ἔξωθεν ἐπεισιόντων εὐπετῶς διαιρεῖται· φθίνει δὴ πᾶν ζῷον ἐν τούτῳ κρατούμενον, γῆράς τε ὀνομάζεται τὸ πάθος. τέλος δέ, ἐπειδὰν τῶν περὶ τὸν μυελὸν τριγώνων οἱ συναρμοσθέντες μηκέτι ἀντέχωσιν δεσμοὶ τῷ πόνῳ διιστάμενοι, μεθιᾶσιν τοὺς τῆς ψυχῆς αὖ δεσμούς.

d3 does not mean "they are handily destroyed," as Zeyl has it, but rather "they are easily torn apart." But the most important point here is the meaning of ὅταν δ' ἡ ῥίζα τῶν τριγώνων χαλᾷ at 81c6–7. Zeyl translates this as "when the roots of the triangles are slackened," without glossing what these "roots of triangles" may refer to.[42] I think it makes little sense to translate *rhiza* as "root" here. When one takes it in a mathematical sense, however, the phrase suddenly gets a relevant meaning. In mathematics, *rhiza* is the base,[43] in this case, the base of our triangles. The sentence ἡ ῥίζα τῶν τριγώνων χαλᾷ means, then, that the base of the triangles is untied, i.e. that they are cut loose in the joints where they clung together. Hence, the triangles themselves are not destroyed, which would be difficult to maintain if indeed they are mathematical figures, but their combinations do fall apart.

To cut things short, it is much easier to argue that in Plato's account of the construction of bodies, "construction" refers to their "structure," and not to their contents—or, in Aristotelian terms: to their form, not to their matter. Paraphrasing Philoponus, one could say that, indeed, Plato was not so *ageōmetrētos* as to say that bodies are made up from two-dimensional surfaces. But that is not, as Philoponus would have it, because Plato is talking *physikōs* here. It is, rather, because the whole account needs to be taken *mathēmatikōs*, and because the referent is not matter, but the formal structures of the body.

Let us conclude. If Plato were indeed saying that geometric atomism is a theory of matter, then Aristotle is certainly right: lines and figures have no bulk or mass—hence, how could the composition of lines and figures lead to the existence of solid bodies? And, indeed, how could mathematics ground physics in this respect? But Aristotle is approaching Plato with the wrong question: he is looking for a theory of the composition of matter and form, focusing on the material component—and, admittedly, Plato did suggest this, by speaking of the world of generation as the receiver of the forms—but Plato himself is not focusing on a material component. His main point is, as I highlighted at the beginning, that bodies cannot come to be ordered out of themselves, but that soul and intellect are needed to accomplish this. Hence, what he is doing is to analyze the order one finds existing in bodies, and bring it back to mathematical structures brought forth by the intelligent design of the Demiurge.

---

42   W. R. L. Lamb (in the Loeb edition) also translates it as "the roots of the triangles," and adds a footnote saying "i.e. the radical structure of the primary triangles," apparently taking *tōn trigōnōn* as an epexegetical genitive.
43   See, e.g., Theon, *Commentaria in Ptolemaei Syntaxin Mathematicam* 637.20. Cf. Ps.-Timaeus 215.12: ῥίζα πάντων καὶ βάσις τῶν ἄλλων ἁ γᾶ.

The material out of which these bodies are composed, i.e. the bulk or mass, or matter, is not part of the question.[44]

This amounts to saying that Plato does not offer a genuine theory of matter. The existence of a material world is taken for granted, and not explained. The receptacle and the triangles may have been some embryonic conceptualizations of it, but all of the inconsistencies and all of the diverse formulations that elicited so many different interpretations are tokens of the simple fact that Plato did not have a clear view on the matter. But, as I have tried to show, that was not Plato's real concern. Timaeus' entire account is set up to show that the truly important causes of the cosmos are soul and intellect. I hope to have made an argument that this is the state of the art we must accept as Plato's, without imposing on him theories or concepts that have been discovered or elaborated after him, even if they were designed to safeguard him against opposing views. Ultimately, to Plato, matter does not matter.

Works Cited

Broadie, Sarah. *Nature and Divinity in Plato's* Timaeus. Cambridge: Cambridge University Press, 2012.

Cornford, Francis M. *Plato's Cosmology: The* Timaeus *of Plato. Translated with a Running Commentary*. London: Kegan Paul, 1937.

Horn, Christoph, Jörn Müller, and Joachim Söder, eds. *Platon Handbuch. Leben—Werk—Wirkung*. Stuttgart-Weimar: J. B. Metzler, 2009.

Johansen, Thomas K. *Plato's Natural Philosophy: A Study of the* Timaeus–Critias. Cambridge: Cambridge University Press, 2004.

Martin, Thomas Henri. *Études sur le* Timée *de Platon* II. Paris: Ladrange Libraire, 1841.

Miller, Dana R. *The Third Kind in Plato's* Timaeus. (*Hypomnemata*, 145). Göttingen: Vandenhoeck & Ruprecht, 2003.

---

44 One may repeat here Broadie's conclusion on Plato's account of the receptacle: "Some may find it disappointing that Plato's concern is conceptually primitive and unsophisticated by comparison with concerns that might have motivated a more controlled and incisive categorial selection," whilst adding that a greater perspicuity would probably not "have advanced the great project of the *Timaeus*, which is to explain nature while thoroughly respecting the basic principle that the cosmos is as superlatively beautiful and excellent, and therefore as stable and harmonious, as anything in the world of becoming can be." (Broadie, *Nature and Divinity in Plato's* Timaeus, 242). The heart of the matter is, I think, that Plato should be approached starting from the questions which he wanted to answer, and not from the questions later interpreters like Aristotle have imposed on him.

Mueller, Ian. "Aristotelian Objections and post-Aristotelian Responses to Plato's Elemental Theory." In *Neoplatonism and the Philosophy of Nature*. Edited by James Wilberding and Christoph Horn. Oxford: Oxford University Press, 2012, +129–146.

Opsomer, Jan. "In Defence of Geometric Atomism: Explaining Elemental Properties." In *Neoplatonism and the Philosophy of Nature*. Edited by James Wilberding and Christoph Horn. Oxford: Oxford University Press, 2012, 147–173.

Saunders, Trevor. *Plato: The* Laws: *Translated with an Introduction*. Harmondsworth: Penguin Books, 1970.

Stocks, John Leofric. *On the Heavens*. Oxford: Clarendon Press, 1922.

Van Riel, Gerd. "Proclus on Matter and Physical Necessity." In *Physics and Philosophy of Nature in Greek Neoplatonism*. Edited by Riccardo Chiaradonna and Franco Trabattoni. Leiden: Brill, 2009, 231–257.

Van Riel, Gerd. "Damascius on Matter." In *Platonism and Aristotelianism (Europaea Memoria*, Reihe 1. Studien, Bd. 85). Edited by Thomas Bénatouïl, Franco Trabattoni and Emanuele Maffi. Hildesheim: Olms, 2011, 189–213.

Van Riel, Gerd. *Plato's Gods*. Aldershot: Ashgate, 2013.

Vitrac, Bernard. "Les mathématiques dans le *Timée* de Platon: le point de vue d'un historien des sciences." *Études platoniciennes* 2 (2006): 11–78.

Williams, Christopher John Fardo. *Philoponus: On Aristotle on Coming-to-Be and Perishing* 1.6–2.4. London: Bloomsbury, 2013.

Zeyl, Donald J. *Plato: Timaeus*. Indianapolis: Hackett, 2000.

An Unnoticed Analogy between the *Timaeus* and the *Laws*

Marwan Rashed

Abstract

The question of the relationship between the *Timaeus* and the so-called "unwritten doctrines" (*agrapha dogmata*) gave rise to many discussions since Antiquity until more recent times. The present paper focuses on what seems to constitute their central point, namely the intermediate position of the *mathēmata*. Aristotle expressly attributes this doctrine to Plato but we don't find it in the dialogues. The paper first recalls the interpretation of the *Timaeus* 55c7–d6 according to which this important passage alludes to the distinction between Forms, *mathēmata* and sensible things. It then proposes a new interpretation of the *Laws* V, 739a1–e7 which shows that a close analogy between the *Timaeus* and the three "constitutions" (*politeiai*) mentioned in the *Laws* is conceivable. This new interpretation has an impact on the overall interpretation of the *Laws*.

Keywords

Plato – *Timaeus* – *Laws* (Plato) – unwritten doctrines (Plato) – mathematics (philosophy of) – political philosophy

The question of the relationship between the *Timaeus* and the so-called "unwritten doctrines" (ἄγραφα δόγματα) has given rise to much discussion in the past, from Antiquity to more recent days.[1] It is not my purport here to deal with the whole range of issues pertaining to it. More narrowly, I will focus on a crucial aspect of these doctrines, namely the intermediary status of the *mathemata*, a theory which Aristotle explicitly attributes to Plato but which we do not find formulated *expressis verbis* anywhere in the dialogues.[2] I shall first briefly

---

1 *Acknowledgments*. A French version of this contribution appeared in *Les Études philosophiques* 181 (2018/1): 115–138. The English version has been published courtesy of Presses Universitaires de France. I would like to thank Thomas Auffret and Chad Jorgenson for their help. Errors are mine.
2 See e.g. Aristotle, *Metaph*. A 6, 987b14–18.

recall my interpretation of an important passage of the *Timaeus* (55c7–d6) which, I presume, is only understandable if we admit that Plato was alluding to the ontological tripartition between Forms, *mathemata* and sensible things. Then, in the light of this passage interpreted this way, I shall turn to the *Laws*, in order to propound a new interpretation of a well-known text from the end of Book v. I shall contend, namely, that there is a close analogy between the ontological tripartition of the *Timaeus* and the three "constitutions" (πολιτεῖαι) that Plato briefly lists at 739a1–e7. This new interpretation, as we shall see, could in turn have some bearing on the interpretation of the *Laws* as a whole.

Let us deal briefly with the *Timaeus*.[3] There are two arguments in favour of the uniqueness of the world in this dialogue. The first one appears in the first part of Timaeus' monologue, the section devoted to the products of the Good.[4] Put roughly, the proof is the following: the sensible world is an imitation of an intelligible paradigm. But this paradigm must be unique. For if it were not, then the unity the sensible world as an image of the intelligible world would not be attached to one of its many units, but to their whole. The world paradigm, in other words, cannot be part of a larger whole, but must encompass *all* of the intelligibles. As previously seen, there is in this proof an apparent difficulty, namely that, despite the fair amount of attention it has received from the part of recent scholars, it turns out to rest on a modern misunderstanding, and a real difficulty which, ironically enough, has remained totally unnoticed.

The "false" difficulty is probably due to the popularity, in the English-speaking world, of G. E. L. Owen's distinction between A- and B-predicates. The B-predicates are shared in common by the Forms and by the sensible objects participating in them; the second level predicates, by contrast, are not. It is because Biped-ness belongs to Humanity that humans are bipeds. On the other hand, the second level predicate "eternal", which is attached to Humanity not *qua* Humanity, but *qua* Form, is not inherited by its many participants.[5] Some scholars thus consider that in the proof of the *Timaeus*, the predicate "unique" should be handled as a second level predicate (an "A-predicate" in Owen's terminology).[6] After all, they say, the Forms as well are unique (there cannot be two Forms of Man, but only one), and that does not impede the

---

3   See Rashed, "Five World Hypothesis."
4   *Tim.* 31a2–b3.
5   Or, in Owen's presentation: "Given any Platonic Idea, at least two and possibly three very different sorts of thing can be said of it. (A) Certain things will be true of it in virtue of its status as an Idea, e.g. that it is immutable. These predicates (call them 'A-predicates') will be true of any Idea whatever. (B) Certain things will be true of it in virtue of the particular concept it represents" (see G. E. L. Owen, "Dialectic and Eristic," 225).
6   For the references, see Rashed, "Five World Hypothesis," 98, n. 12.

particulars sharing in them from being many (there are many men). But this objection is mistaken. On their view, it is not *qua* totality that the intelligible totality is unique, but *qua* intelligible. But this is to confuse the fact of being unique in kind and the fact of being an all-encompassing totality. The fact of being unique is relational: there is no other thing to which the thing we are considering is connected by a relation of similarity. By contrast, the fact of being all-encompassing is an internal determination, i.e., in Owen's typology, a B-predicate, exactly like "humanness" for the Form of Man. There can be no absolute separation in the intelligible realm, because the different Forms constituting it are inseparable from one another. If, by way of consequence, something must partake of it *qua* all-encompassing totality, this participant must encompass in itself everything there is—at its subordinate level at least. Hence, Plato's proof is perfectly correct.

This superficial difficulty, however, conceals a deeper one. This proof has taken for granted that we should posit a clear-cut separation between two realms, the intelligible and the sensible. But nothing has been said about their eventual relationship. In other words, we have proved that under two strong assumptions—that of a separation between the Intelligible and the Sensible, and that of an all-encompassing intelligible living being—the sensible world ought to be unique. But we are thus left with another serious danger, that of assuming two worlds, an intelligible world and a sensible one. Having saved the uniqueness of the sensible world, we now run the risk of cutting it off from its paradigm. The totality of what there is will then turn out to be nothing but a rhapsody or, in Aristotle's words (against Speusippus), a bad tragedy composed of unconnected episodes.[7] I cannot, by any stretch of the imagination, see how Plato could not have been aware of this peril. All the more so, since *nowhere* in his dialogues does he ever speak of what was later to become a customary way of designating the νοητὸν ζῷον: namely, as the so-called "intelligible world."

This apparent flaw explains, in my view, the otherwise strange fact that Plato, some pages later, alludes again to the uniqueness of the world. The text is so brief that we can translate it again:[8]

> Now, if anyone, taking all these things into account, should raise the pertinent question, whether the number of worlds should be called indefinite

---

7 See Aristotle, *Metaph.* XII 10, 1075b37–1076a4 and XIV 3, 1090b13–20.

8 *Tim.* 55c7–d6: "Ἃ δή τις εἰ πάντα λογιζόμενος ἐμμελῶς ἀπορεῖ πότερον ἀπείρους χρὴ κόσμους εἶναι λέγειν ἢ πέρας ἔχοντας, τὸ μὲν [d] ἀπείρους ἡγήσαιτ' ἂν ὄντως ἀπείρου τινὸς εἶναι δόγμα ὧν ἔμπειρον χρεὼν εἶναι, πότερον δὲ ἕνα ἢ πέντε αὐτοὺς ἀληθείᾳ πεφυκότας λέγειν ποτὲ προσήκει, μᾶλλον ἂν ταύτῃ στὰς εἰκότως διαπορήσαι. τὸ μὲν οὖν δὴ παρ' ἡμῶν ἕνα αὐτὸν κατὰ τὸν εἰκότα λόγον πεφυκότα μηνύει θεόν, ἄλλος δὲ εἰς ἄλλα πῃ βλέψας ἕτερα δοξάσει.

or limited, he would judge that to call them indefinite is the opinion of one who is indeed indefinite about matters on which he ought to be definitely informed. But whether it is proper to speak of them as being really one or five, he might, if he stopped short there, more reasonably feel a doubt. As to ourselves, however, some god gives us a sign that the world by nature is one, according to the probable account; but another, looking to other considerations, will judge differently.

What are "these things"? I guess that they consist of all the kinds of entities that have been mentioned so far. Plato has dealt with moved solids, with geometrical solids, with surfaces, and, rather elusively, with mysterious things of a still higher rank, close to the God.[9] These objects, in their very constitution, have the feature of being strictly linked to one another by a relation of priority and posteriority. An object is prior to another if its notion is implied in that of the other without the other's notion being implied in its own. For instance, a surface is prior to a mathematical solid because the notion of a solid is not to be grasped without that of a surface, but not the other way round. On the interpretation that I have suggested and defended elsewhere,[10] Plato is now alluding to these different classes of objects, and thus implicitly proposing a solution to the aporia stemming from his first proof of the uniqueness of the world. Plato's message would be the following: there is no brutal scission between the intelligible and the sensible, but a succession of different ontological levels, beginning with the Forms and ending with the sensible bodies. These two domains are separated by the mathematical realm, itself consisting of three classes: numbers, surfaces, solids. It is in the tacit denial that the lines could represent by themselves an ontological class distinct from that of the numbers that we find the essential intuition of Plato's mathematical ontology. For this denial is part and parcel of Plato's conception of logistic as a theory of pure ratios, either finite or, in the case of the constitutive algorithms of the quadratic surds, infinite. What Plato is saying here is that it is extremely difficult to argue for the articulation in a single whole of these five ontological classes. We need a divine sign in order to be sure that they form a single world, rather than five distinct worlds connected to one another.

---

9   See below, pp. 208–209, for the exact passages.
10 Rashed, "Plato's five world hypothesis."

As announced in the introduction, I would like in the present chapter to confirm and enrich this analysis by taking the *Laws* into account. Let us first cite in full the text on the three constitutions:[11]

> Our next move in this business of legislation must be—like the moving of a man on the board from the "sacred line"—so singular that it may surprise you on a first hearing. Yet reflection and practical experience will make it clear that a society is likely to enjoy but a second-best constitution. Some of us may be dissatisfied with such a society from their unfamiliarity with the situation of a legislator who does not possess autocratic power, but the procedure of strict exactitude is to discriminate a best constitution, a second-best, and a third-best, and then to leave the choice between them to the party responsible for the community. Accordingly, I propose that we should adopt this method in our present proceedings, once we shall have recalled the best, second-best, and third-best constitutions. Let us leave the choice between them to Clinias in the present case, or to any one else who may at any time come to the task of selection with a desire to incorporate what he values in his own native institutions to suit his own taste.

11   *Laws* v 739a1–e7: Ἡ δὴ τὸ μετὰ τοῦτο φορά, καθάπερ πεττῶν ἀφ' ἱεροῦ, τῆς τῶν νόμων κατασκευῆς, ἀήθης οὖσα, τάχ' ἂν θαυμάσαι τὸν ἀκούοντα τὸ πρῶτον ποιήσειεν· οὐ μὴν ἀλλ' ἀναλογιζομένῳ καὶ πειρωμένῳ φανεῖται δευτέρως ἂν πόλις οἰκεῖσθαι πρὸς τὸ βέλτιστον. τάχα δ' οὐκ ἄν τις προσδέξαιτο αὐτὴν διὰ τὸ μὴ σύνηθες νομοθέτῃ μὴ τυραννοῦντι· τὸ δ' ἔστιν ὀρθότατον εἰπεῖν μὲν τὴν ἀρίστην πολιτείαν καὶ δευτέραν καὶ τρίτην, [b] δοῦναι δὲ εἰπόντα αἵρεσιν ἑκάστῳ τῷ τῆς συνοικήσεως κυρίῳ. ποιῶμεν δὴ κατὰ τοῦτον τὸν λόγον καὶ τὰ νῦν ἡμεῖς, εἰπόντες ἀρετῇ πρώτην πολιτείαν καὶ δευτέραν καὶ τρίτην· τὴν δὲ αἵρεσιν Κλεινίᾳ τε ἀποδιδῶμεν τὰ νῦν καὶ εἴ τις ἄλλος ἀεί ποτε ἐθελήσειεν ἐπὶ τὴν τῶν τοιούτων ἐκλογὴν ἐλθὼν κατὰ τὸν ἑαυτοῦ τρόπον ἀπονείμασθαι τὸ φίλον αὐτῷ τῆς αὑτοῦ πατρίδος.
      Πρώτη μὲν τοίνυν πόλις τέ ἐστιν καὶ πολιτεία καὶ νόμοι [c] ἄριστοι, ὅπου τὸ πάλαι λεγόμενον ἂν γίγνηται κατὰ πᾶσαν τὴν πόλιν ὅτι μάλιστα· λέγεται δὲ ὡς ὄντως ἐστὶ κοινὰ τὰ φίλων. τοῦτ' οὖν εἴτε που νῦν ἔστιν εἴτ' ἔσται ποτέ – κοινὰς μὲν γυναῖκας, κοινοὺς δὲ εἶναι παῖδας, κοινὰ δὲ χρήματα σύμπαντα – καὶ πάσῃ μηχανῇ τὸ λεγόμενον ἴδιον πανταχόθεν ἐκ τοῦ βίου ἅπαν ἐξῄρηται, μεμηχάνηται δ' εἰς τὸ δυνατὸν καὶ τὰ φύσει ἴδια κοινὰ ἀμῇ γέ πῃ γεγονέναι, οἷον ὄμματα καὶ ὦτα καὶ χεῖρας κοινὰ μὲν ὁρᾶν δοκεῖν καὶ [d] ἀκούειν καὶ πράττειν, ἐπαινεῖν τ' αὖ καὶ ψέγειν καθ' ἓν ὅτι μάλιστα σύμπαντας ἐπὶ τοῖς αὐτοῖς χαίροντας καὶ λυπουμένους, καὶ κατὰ δύναμιν οἵτινες νόμοι μίαν ὅτι μάλιστα πόλιν ἀπεργάζονται, τούτων ὑπερβολῇ πρὸς ἀρετὴν οὐδείς ποτε ὅρον ἄλλον θέμενος ὀρθότερον οὐδὲ βελτίω θήσεται. ἡ μὲν δὴ τοιαύτη πόλις, εἴτε που θεοὶ ἢ παῖδες θεῶν αὐτὴν οἰκοῦσι πλείους ἑνός, οὕτω διαζῶντες εὐφραινόμενοι κατοι[e]κοῦσι· διὸ δὴ παράδειγμά γε πολιτείας οὐκ ἄλλῃ χρὴ σκοπεῖν, ἀλλ' ἐχομένους ταύτης τὴν ὅτι μάλιστα τοιαύτην ζητεῖν κατὰ δύναμιν. ἣν δὲ νῦν ἡμεῖς ἐπικεχειρήκαμεν, εἴη τε ἂν γενομένη πως ἀθανασίας ἐγγύτατα καὶ ἡ μία δευτέρως· τρίτην δὲ μετὰ ταῦτα, ἐὰν θεὸς ἐθέλῃ, διαπερανούμεθα. νῦν δ' οὖν ταύτην τίνα λέγομεν καὶ πῶς γενομένην ἂν τοιαύτην;

> The best society, then, that with the best constitution and code of law, is one where the old saying is most universally true on the whole society. I mean the saying that "friends'" property is indeed common property. If there is now on earth, or ever should be, such a society—a community in women-folk, in children, in all possessions whatsoever, if all means have been taken to eliminate everything we mean by the word ownership from life; if all possible means have been taken to make even what nature has made our own in some sense common property, I mean, if our eyes, ears, and hands seem to see, hear, act, in the common service; if, moreover, we all approve and condemn in perfect unison and derive pleasure and pain from the same sources—in a word, when the institutions of a society make it most utterly one, that is a criterion of their excellence than which no truer or better will ever be found. If there is anywhere such a city, with a number of gods, or sons of gods, for its inhabitants, they dwell there thus in all joyousness of life. Whence for the pattern of a constitution we should look to no other quarter, but cleave to this and strive to come as near it as may be in our state. That which we have now finished handling, were it once brought to the birth, would be in its fashion the nearest approach to immortality and truly one in a secondary degree; of the third, under Heaven's favour, we will treat hereafter, for the present, what, in any case, is this system we speak of, and how may it come to be what it is?

This text is extremely puzzling and, as far as I am aware, has never been explained in a satisfactory way by scholars. It gives rise to three main questions that we must address before engaging in a comparison with the *Timaeus*: (i) Is it really the case that the three constitutions are *each* a *distinct* object of choice for the legislator, or do they only describe three correlated "aspects," whatever that may mean, of the (single) best possible constitution for humans? (ii) To which category does the constitution dealt with at length in the *Laws* belong? In other words, and to judge from what is actually said at the end of the passage, is Plato's purport to give us a full discussion of the *second-best* or of the *third-best* constitution? (iii) What is the *difference* between the second-best and the third-best constitution?

Let us address these three questions.

(i) *Is it really the case that the three constitutions are each a distinct object of choice for the legislator?*

Curiously enough, this question seems never to have been asked by scholars. It is far from certain, however, that the text should be read in the traditional way, i.e. as stating that the legislator must choose *one of* the three constitutions mentioned by the Athenian. It is indisputable that the legislator is confronted with a real choice. The first paragraph speaks of a αἵρεσις, a "choice" that will be left to "the party responsible for the community" and, more specifically, to Clinias. And there is of course no choice which is not also a real choice. You are unlikely to propose to your little nephew a choice between the Platonic Idea of a candy and a sensible candy which falls short of being as good as the Ideal Candy. The only real choice will take place between the artisanal candy with the best possible flavour, bought from the best sweet shop in town, and the industrial candy from the supermarket. They both exist. The first is not a Platonic Idea, but it has been produced according to the rules of the art, while the other is not necessarily disgusting, but surely not as good as the former.

The same argument applies to cities as well as to candies. In order for it to be an object of choice, the "ideal" city must be "ideal" in a loose sense: it is a city whose existence is both internally possible *for us* and factually out of *our* reach. Let's imagine that the "ideal" candy exists only in Australia, while your little nephew lives in Europe. In some sense, it is *possible* to get one for him. You just have to own a supersonic jet and to send it to Australia in order to bring the candy back; in some other sense (possibility for "normal" or, better, "real" people), this is *impossible*. All the same for the "ideal" constitution. Its realization is *possible* because the sons of the Gods can manage to produce one such (communist) city at the top of Mount Olympus; it is *impossible*, on the other hand, because we "real" humans, who do not have enough lung capacity to dwell durably on such summits, are unable to organize our political regime this way.

It is probably with similar considerations in mind that recent interpreters of the *Laws* tend to insist on the reality of the terms of the choice. André Laks, for instance, writes that Plato "opt[e] clairement, en particulier au livre v [sc. of the *Laws*], pour une interprétation de la *République* en termes de possibilité réelle." And he adds: "il n'y aurait pas de sens, sinon, à préconiser un « retrait » par rapport aux mesures qu'elle adopte."[12] His argument seems thus to be the following: our text of the *Laws* suggests that we should not adopt the communist constitution of the *Republic*, but another one, whose program is less ambitious than the first. As a consequence, we should not interpret this adoption of the second-best regime as a simple way of *realizing* the first but, rather, as a choice of *another* model. The first constitution is something like an Australian candy: in a real sense possible to acquire, but actually impossible.

---

12 A. Laks, *Médiation et Coercition*, 42. Laks actually writes "elles adoptent," but this is a *lapsus calami* for "elle adopte," sc. *la République*. I am grateful to André Laks for confirming this to me *per lit*.

On this interpretation, we should expect to find the same kind of distinction between the second-best and the third-best constitution. According to André Laks, however, "[s]i cette troisième cité a peut-être quelque chose à voir avec la cité appelée à prendre naissance, dans un au-delà du dialogue, sur le territoire de la Magnésie crétoise, elle représente avant tout la série des cités possibles qui pourraient naître, dans des conditions différentes de celles qu'offre la colonie cnossienne, et que Platon ne spécifie pas."[13] Or, as he clearly puts it elsewhere : "La troisième cité représente un certain rapport entre la finalité recherchée (la réalisation du meilleur) et le matériau dont la législation dispose pour y parvenir (les circonstances géographiques, historiques, politiques)."[14] If I correctly understand these two statements, Laks does not hold that we could *choose* between the second and the third constitution. He rather thinks that the only difference between them is that the third fleshes out the second by implementing its general design. The second constitution contains the general principles of existence for the best possible city *for us*. The third constitution plunges these general principles into concrete existence by "incarnating" them in a given place, at a given time, for a given people, etc. In this case, however, there is a strong asymmetry between the relation of the second city to the first and the relation of the third city to the second. Whereas the first and the second cities are two distinct *models*—the former possible for gods but not for men, the second humanly possible—the third city is nothing but the concrete instantiation of the second one, and not a third model of its own. I find this unlikely, because in the first paragraph of our quote, Plato is not suggesting any distinction of status between the three constitutions. At both places where they appear, they are clearly put on a par.[15] I would thus tend to favour an interpretation which would not introduce such a break between the two prior constitutions and the third.

It can scarcely be denied, given Plato's insistence throughout this paragraph, that the legislator is supposed to choose *one* constitution (i.e. one constitution *only*, otherwise this procedure would not be a choice). But is it really the case that the legislator has to choose between *one of the three constitutions*

---

13   Laks, *Médiation et Coercition*, 41.
14   Laks, *Lois et Persuasion*, 471 (quoted by Castel-Bouchouchi, *Les Lois*, 345–346, who endorses his interpretation: "[...] dans un cas on examine une possibilité théorique, et dans l'autre on fait allusion à une possibilité réelle: l'Athénien ne s'engage pas à 'réaliser effectivement' la cité, mais à 'achever son discours' plus tard en prenant en compte les données concrètes").
15   See 739a6–b1 (τὸ δ' ἔστιν ὀρθότατον εἰπεῖν μὲν τὴν ἀρίστην πολιτείαν καὶ δευτέραν καὶ τρίτην, δοῦναι δὲ εἰπόντα αἵρεσιν ἑκάστῳ τῷ τῆς συνοικήσεως κυρίῳ) and 739b2–3 (ποιῶμεν δὴ κατὰ τοῦτον τὸν λόγον καὶ τὰ νῦν ἡμεῖς, εἰπόντες ἀρετῇ πρώτην πολιτείαν καὶ δευτέραν καὶ τρίτην).

mentioned as against the others? Not necessarily, if they actually form a single unity.[16] Even if this eventuality does not seem to have been envisaged by previous scholars, the implicit meaning of the passage may very well be that the legislator, once he has been told about the Athenian's three constitutions, will have to choose between the unity they form together, and *other* constitutions, which were so numerous in Greece at that time. It will be objected that this is not the most natural way of reading the passage. I shall reply, on the contrary, that it is typical of Plato's art of writing to mislead the superficial reader in this way: *"Three constitutions?—Yes—A choice?—For sure—A choice between these three constitutions?—Not at all, my dear reader in a hurry, but a choice between these three constitutions taken as a whole and any constitution you might pick out during a tour in Greece and Magna Graecia."* The message of the Athenian to Clinias and Megillos is clear. He will only give them a description of the three constitutions. Then, it will be *their* decision, *not his*, either to adopt these three constitutions (in a sense that remains to be defined), or to keep legislating according to the old traditions at their disposal (like all other legislators at their time).[17]

An element of confirmation can be gained from what follows. At 539e1–3, Plato does not say a single word about the fact that the first and the second cities could form an alternative. The second is presented as an *approximation* to the first. It would be entirely natural, under these conditions, if the three constitutions were three "stages," three theoretical "moments," giving rise to the full description of *the* best city. The first city would provide us with the divine παράδειγμα, the second with its best human approximation and the third with the peculiar data to which this best human approximation must be applied. We shall come back to this point later. For the time being, let us just stress that it is not strictly necessary to postulate that we have to choose one of the three constitutions mentioned. On the contrary, the passage, when we read it in its continuity, seems to exclude this interpretation.

(ii) *To judge from what is actually said at the end of the passage, is Plato's purport in the* Laws *to give us a full discussion of the* second-best *or of the* third-best *constitution?*

Much uncertainty has surrounded the end of the passage. Let us quote it in Greek:

---

16   I am grateful to Thomas Auffret for having discussed this issue with me, and for the suggested solution.
17   As is well-known, the school of Aristotle spent much effort collecting and describing these constitutions.

[e1] διὸ δὴ παράδειγμά γε πολιτείας οὐκ ἄλλῃ χρὴ [2] σκοπεῖν, ἀλλ' ἐχομένους ταύτης τὴν ὅτι μάλιστα τοιαύτην [3] ζητεῖν κατὰ δύναμιν. ἣν δὲ νῦν ἡμεῖς ἐπικεχειρήκαμεν, εἴη [4] τε ἂν γενομένη πως ἀθανασίας ἐγγύτατα καὶ ἡ μία δευτέρως· [5] τρίτην δὲ μετὰ ταῦτα, ἐὰν θεὸς ἐθέλῃ, διαπερανούμεθα. [6] νῦν δ' οὖν ταύτην τίνα λέγομεν καὶ πῶς γενομένην ἂν [7] τοιαύτην;

It is not difficult to recognize the first constitution in the "pattern of a constitution" (παράδειγμα πολιτείας). As we have just seen, the constitution which is "most similar" (ὅτι μάλιστα τοιαύτην) to it is the second one. "We have just now finished handling it" (νῦν [...] ἐπικεχειρήκαμεν, perfect tense). It is "the nearest approach to immortality" and "truly one in a secondary degree" (ἡ μία δευτέρως). As for the "third constitution" (τρίτην) we shall bring it to an end (διαπερανούμεθα) *Deo volente*. Then follows the last sentence of the passage: "for the present, what, in any case, is this system (ταύτην) we speak of, and how may it come to be what it is?"

Besides minor inaccuracies in the rendering of these lines, two more serious shortcomings affect the general interpretation of the passage in some modern translations and commentaries. The first pertains to the perfect ἐπικεχειρήκαμεν, the second to the antecedent of ταύτην. As to the first issue, the perfect tense leaves no place to doubt. In the literary fiction, the Athenian considers that the attempt to deal with the second city is already behind us. And the νῦν indicates that this treatment has not been made in a remote past, but "right now," hence at least very recently. In other words, it should be possible to find it in the immediate context of what precedes.

Concerning the second issue, some translators feel the need to render the simple pronoun ταύτην as if it were referring to the *second* city. This is, for instance, what we find in Des Places' translation for the Budé series ("Enfin, pour le moment, comment définirons-nous la seconde cité, et comment peut-elle avoir pris cette forme?")[18] or, more recently, in Schöpsdau's translation ("Doch im Augenblick *geht es darum*: wie beschreiben wir diesen *zweitbesten* Staat, und wie könnte er in dieser Form verwirklicht werden?")[19] If not excluded from a strictly grammatical point of view, this construction is at least very implausible. For ταύτην is more likely to be related to the last feminine word in the sentence. In the present case, it should pick up τρίτην (l. 5) rather than ἣν δὲ (l. 3). Moreover, διαπερανούμεθα is in the future. The completion of the third city will be achieved *later*. The first person plural is ambiguous. If it is interpreted strictly, then the Athenian is speaking of the *description*, not of the *realization*

---

18 See des Places (ed. and trans.), *Platon: Œuvres Complètes*, 96.
19 See Schöpsdau (ed. and trans.), *Platon, Gesetze Buch I–VI*, 317.

of the third city (since it has just been said, and will be confirmed at the end of the *Laws*,[20] that the Athenian does not participate in the effective realization of the Magnesian city). If, on the other hand, we take it in a more relaxed way, then the first person plural does not signify very much. The Athenian would only be saying that *some* of us, i.e. *one of you*, will achieve the foundation of the new city in the future.

What about the last sentence? There is not the slightest hint here that Plato is alluding to the second city. We must first address a textual problem: should we adopt the reading "we say now" (λέγομεν, with ms. O and ms. A after correction by the first hand) or the reading "let us say now" (λέγωμεν, with ms. A before deletion)? Mss A and O are ancient and venerable. None of them is really better than the other, so we should decide which reading to retain on more internal grounds. The interpretation of the subjunctive λέγωμεν runs smoothly: "let us now say which is this city and how [...]." With the subjunctive, the sentence announces a forthcoming treatment and the opposition between the second and the third city is clearly expressed in the tense: the second city has just been handled. From now on begins the treatment of the third city; may God give us the strength to bring it to an end. If, on the other hand, we adopt the indicative λέγομεν, the syntax is harsher. The accusative ταύτην will result from an attraction, either from τρίτην a line before, or from τίνα. The translation will be: "But now, then, this city, of which kind do we say that it is, and how may it come to be such?" I see no way to gain certainty about which version was written by Plato. The editors, who adopt the indicative λέγομεν, might be right, since this makes the text slightly more difficult. But the subjunctive is surely not impossible. Three arguments in its favour are worth considering: (i) First, ms. O is frequently mistaken about the length of the [o].[21] (ii) Secondly, the confusion between *omicron* and *omega* is very common in the manuscripts *in general*. To decide which text to adopt, then, is not only a matter of textual transmission, but also of interpretation. (iii) There were perhaps reasons, for ancient editors, as well as for modern interpreters, to read λέγομεν rather than λέγωμεν. For a correct reading of the

---

20 See *Laws* XII 969c4–d3.
21 See for instance 738a2 λέγωμεν A recte et in marg. O: λέγομεν O; 741b2–3: τὸν εἰρημένον A *recte et in marg*. O: τῶν εἰρημένων O. The independent value of the correction in A is rather weak, because it seems to rely on a source which was almost identical to O. See Des Places, *Les Lois*, vol. I, ccx: "[...] j'ai pu constater que partout où O¹ et Oᶜ étaient d'accord avec une correction de A, celle-ci était de première main (Aᶜ); y avait-il, au contraire, désaccord entre O ou Oᶜ et la correction de A, celle-ci était d'une main différente et vraisemblablement plus tardive (A² ou a) tandis que O restait fidèle à A *ante correctionem*."

ταύτην (as referring to τρίτην) necessarily implies that the subjunctive launches the treatment of the third city. This connexion is weaker, on the other hand, with the indicative, since the meaning of the sentence as a whole becomes blurred. I would thus tentatively suggest, contrary to modern editors, to print the subjunctive λέγωμεν in the text.

Fortunately none of this makes much difference in terms of interpretation. For the inceptive value of the subjunctive is also to be found if we adopt the other text. Even if we retain λέγομεν, the Athenian asks a vivid question, addressing the new topic of the third constitution. He will deal with it immediately afterwards, by first describing the division of lands and houses (Νειμάσθων μὲν δὴ πρῶτον γῆν τε καὶ οἰκίας).

(iii) What is the difference between the second-best and the third-best constitution?

At this stage the first question which suggests itself is the following: why do serious scholars adopt such counter-intuitive constructions of this passage, which, from a philological point of view, is rather plain? Basically, I suggest, because they do not want to equate the third city with the city described in the *Laws*. It is necessary, therefore, to attribute this role to the second city, so as to construct τρίτην δὲ μετὰ ταῦτα, ἐὰν θεὸς ἐθέλῃ, διαπερανούμεθα as a mere parenthesis. But with the interpretation I propose of the whole passage, the second city has *already* been dealt with at this stage, while the discussion of the third one is *still to come*. The lines 739e1–7 are the formal turning point between the treatment of the second and the treatment of the third city.

We are thus facing an aporia, which can be put as follows: with a more correct and natural reading of the Greek, the denotation of the second and third constitutions turns out to be somewhat mysterious. The second city has been dealt with already; but where? And if the *Laws* deals with the third constitution, without however telling us anything about the concrete details which seem to belong to this stage of the description, what will be the difference between the second and the third constitution? If, on the other hand, we equate the city described in the *Laws* with the second city of our passage and postpone the treatment of the third city to some undetermined future (e.g. the future of the discussion between the three old men, the future of the realization of the legislative project, a future outside the fiction of the dialogue), the interpretative difficulties are apparently resolved, but the meaning of the seven Greek lines becomes barely understandable.

Before presenting my own solution, I would like to say a few words about the interpretation of Henri Margueritte, such as we can reconstruct it from a text in which his pupil Jacques Brunschwig comments on a *mémoire*, written by his cousin Pierre Vidal-Naquet at the time when he was following Margueritte's seminar at the École Pratique des Hautes Études. Here is the description of this interpretation as given by Brunschwig:[22]

> L'interprétation généralement retenue pour ce passage consiste [...] à identifier la « cité seconde » avec la cité décrite dans les *Lois*, à laquelle renverrait l'expression « la cité que nous venons d'esquisser »; quant à la « cité troisième », dont la description paraît être renvoyée à un avenir indéterminé, les commentateurs se partagent: une cité concrètement réalisée, à la différence des deux précédentes? Les détails d'application de la législation, tels qu'ils sont donnés dans les *Lois* elles-mêmes? Un ouvrage projeté, mais jamais écrit? Pierre met l'accent, lui, sur la différence entre *epikekheirêkamen* (« nous venons d'esquisser ») et *diaperanoumetha* (« nous poursuivrons jusqu'au bout »), et propose en conséquence d'identifier la « cité troisième », celle dont on va poursuivre la description « jusqu'au bout », avec la cité des *Lois* elle-même; quant à la « cité seconde », elle est identifiée avec celle qui n'est effectivement qu'« esquissée » (plus que cursivement, il faut l'avouer) dans les seules lignes 739e 2–3 (« celle qui ressemble le plus possible » au modèle fourni par la « cité première »).

Margueritte's interpretation is clever, because it stands alone in offering a precise suggestion as to the passage to which the verb ἐπικεχειρήκαμεν might be referring. The problem with this interpretation, however, is that this previous passage consists of only half a line—more precisely, of a sequence of four words: τὴν ὅτι μάλιστα τοιαύτην. By saying that the second city is *the best possible approximation* of the first, the Athenian would have "sketched" its nature, so that he could now engage in a full description of the third city. This suggestion, of course, is hardly convincing. As Brunschwig notes with a pinch of friendly teasing, such a description would have been made "plus que cursivement, il faut l'avouer." Yet, we cannot but admire Margueritte and Vidal-Naquet for having been sensitive to the meaning of the Greek tenses.[23]

It is now time to suggest a way of solving the present aporia. My solution rests on a similarity to which Glenn Morrow was, to my knowledge, the first

---

22   Brunschwig, "Le philosophe," 138–153.
23   In spite of my beloved master's remark (see Brunschwig, "Le philosophe," 148, n. 48), I fail to see why the phrase *Deo volente* (ἐὰν θεὸς ἐθέλῃ) should be counted as a hint in favour of the orthodox interpretation. At five places in the *Laws*, it refers to the completion of what is being *said*. See 632e7, 688e2, (739e5), 752a8, 859b3. The single exception is 778b7, where the phrase is likely to be an allusion to the material foundation of the city.

to draw attention.[24] It is the similarity of structure that we can reconstruct between the cosmology of the *Timaeus* and the legislation of the *Laws*. In a paper published in 1953, Morrow writes:[25]

> I suggest that a better clue to understanding the *Laws* and its relation to the political ideal of the *Republic* is to be found in the *Timaeus*, more particularly in the work of the Demiurge described there. The *Timaeus* belongs to the same period of Plato's life. Like the *Laws*, it is sharply distinct, both in style and in content, from the works of Plato's middle age. In no other dialogue had Plato ever attempted to deal seriously and systematically with the material of empirical science. What we have in the earlier dialogues touching this point is that the world of Becoming imitates and participates in the Ideas; just how it does so is nowhere discussed, and only rarely, and as it were incidentally, is there any hint of the implications and presuppositions involved in this theory of the two worlds, the world of ideal Forms and the world of imperfect imitations. But these are precisely the great matters discussed in the *Timaeus*. The bridge between the two worlds is a metaphor—the metaphor of the cosmic Demiurge, or Craftsman, who by his knowledge of the ideal Forms and his acquaintance with the materials he has to work with constructs a world in the likeness of the ideal, as nearly as his materials will permit him.

Since Morrow's article, this scheme has been further scrutinized by André Laks in several contributions devoted to the *Laws*. Laks writes in particular:[26]

> Both dialogues rely on a similar pattern. The 'model' to which the craftsman-demiurge looks in the *Timaeus* (the Forms) has its analogue in the *Laws* in the political model of the 'first city'; to the *Timaeus*' material 'receptacle' (the *chōra*), out of which the elementary triangles and the four elements will emerge, corresponds the human material that the legislator must shape into a political body. Even more striking is the fact that the material *chōra* of the *Timaeus* is identical with 'necessity', for the legislator of the *Laws* must also grapple with necessity (e.g. 857e10–858a6), which marks the limit of his actions.

---

24 Even if it was already implicit in Robin, *Platon*, Paris, 226–228, who had the additional merit, from the point of view of the interpretation I am proposing, of connecting the mathematical partition of the city in the *Laws* to that of the heavens in the *Timaeus*.
25 Morrow, "Demiurge in Politics," 7–8.
26 Laks, "The *Laws*," 273. See also, by the same, in French (basically the same text, with some variants): *Médiation et coercition*, 41 and "Prodige et médiation", 22.

Morrow and Laks are in agreement about the way in which we should understand the analogy between the *Timaeus* and the *Laws*. According to them, there are only two realms: the intelligible paradigm on the one hand, the sensible imitation on the other. Laks draws attention to an important element besides, namely the parallel between the "model" of the Demiurge and the "model" of the first city. This fact, however, does not lead him to modify his general interpretation of the three cities as much as it could have done. Let us expand on it a little more. If there is a way to construct an analogy between the paradigm in the *Timaeus* and the first city in the *Laws* (which indeed is explicitly described as a 'paradigm', παράδειγμα, at 739e1), we should be able to connect the second and third cities of the *Laws* to other ontological realms of the *Timaeus*. Such indeed will be my working hypothesis: the second city corresponds to the intermediary realm of the *mathēmata*, and the third city to the realm of the χώρα.

In order to confirm this, we should first be able to find something clearly mathematical in the immediate context of the text of *Laws* v. It is this mathematical evidence that the νῦν ἐπικεχειρήκαμεν will be referring to, allowing us to associate the second city with the *mathēmata*. We will not have to look for this evidence very long. One of the most important passage of the *Laws* in terms of mathematical learning appears *one* page earlier. Let us quote it in full:[27]

---

27   *Laws* v 737c1–738b1: Τίς οὖν δὴ τρόπος ἂν εἴη τῆς ὀρθῆς διανομῆς; πρῶτον μὲν τὸν αὐτῶν ὄγκον τοῦ ἀριθμοῦ δεῖ τάξασθαι, πόσον εἶναι χρεών· μετὰ δὲ τοῦτο τὴν διανομὴν τῶν πολιτῶν, καθ' ὁπόσα μέρη πλήθει καὶ ὁπηλίκα διαιρετέον αὐτούς, ἀνομολογητέον· ἐπὶ δὲ ταῦτα τήν τε γῆν καὶ τὰς οἰκήσεις ὅτι μάλιστα ἴσας ἐπινεμητέον. ὄγκος δὴ πλήθους ἱκανὸς οὐκ ἄλλως ὀρθῶς γίγνοιτ' ἂν λεχθεὶς ἢ πρὸς τὴν γῆν καὶ πρὸς τὰς τῶν [d] πλησιοχώρων πόλεις· γῆ μὲν ὁπόση πόσους σώφρονας ὄντας ἱκανὴ τρέφειν, πλείονος δὲ οὐδὲν προσδεῖ, πλήθους δέ, ὁπόσοι τοὺς προσχώρους ἀδικοῦντάς τε αὐτοὺς ἀμύνασθαι δυνατοὶ καὶ γείτοσιν ἑαυτῶν ἀδικουμένοις βοηθῆσαι μὴ παντάπασιν ἀπόρως δύναιντ' ἄν. ταῦτα δέ, ἰδόντες τὴν χώραν καὶ τοὺς γείτονας, ὁριούμεθα ἔργῳ καὶ λόγοις· νῦν δὲ σχήματος ἕνεκα καὶ ὑπογραφῆς, ἵνα περαίνηται, πρὸς τὴν νομοθεσίαν ὁ λόγος ἴτω. Πεντάκις μὲν χίλιοι ἔστωσαν καὶ τετταράκοντα, ἀριθμοῦ τινος ἕνεκα προσήκοντος, γεωμόροι τε καὶ ἀμυνοῦντες τῇ νομῇ· γῆ δὲ καὶ οἰκήσεις ὡσαύτως τὰ αὐτὰ μέρη διανεμηθήτων, γενόμενα ἀνὴρ καὶ κλῆρος συννομή. δύο μὲν δὴ μέρη τοῦ παντὸς ἀριθμοῦ τὸ πρῶτον νεμηθήτω, μετὰ δὲ ταῦτα τρία τὸν αὐτόν· πέφυκε γὰρ καὶ τέτταρα καὶ πέντε καὶ μέχρι τῶν δέκα ἐφεξῆς. δεῖ δὴ περὶ ἀριθμῶν τό γε τοσοῦτον πάντα [a] ἄνδρα νομοθετοῦντα νενοηκέναι, τίς ἀριθμὸς καὶ ποῖος πάσαις πόλεσιν χρησιμώτατος ἂν εἴη. λέγωμεν δὴ τὸν πλείστας καὶ ἐφεξῆς μάλιστα διανομὰς ἐν αὑτῷ κεκτημένον. ὁ μὲν δὴ πᾶς εἰς πάντα πάσας τομὰς εἴληχεν· ὁ δὲ τῶν τετταράκοντα καὶ πεντακισχιλίων εἴς τε πόλεμον καὶ ὅσα κατ' εἰρήνην πρὸς ἅπαντα τὰ συμβόλαια καὶ κοινωνήματα, εἰσφορῶν τε πέρι καὶ διανομῶν, οὐ πλείους μιᾶς δεουσῶν ἑξήκοντα δύναιτ' ἂν τέμνεσθαι τομῶν, συνεχεῖς δὲ ἀπὸ μιᾶς [b] μέχρι τῶν δέκα.

> What, then would be the right method of distribution? First, we must fix the total number of citizens at the suitable figure; next we must come to an agreement about their distribution, the number and size of the sections into which they should be subdivided; the land and houses should be partitioned among these sections as equally as may be. What would be a satisfactory total for the population is more than can be rightly said without consideration of the territory and the neighbouring communities. The territory should be large enough for the adequate maintenance of a certain number of men of modest ambitions, and no larger; the population should be sufficient to defend themselves against wrongs from societies on their borders, and to assist their neighbours when wronged to some purpose. These points we will settle, practically and theoretically, by an inspection of the territory and its neighbours, but for the present our argument may proceed to the completion of our code of laws, in outline as a general sketch.
>
> Let us assume—to take a convenient number—that we have five thousand and forty landholders, who can be armed to fight for their holdings, and that the territory and houses are likewise divided among the same number, so that there will be one man to one holding. Let this total be divided first by two, and then by three; in fact it will permit of division by four, five, and the successive integers up to ten. Of course anyone who is acting as a legislator must be at least familiar enough with figures to understand what number, or kind of number, will prove most useful in a given State. Accordingly we will select that which has the greatest number of immediately successive divisions. The whole integer-series, of course, admits division by any number and with any quotient, while our 5040 can be divided, for purposes of war, or to suit the engagements and combinations of peace, in the matter of taxes to be levied and public distributions to be made, into fifty-nine quotients and no more, ten of them, from unity onwards, being successive.

We should refrain from thinking that in this passage, Plato contents himself with displaying some piece of ludicrous mathematical fantasy. The number 5040, because of its remarkable properties of divisibility, is the backbone of every durable city. Plato will state this a little below, at the end of book V:[28]

> Our immediate concern, now that we have resolved on the division into twelve parts, must be precisely to see in what conspicuous fashion these

---

28   *Laws* V 746d–747b.

twelve parts, admitting, as they do, such a multitude of further divisions, with the subsequent groups which arise from them, down to the five thousand and forty individuals—this will give us our brotherhoods, wards, and parishes, as well as our divisions of battle and columns of route, not to mention our currency and measures of capacity, dry and liquid and of weight—to see, I say, how all these details must be legally determined so as to fit in and harmonize with each other. There is a further fear we must dismiss, apprehension of a possible reputation for finicking pedantry if the law enacts that no utensil whatever in the possession of a citizen shall be of other than the standard size. The legislator must take it as a general principle that there is a universal usefulness in the subdivisions and complications of numbers, whether these complications are exhibited in pure numbers, in lengths and depths, or again in musical notes and motions whether of rectilinear ascent and descent or of revolution. All must be kept in view by the legislator in his injunction to all citizens, never, so far as they can help it, to rest short of this numerical standardization. For alike in domestic and public life and in all the arts and crafts there is no other single branch of education which has the same potent efficacy as the theory of numbers; but its greatest recommendation is that it rouses the naturally drowsy and dull, and makes him quick, retentive and shrewd—a miraculous improvement of cultivation upon his native parts.

And again, for inattentive readers, in the course of book VI:[29]

> We may open the legislation which is now to follow in some such way as this, with religion as our starting-point. We must first return to our number of 5040 and the various convenient subdivisions we find both in this total and in the constituent tribe, which was, you will remember, by assumption one-twelfth of the whole, and is thus the exact product of one-and-twenty by twenty. Now our total number permits of division by twelve, and so likewise does that of the tribe, so each such division must be thought of as a sacred thing, a gift of Heaven corresponding with the months of the year and the revolution of the universe. This, in fact, is why all communities are under the sway of an instinct which consecrates them, though some authorities perhaps have made a truer division than others, and been more fortunate in the result of the consecration. For our own part, our present point is that we were justified in our preference for the number 5040, as it is divisible by every integer from 1 to 12 with the

---

29   *Laws* VI 771a–c.

exception of 11, and that can be very readily put right, since one way of mending it is to set two hearths on one side. That the fact is so could be proved in a very few words if we had the leisure.

These passages show that Plato is extremely serious when he affirms that the whole social and political organization of his city must depend on the number 5040, because this number has many dividers, i.e. 59. What is the point at stake? Since Mersenne,[30] we know that Plato is alluding here to a theorem of number theory, which gives the rule for reckoning the number of dividers of any given integer.[31] We can formulate and prove it as follows:

- THEOREM: let us suppose that $n = \prod m_i^{p_i}$ (with m_i and p_i integers and m_i prime numbers); then if we call $\Sigma(n)$ the number of the dividers of n (1 excepted), we have:

$$\Sigma(n) = \prod(p_i+1) - 1.$$

- PROOF: let us first suppose that $n = b^i c^j$, b and c being two prime numbers and i and j two integers. We can represent the entire set of the dividers of n by means of the following table:

1	c	...	c^j
b	bc	$b...$	bc^j
...	... c	... ...	... c^j
b^i	$b^i c$	$b^i ...$	$b^i c^j$

We know, moreover, that if a number divides the divider of an integer, it also divides this integer. Reciprocally, we know that "if two numbers by multiplying one another make some number, and any prime number measure the product, it will also measure one of the original numbers" (Euclid, *Elements* VII 30). Thus, by an iteration of the same process, we can prove the theorem for the potencies of as many prime numbers as we wish. It will be enough, for each new divider (d^k, etc.), to put the factors previously obtained on a row starting with 1 on the left, and the different factors of the new divider d^k (i.e. $d, d^2, ..., d^k$) in a column under the 1 on the left. In the present case, each row of the new table

---

30   See Dickson, *Theory of Numbers*, Vol. 1, 51 (quoted by J. Itard, see following note).
31   See Itard, *Euclide*, Paris, 68–69: "Platon sait que le nombre 5040 a 59 parties, lesquelles se succèdent de 1 à 10 d'une façon continue, et que le reste de sa division par 11 est 2. La recherche des diviseurs d'un nombre donné est donc au moment de la rédaction des *Lois* un problème banal."

will contain $(i+1).(j+1)$ elements and each column $(k+1)$ elements. The new table of the factors of the product $b^i.c^j.d^k$ will therefore contain $((i+1).(j+1).(k+1))-1$ elements. This procedure can be iterated for the potencies of as many factors as we wish. If we call $(T_n)_{n\geq 0}$ the series of our tables and $(R_n)_{n\geq 0}$ the series of our top rows, we shall, at each new stage of the process, write the previous table T_n under the form of the row R_{n+1} of the new table T_{n+1}.

Let us turn to Plato's example again. Since $5040 = 2^4.3^2.5.7$, we have:

$$\Sigma(5040) = (4+1)(2+1)(1+1)(1+1) - 1 = 5.3.2.2 - 1 = 60 - 1 = 59.$$

Thus, the mathematical theorem to which Plato alludes in the *Laws* is far from being trivial. It is none other than the Greek formulation of the so-called "fundamental theorem of arithmetic," which states that every integer greater than 1 either is prime itself or is the product of prime numbers in exactly one way (only the order of the primes in the product being arbitrary). It has long been recognized that Prop. VII 30–32 of Euclid's *Elements* basically correspond to the unique factorization theorem. There has been much dispute over the historical context of the theory expounded in Book VII of the *Elements*. Despite the fact that it has become fashionable in recent years among historians of Greek mathematics (especially in circles rather foreign to Plato's art of writing) to consider doubtful even the most obvious evidence, I remain convinced by Zeuthen's interpretation, according to which Theaetetus' researches in arithmetic is lurking in the background of Euclid's Book VII.[32] More generally, Zeuthen's periodization seems to me the only one able to account for the first pages of the *Theaetetus*, in which Plato clearly distinguishes between knowledge of the irrationality of the diameter of the square, which is already considered old, on the one hand, geometrical proofs by Theodorus of Cyrene of the irrationality of $\sqrt{3}$, $\sqrt{5}$ ... $\sqrt{17}$ on the other, and, finally, the general treatment of irrationality which the young Theaetetus is about to provide.

We may express Zeuthen's general reconstruction of the history of Greek arithmetic in the 5th and 4th centuries by resorting to a handy periodization into four stages, such as the one proposed by O. Becker.[33] Becker first distinguishes what he calls the "*altpythagoreische Stufe*." This stage is characterized

---

[32] See H.-G. Zeuthen, "Sur la constitution des livres arithmétiques." The main lines of Zeuthen's reconstruction, concerning the role of Theaetetus in the constitution of the core of the arithmetical books in particular, has been accepted by such scholars as (to quote but a few) Sachs, Toeplitz, Becker, Heath (who, after having considered the substance of the arithmetical book Pythagorean, made a *retractatio* at the end of his life), Knorr, and Thomas.

[33] See Becker, "Lehre," 550–553.

by its "dyadic" nature, based on the opposition of the even and the odd. Becker goes as far as to deny that the factorization of any number into prime numbers was already known. Perhaps might it be more prudent to say, with Zeuthen[34], that it was of no peculiar relevance. At any rate, the incommensurability of the diameter of the square was still proved, at this first stage, by means of the odd and the even. Proportions were not considered from this arithmetical point of view. They were dealt with in musical and geometrical contexts, and they were essentially rational.

Becker's (i.e. Zeuthen's) second stage consists in the arithmetic of Theodorus of Cyrene. All we can reconstruct from it must be gained from Plato's *Theaetetus*. The presentation here provided of Theodorus' treatment of the surds from $\sqrt{3}$ to $\sqrt{17}$ suggests an attempt to define irrationality in terms of incommensurability (rather than ineffability), i.e. by considerations pertaining to measure. The mathematical procedure lying behind this change is that of the ἀνταναίρεσις of homogeneous magnitudes.

After Theodorus (and before Eudoxus' formal definition of the equality of ratios, which we do not have to consider for present purposes) comes his pupil Theaetetus. Theaetetus is the first mathematician who tried to address the question of irrationality in all its generality. The results of his work are preserved in Euclid's *Elements*, Book X, which in turn are based on theorems recorded in the arithmetical books (VII–IX). The crucial issue, from this point of view, is Theatetus' demonstration of the unique factorization theorem. In Zeuthen's words:

> Notre commentaire du VIIe livre a mis en relief la volonté d'établir le fondement d'une démonstration exacte des conditions nécessaires et suffisantes de la rationalité des racines de fractions et de nombres entiers, et on a vu qu'à cet effet il fallait établir des théorèmes sur l'univocité de la décomposition d'un nombre entier en facteurs premiers.[35]

And a little later:

> Dans ces conditions, l'invention des définitions du VIIe livre et des démonstrations qu'elles rendent possibles était une innovation de haute valeur. Elle devait être appréciée aussi à l'époque où elle a été faite et où l'on avait déjà reconnu l'insuffisance des anciennes démonstrations.

---

34   Zeuthen, "Sur la constitution des livres arithmétiques," 418.
35   Zeuthen, "Sur la constitution des livres arithmétiques," 417–418.

Elle serait donc digne de l'éloge de Platon, qui attribue à Théétète la découverte des vérités démontrées dans ce VIIe livre, et dont aucune autre démonstration nous est conservée.[36]

On Zeuthen's interpretation, then, the unique factorization theorem was the keystone of Theaetetus' arithmetic, in particular of his "higher" theory of irrationality such as we can reconstruct it from Book X of the *Elements*. By recording, in the passage of the *Laws*, the "constructive" side of the theorem, Plato was subtly alluding to the epistemological relevance of this "new" number theory, put forward by Theaetetus, for the project of building a coherent intermediary level between the "paradigm" and the third city (i.e. the city of the *Laws*).

The correlation between Theaetetus' fundamental theorem and the mathematical riddle of the factorization of 5040 in the *Laws* had initially been seen by Toeplitz, followed by Becker.[37] But in the absence of further considerations pertaining to the structure of the *Laws* as a whole and its relationship to the *Timaeus*, this fact was condemned to remain partial and isolated, appearing at best as a testimony of Plato's acquaintance with Theaetetus' research.[38] Now that we have proposed to see in the relation between 5040 and its 59 dividers the purest expression of the "second city," the parallel between the *Laws* and Theaetetus' arithmetic becomes much more significant. The point at stake is not just, as will be said later in the seventh book of the *Laws*,[39] that the citizens of the Cretan city must be acquainted with mathematical irrationality. More profoundly, Plato stresses the fact that the "third city" itself would lack all harmony, order, and beauty, if its relationship to the "paradigm" constituted by the "first city" were not mediated by the second

---

36   Zeuthen, "Sur la constitution des livres arithmétiques," 420.
37   See H. Rademacher and O. Toeplitz, *Von Zahlen und Figuren*, B101–102, who write in particular, 101: "Daß die Alten mehr gewußt habe, als bei EUKLID aufgeführt ist, läßt ein wenig beachtete Stelle im 5. Buch von PLATONS Gesetzen ahnen." Becker's reconstitution, "Lehre vom Geraden und Ungeraden," 552–553, does not add anything new to Toeplitz' reconstitution. The philosophical importance of Theaetetus' presence in the *Laws* has also been stressed recently by Auffret, *Mesure et Juste Mesure chez Platon*, 227–229. By contrast, Brumbaugh's interpretation of the passage of the *Laws* according to which Plato empirically reckoned the dividers of 7! seems to me very unlikely (see Brumbaugh, *Plato's Mathematical Imagination*, 61–62). For, as Rademacher and Toeplitz, *Von Zahlen und Figuren*, 102, rightly note: "Die für PLATONS Sprachgebrauch ungewöhnlich umständliche Umschreibung der Zahl 59 als 60–1 und die Anweisung, der Gesetzgeber müsse mit dieser Sache allgemein Bescheid wissen, lassen also vermuten, daß PLATON selbst damit Bescheid gewußt hat."
38   If not, as in Itard's analysis (see above, p. 204, n. 31), of Plato's mathematical culture in general.
39   See *Laws* VII 819a8–820d2.

city understood as a set of mathematical relations permitted by Theaetetus' theory of numbers. As aptly put by Toeplitz, Plato recommends "die Zahl der Ackerlose und der Grundeigentümer in einem neu zu gründenden Staat so zu wählen, daß sie möglichst viele Teiler habe, etwa gleich 5040, das 60–1 Teiler habe; der Gesetzgeber müsse so viel Arithmetik verstehen, daß er je nach den Größenverhältnissen der Stadt das passend einrichten könne."[40]

The similarities between the *Timaeus* and the *Laws* shed light on both works. For in both cases, the intermediary level consists of a mathematical realm whose structure and completion have been established by Theaetetus' recent research. In the case of the *Timaeus*, the intermediary beings *par excellence* were the five regular solids, whose construction is known to have been achieved by the young mathematician. In the case of the *Laws*, Plato makes an allusion to Theaetetus' achievements in number theory. Such a strong parallel is all the more striking since there is, as is well-known, a deep connection between Theaetetus' arithmetical research on irrationality and his discoveries in the field of solid geometry. Moreover, in the case of the "five worlds," if the interpretation I have suggested is correct, the core of the riddle consisted in Plato's tacit exclusion of the lines from his own mathematical ontology, a move that was part and parcel of his endorsement of Theaetetus' treatment of irrational magnitudes by means of continued fractions. It is clear, therefore, that Plato himself was aware of the connection between both sides of Theaetetus' researches.

As a final remark, I would like to draw attention to an analogy in the textual presentation of, so to say, the "fundamental riddle" in the *Timaeus* and the *Laws*. In the former dialogue, Timaeus of Locri introduces his enigma with the words "Now, if anyone, taking all these things into account (ἃ δή τις εἰ πάντα λογιζόμενος), should raise the pertinent question, whether […]." In the latter, the Athenian says: "Our next move (ἡ δὴ τὸ μετὰ τοῦτο φορά) in this business of legislation must be—like the moving of a man on the board from the 'sacred line'—so singular that it may surprise you on a first hearing. Yet reflection and practical experience (ἀναλογιζομένῳ καὶ πειρωμένῳ) will make it clear that […]." In both texts, then, Plato asks his reader to reflect on (cf. λογιζόμενος, ἀναλογιζομένῳ) something he has already said. In the case of the *Timaeus*, the solution to the riddle lurks at 53c4–54d7:

> First then, it must be obvious to anyone that fire, earth, water and air are bodies, and all body has volume. Volume, again, is necessarily enclosed by surface, and rectilinear surface is composed of triangles. All

---

40 Rademacher and Toeplitz, *Von Zahlen und Figuren*, 100.

triangles are derived from two, and each of these has one right angle and two acute. One them has, on either side, half a right angle, subtended by equal sides, the other unequal parts of a right angle, subtended by unequal sides. So we postulate this as the source of fire and the other bodies, as we follow our argument which combines necessity with probability. What still more remote sources there may be is known to God and such men as God loves.[41]

This text mentions the five would-be worlds of 55c–d: the four sensible bodies, the four mathematical solids attached to them, the surfaces and, still higher on the scale of reality (this is the difficult point left to the reader), the mathematical numbers and the Forms (both explicitly mentioned a little earlier, at 51b6–e6; see also 53b5: εἴδεσί τε καὶ ἀριθμοῖς). There is a trap, however, intentionally left by Plato to lead his non-mathematician reader astray (ἀγεωμέτρητος μηδεὶς εἰσίτω [...]): after mentioning in so many letters the five ontological classes forming by their association his unique world, Plato devotes an entire page to the description of the *five* regular solids. From Plutarch through to modern scholars, this has led many readers into error, as soon as they tried to connect each possible world to a peculiar solid, without realizing that in order for a *world* (κόσμος), i.e. a perfectly organized totality, to be really such, it ought to have the physical constitution described by Plato for *our* world.

Mutatis mutandis, we can make the same remark in the case of the *Laws*. As in the *Timaeus*, the riddle of the three constitutions is separated from its solution—itself concealed to the non-mathematical reader—by an appendix which could easily mislead us. For immediately after mentioning 5040 and its manifold factorization, Plato proceeds to the examination of the rules to follow in matters of religious property. Our city must leave untouched the old customs thereabout.[42] *Prima facie*, Plato draws a direct

---

41 Πρῶτον μὲν δὴ πῦρ καὶ γῆ καὶ ὕδωρ καὶ ἀὴρ ὅτι σώματά ἐστι, δῆλόν που καὶ παντί· τὸ δὲ τοῦ σώματος εἶδος πᾶν καὶ βάθος ἔχει. τὸ δὲ βάθος αὖ πᾶσα ἀνάγκη τὴν ἐπίπεδον περιειληφέναι φύσιν· ἡ δὲ ὀρθὴ τῆς ἐπιπέδου βάσεως ἐκ τριγώνων συνέστηκεν. τὰ δὲ τρίγωνα πάντα ἐκ δυοῖν ἄρ[δ]χεται τριγώνοιν, μίαν μὲν ὀρθὴν ἔχοντος ἑκατέρου γωνίαν, τὰς δὲ ὀξείας· ὧν τὸ μὲν ἕτερον ἑκατέρωθεν ἔχει μέρος γωνίας ὀρθῆς πλευραῖς ἴσαις διῃρημένης, τὸ δ' ἕτερον ἀνίσοις ἄνισα μέρη νενεμημένης. ταύτην δὴ πυρὸς ἀρχὴν καὶ τῶν ἄλλων σωμάτων ὑποτιθέμεθα κατὰ τὸν μετ' ἀνάγκης εἰκότα λόγον πορευόμενοι· τὰς δ' ἔτι τούτων ἀρχὰς ἄνωθεν θεὸς οἶδεν καὶ ἀνδρῶν ὅς ἂν ἐκείνῳ φίλος ᾖ.

42 *Laws* v 738b2–e8: "These facts of number, then, must be thoroughly mastered at leisure by those whose business the law will make it to understand them—they will find them exactly as I have stated them—and they must be mentioned by the founder of a city, for the reason I shall now give (τῶνδε ἕνεκα). Whether a new foundation is to be created

connection between the gods and the legislative procedure. We should follow the divine indications and build our new city accordingly. In the context of the "three constitutions," this cannot but suggest that our city is the second one. Since Plato is about to describe the first city as divine, and the second city as the first's best possible approximation, it would be very natural indeed to equate the second city with the bulk of those prescriptions emanating from the gods. But no! The city to be founded (or restored) is the *third* one, the second one being purely mathematical. What Plato says is only that, *except* for what pertains to temple property (where inspiration suggested by divine oracles must be followed), we should resort to rational, i.e. *mathematical*, partitions. In other words, the expression τῶνδε ἕνεκα, at 738b4, announces the *whole* development to follow, including the text about the three constitutions, not just the rules about the gods' properties. The religious law itself, moreover, must be turned as much as possible to the benefit of the mathematical scheme and its concern for order, regularity, measure, and—ultimately—unity. Plato's strategy as an author is identical in both passages, in the *Timaeus* and in the *Laws*.

To conclude, let us briefly sketch the whole range of analogies between the cosmic and the civil foundation:

> from the outset or an old one restored, in the matter of gods and their sanctuaries—what temples must be founded in a given community, and to what gods or spirits they should be dedicated—no man of sense will presume to disturb convictions inspired from Delphi, Dodona, the oracle of Ammon, or by old traditions of any kind of divine appearances or reported divine revelations, when those convictions have led to the establishment of sacrifice and ritual (whether original and indigenous, or borrowed from Etruria, Cyprus, or elsewhere), the consequent consecration by the tradition of oracles, statues, altars, and shrines, and the provision for each of these of its sacred precinct. A legislator should avoid the slightest interference with all such matters; he should assign every district patron god, or spirit, or hero, as the case may be, and his first step in the subdivision of a territory should be to assign to each of them his special precinct with all appertaining dues. His purpose in this will be that the convocations of the various sections at stated periods may provide opportunities for the satisfaction of their various needs, and that the festivities may give occasion for mutual friendliness, familiarity, and acquaintance. There is indeed no such boon for a society as this familiar knowledge of citizen by citizen. For where men have no light on each other's characters, but are in the dark on the subject, no one will ever reach the rank or office he deserves, or get the justice which is his proper due. Hence in every society it should always be the endeavour of every citizen, before anything else, to prove himself to all his neighbours no counterfeit, but a man of sterling sincerity, and not to be imposed on by any counterfeiting in others."

	Timaeus	*Laws*
fundamental riddle	five worlds (55c–d)	three cities (V 739a–d)
paradigm	intelligible living being	*First city*, as described in the *Republic*
intermediary	mathematical entities	*Second city*, or the whole set of relations between the dividers of 5040 (= 7!) (V 737c–738b)
mathematicall theory	Theaetetus' construction of the five regular solids	Theaetetus' theory of irrational magnitudes
textual trap	the five solids	divine inspiration
foundational instance	the five solids	Legislator
image plunged in time	sensible living being	*Third city*
space of realization	χώρα as "place"	χώρα as "territory"
modality	necessity	necessity

Works Cited

Auffret, Thomas. *Mesure et Juste Mesure chez Platon*. Thèse de doctorat de l'Université Paris-1 Panthéon Sorbonne, 2014.

Becker, Oskar. "Die Lehre vom Geraden und Ungeraden im Neunten Buch der Euklidischen Elemente. (Versuch einer Wiederherstellung in der ursprünglicher Gestalt)." *Quellen und Studien zur Geschichte der Mathematik, Astronomie und Physik* 3 (1936): 533–553.

Brumbaugh, R. S. *Plato's Mathematical Imagination*, Bloomington: Indiana University Press, 1954.

Brunschwig, Jacques. "Le philosophe, héros secret de l'historien?" In *Pierre Vidal-Naquet, un historien dans la cite*. Edited by François Hartog et al., Paris: La Découverte, 2007.

Castel-Bouchouchi, Anissa. *Platon: Les Lois*. Paris: Folio, 1997.

Des Places, Édouard. *Platon: Œuvres Complètes*, t. XI (2ᵉ partie): *Les Lois, livres III–IV*, ed. and transl. by Édouard des Places. Paris: Les Belles Lettres, 1951.

Dickson, Leonard, E. *History of the Theory of Numbers*, 3 Vol. Washington: Carnegie Institute of Washington, 1919.

Itard, Jean. *Les livres arithmétiques d'Euclide*. Paris: A. Blanchard, 1961.

Laks, André. *Lois et Persuasion. Recherche sur la structure de la pensée platonicienne*. Thèse d'État, Paris: Université de Paris-IV-Sorbonne, 1988.

Laks, André. "The *Laws*." In *Greek and Roman Political Thought*. Edited by Christopher Rowe and Malcolm Schofield. Cambridge: Cambridge University Press, 2000, 258–292.

Laks, André. *Médiation et Coercition. Pour une lecture des* Lois *de Platon*. Lille: Presses Universitaires du Septentrion, 2005.

Morrow, G. R. "The Demiurge in Politics: the *Timaeus* and the *Laws*." *Proceedings and Addresses of the American Philosophical Association*, 27 (1953–1954): 5–23.

Owen, G. E. L. "Dialectic and Eristic in the Treatment of the Forms" In *Logic, Science and Dialectic: Collected Papers in Greek Philosophy*. Ithaca: Cornell University Press, 1986.

Rademacher, Hans and Otto Toeplitz. *Von Zahlen und Figuren*. Berlin: Springer, 1930.

Rashed, Marwan. "Plato's Five World Hypothesis (*Ti.* 55cd), Mathematics and Universals." In *Universals in Ancient Philosophy*. Edited by Riccardo Chiaradonna and Gabriele Galluzzo. Pisa: Edizioni della Normale, 2013, 87–112.

Robin, Léon. *Platon*. Paris: Presses Universitaires de France, 1935.

Schöpsdau, Klaus. *Platon, Gesetze Buch I–VI* (*Platon, Werke in acht Bänden*, ed. by Gunther Eigler, Band 8,1), transl. by Klaus Schöpsdau. Second edition. Darmstadt: Wissenschaftliche Buchgesellschaft, 1990.

Zeuthen, H.-G. "Notes sur l'histoire des mathématiques. viii. Sur la constitution des livres arithmétiques des *Éléments* d'Euclide et leur rapport à la question de l'irrationalité." *Oversigt over det kgl. Danske videnskabernes selskabs forhandlinger* (1910): 395–435.

What is Perceptible in Plato's *Timaeus*?

Filip Karfík

Abstract

Plato's *Timaeus* offers an elaborate theory of sense-perception. It is defined in terms of an opinion accompanied by irrational sensation. In humans, sensation is a physiological process occurring in the ensouled body through the agency of the mortal kind of soul whereas opinion is a judgement passed on this process by the rational kind of soul. The sensation itself is a result of the clash between different bodies defined in terms of masses of minuscule regular solids of fire, air, water, and earth, themselves composed of two kinds of triangles. Clashes between bodies cause dissolution and reconfiguration of these solids. These processes can be described mathematically but, to the human soul, they appear as different *qualia*. Perceptible *qualia* are not subject-independent properties. Nevertheless, there must be intelligible Forms of them on which true judgements about them are based.

Keywords

Plato – *Timaeus* – sense-perception – sensation – *qualia* – Forms

1   Introduction

Sense-perception is an important topic in Plato's *Timaeus*. After all, the main object of Timaeus' speech is to give an account of the "visible and tangible world,"[1] as he puts it at the outset, or of the "perceptible god,"[2] as he prefers to call this world at the end of his contribution to the feast of speeches given in reward of Socrates' account of the best form of society.[3] This task involves an explanation of the perceptible characteristics of the world, on the one hand, and of cognition grasping them, on the other.

A theory of sense-perception giving an account both of what is perceptible and of what is perceiving, constitutes an essential part of Timaeus' discourse

---

1   *Tim.* 28b3–7: *kosmos* [...] *horatos* [...] *haptos te*.
2   *Tim.* 92c7: *theos aisthētos*.
3   Cf. *Tim.* 17a–20d.

on "the nature of the universe"[4] and is by no means a mere appendix to it. If we take a look at the disposition of the whole of Timaeus' speech, we realise the importance of this topic. Not only is it present from the beginning until the end, but each of its two main parts are, in a way, structured around it. In the first part, dealing with the making of the world by the Demiurge, the construction of the body of the universe aims at making this body "visible and tangible"[5] while the constitution of the world soul is designed to put this soul into contact with both what is "perceptible"[6] and what is "rational."[7] The second part of Timaeus' speech, which deals with the making of mortal living beings by the aids of the Demiurge, pays even more attention to sense-perception. As a matter of fact, the whole fabric of the human body aims at making different kinds of sense-perception possible. Moreover, an elaborated account of the nature of bodies in general (47e3–61c2) interrupts the description of the sensory organs of the human body in order to provide the foundations for the explanation of the nature and mechanism of sense-perception. This explanation itself then encompasses a detailed theory of perceptible characteristics of bodies (61c3–68d7) and a corresponding theory of the psychological and physiological conditions of different kinds of sense-perception by human beings, animals, and, to some degree, also plants (69c5–77c5).

Surprisingly, sense-perception as a topic of its own has not attracted much attention in recent scholarship on the *Timaeus*,[8] except for a comprehensive and highly accurate account published by Luc Brisson in 1999[9] and several articles about particular senses.[10] There is indeed little that can be added to, or emended in, Brisson's brilliant account. A puzzling question, however, is worth to be dwelt upon that may occur to our mind once we have understood how Plato's theory of sense-perception in the *Timaeus* works and what it means. This question is: What is the nature of perceptible characteristics and how it is that we have a kind of knowledge of them?

---

4 *Tim.* 27a4: *peri physeōs tou pantos.*
5 *Tim.* 31b5–6 and 32b8.
6 *Tim.* 37b6: *to aisthēton.*
7 *Tim.* 37c1: *to logistikon.*
8 From two more recent monographs on the *Timaeus*, Johansen, *Plato's Natural Philosophy*, pays some attention to sense-perception in dealing mainly with the teleological account of vision (160–176), while Broadie, *Nature and Divinity in Plato's* Timaeus, does not even include sense-perception in the general index to her book.
9 Brisson, "Plato's Theory of Sense Perception in the *Timaeus*: How it Works and What it Means."
10 Ierodiakonou, "Plato's Theory of Colours in the *Timaeus*," and Lautner, "The *Timaeus* on Sounds and Hearing with some Implications for Plato's General Account of Sense-Perception."

2 A Caveat

Let me begin with a terminological observation. A perceptible characteristic is what is called *aisthēton*.[11] A cognitive act relating to it bears a somewhat mysterious complex name *doxa met' aisthēseōs alogou*:[12] "opinion accompanied by irrational sensation." Since the cognitive act relating to perceptible characteristics is called *doxa*, "opinion,"[13] the "perceptible," *aisthēton*, may also be termed *doxaston*, "opinable."[14] It is important to note and to keep in mind the distinction between opinion and sensation: the cognitive act that grasps a perceptible characteristic is not called *aisthēsis*, sensation, but *doxa*, opinion. It involves sensation but sensation is "irrational," i.e. it is not a cognitive act. We should therefore be very careful in translating these terms. If by sense-perception we mean the cognitive grasp of a perceptible characteristic, then Plato's term for it in the *Timaeus* is not "sensation" but "opinion accompanied by irrational sensation." Consequently, in what follows, I will always render *aisthēsis* with "sensation" while, in speaking about "sense-perception," I will refer to what, in Timaeus' terms, is an opinion involving sensation.[15]

3 Bodies and Souls

Perceptible characteristics, Timaeus tells his listeners initially, such as "visible" (*horaton*) and "tangible" (*hapton*) go along with body (*sōma*).[16] Two kinds of bodily stuff (*sōmatoeides*) are particularly important from this point of view: fire (*pyr*) and earth (*gē*). Nothing, Timaeus claims, can be visible without fire nor can anything be tangible without earth.[17] Another two bodies, air (*aēr*) and water (*hydōr*), will turn out to be necessary conditions for audible, olfactory, and gustatory characteristics.[18]

---

11 *Tim.* 28b8: *ta toiauta aisthēta*.
12 *Tim.* 28a2–3, cf. also 52c7.
13 *Tim.* 28c1, 37b8, 51d4, 51d6, 52a7, 77b5.
14 *Tim.* 28a3.
15 Pace Brisson, "Sense Perception," who uses both terms, sensation and sense-perception, as interchangeble.
16 *Tim.* 28b7–8.
17 *Tim.* 31b3–6.
18 *Tim.* 32b3–4, 55d6–56b6, 58d1–5, 65b4–67a6. Cf. Brisson, "Sense Perception," 154. Here, Brisson states that touch takes place in relation to four elements, referring to 61d–65b. But 30b4–8 makes it clear that touch relates basically to earth as vision does to fire. Audition relates to air, taste to water and olfaction to water changing into air or air changing into water, as Brisson states. On olfaction see also Vlastos, *Platonic Studies*, 366–378.

Cognition of perceptible characteristics, on the other hand, is something which Timaeus ascribes to the soul. There is no cognition of this sort where there is no impact of bodies on a soul, as we will learn from him later in his account.[19]

There are, however, according to Timaeus, different kinds of soul: (1) the universal soul or world soul,[20] (2) particular souls of humans and animals[21] and (3) a mortal kind of soul present in bodies of humans, animals and plants.[22] The world soul and particular souls of humans and animals are immortal[23] and they are by nature rational,[24] though they animate mortal bodies[25] and, for this very reason, become temporarily irrational, i.e. unable to perform, or to perform properly, the act of reasoning.[26] On the other hand, the mortal kind of the soul is not only itself perishable like the body it is fastened into[27] but in addition to this it is in itself irrational, i.e. by nature unable to reason.

To which of these kinds of the soul, we may ask, does Timaeus ascribe the cognition of perceptible characteristics? No doubt he attributes such cognition to the immortal and rational world soul which brings forth "opinions and beliefs" (*doxai kai pisteis*) concerning "the perceptible" (*to aisthēton*).[28] As for humans, animals and plants, the matter seems to be more complex. In principle, to bring forth an "opinion" is always an act of a rational soul. Hence, only humans and animals will be able to form opinions about perceptible characteristics while plants, which have "no share in opinion, reasoning and intellection," will not.[29] Still, even plants, being endowed with a kind of mortal soul, namely the appetitive part (*to epithymētikon*),[30] will experience some "sensation" (*aisthēsis*).[31] On the other hand, humans and animals will be able to form

---

On the academic doctrine of the coordination between senses and elements see Baltes, "Die Zuordnung der Elemente zu den Sinnen bei Poseidonios und ihre Herkunft aus der alten Akademie."

19 *Tim.* 64a6–c7.
20 *Tim.* 34b3–37c5.
21 *Tim.* 41b6–44d2, 69c5–6, 73c6–d2.
22 *Tim.* 69c7–72b5 (for humans), 77a3–c5 (for plants), 91e4–6 (for animals).
23 *Tim.* 36e4–5, 41d1, 43a4–5.
24 *Tim.* 36e3–c5, 41d4–7, 43a3–4, 44b1–c1, 44d3.
25 *Tim.* 69c2, 81d4–e5.
26 *Tim.* 43a4–44c4.
27 This is why the mortal kind of the soul is fabricated by lesser gods, not by the Demiurge himself, cf. 41c2–d3, 42e5–43a6 and 69c3–8.
28 *Tim.* 37b6–8.
29 *Tim.* 77b5: ᾧ δόξης μὲν λογισμοῦ τε καὶ νοῦ μέτεστιν τὸ μηδέν.
30 *Tim.* 69e5–70a2, 70d7 and 77b3–4.
31 *Tim.* 77b5–6.

opinions on perceptible characteristics only due "sensations" (*aisthēseis*)[32] that are somehow dependent on the presence of a mortal kind of the soul in their body and are in themselves irrational. Thus, cognition of perceptible characteristics defined as "opinion accompanied by irrational sensation" will only be ascribable to particular rational souls insofar as they are linked with the mortal kind of soul in a mortal body.

4   Corpuscles and Masses

Let me for the sake of brevity leave aside the world soul's cognitive powers, as well as the question of the function of the mortal parts of the soul, and focus on how Timaeus describes the perceptible characteristics in relation to human cognition. I have said that they relate to four kinds of bodies. I must now qualify this statement. Bodies, on Timaeus' theory, are geometrically shaped structures each of which, taken separately, is so minuscule as to be invisible for us.[33] Fire is a pyramid, earth is a cube, water is an icosahedron, and air an octahedron.

Each of these minuscule regular solids is itself composed of a number of elementary triangles into which it can be dissolved. Three of them, fire, water, and air, are compounded of and can be dissolved into a single kind of triangle, the equilateral, and can thus transmute into one another, while earth, being compounded of another kind of triangle, the isosceles, if it is dissolved, can only form earth.[34] Both kinds of triangles exist in different sizes[35] but all of them are so minuscule that none of the particular corpuscles of fire, earth, water, and air, despite differences in size between them, is perceptible for us. The only thing we can perceive—or "see" as Timaeus puts it per metonymy— are "masses" (*onkoi*) of many such corpuscles put together.[36] These masses can be of very different types since there is great variety of mixtures between innumerable corpuscles of four different kinds in different sizes.[37] Thus what we perceive are not characteristics of particular corpuscles, such as the number of their vertices, the size of their surfaces, the nature of the angles between

---

32   *Tim.* 43c6.
33   *Tim.* 56b7–c3.
34   *Tim.* 53c4–57c6. Cf. Vlastos, *Plato's Universe*, pp. 66–97, and Bodnár, "Matter or Size, Texture, and Resilience: The Variety of Elemental Forms in Plato's *Timaeus*."
35   *Tim.* 57c8–d3.
36   *Tim.* 56c2–3.
37   *Tim.* 57d2–5.

their edges and their sides but something related to various masses of such corpuscles.

What is this something? On this issue, Timaeus is most explicit and the answer he gives is a complex one.

5 Movements

Masses of elementary bodies, i.e. corpuscles of four elements, are not stable but in motion.[38] Their movement is caused by their reciprocal contact and the differences between them. Whenever bodies that are not equal one to another come into contact, Timaeus tells us, they move.[39] This movement will be not a simple locomotion of corpuscles and their masses from one place to another. It will affect the very consistence of the elementary bodies, by dissolving them into their triangular constituents and by regrouping these constituents, such that the masses that clash in this way one with another will transform their structure and become different from what they were before the clash. These transformations will occur in accordance with the mathematical properties of elementary bodies involved in the clashing masses, depending on their kinds, sizes and numbers. Let me quote Timaeus' description of such processes:

> When one of the other kinds is enveloped in fire and cut up by the sharpness of its angles and edges, then, if it is recombined into the shape of fire, there is an end to the cutting up; for no kind which is homogeneous and identical can effect any change in (*metabolēn empoiēsai*), or suffer any change from (*pathein*), that which is in the same condition as itself. But so long as, passing into some other kind, a weaker body is contending (*machētai*) with a stronger, the resolution does not come to an end. And, on the other hand, when a few smaller particles are enveloped in a large number of bigger ones and are being shattered and quenched, then, if they consent to combine into the figure of the prevailing kind, the quenching process comes to an end: from fire comes air, from air, water. But if they (the smaller particles) are on their way to these (air or water), and one of the other kinds meets them and comes into conflict, the process of their resolution does not stop until either they are wholly dissolved by the thrusting and escape to their kindred, or they are

---

38   *Tim.* 57d7–c4.
39   Ibid.

overcome and a number of them form a single body uniform with the victorious body and take up their abode with it.[40]

transl. Cornford

Sense-perception relates to masses of elementary corpuscles undergoing such transformations. This means that what it grasps is not a stable thing or structure. It is a movement, a change, a process that occurs between different factors entering into it and being transformed through it.

6 Mathematical Formulas

These processes—which are depicted in terms of a battle between masses of elemental corpuscles—can be captured by mathematical formulas. A number of corpuscles of a particular kind are transformed into a number of corpuscles of a different kind or even of the same kind. In principle, it must be possible, for every process, to establish an equation with a *status quo ante bellum* on the one side and a *status quo post bellum* on the other, as Timaeus himself suggests:

When water is divided into parts by fire, or again by air, it is possible for one particle of fire and two of air to arise by combination.[41]

transl. Cornford

Let us put it this way: $20^{\text{water}} = 4^{\text{fire}} + (2 \times 8^{\text{air}})$, if we count the surfaces of the icosahedron, tetrahedron and two octahedral, or this way: $120^{\text{water}} = 24^{\text{fire}} + (2 \times 48^{\text{air}})$, if we count the elementary triangles of which these surfaces are compounded.

And the fragments of air, from a single particle that is dissolved, can become two particles of fire.[42]

transl. Cornford

Let us put it this way: $8^{\text{air}} = 2 \times 4^{\text{fire}}$ or this way correspondingly: $48^{\text{air}} = 2 \times 24^{\text{fire}}$.

Even if more complex formulas would be needed for transformations of mixed masses into one another, such formulas can be established. They do not really grasp the process as such but they fix the *status quo ante* and the *status*

---

40 *Tim.* 56e8–57b7.
41 *Tim.* 56d5–e1.
42 *Tim.* 56e1–2.

quo post of it while determining the process itself as a relation of equality between these two states. If nothing else, this is enough to make such processes accessible to reason. In this way, these processes are calculable. This is something the Demiurge needs in order to make them follow his designs.[43] Human beings, however, do not calculate mathematical formulas. Instead, they perceive characteristics of a quite different nature.

7 Pathēmata

Transformations of bodily masses that can be fixed by means of mathematical equations are nevertheless processes in which these masses act one upon another. Depending on whether the corpuscles they are compounded from "win" or "lose" the battle, i.e. whether they persist or are dissolved, they play the part of an active or of a passive factor. Either they "effect a change" (*metabolēn empoiēsai*) or they "undergo"' it (*pathein*).[44] Accordingly, they are described either as "that which acts" (*to drōn*,[45] *to poioun*[46]) or as "that which is acted upon" (*to pathon*)[47] while the process occurring between them is termed *pathos*[48] or *pathēma*.[49] The latter term, in particular, is used to describe the process itself.

It is worth paying attention to the different ways in which Timaeus uses this term.

(1) It can be used in the general sense of any process of transformation occurring between different bodily masses, independently of whether it is or not perceived by somebody, i.e. by a soul.[50]

(2) Most frequently, however, it is used to name those processes of this kind that eventually enter into the perceptual field of a human being.[51] These are processes of transformation that affect an ensouled human body. These *pathēmata*, Timaeus tells us, are nothing other than movements (*kinēseis*) produced in a human body by various bodily masses hitting its various parts.[52] These movements run through the human body in ways Timaeus

---

43 Cf. *Tim.* 47e4–48a5, 56c3–7, 68d2–69c3.
44 *Tim.* 57a4–5.
45 *Tim.* 62b6, 64e5, 65b5, 65b7, 65d6. For the pair *paschon-drōn* see also 33d1.
46 *Tim.* 64b6.
47 *Tim.* 63c3, 65b6.
48 *Tim.* 58e7, 62b5.
49 Cf. the notes 53–55, 57, 59 below.
50 *Tim.* 57c1, 64a6–7
51 *Tim.* 42a6, 43b7, 44a8, 61c5 etc.
52 *Tim.* 43b5–c5, 64e6.

specifies later in his account. If they reach the circular movements of the rational soul performing in the brain, we call them—precisely because they reach the soul, as Timaeus stresses—sensations (*aisthēseis*).[53] Sensations are thus movements (*kinēseis*) in the sense of processes of transformation of elementary corpuscles (*pathēmata*) if they occur between a bodily mass and a human body and if they reach a rational soul. (Qualifications or modifications of this definition of sensation will be needed for animals and plants.) In order to distinguish these *pathēmata* from *pathēmata* in the general sense (1) Timaeus also terms them "those *pathēmata* that provide sensation" (τὰ παθήματα ὅσα αἰσθητικά).[54]

(3) The term *pathēma*, along with its cognate *pathos*, is used also to designate what human beings perceive, i.e. the perceptible characteristics *as they appear to us*.[55] In listing them, Timaeus distributes them into three groups: (i) those that are common to the whole body, (ii) those that are particular to specific parts of the body, and (iii) those that occur together with both aforementioned kinds (i) and (ii).[56] He first treats the common ones (61d5–64a1), then those occurring together with both the common and particular ones (64a2–65b6) and finally those occurring only in particular parts of our body (65b6–68d7). Here is the list of these *pathēmata* or *aisthēseis*:[57]

(i) sensations common to the whole body:
   hot/cold, hard/soft, heavy/light, smooth/rough[58]
(ii) sensations accompanying the common, as well as the particular sensations:
   pleasurable/painful[59]
(iii) sensations occurring in parts of the body:
   – affecting the tongue: astringent/harsh, acrid/saline,[60] pungent, acid, sweet[61]
   – affecting the nostrils: nameless diversity of pleasurable/painful[62] scents

---

53   *Tim.* 43c6–d2.
54   *Tim.* 61d1.
55   *Tim.* 65d4: φαίνεται.
56   *Tim.* 64a1–6, 65b4–c1.
57   Cf. Brisson, "Sense Perception," 154. The English translation of the corresponding Greek terms is Cornford's.
58   θερμόν/ψυχρόν, σκληρόν/μαλακόν, βαρύ/κοῦφον[ἐλαφρόν], λεῖον/τραχύ.
59   ἡδύ/ἀλγεινόν or ἡδονή/λύπη.
60   *Pace* Brisson "Sense Perception," 154, who translates it by "agreeable." I take it that ἁλικά (65e3) is the opposite of πικρά.
61   στρυφνά/αὐστηρά, πικρά/ἁλυκά, δριμέα, ὀξύ/γλυκύ.
62   ἡδύ/λυπηρόν.

- concerning hearing: high/low, smooth/harsh, loud/soft[63]
- concerning sight: white/black, bright/red[64] and their mixtures: golden, purple, dark violet, tawny, grey, white yellow, dark blue, blue green, green[65]

In this sense, *pathēmata* or *pathē* are what we "perceive" in discerning characteristics that appear to us and in attributing to most of them (except for scents) different names. In other words, they are what constitute the object of sense-perception defined as "opinion accompanied by irrational sensation." "Irrational sensation" is a given *pathēma* while "opinion" is a judgement that a rational soul passes on it, once this *pathēma* has reached the soul's revolutions in one's brain.

8   What Happens and What Appears

Let us now reflect for a while on what happens in an act of sense-perception explained in this way. A *pathēma* that becomes an *aisthēsis* in reaching the rational soul through the intermediary of sentient tissues of a living body is a movement or process consisting in transformations of corpuscles of elements due to clashes between masses of them. As such it is something that occurs between different terms. We have seen that, due to the mathematical properties of the corpuscles, such a process is describable by the means of mathematical equations. As such, it is conceived of as a sort of complex relation. A quantity of corpuscles of specific kinds acting upon another quantity of corpuscles of different specific kinds produces as a result a different configuration, both in amounts and in kinds, of corpuscles. If this happens between an external bodily mass and a part of a sentient body, the process which allows for a mathematical formula will *appear* to us as a specific perceptible characteristic, e.g. as *hot* to our flesh, as *harsh* to our tongue, or as *white* to our sight.[66]

Note that in the case of these three characteristics Timaeus expressly establishes the following equation:

hot: flesh = harsh: tongue = white: sight

---

63 (ἀκοή) ὀξεῖα/βαρυτέρα, ὁμαλή τε καὶ λεῖα/τραχεῖα, πολλή/σμικρά.
64 λευκόν/μελάν, (λαμπρόν τε καὶ) στίλβον/ἐρυθρόν.
65 ξανθόν, ἁλουργόν, ὄρφνινον, πυρρόν, φαιόν, ὠχρόν, κυανοῦν, γλαυκόν, πράσιον.
66 *Tim.* 67d2–e4.

This does not mean that the same bodily mass of a given structure will produce different effects in acting upon different senses of our body, though this may also be true. Rather it means that whenever the same ratio occurs between the structure of a given external bodily mass and that of a given sense organ of our body, it will produce effects that are analogous. But the fact remains that they will *appear* to us as different characteristics for which we will use different names in identifying them.

Let us also take into account the following feature of Timaeus' account. In the case of scents, what is acting upon our nostrils are intermediary states of masses of water changing into air or masses of air changing into water, i.e. the *status quo ante* of this process is itself a process half a way of a transformation. What acts upon our nostrils is strictly speaking neither air nor water nor any other element but a certain quantity of elementary triangles into which a mass of air or water is dissolved in the process of regrouping into a mass of the other of these two elements respectively.[67]

What I want to stress by these examples are three points concerning the characteristics appearing to us: (1) what these characteristics reveal to us are not properties of particular bodies but *relations* between different bodily masses; (2) these relations, though they may be fixed by mathematical formulas, are not static structures but *processes of change*; (3) these processes of change *appear to us* not as such relations and processes but as characteristics for which the term *qualia* would be most fitting though Timaeus does not use it.[68] These *qualia* do not appear as something stable, either. On the contrary, they turn, melt, merge, and verge one into another. Nevertheless, they possess enough of stability and determinacy to be discerned one from another and recognized as specific kinds, e.g. the colour red, a low sound, or a sweet taste.

9   Pattern and Change

This reflection raises several questions. One of them is the following: Why it is that, apparently, something else *happens* (namely a transformation of different bodily masses due to their clashing) and something else *appears* to us (a perceptible *quale*)? Let me try to give a tentative answer to this question.

What happens when perceptible *qualia* appear to us is a process that allows for mathematical description. This description does not, however, grasp it insofar as it is a process but rather insofar as it is static. It grasps a pattern of what

---

67   *Tim.* 66d1–67a1.
68   Though cf. 50a1–3.

happens. Such a grasp is an act of reasoning and the pattern grasped in this way, the mathematical formula, is an intelligible object. As satisfactory as such a cognitive act may be in terms of knowledge of what happens, there is something in the nature of the process that escapes the grasp of such a cognitive act. If there was not, there would be an entirely intelligible object in front of us. It is not easy to say what this something is, but we may guess that it will be the passage itself between the two sides of the equation expressing the change of one bodily mass into another. The mathematical formula fixes this passage as a relation of equality. But equality is a relationship between the *status quo ante* and the *status quo post* whereas the *passage* between them—the battle itself—is of another nature, that of *change*, of *becoming different* rather than of *being equal.* Reasoning lays hold of the relation of equality, but the process of becoming different escapes its grasp.

If processes of transformation affecting bodily masses ought to be apprehended in what distinguishes them from intelligible patterns that make them accessible to reason, they must present themselves in another garb to another kind of cognition. This is why they *appear to opinion* as perceptible *qualia* instead of being thought by reason in terms of mathematical objects. Or to put it the other way around: in becoming processes of change that occur in particular places, mathematical formulas must change their nature and become something less definite than numbers and geometrical figures, though still specific enough to be distinguishable and nameable. This is why they do not present themselves to the soul as mathematical formulas, but as perceptible *qualia*.

10   Forms of Perceptible *Qualia*?

Another question is this: How it is that we identify and name perceptible *qualia* that appear to us? Let me sketch three possible answers to this question.

(1) The first one is that we grasp the mathematical formula of every perceptible *quale* that occurs to us, i.e. we make the calculus of processes affecting our body and assign to different formulas thus uncovered the corresponding names. This, however, does not seem to be Timaeus' theory since he suggests that such a calculus, though it may constitute a pleasurable pastime,[69] should it be applied to the whole range of perceptible *qualia*, would surpass human capacity being something which is only in the power of the Demiurge.[70]

---

69 *Tim.* 59c5–d2.
70 *Tim.* 62d2–7.

(2) Another possible answer is to suppose that there are intelligible Forms of perceptible *qualia* which make it possible for rational soul to recognize them and to assign to them the right names. This explanation of the cognition of perceptible characteristics is supported by the fact that, according to Timaeus' descriptions of sense-perception by the world soul and by human beings, the whole of the rational soul, including the Circle of the Same which is responsible for the cognition of intelligibles, is involved in every act of true opinion (*doxa alēthēs*) concerning sensations (*aisthēseis*).[71] This hypothesis (a hypothesis it must remain because Timaeus is by no means explicit on this issue) may, however, turn out to be a source of further puzzlement. Let me state some of the difficulties to which it gives rise. First, we would have to assume that there are Forms of all of the perceptible *qualia* listed above, including colours, pleasures and pains and tactile sensations. Second, there would be Forms of processes occurring between active and passive factors. Third, mathematical formulas that capture these processes would not be identical with these Forms but would constitute the means by which the Demiurge makes the clashing bodily masses resemble the intelligible models of such clashes.

(3) If we shrink away from the latter hypothesis, having rejected the first possible answer to our question, the only remaining basis for attributing names to the perceptible *qualia* would be some sort of convention, like in Parmenides' account of the opinions of ignorant mortals.[72] As a matter of fact, there would be no criterion enabling us to form a true opinion. This is evidently not Timaeus' theory since he allows for the difference between a true and a false opinion concerning sensations.[73]

Shall we, then, go for the second option, notwithstanding the puzzling questions mentioned? Interestingly, in the philosophical passage of the *Seventh Letter*, regardless of whether it is authentic or not, there is a list of different kinds of true beings which, as they are in themselves, are to be distinguished from their respective names, definitions, images and kinds of cognition. Among these objects the author of the letter quotes also "colour" (*chroa*) and "all acting and being acted upon" (*poiēmata kai pathēmata sympanta*).[74] Whoever the author was, he or she chose this option. And so can we.

---

71 *Tim.* 37a6–c5 and 43c7–44c4.
72 Cf. Parmenides, fr. B 8.50–61 Diels-Kranz (= D 8.55–66 Laks-Most).
73 Cf. *Tim.* 37b7 and 43b5–44b1.
74 *Ep.* VII 342d4 and d8.

11　Are Perceptible *Qualia* Subject-Independent?

Finally, in light of everything that has been said in the previous pages, we may ask whether perceptible *qualia*, according to the theory put forward in Plato's *Timaeus*, are objective, i.e. subject-independent properties of the things perceived. We must answer this question in the negative. As we have seen, what is perceived are processes of change that occur between particular masses of elemental corpuscles on the one hand and sentient tissues of human or animal body on the other. There is no perceptible *quale* unless there is such a process of change and unless this process affects a rational soul.[75] Thus, the redness of a rose, for instance, is characteristic not of this particular rose in itself, but of the impact this kind of rose has upon the eye of a human being. The same kind of rose may have a different impact on the eye of an animal different from human beings, as it has also a different impact on an human eye which does not function properly due to a deficiency in its physiology. Thus the colour red comes about only in typical processes of interaction between bodily masses of a specific kind with sentient tissues of a specific kind. Perceptible *qualia* are phenomena dependent on the encounter between things perceived and beings perceiving these things. Consequently, unlike geometrical characteristics of the things perceived, they do not constitute intrinsic properties of these things. In this respect, Plato's account of what is perceptible is in agreement with that of Democritus rather than with that of Aristotle. This does not preclude, however, that, in addition to the possibility of capturing the processes that underlie the occurence of perceptible *qualia* through mathematical formulas, there exist intelligible Forms that provide a basis for naming these *qualia* correctly.

Works Cited

Baltes, Matthias. "Die Zuordnung der Elemente zu den Sinnen bei Poseidonios und ihre Herkunft aus der alten Akademie." *Philologus* 122, (1978): 183–196. Reprint in id., ΔΙΑΝΟΗΜΑΤΑ. *Kleine Schriften zu Platon und zum Platonismus*. Stuttgart: B. G. Teubner, 1999, 33–50.

Bodnár, Istvan. "Matter or Size, Texture, and Resilience: The Variety of Elemental Forms in Plato's *Timaeus*." *Rhizai* v/1 (2008): 9–34.

---

[75] Note that animals too, as well as human children, possess rational souls, though more or less dysfunctional, cf. *Tim.* 43a–44a (for children) and 91d–92c (for animals).

Brisson, Luc. "Plato's Theory of Sense-Perception in the *Timaeus*: How it Works and What it Means." With "Commentary on Brisson," by D. R. Miller. In *Proceedings of the Boston Area Colloquium in Ancient Philosophy*, vol. XIII, 1997. Edited by John Cleary and Gary Gurtler. Leiden: Brill, 1999, 177–185.

Broadie, Sarah. *Nature and Divinity in Plato's* Timaeus. Cambridge: Cambridge University Press, 2012.

Johansen, Thomas K. *Plato's Natural Philosophy: A Study of the* Timaeus-Critias. Cambridge: Cambridge University Press, 2004.

Ierodiakonou, Katerina. "Plato's Theory of Colours in the *Timaeus*," *Rhizai* II/2 (2005): 219–233.

Lautner, Péter. "The *Timaeus* on Sounds and Hearing with some Implications for Plato's General Account of Sense-Perception." *Rhizai* II/2, (2005): 235–253.

Vlastos, Gregory. *Platonic Studies*. Princeton: Princeton University Press, 1981.

Vlastos, Gregory. *Plato's Universe*. Seattle: University of Washington Press, 1975. Reprinted with a new introduction by Luc Brisson. Las Vegas: Parmenides Publishers, 2005.

Plato on Illness in the *Phaedo*, the *Republic*, and the *Timaeus*

Gábor Betegh

Abstract

As we learn from Phaedo, Plato could not be present at the important philosophical conversation that took place on Socrates' last day, because he was ill, just as the unnamed fourth guest missed Timaeus' great speech because he was unwell. Starting from these two cases, and then by bringing in Plato's remarks on illness in the *Republic*, the paper argues that for Plato illness is bad because it reduces the person's agency in such a way that she cannot perform her key functions and tasks, and carry on with her long- or short-term projects. How can such disruptions be prevented and cured? In the *Timaeus*, the cosmos provides an example of an embodied living being who never gets ill, and whose body never disrupts the cognitive activities of its soul. The cosmos is eternally healthy because it constitutes a self-sustaining homeostatic system, in which the motions of the soul also guarantee the incessant well-balanced, metabolism of its body. This is unavailable to human beings, not only because we are not closed systems, but also because the motions of our rational soul do not directly regulate our metabolism. However, studying the cyclical physical processes in the cosmos, and their counterparts in the human organism, we can learn how to emulate, as far as possible, the regulated metabolism of the cosmos, and thereby become our own doctors.

Keywords

Plato – *Phaedo* – *Republic* – *Timaeus* – illness – health – Asclepius – cosmos – world soul – world body – metabolism – body – soul

1

Plato informs us about only two events from his life in his dialogues.[1] First, that he was present at the trial of Socrates (*Apol.* 34a1; and 38b6), and second that

---

[1] I had the opportunity to present different versions of this paper in Prague, Chicago, Budapest, London, Edinburgh, and St Andrews. I thank my audiences for helpful comments. I am

he was not present in the prison on Socrates' final day. When Echecrates asks Phaedo who was there, Phaedo lists seven Athenians by name, mentions some other locals,[2] and finally adds: "But Plato was ill, I think" (Πλάτων δὲ οἶμαι ἠσθένει, 59b10). Commentators, ancient and modern, have come up with various suggestions as to why Plato wanted to remind his readers of his absence. The most popular explanation is that in this way Plato declined responsibility for the exactness of the description of the event and the discussion, pointing out that he was not a witness himself.[3]

Be that as it may, Plato indicates the cause of his absence as well: he was ill, or at least so Phaedo believes. There has been some discussion as to whether Plato was indeed suffering from a bout of ill health or whether it was just an excuse.[4] This is one of the many historical questions that, I think, we will never be in a position to answer conclusively. Yet, there is a further notable point, which, to the best of my knowledge has not received much, if any, attention. Plato's illness, no matter whether historically true or false, is a powerful illustration for one of the central topics of the dialogue.[5] Socrates' central claim that triggers the entire discussion is that the body is a constant nuisance and hindrance for anyone who is truly dedicated to philosophy. As Socrates states at a later point of the discussion:

[...] ἕως ἂν τὸ σῶμα ἔχωμεν καὶ συμπεφυρμένη ᾖ ἡμῶν ἡ ψυχὴ μετὰ τοιούτου κακοῦ, οὐ μή ποτε κτησώμεθα ἱκανῶς οὗ ἐπιθυμοῦμεν· φαμὲν δὲ τοῦτο εἶναι τὸ ἀληθές. μυρίας μὲν γὰρ ἡμῖν ἀσχολίας παρέχει τὸ σῶμα διὰ τὴν ἀναγκαίαν τροφήν· ἔτι δέ, ἄν τινες νόσοι προσπέσωσιν, ἐμποδίζουσιν ἡμῶν τὴν τοῦ ὄντος

---

particularly grateful to István Bodnár, Victor Caston, Yahei Kanayama, Filip Karfík, David Sedley, and an anonymous referee for their feedback.

2 Cf. Most, "A Cock for Asclepius," 106, on the possible importance of the specific way in which the list of attendees is constructed.
3 E.g. Burnet, *Phaedo*, ix; Gallop, *Phaedo*, ad loc. This basic agreement notwithstanding, they can still disagree about whether Phaedo's report has anything to do with historical reality or is simply Plato's own literary creation (e.g. Burnet, *Phaedo*, ix). To this, I would add that his presence would have put Plato, as the writer of the *Phaedo*, in quite a quandary. On the one hand, his chosen methodology would have barred him from speaking in his own voice as a participant in the dialogue. On the other hand, it would have been equally awkward to make himself a silent character, who had nothing to contribute to these key questions, and who was not addressed by Socrates in some special way.
4 For a sceptical view, see e.g. Guthrie, *A History of Greek Philosophy: Volume 3, the Fifth Century Enlightenment*, 489 n. 2; *contra* e.g. Wilamowitz, *Platon*², 325 n. 1 and Most, "A Cock for Asclepius."
5 Interestingly, there is no trace of a Neoplatonic discussion of Plato's illness apart from Proclus' mention of it in his commentary on the *Timaeus*, *In Tim.* I 23.4–11. Cf.: Gertz, *Death and Immortality in Late Neoplatonism*, 24.

θήραν. ἐρώτων δὲ καὶ ἐπιθυμιῶν καὶ φόβων καὶ εἰδώλων παντοδαπῶν καὶ φλυ-
αρίας ἐμπίμπλησιν ἡμᾶς πολλῆς, ὥστε τὸ λεγόμενον ὡς ἀληθῶς τῷ ὄντι ὑπ'
αὐτοῦ οὐδὲ φρονῆσαι ἡμῖν ἐγγίγνεται οὐδέποτε οὐδέν.

[...] as long as we have the body and our soul is fused with bodily evil, we'll never properly acquire what we desire, namely, as we would say, the truth. For the body detains us in countless ways because of the sustenance it needs. *Besides, should certain diseases attack it, they impede our hunt for reality.* The body fills us up with loves, desires, fears and fantasies of every kind, and a great deal of nonsense, with the result that it really and truly, as the saying goes, makes it impossible for us even to think about anything at any moment.
    66b5–c5, my emphasis[6]

Plato's illness is a case in point. Because he was ill, Plato was not only bereft of the opportunity to say farewell to his beloved teacher, but also missed an important philosophical discussion. What Socrates' arguments in the *Phaedo* show is precisely that Plato's illness is, at least temporarily, the cause of the greatest bad for him, in so far as it deprives him of the greatest good: it prevents him, at least temporarily, from doing philosophy or at least to participate at an important philosophical conversation. Conversely, Plato's illness is a very concrete and powerful reminder of the fact that Socrates is right: the body can effectively obstruct the soul in pursuing its most important project.

But Plato was apparently not the only one who missed a fascinating philosophical discussion because of falling ill. Remember the opening words of the *Timaeus* (17a1–5):

ΣΩ. Εἷς, δύο, τρεῖς· ὁ δὲ δὴ τέταρτος ἡμῖν, ὦ φίλε Τίμαιε, ποῦ τῶν χθὲς μὲν δαι-
τυμόνων, τὰ νῦν δὲ ἑστιατόρων;
ΤΙ. Ἀσθένειά τις αὐτῷ συνέπεσεν, ὦ Σώκρατες· οὐ γὰρ ἂν ἑκὼν τῆσδε ἀπελεί-
πετο τῆς συνουσίας.

Socr. One, two, three ... Where's number four, Timaeus? The four of you were my guests yesterday and today I'm to be yours.
Tim. He came down with some illness, Socrates. He would not have missed our meeting willingly.[7]

---

6 All Greek texts are from the OCT. Translations from the *Phaedo* are from Sedley and Long, eds., *Plato: Meno and Phaedo,* with occasional modifications.
7 Translations from the *Timaeus* are from Cornford with occasional modifications.

Here, the last sentence clearly indicates that the bodily condition of the unnamed guest is an impediment for him: it prevented him from doing something he planned to do and found important.

I would like to suggest that the similarity between the predicament of these two characters is not accidental.[8] As scholars have noted, and as I have argued elsewhere,[9] there are strong thematic links that connect the *Phaedo* and the *Timaeus*. One of these shared topics is precisely the soul-body relationship. As has often been pointed out, the *Timaeus* expounds a novel, less austere conception of the body, and, closely related to this, of the possibilities and limitations of embodied existence.[10] I will try to argue that this has important ramifications for the way in which we think about illness. To begin with, in the framework of the *Timaeus*, illness will not be simply a powerful demonstration of the troubles caused by embodiment. More importantly, it will present a pressing philosophical problem: if the body is indeed teleologically created for us by divine beings, why does it still get ill? But as I shall also show, the *Timaeus* brings a number of other novel elements into the picture, not least because of its cosmological framework, and its conception of the cosmos as an embodied, intelligent, divine being.

All in all, what I would like to show is that in these two dialogues we start out with characters falling ill, and unable to attend a philosophical discussion. But, at the end, these two texts invite us to think in somewhat different ways about the nature of the bad that illness brings to us, and, connectedly, what the proper attitude towards illness is. In the rest of this paper, I would like to explore what these differences consist in. I shall speak more briefly about the problems raised by the *Phaedo*, and touch upon the discussion of illness in the *Republic*, before turning to a more detailed analysis of certain aspects of the conceptualisation of illness and health, in the *Timaeus*.

---

8 Not surprisingly, the identity of this unnamed character has been the subject of some speculation. Most recently Mary Louise Gill, "Plato's Unfinished Trilogy: *Timaeus-Critias-Hermocrates*" and David Sedley, "*Timaeus* as Vehicle for Platonic Doctrine" have argued, independently of each other, and for different and partially incompatible reasons, that the unnamed character is Plato himself. The suggestion was already made in antiquity by Dercyllides (Proclus, *In Tim.* I 20.7–9).

9 Betegh, "Tale, theology, and teleology in the *Phaedo*," and "Cosmic and Human Cognition in the *Timaeus*."

10 See, most recently, Jorgenson, *The Embodied Soul in Plato's Later Thought*, esp. ch. 3.

2

The first thing worthy of note is that Plato, in all of his dialogues, agrees with the common conception that illness is something bad and inherently undesirable. Plato is of course entirely capable of coming up with strongly revisionary accounts of evaluative concepts. The *Phaedo* itself offers a number of examples of such revisionary moves. Most notoriously, it turns out that from the philosopher's perspective, and for the philosopher, death is not at all a bad thing, whereas bodily pleasures turn out to be hardly, if at all, better than pain.[11] Elsewhere, we also learn that punishment can be a good thing (e.g. *Gorg.* 478a; *Rep.* 591b). Illness however is apparently not subjected to any such reevaluation. Plato agrees with the many that illness is inherently bad.[12] Perhaps the best you can say about illness is that it is one of the things in the face of which you can display courage—as Socrates says in the *Laches* (191d–e). But, surely, this does not make it good in itself, just as it does not make a precarious military situation or a ravaging storm at sea good or desirable, just because one can behave courageously in relation to them.[13]

It is however not quite so obvious *why exactly* illness is bad. An immediate answer could come from the fact that illness is the privation of health, which, other things being equal, is a good thing. Yet, as the predicament of Plato and the unnamed character in the *Timaeus* reminds us, illness is bad not only in general and in abstract terms as the privation of health, but also in its very concrete, immediate effects. Illness is bad in so far as it is a debilitating condition that *reduces our agency*. Plato and the unnamed character of the *Timaeus* wanted to be there, but they could not because of their medical condition. In fact, Plato makes clear in a number of dialogues that illness has the power to thwart our most important projects, and can make our life miserable, to such an extent that it can render life quite simply not worth living. As Socrates points out in the *Gorgias*, the ship's captain can actually harm a person by

---

11 The distinction between pure and impure pleasures is less emphatic in the *Phaedo* than in the *Republic* and the *Philebus*. Nonetheless, at 64d Socrates notes that bodily pleasures are "so-called" pleasures, and at 83c he remarks that violent pleasures are intense but are not true. Finally, at 114c he distinguishes the pleasures of learning from other types of pleasure, and gives approval to it.

12 Cf. e.g. *Charm.* 164 a–b, 165c–d; *Gorg.* 478b; Cf. also *Eryx.* 397a–b; *Alc.* I 108.

13 The only possible exception I found is *Laws* V 728d–e, where the Athenian says that the legislator will consider that "the body to value [is] not the one which is beautiful, or strong, or swift, or large, or even healthy—though that is the answer many people would expect. Nor again is it their opposites" (trans. Griffith). Cf. also Chrysippus' objection as transmitted by Plutarch *De Stoic. repugn.* 1040d1–3: ἐν δὲ τοῖς πρὸς Πλάτωνα κατηγοpῶν αὐτοῦ δοκοῦντος ἀγαθὸν ἀπολιπεῖν τὴν ὑγίειαν.

saving him from drowning, if that person is afflicted with some grave and incurable physical illness.[14] For such a person, it is better to go to a watery grave than to continue living. This is also why Socrates in Book 3 of the *Republic* argues that doctors ought to take Asclepius as their role model, in so far as the healing god never aimed at the prolongation of biological life for its own sake, and provided treatment only to people who had a reasonable chance of living a full, meaningful, useful life, in which they could carry on their life projects.

But one might want to pursue this issue further, and ask in what way illness has this power over us? In what way can it dash our projects temporarily, as in the case of Plato and (we hope) of the unnamed character of the *Timaeus*, or permanently and fatally, as in the case of those whom doctors and ship captains should rather let die?

On the basis of this set of examples, we might start formulating an answer along the following lines. Illness is bad because it is a temporary or permanent disruption of the normal condition of the organism, so that the person cannot perform his or her key functions and tasks, and carry on with his or her long- or short-term projects. Importantly, this conception of illness as a malfunction is obviously parasitic on the notion of proper functioning. Now, fully in line with the strict distribution of *erga*, tasks, and functions, Plato, at least in the *Republic*, appears to maintain a non-generalisable conception of illness as a malfunction. Malfunction is always relative to the specific function of the subject. A person might be considered ill in so far as he is unable to perform his function in society due to a bodily condition. But the same bodily condition might not count as a malfunction, and hence an illness, if it does not hinder another person fulfilling his specific function.[15] It will turn out, then, that although Plato agrees with the common evaluation of illness as something bad, he bases his evaluation on a revisionary conception of what really counts as illness for the individual.[16]

As Socrates says in the *Republic*, Asclepius "knew that in a well-run society each citizen has his own appointed function that he must perform, and that no one can afford to spend his whole life being ill and being treated by doctors" (εἰδὼς ὅτι πᾶσι τοῖς εὐνομουμένοις ἔργον τι ἑκάστῳ ἐν τῇ πόλει προστέτακται, ὃ ἀναγκαῖον ἐργάζεσθαι, καὶ οὐδενὶ σχολὴ διὰ βίου κάμνειν ἰατρευομένῳ, 406c3–5, trans. Griffith, modified). This is what Asclepius himself was well aware of, but

---

14   *Gorg.* 511e–512a; cf. also *Crito* 47c–48a.
15   This is thus a more restricted notion of function than the one that figures in Boorsean conceptions of illness, which focus on species-specific functions falling below the population mean (Boorse, "Health as a theoretical concept," and "A Rebuttal on Health").
16   This is a revision of what counts as illness, and not whether or not illness, so understood, is bad.

subsequent generations of doctors, even in the school of Asclepius, have ignored. Socrates then continues with the example of the carpenter who only cares to be treated by a doctor if there is a reasonable chance that the cure will enable him "to become healthy and get on with his life and do his own work" (ὑγιὴς γενόμενος ζῇ τὰ ἑαυτοῦ πράττων, 406e2). Our carpenter has a laudable attitude towards his medical condition, Socrates explains, because "[h]e had a certain function to perform [...] and his life was worth nothing to him if he couldn't perform it" (τι αὐτῷ ἔργον, ὃ εἰ μὴ πράττοι, οὐκ ἐλυσιτέλει ζῆν, 407a1–2).[17] This contrasts with the mistaken and harmful attitude of Herodicus who had to give up his job as an athletic coach because he became an invalid, but instead of giving up his life, he became the originator of the bad type of medicine which prioritizes the conservation of life for its own sake.[18]

A serious hand injury can thus render the carpenter temporarily unable to fulfil his tasks, while losing an arm can permanently incapacitate him, so that, if he has the correct attitude, he prefers to die. Note, however, that the very same medical condition might not hinder someone with a different *ergon* from carrying on doing *his* job. For instance, a *paidagogos* could still accompany the child in his care to school, or the left-handed scribe could continue copying his scrolls with his right hand temporarily or permanently affected. Even more to the point, the philosopher could continue a contemplative life even if he was injured or lost a limb. Indeed, Epictetus' crippled leg made him unfit for certain tasks and functions, but did not prevent him from being a philosopher. And, as we know from the *Republic*, Theages had a bodily illness (τοῦ σώματος νοσοτροφία, 496c2) that prevented him from becoming a politician, but that still allowed him to carry on doing philosophy.

---

17 Plato would thus agree with Havi Carel when she writes that "illness is not just an impairment of a certain organ or physiological function. Rather, it affects the entire person and her relationship with both physical and social environment." On the other hand, he would emphatically reply in the negative to Carel's question: "when seriously constrained by ill health, be that of chronic illness, terminal illness or disability, can one still be happy?"(Carel, "Can I Be Ill and Happy?" 96). For a charitable reading of the *Republic* passage see esp. Reeve, *Philosopher-Kings: The Argument of Plato's Republic*, 213–215; Ferrari, ed., *The Cambridge Companion to Plato's Republic*, 173–4; cf. also Levin, *Plato's Rivalry with Medicine: A Struggle and its Dissolution*, 119.

18 The recommendation voiced by Socrates thus differs from the more widespread practice according to which those patients who were considered hopeless were not treated further, but were left to the care of the family. As we can see from the case of Herodicus, this practice still allows giving treatment to patients whose lives can be saved, and who can continue to live a relatively active life, but who would be left with a permanent impairment which would hinder them to continue to fulfil what, on Socrates' account, is their natural proper function in society.

If it is not injuring or losing a limb, or becoming crippled, that prevents the philosopher from doing his specific *ergon*, what is it? The most obvious answer is intense pain. The carpenter might find it extremely difficult to concentrate on the half-ready couch in his workshop when he is having a migraine attack, and the finished product might well show signs of his reduced level of attention. But he can, even if with serious efforts, finish the job. Just as the *paidagogos* suffering from a bad toothache is likely to find a rowdy child even more irritating, and probably lose his temper more easily—but it would still not prevent him from finding the way to school and then ushering the boy back home. Intense pain on the other hand makes it well-nigh impossible for the philosopher to accomplish his *ergon*. It seems that in contrast to other occupations, a bodily condition is debilitating for the philosopher primarily because, and in so far as, it causes acute pain.[19]

I would like to suggest that this is precisely why there is strikingly little on illness itself in the *Phaedo*, and the little we do get shows a somewhat ambiguous attitude. As we have seen, disease is on Socrates' list in his grand tirade against the body (*Phd.* 66b5–c5), and as I have argued, the reference to Plato's illness is a good illustration of the way in which the body can (temporarily) hinder someone to do philosophy and attend important philosophical discussions. But then Socrates does not elaborate on the deleterious effects of medical conditions, whereas he explains in considerable detail why perception, pleasure and pain can hinder or even block our quest for the truth. Indeed, the whole discussion starts with Socrates' musing remarks on the relationship between pleasure and pain, as the fetters are removed from his ankle and wrist, about which he even goes on to compose a little myth in the manner of Aesop (60b–c).[20] In contrast with the focus on pleasure and pain, Socrates never gives an account in the *Phaedo* of the way in which illness can affect the soul's proper functioning, conceived as the search for truth through the contemplation of transcendent Forms.[21] It is never made explicit in the text, and therefore I can only tentatively suggest that in the framework of the *Phaedo*, illness has the power of "impeding our hunt for reality" (ἐμποδίζουσιν ἡμῶν τὴν

---

19   I found the most instructive treatment of pain in Plato in Evans, "Plato and the Meaning of Pain." Obviously, other unpleasant aspects of illnesses can prevent a philosopher to attend social gatherings where interesting philosophical discussions take place; but in these cases, he is prevented to attend the event not *qua* philosopher.

20   On "Aesop'" myth, see Betegh, "Tale, Theology, and Teleology." Remarkably, Socrates appears to say here that pleasure and pain are opposites, whereas in the *Gorgias* (495e–497a) he says that they cannot be opposites.

21   On how pleasures and pains affect negatively the soul's proper activity, see Ebrey, "The Asceticism of the *Phaedo*: Pleasure, Purification, and the Soul's Proper Activity."

τοῦ ὄντος θήραν, 66c1–2) primarily in so far as it causes pain. It is through the experience of intense pain that illness misleads us into thinking that the body is something really real. As most of us unfortunately know from experience, the feeling of intense pain has a particularly pressing immediacy. It evinces with singular sharpness that we have a body, and throws into relief the power our bodies can have over us, what we can, and what we cannot do. Pain, just like bodily pleasure, draws our attention to our own body, and thereby "rivets and pins" the soul to the body.[22]

These considerations might also have some bearing on the recent debate on the ascetic vs. evaluative interpretation of the *Phaedo*. Very briefly, on the ascetic reading, favoured most recently by Travis Butler and David Ebrey,[23] Socrates recommends that we ought to do whatever is in our power to avoid pain and pleasure. By contrast, on the evaluative reading, defended by Raphael Woolf and Daniel Russell, what Socrates advocates is not to change our behaviour, but rather to change our attitude: instead of actively seeking and practicing austere abstinence, we ought to have the correct evaluative attitude towards corporeal pleasures and pains, by not attaching any importance to them.[24] Now as Raphael Woolf's nuanced analysis shows, I think, conclusively, the *Phaedo* offers textual clues for both readings. On the whole, the *Phaedo* does suggest that the fewer and lesser bodily pleasures and pains we experience the better off we are, and therefore we should try to avoid situations and activities in which we encounter them. This is so because, no matter what, bodily pleasures and pains do have a power over us, and do "rivet and nail" the soul to the body. On the other hand—and this is where I rather agree with the evaluative reading—the active avoidance of pleasure and pain ought not become a programme and goal in itself. If we concentrate too much on how to steer clear of pleasures and pains, we might end up focusing once again on the body in this roundabout, negative way, instead of doing philosophy. In any case, we will encounter some pleasures and pains, so we'd better also develop the correct attitude towards them in order to minimise their effect on us.

Be that as it may, illness in its relation to pain might well create a problem for the ascetic view. It is, I think, not by chance that asceticism in general, and

---

22 The comparison with Carel, "Ill and Happy," 100, is once again helpful: "Whereas it is normally taken for granted that the body is a healthy functioning element contributing silently to the execution of projects (with the body perceived as transparent and inconspicuous), in illness the body comes to the fore and its pain and incapacity directly affect the agency of the person."
23 Butler, "A Riveting Argument in Favor of Asceticism in the *Phaedo*"; Ebrey, "Asceticism of the *Phaedo*."
24 Woolf, "The Practice of a Philosopher"; Russell, *Plato on Pleasure and the Good Life*, ch. 3.

ascetic readings of the *Phaedo* in particular, concentrate primarily on the active avoidance of *pleasure*. It is relatively easy to see how one can actively avoid pleasure: one does not accept invitations to lavish feasts, leads an abstemious life, does not engage in sex, or only for the sake of securing heirs, and so forth. It is considerably less obvious how one can actively avoid pain *without* paying at least some attention to the body. Avoiding lavish feasts and leading an abstemious life will not do in itself. To maintain health and to prevent the onset of illness, eating and drinking less, and less pleasurably, can help, but is not enough. At the very least, the restrained diet should also be a fairly balanced one, and to make it balanced will require some attention. Similarly, a modicum of exercise, and therefore some time and attention paid to the body, will be needed. So while I agree that the ascetic reading of the *Phaedo* has a strong appeal, I think it is far from obvious how to reconcile the project of strictly leaving the body behind as far as possible with the active avoidance of pain and, relatedly, the active prevention of illness.

Small surprise, then, that immediately before he turns to the correct attitude towards health and medicine, Socrates in the *Republic* does spend some time setting down the guidelines for the correct, balanced diet and regimen for the guardians. And in this discussion maintaining bodily health and strength does have a role.[25] This appears to be a recognition that if one wants to avoid illness and the consequent debilitating pain, it will not suffice to say that one must avoid pleasurable meals and drinks.

Note also, that Socrates in the *Republic* contrasts injuries and seasonal diseases with such medical conditions as are caused by idleness, lack of moderation in food and drink, or a licentious life style.[26] Clearly, we cannot be held responsible for medical conditions inflicted on us by such external causes as injuries and illnesses caused by extreme weather conditions.[27]

---

25   *Rep.* III 402e–405a.
26   *Rep.* III 405c8–d4: "And don't you think it's a disgrace," I asked, "to need medical attention, not as a result of injuries or the onset of some seasonal illness, but because our inactivity, and a routine such as we have described, have filled us up with gas and ooze, like a marsh, and compelled those clever doctors of the school of Asclepius to invent names like "wind" and "flux" for our diseases?" (Τὸ δὲ ἰατρικῆς, ἦν δ' ἐγώ, δεῖσθαι ὅτι μὴ τραυμάτων ἕνεκα ἤ τινων ἐπετείων νοσημάτων ἐπιπεσόντων, ἀλλὰ δι' ἀργίαν τε καὶ δίαιταν οἵαν διήλθομεν, ῥευμάτων τε καὶ πνευμάτων ὥσπερ λίμνας ἐμπιμπλαμένους φύσας τε καὶ κατάρρους νοσήμασιν ὀνόματα τίθεσθαι ἀναγκάζειν τοὺς κομψοὺς Ἀσκληπιάδας, οὐκ αἰσχρὸν δοκεῖ;)
27   In the final myth of the *Phaedo*, when he describes the vastly superior conditions on the real surface of earth and comparing it to our condition, Socrates says the following: "Their seasons are temperate in such a way that they are free of illness and live for a much longer time than the people here." (τὰς δὲ ὥρας αὐτοῖς κρᾶσιν ἔχειν τοιαύτην ὥστε ἐκείνους ἀνόσους

Moreover, Socrates in the *Republic* also recommends that the guardians should be exposed to "hardship, pain, and trial," as well as pleasure and other temptations (413d–414a; cf. 503a). This, however, should only serve as a *test* of the steadfastness of their character. As far as I can see, it is never suggested that they should be made to experience some measure of pleasure and pain, and especially not illness, in order to immunise them.

Let me close this cursory treatment of the *Phaedo* and its relation to the *Republic* with a brief remark on Asclepius. Before ending his earthly life, Socrates famously reminded his friends not to forget to sacrifice a cockerel they owe to Asclepius (ᾮ Κρίτων, ἔφη, τῷ Ἀσκληπιῷ ὀφείλομεν ἀλεκτρυόνα, *Phd.* 118a7–8). This enigmatic, but surely significant utterance, has provoked a great deal of speculation ever since antiquity. As opposed to the most widespread view according to which Socrates refers to his own imminent recovery from embodiment conceived as an illness, Glenn Most and, more recently, Yahei Kanayama have suggested that through Socrates' remark, Plato refers to his own recuperation from the medical condition which prevented him from being present at that very occasion.[28] It seems to me that no matter whether the reference is to Socrates or to Plato, the essential point is that Asclepius is thanked here not simply for a successful recovery, but more specifically, because he has performed exactly that role for which he is hailed in the *Republic*. His intervention made it possible for a person to continue the project which has defined that person's life, and in which the person has been hindered by his bodily condition.

3

It is time to turn to the *Timaeus*. As stated at the outset, I will attempt to explore the ways in which Timaeus' account of illness differs from what we have seen in the *Phaedo* and the *Republic*. I will argue that the account of illness in the *Timaeus* is more immediately linked to an account of bodily health and, in particular, to an examination of the conditions and maintenance of bodily health. Moreover, I will try to show that Timaeus, true to Plato's characteristic method, proceeds by setting out a divine paradigm, which in this case is a continuously healthy embodied divine organism—the cosmos itself. Timaeus describes why the cosmos is able to retain its health unfailingly, why the good health of the

---

εἶναι καὶ χρόνον τε ζῆν πολὺ πλείω τῶν ἐνθάδε [...], *Phd.* 111b1–6). Temperate climatic conditions can reduce illness and prolong life.

28 Most, "A Cock for Asclepius"; Kanayama, "Socrates' Last Words."

divine organism is inherently unattainable for us, and why and how the health of the cosmic god can still serve for us as a normative ideal that we ought to emulate. The passage in which Timaeus formulates the ideal of "becoming like god" towards the very end of the dialogue (90a–c) has been discussed extensively by scholars in recent years.[29] However, these discussions have almost exclusively focused on the way in which our rational souls ought to emulate their divine cosmic counterpart to achieve the best human life. Ultimately, I will try to show that even though the relationship between the cosmic and the human souls is without doubt the centrally important aspect of the goal of human life, Timaeus conceives the maintenance of bodily health as a lower form of *homoiōsis theōi*—or, more precisely, as an ancillary part of the more comprehensive normative programme of becoming like god. Just as our souls should emulate the cosmic soul, our bodies should also emulate the cosmic body. Just as madness, irrationality, and other forms of psychic dysfunctions can be described as diverging from the cosmic divine model, so also is illness a deviation from a state in which the functioning of our bodies matches, as far as possible, the functioning of the cosmic body. As must be evident already from this prefatory summary, I will attempt to show that while Timaeus' account of health and illness builds on familiar Platonic themes and patterns, it departs in important ways from the picture of illness, and the correct attitude towards it, that we get from the *Phaedo* and the *Republic*.

Let us start with some uncontroversial points. As a number of recent studies have argued, the *Timaeus* evinces a markedly different approach towards the body. Among others, Thomas Johansen, Sarah Broadie and Gabriela Roxana Carone have offered illuminating analyses of the fact that in Timaeus' account both the basic structure of the corporeal realm—the geometrical construction of the four elementary bodies—and the anatomy and physiology of the human organism are the results of divine creation aiming at the best, the most orderly, and the most beautiful.[30] In particular, the body of human beings is constructed by the auxiliaries of the Demiurge in order to be of service to the rational soul. However, from our present perspective, the fact remains—and Timaeus fully acknowledges it—that despite all the divine care and attention devoted to the construction of the human body, we still do get ill. Timaeus ultimately agrees with the Socrates of the *Phaedo* that even if the human body was constructed with a view to the interest of the rational soul, it keeps causing

---

29   See in particular the seminal paper by Sedley, "The Ideal of Godlikeness."
30   Johansen, *Plato's Natural Philosophy*; Broadie, *Nature and Divinity in Plato's Timaeus*; Carone, *Plato's Cosmology and its Ethical Dimension*.

problems for the soul and can hinder it in pursuing its projects and carrying out its proper activity. Just think of what happened to our unnamed guest.

Given the overarching teleological framework, and the consequent attention paid to the functioning of the human body, the causes of illness have to be explained in order to fit the failings of our body into the theodicy of the *Timaeus*. It should not come as a surprise, then, that the *Timaeus* contains Plato's most detailed account of diseases (*Tim.* 81a–87a). This formerly neglected part of the dialogue has recently been subject to valuable discussions, which have made clearer Plato's relationship to the medical tradition, and have tried to come to grips with Timaeus' striking claims about the physiological origins of psychological illnesses and alleged moral vices.[31] As it will be clear from my own discussion, I have greatly benefited from these studies. I would however like to approach the issue from a somewhat different angle, as I outlined in my introductory paragraph to this section.

What is particularly striking in Timaeus' account is that it shows that embodied life as such is not necessarily a curse. Indeed, Timaeus describes in great detail a corporeal organism which lives a fully happy, contemplative life. As he explains, the cosmos is a divine living being, which starts its life when its body becomes animated by its soul:

> Ἐπεὶ δὲ κατὰ νοῦν τῷ συνιστάντι πᾶσα ἡ τῆς ψυχῆς σύστασις ἐγεγένητο, μετὰ τοῦτο πᾶν τὸ σωματοειδὲς ἐντὸς αὐτῆς ἐτεκταίνετο καὶ μέσον μέσῃ συναγαγὼν προσήρμοττεν· ἡ δ' ἐκ μέσου πρὸς τὸν ἔσχατον οὐρανὸν πάντῃ διαπλακεῖσα κύκλῳ τε αὐτὸν ἔξωθεν περικαλύψασα, αὐτὴ ἐν αὑτῇ στρεφομένη, θείαν ἀρχὴν ἤρξατο ἀπαύστου καὶ ἔμφρονος βίου πρὸς τὸν σύμπαντα χρόνον.

> When the whole fabric of the soul had been finished to its maker's mind, he next began to fashion within the soul all that is bodily, and brought the two together, fitting them centre to centre. And the soul, being everywhere interwoven from the centre to the outermost heaven and enveloping the heaven all round on the outside, revolving within its own limit, made a divine beginning of ceaseless and intelligent life for all time.
>
> 36d7–e5

---

31 Cf., most recently, Ayache, "Est-il vraiment question d'art médical dans le *Timée*?"; Vegetti, *La Medicina in Platone*; Mackenzie, *Plato on Punishment*; Gill, "The Body's Fault ? Plato's *Timaeus* on Psychic Illness"; Lloyd, *In the Grip of Disease: Studies in the Greek Imagination*: ch. 6; Lautner, "Plato's Account of the Diseases of the Soul in *Timaeus* 86b1–87b9"; Sassi, "Mental Illness, Moral Error, and Responsibility in the Late Plato," and Jorgenson in this volume. From the earlier literature, see e.g. Abel, "Plato und die Medizin seiner Zeit."

Due to the Demiurge's providential planning and manufacturing (to which we shall shortly return), the life of the cosmos is eternal. Yet, as we have learnt from the *Republic*, longevity is not an aim in itself. What matters is that throughout its eternal embodied life, the soul of the cosmos is able to engage in the highest form of cognitive activity and live an intelligent life (*emphrōn bios*), apparently without being disrupted or hindered by its body. Indeed, immediately after this statement about the beginning of the intelligent life of the cosmos, Timaeus also describes in detail the cognitive activities of the cosmic soul, and explains that the soul of the cosmos formulates unfailingly true opinions and convictions about objects that come to be, and knowledge and understanding about intelligible eternal objects (ὅταν μὲν περὶ τὸ αἰσθητὸν γίγνηται καὶ ὁ τοῦ θατέρου κύκλος ὀρθὸς ἰὼν εἰς πᾶσαν αὐτοῦ τὴν ψυχὴν διαγγείλῃ, δόξαι καὶ πίστεις γίγνονται βέβαιοι καὶ ἀληθεῖς, ὅταν δὲ αὖ περὶ τὸ λογιστικὸν ᾖ καὶ ὁ τοῦ ταὐτοῦ κύκλος εὔτροχος ὢν αὐτὰ μηνύσῃ, νοῦς ἐπιστήμη τε ἐξ ἀνάγκης ἀποτελεῖται, 37b6–c4). What is more, the cosmos is not the only divine compound of body and soul. For Timaeus maintains that the stars and planets, and even the earth we tread on, are corporeal gods, who live their divinely happy, contemplative life forever.[32] If so, we are literally surrounded by such embodied living beings, who are immersed in their thoughts, apparently undisturbed by their bodies, and formulate true *logoi*, opinions and convictions, as well as understanding and knowledge. So even though they are eternally tied to their bodies, the souls of the cosmos, and these other cosmic gods, are thus able to perform undisturbed and uninterrupted what, according to the *Phaedo*, the proper activity and *ergon* of the soul is.[33]

That it is possible for an embodied being to lead such a life was not, I think, considered seriously by the Socrates of the *Phaedo*.[34] As Socrates complained, "as long as we have the body and our soul is fused with bodily evil, we'll never properly acquire what we desire, namely, as we would say, the truth" (66b). So how can the soul of the cosmos remain undisturbed by its body, avoid that its body constantly interrupts and hassles it, so that it can continue its cognitive activity at the highest level, and "acquire the truth"? If we want to get closer to the truth during our incarnate existence, our primary concern should be to

---

32   For the cognitive activity of the heavenly bodies, cf. 40a7–b2: κινήσεις δὲ δύο προσῆψεν ἑκάστῳ, τὴν μὲν ἐν ταὐτῷ κατὰ ταὐτά, περὶ τῶν αὐτῶν ἀεὶ τὰ αὐτὰ ἑαυτῷ διανοουμένῳ, τὴν δὲ εἰς τὸ πρόσθεν, ὑπὸ τῆς ταὐτοῦ καὶ ὁμοίου περιφορᾶς κρατουμένῳ. On the metaphysics of corporeal gods of the *Timaeus*, see now Broadie, "Corporeal Gods, with Reference to Plato and Aristotle." In the *Phaedrus* (246c5–d2) Socrates expresses strong scepticism about the possibility of such immortal divine beings who are compounds of body and soul.

33   On the proper activity of the soul in the *Phaedo*, see Ebrey, "Asceticism of the *Phaedo*."

34   With the possible exception of the "aether dwellers."

try to approximate with our own rational souls the state of the cosmic soul, the celestial counterpart of our rational souls (90a–c). However, this is surely not enough, because we should also try to protect the rational soul from the deleterious influences of the body—the ones the Socrates of the *Phaedo* railed at. We therefore ought to examine how the body of the world functions so that it manages not to pester its soul, and we should also try to approximate, as far as possible, the state of the body of the cosmos, so that our bodies disturb and hassle, as little as possible, our own rational souls.

How can the cosmos be free from bodily ills? First of all, the Demiurge made sure that the cosmos is not vulnerable to ageing[35] and illness (*agērōn kai anoson*) by using up all the elements in its construction:

> Τῶν δὲ δὴ τεττάρων ἓν ὅλον ἕκαστον εἴληφεν ἡ τοῦ κόσμου σύστασις. ἐκ γὰρ πυρὸς παντὸς ὕδατός τε καὶ ἀέρος καὶ γῆς συνέστησεν αὐτὸν ὁ συνιστάς, μέρος οὐδὲν οὐδενὸς οὐδὲ δύναμιν ἔξωθεν ὑπολιπών, τάδε διανοηθείς, πρῶτον μὲν ἵνα ὅλον ὅτι μάλιστα ζῷον τέλεον ἐκ τελέων τῶν μερῶν εἴη, πρὸς δὲ τούτοις ἕν, ἅτε οὐχ ὑπολελειμμένων ἐξ ὧν ἄλλο τοιοῦτον γένοιτ' ἄν, ἔτι δὲ ἵν' ἀγήρων καὶ ἄνοσον ᾖ, κατανοῶν ὡς συστάτῳ σώματι θερμὰ καὶ ψυχρὰ καὶ πάνθ' ὅσα δυνάμεις ἰσχυρὰς ἔχει περιιστάμενα ἔξωθεν καὶ προσπίπτοντα ἀκαίρως λύει καὶ νόσους γῆράς τε ἐπάγοντα φθίνειν ποιεῖ.

Now the frame of the world took up the whole of each of these four [*viz.* the four elements]; he who put it together made it consist of all the fire and water and air and earth, leaving no part or power of anyone of them outside. This was his intent: first, that it might be in the fullest measure

---

35 The reference to aging is remarkable. As we shall see below, Timaeus thinks that it is possible to lead a human life without falling ill, and, what is more, one can reach a natural death without being ill (81b–e, see also below). Just as important, there is no suggestion in Plato that elderly people would be less apt to do philosophy—if anything, quite the opposite. So why is this "ageist" remark by Timaeus? I would tentatively suggest an answer along the following lines. Aging, even if the person remains completely healthy, is marked by a shift in the physiological characteristics of the body; for instance, by a shift in the dry-wet axis. Such a combination of a dynamic equilibrium of the opposites, combined with a gradual shift in the proportion of one or more pairs of opposites is conceivable at the cosmic level as well. For instance, although according to Anaximander's fragment DK B 1 there is a dynamic equilibrium between pairs of opposites, according to some testimonies the cosmos is gradually becoming hotter and dryer (e.g., Aristotle, *Meteor.* 353b6 ff. and DK A 27; cf. Fredeudenthal, "The Theory of the Opposites and an Ordered Universe: Physics and Metaphysics in Anaximander," 217–225). By saying that the cosmos is "unageing", Timaeus might indicate that there is no such shift in the dynamic equilibrium which characterizes the physiology of the cosmos (on which see more below).

a living being whole and complete, of complete parts; next, that it might be single, nothing being left over, out of which such another might come into being; and moreover that it might be free from age and sickness. For he perceived that, if a body be composite, when hot things and cold and all things that have strong powers beset that body and attack it from without, they bring it to untimely dissolution and cause it to waste away by bringing upon it sickness and age. For this reason and so considering, he fashioned it as a single whole consisting of all these wholes, complete and free from age and sickness.

32c5–33a6

By leaving none of the corporeal elements outside of the cosmos, the Demiurge has ensured that no external harm will afflict it. So no wounds or injuries endanger the well-being of the cosmic organism. Moreover, it will not be subject to the harmful effects of the opposites, such as the hot and the cold. So no "seasonal illnesses," due to extreme weather conditions.

How do *we* fare in that respect? The younger gods who designed and fabricated our bodies did their best to protect us from the type of external effects that the cosmos is entirely free from. This is why they covered the marrow with hard bones, and wrapped the bones in flesh, in order to protect us from injuries and the effects of excessive heat and cold (74b7–c5). Given that flesh would be too thick a covering for the head, the gods resourcefully enveloped it in skin and hair, once again in order to protect it from injuries and extreme weather conditions, as far as possible, but without hindering cognition (75e–76d). But all these efforts can only mitigate our vulnerability to external effects, and Timaeus ultimately agrees with the Socrates of the *Republic* that whatever we do, we can still be victims of injuries and seasonal illnesses. But this is the type of physical ill that can happen to us, but for which neither the auxiliaries of the Demiurge, nor we can be held responsible.

However, the fact that there is nothing left outside the cosmos has further momentous consequences of a positive nature. Timaeus continues by pointing out, quite reasonably, that the cosmos can dispense with sense organs because there is nothing external to it to see or hear. So, no injuries and seasonal illnesses, and, moreover, no hassle with perception. By using up all of the elements, and thus making the cosmos complete, the Demiurge killed two birds with one stone. There is however a third bird:

πνεῦμά τε οὐκ ἦν περιεστὸς δεόμενον ἀναπνοῆς, οὐδ' αὖ τινος ἐπιδεὲς ἦν ὀργάνου σχεῖν ᾧ τὴν μὲν εἰς ἑαυτὸ τροφὴν δέξοιτο, τὴν δὲ πρότερον ἐξικμασμένην ἀποπέμψοι πάλιν. ἀπῄει τε γὰρ οὐδὲν οὐδὲ προσῄειν αὐτῷ ποθεν—οὐδὲ γὰρ ἦν—αὐτὸ γὰρ ἑαυτῷ τροφὴν τὴν ἑαυτοῦ φθίσιν παρέχον καὶ πάντα ἐν ἑαυτῷ καὶ ὑφ' ἑαυτοῦ πάσχον καὶ δρῶν ἐκ τέχνης γέγονεν· ἡγήσατο γὰρ αὐτὸ ὁ συνθεὶς αὔταρκες ὂν ἄμεινον ἔσεσθαι μᾶλλον ἢ προσδεὲς ἄλλων.

There was no surrounding air (*pneuma*) to require breathing, nor yet was it in need of any organ by which to receive food into itself or to discharge it again when drained of its juices. For nothing went out or came into it from anywhere, since there was nothing: it was designed to feed itself on its own waste and to act and be acted upon entirely by itself and within itself; because its creator thought that it would be better self-sufficient, rather than dependent upon anything else.

33c3–d3

Negatively, the cosmos is thus not vulnerable to harmful external influences. Positively, the cosmos is self-sufficient (*autarkes*). Importantly, this *autarkeia* is not described as a static state, but the cyclical process of the intertransformation and relocation of elements. Moreover, it is not simply a cyclical process, but it is described in terms of an internal activity of nourishment and excretion; in a word, the *metabolism* of the cosmos as a living organism. As we shall shortly see—barring injuries and seasonal illnesses—all morbid states of the human organism are derivable from a disruption of the balance of metabolism. And, as we shall also see, this is precisely the single most important cause of illness that we can also do something about.

But how does the cosmos maintain the complete, uninterrupted regularity of its metabolism? For if we could understand that, and apply it to our own bodies, we could also, so far as it is possible for us, prevent ourselves from falling ill. Most commentators assume that the *autarkeia* of the cosmos means that the Demiurge created the body of the world in such a way that it can recycle its waste into its nourishment, such that the *body* of the cosmos constitutes a self-sustaining homeostatic system. What renders this reading *prima facie* attractive is that it exempts the soul of the world from any care for its body: physical processes constituting the metabolism of the cosmos, on this view, run on their own, without any attention required from the soul of the cosmos. On this reading, the soul of the cosmos can be completely immersed in contemplation, because its body is designed in such a way that it does not need any care or maintenance.

It seems to me however that what Timaeus wants to say is that the self-sustaining homeostatic system is not the body of the world taken in itself, but rather the cosmic organism as a whole, conceived as a compound of body and soul. Timaeus in this respect agrees with speakers of other Platonic dialogues, such as the *Gorgias* and the *Statesman*: if the body is left to its own devices, it will gradually fall into disarray, no matter how well it was organised at the beginning.[36]

So, if the body of the cosmos does not constitute a self-regulating system in and of itself, how is the incessant, cyclical, well-balanced, metabolism of the cosmic god maintained? First of all, it is ultimately due to the *periodos*, the circular motion of the circles of the world soul,[37] that the body of the world does not reach either a static state of complete homogeneity, or a similarly static state in which the four elements would be arranged in four homogeneous concentric circles. The circular motion of the world soul, enveloping the body of the cosmos from the outside, presses the elementary particles together by the centripetal force of its rotation. Because of this pressure, there are no empty spaces between the particles. Moreover, due to this pressure, the sharp-edged fire particles cut up the other types of particles, opening up a pass-way for the other elements as well. This process ensures that all four elements, and all the differently sized varieties of the four elements, reach their proper places, without however letting them reach a homogeneous static state (58a4–c4). As Timaeus summarises the outcome:

ἡ δὴ τῆς πιλήσεως σύνοδος τὰ σμικρὰ εἰς τὰ τῶν μεγάλων διάκενα συνωθεῖ. σμικρῶν οὖν παρὰ μεγάλα τιθεμένων καὶ τῶν ἐλαττόνων τὰ μείζονα διακρινόντων, τῶν δὲ μειζόνων ἐκεῖνα συγκρινόντων, πάντ' ἄνω κάτω μεταφέρεται πρὸς τοὺς ἑαυτῶν τόπους· μεταβάλλον γὰρ τὸ μέγεθος ἕκαστον καὶ τὴν τόπων μεταβάλλει στάσιν. οὕτω δὴ διὰ ταῦτά τε ἡ τῆς ἀνωμαλότητος διασῳζομένη γένεσις ἀεὶ τὴν ἀεὶ κίνησιν τούτων οὖσαν ἐσομένην τε ἐνδελεχῶς παρέχεται.

So the coming-together involved in the condensing process thrusts the small bodies together into the interstices between the large ones. Accordingly, when the small are set alongside the large, and the lesser disintegrate the larger, while the larger cause the lesser to combine, all are changing the direction of their movement, this way and that, towards their own regions; for each, in changing its size, changes also the situation of its region. In this way, then, and by these means there is a perpetual

---

36 Cf. esp. *Polit.* 269d–e, and 273b; cf. also *Crat.* 399e–400a.
37 I agree with Karfík, *Die Beseelung des Kosmos. Untersuchungen zur Seelenlehre, Kosmologie und Theologie in Platons Phaidon und Timaios*, 165–170 and 179–180, (and Archer-Hind's translation) that, *pace* Taylor, Cornford and Zeyl, *periodos* at 58a5 must refer to the circular *motion* of the world soul. The following analysis owes much to Karfík's very perceptive discussion.

safeguard for the occurrence of that heterogeneity which provides that the perpetual motion of these bodies is and shall be without cessation.
58b4–c4

Moreover, to the regular rotation of the whole cosmos caused by the Circle of the Same, we should add the more complex movements of the planets riding on the circles of the Different. Most important among these are the Sun, the Moon, and the Earth, conceived as the primary "organs" of time. The Sun in particular is responsible for the seasons, whereas the Earth is hailed not only as our nurse or nourisher (*trophos*) but also as "the guardian and *demiurgos* of night and day" (φύλακα καὶ δημιουργὸν νυκτός τε καὶ ἡμέρας, 40b9–10). It is by ensuring the regularity of seasons, that the celestial gods can fulfil the task assigned to them by the Demiurge "to bring mortal living beings to birth, feed them, and cause them to grow" (ἀπεργάζεσθε ζῷα καὶ γεννᾶτε τροφήν τε διδόντες αὐξάνετε καὶ φθίνοντα πάλιν δέχεσθε, 41d2–3). So in addition to the elemental processes guaranteed by the Circle of the Same, the planets on the Circle of the Different, together with the Earth, are responsible for the regularity of the daily and seasonal cycles, and consequently for the dynamic, cyclical balance between the hot and the cold, the wet and the dry. The movements of the circles of the Same and the Different, in conjunction with the Earth, jointly guarantee that the metabolism of the world's body remain constant and well-balanced.[38]

The real importance of this description from our present perspective becomes clear only at a later point of the dialogue, when Timaeus turns to offer his detailed explanation and classification of human illnesses. The physical and physiological explanations are complex, and a number of specific details are obscure. The general outlines are, however, clear, and are fully sufficient for our present purposes. Here is Timaeus' first general characterisation of illness:[39]

Τὸ δὲ τῶν νόσων ὅθεν συνίσταται, δῆλόν που καὶ παντί. τεττάρων γὰρ ὄντων γενῶν ἐξ ὧν συμπέπηγεν τὸ σῶμα, γῆς πυρὸς ὕδατός τε καὶ ἀέρος, τούτων

---

38 All this is of course quite reminiscent of those passages in which Aristotle speaks about the Sun and the heavens as the maintainers of the perpetual cosmic motion and cyclical inter-transformation of the elements, counter-acting the elements natural tendency to go to their respective natural places (*De gen. et corr.* 336a14–18; cf. also *Phys.* 194a13; *Met.* 1071a11–17).

39 On Timaeus' description and categorisation of illnesses, see in particular Miller, "The Aetiology of Disease in Plato's *Timaeus*," and Grams, "Medical Theory in Plato's *Timaeus*." I have been persuaded by the arguments of Prince, "The Metaphysics of Bodily Health and Disease in Plato's *Timaeus*," that the three categories of illness are not at the same level, but the first category described at 82a1–b7 is the general genus of which the second and third categories, described at 82b8–84c7 and 84d2–86a8 respectively, are species.

ἡ παρὰ φύσιν πλεονεξία καὶ ἔνδεια καὶ τῆς χώρας μετάστασις ἐξ οἰκείας ἐπ᾽ ἀλλοτρίαν γιγνομένη, πυρός τε αὖ καὶ τῶν ἑτέρων ἐπειδὴ γένη πλείονα ἑνὸς ὄντα τυγχάνει, τὸ μὴ προσῆκον ἕκαστον ἑαυτῷ προσλαμβάνειν, καὶ πάνθ᾽ ὅσα τοιαῦτα, στάσεις καὶ νόσους παρέχει· παρὰ φύσιν γὰρ ἑκάστου γιγνομένου καὶ μεθισταμένου θερμαίνεται μὲν ὅσα ἂν πρότερον ψύχηται, ξηρὰ δὲ ὄντα εἰς ὕστερον γίγνεται νοτερά, καὶ κοῦφα δὴ καὶ βαρέα, καὶ πάσας πάντη μεταβολὰς δέχεται. μόνως γὰρ δή, φαμέν, ταὐτὸν ταὐτῷ κατὰ ταὐτὸν καὶ ὡσαύτως καὶ ἀνὰ λόγον προσγιγνόμενον καὶ ἀπογιγνόμενον ἐάσει ταὐτὸν ὂν αὐτῷ σῶν καὶ ὑγιὲς μένειν· ὃ δ᾽ ἂν πλημμελήσῃ τι τούτων ἐκτὸς ἀπιὸν ἢ προσιόν, ἀλλοιότητας παμποικίλας καὶ νόσους φθοράς τε ἀπείρους παρέξεται.

The origin of diseases is no doubt evident to all. Since there are four kinds which compose the body, earth, fire, water, and air, disorders and diseases arise from the unnatural prevalence or deficiency of these, or from their migration from their own proper place to an alien one; or again, since there are several varieties of fire and the rest, from any bodily part's taking in an unsuitable variety, and from all other causes of this kind. For when anyone of the kinds is formed or shifts its place contrary to nature, parts that were formerly cold are heated, the dry become moist, and so also with the light and the heavy, and they undergo changes of every kind. The only way, as we hold, in which any part can be left unchanged and sound and healthy is that the same thing should be coming to it and departing from it with constant observance of uniformity and due proportion; any element that trespasses beyond these limits in its in-coming or passing out will give rise to a great variety of alterations and to diseases and corruptions without number.

82a1–b7

The ultimate cause of illness is thus the breakdown of precisely that kind of constant, but well-regulated motion, interchange, and inter-transformation of elements, and their various kinds, as well as the balanced distribution of hot and cold and wet and dry, that is guaranteed at the cosmic level by the motions of the world soul. At the other extreme, what characterises the physiology of the new-born baby is precisely the complete imbalance of all these elementary motions (42e–44d). This chaotic imbalance of metabolism, characterised by particles aggressively entering and leaving the body, also disrupts the regular motions of the rational soul of the baby—so much so that its two circles become completely distorted, almost broken up. The circle of the different starts to revolve in the opposite direction, whereas the circle of the same stops moving altogether. If this state of the infant is not properly taken care of, it can lead to *amathia*, stupidity, what Timaeus describes as the greatest illness (*tēn megistēn* [...] *noson*, 44c1). This description confirms once again that a well-ordered metabolism is the key to maintaining or regaining health, whereas a serious imbalance of metabolism is a pathological state which can lead to the most serious cognitive impairment and psychological problems.

Now, as we have seen, metabolism at the cosmic level is regulated by the movements of the world soul. But doesn't this mean that the world soul does after all need to busy itself with maintaining the physical-physiological processes in its body, and thereby gets distracted in its cognitive activity? I think not. What is so special about the world soul is that its regular revolutions *both* constitute its cognitive activity *and* guarantee the health of the world's body. It is by the same motions that the soul fulfils its proper *ergon* of cognising and formulating knowledge and understanding about eternal, indivisible, always self-same forms, and true opinions about divisible corporeal beings, *and* that it keeps the body of the world in good condition. By performing what it most desires to do in and of itself, the world soul also takes care of the health of its body. No extra attention to the body is needed.

The crucial point is that by thinking its eternal thoughts, the world soul at the same time, and by the same movements, also keeps its body perfectly fit. Unfortunately, we human beings are constitutionally, or rather anatomically, incapable of performing this feat. Our rational soul is not such that it would be able to regulate the physiological processes of our body simply by contemplation.

So if it is not by the movements of our rational soul, how is our metabolism regulated and maintained? But, even before that, why is the human body not self-sustaining and *autarkes*? For, from the mere fact that there are things external to the human body, it does not immediately follow that the human organism could not be a self-sustaining, closed system. I see no reason in principle why the elements *within* the body could not simply transform into one another, in a cyclical fashion, as they do it in the cosmic body. In other words, why do we need to have nourishment from the outside, and why do we in turn excrete matter?

Timeaus' answer is that it is so because the body is constantly being bombarded by particles from the outside. These particles, primarily of fire and air, dissolve parts of the tissues of the organism, and thereby create a constant depletion and wasting-away (ὑπὸ τούτων τηκόμενον κενούμενόν τ' ἔφθινεν, βοήθειαν αὐτῷ θεοὶ μηχανῶνται, 77a2–3) that needs to be replenished by sustenance from the outside.[40] The process is described in considerable detail, but I will

---

40 Cf. Miller, "Aetiology of Disease," 177 and Karfík, "The Constitution of the Human Body in Plato's *Timaeus*," 170.

now skip over many subtleties and niceties. The gods designed the gastrointestinal tract in order that it processes the food and drink entering the body. By the force of fire in the belly, the nourishment is melted and broken down into particles that are appropriate to replenish the depleted tissues. These particles are then transported to their respective destinations by the blood flow. This is how healthy, balanced metabolism works. If it could be maintained, we could retain our health even if not quite in the way the cosmos does.

But we still don't know what regulates metabolism in the human organism. This whole complex I described in the previous paragraph is likened to an irrigation system and, as Timaeus explains, this system needs a pump. This is why we breathe. We breathe in order to keep this whole elaborate process of the digestion of nourishment and the transportation of the elements to their proper places in operation (for a summary, see 78e4–79a4). We understand then that, in the final account, breathing is the process that maintains and regulates metabolism.

However, breathing is neither caused nor operated by the rational soul. The motions of the circles of our rational soul, and our concomitant cognitive activities, have nothing to do with respiration, and thereby have no immediate role in maintaining and regulating our metabolism.[41] Even more interestingly, breathing is not regulated by the lower, mortal soul parts either. Indeed, it is striking how little we learn about the function and functioning of the lowest part of the soul. It is introduced as the soul the desires of which are directed at food and drink and other bodily needs (τὸ δὲ δὴ σίτων τε καὶ ποτῶν ἐπιθυμητικὸν τῆς ψυχῆς καὶ ὅσων ἔνδειαν διὰ τὴν τοῦ σώματος ἴσχει φύσιν, 70d7–8), but then we learn next to nothing about how this desire contributes to our nourishment and metabolism. Timaeus describes the anatomical location of this soul, and launches into an elaborate discussion of the quasi-cognitive function of this soul—via the liver—in receiving dream and divinatory images (71a–72c), as well as commands, in the form of mirror images, from the rational soul.

If not the lowest soul, what part of the organism is responsible for regulating breathing and metabolism? In order to explain the driving force that keeps us breathing, Timaeus introduces what I take to be the most eccentric feature of his entire anatomical and physiological theory: an invisible respiratory organ, composed of air and fire, which to the best of my knowledge, is entirely Plato's invention, with no parallel in the medical tradition. This organ is likened in a complex and far from pellucid analogy to a *kyrtos*, which is some sort of basket used to catch fish. This fishing instrument consists of a cavity (*kytos*) delimited

---

41   Remarkably, at this point Timaeus is just a step away from the view that by focusing on our breathing, and by making it regular, we can positively influence our overall bodily state.

by a plaited structure (*plegma*), on which there are two entrances (*enkyrtia*) so that the fish can enter through the entrances, but are then get trapped in the cavity.[42] The entrances of this device are likened to the nose and the mouth, the cavity of it to the lungs and the stomach, and the mesh to a body composed of air and fire (78b4). More precisely, the rays (78e2, *aktines*), of fire are analogous to the plait (see esp. 79d4: ἐκ πυρὸς πεπλέχθαι πᾶν) and their interstices are filled with air. This mesh-like body is of a tubular shape and wraps the hollow organs of the lungs and stomach.[43] Now, just as the mesh of the *kyrtos* entraps the fish, but lets water through, the walls of this organ in the human body traps food and drink, but is permeable for the more fine-grained fire and air particles.

Timaeus moreover explains that air enters and exits the body not only through the nose and the mouth, but also through pores on the skin (78d1–e2).[44] Given the absence of vacuum, the particles of air push the ones in front of them, whereas their places have to be filled by those that are after them. I inhale not because my lungs expand, but because there are particles of air coming out of the pores of my body, which thrust the air around my nose, and push the particles of air into the entrance of the *kyrtos*-like organ. But as these particles enter the internal cavity, my chest expands, while the air which surrounds my chest sinks into my body through the pores. Now the place previously occupied by the particles of air surrounding my body cannot be left empty, so it gets filled by the air which is inside, and which can now exit my body through the nostrils. This is why I breathe out, and not because my muscles compress my lungs.

At this point the interpretation of the passage becomes particularly unclear and vexed.[45] What seems relatively uncontroversial is that the regular alternation of the influx and egress of air moves with it the internal mesh composed of the rays of fire, so that the internal fiery part also keeps expanding

---

42   *Tim.* 78b2–c1. For a recent analysis of this difficult passage, see Pelavski, "Physiology in Plato's *Timaeus*: Irrigation, Digestion and Respiration," with important corrections to Cornford's extensive and otherwise informative discussion (Cornford, *Plato's Cosmology*, 308–313). In particular, Pelavski warns us from unduly pressing the analogy between the form and structure of the *kyrtos* and the anatomy of the respiratory organ, instead of focusing on the functional aspect of the analogy. See also Karfík, "Human Body."

43   I have been persuaded by Pelavski that at least this part of the respiratory-digestive organ is entirely inside the trunk, and does not need to pass through the body and envelope the trunk from the *outside* as Cornford has maintained.

44   I agree with the majority of interpreters that the air entering through the pores reaches the air in the *kyrtos* against Pelavski's suggestion that the pores lead to cul-de-sacs (Pelavski, "Physiology," 69).

45   For the main interpretative options, see Cornford, *Plato's Cosmology*, 308–313; Joubaud, *Le corps humain dans la philosophie platonicienne: étude à partir du Timée*, 67–71; Pelavski, "Physiology," 68–73.

and contracting. The fire thus set in motion breaks down and dissolves the nourishment entrapped in the stomach, and pushes the processed particles into the flow of blood, which then transports them to the appropriate parts of the body to replenish their tissues (78e6–80d7). This is how the oscillation of air in the respiratory organ keeps our metabolism in operation.

Without going into further details, let me highlight three points.[46] First, the functioning of the respiratory organ is based on two physical principles. One, on the movement of particles in the absence of vacuum, which is called *periōsis* by Timaeus. Two, that the air becoming hot and fiery inside the body wants to go outside to rejoin its cosmic like (79c7–e3).[47] Now, as we have seen, both the absence of void, and the overall tendency of elements towards their own places—and in particular the motion of fire within the cosmos—are ultimately due to the motions of the world soul. (Note, that the connection between the physical effects of the motions of the world soul and physiological processes is far from being so clear-cut in other cases.) This means that the process of respiration is closely dependent on the physical corollaries of the motions of the world soul. Although it is not directly observable, the motions of the world soul not only regulate the metabolism of the world's body, but also contribute to human metabolism.

My second point is that, remarkably, Timaeus makes it very explicit that in designing the digestive apparatus the younger gods aimed at imitating the motions of the elements in the cosmos:

> ὁ δὲ τρόπος τῆς πληρώσεως ἀποχωρήσεώς τε γίγνεται καθάπερ ἐν τῷ παντὶ παντὸς ἡ φορὰ γέγονεν, ἣν τὸ συγγενὲς πᾶν φέρεται πρὸς ἑαυτό. τὰ μὲν γὰρ δὴ περιεστῶτα ἐκτὸς ἡμᾶς τήκει τε ἀεὶ καὶ διανέμει πρὸς ἕκαστον εἶδος τὸ ὁμόφυλον ἀποπέμποντα, τὰ δὲ ἔναιμα αὖ, κερματισθέντα ἐντὸς παρ' ἡμῖν καὶ περιειλημμένα ὥσπερ ὑπ' οὐρανοῦ συνεστῶτος ἑκάστου τοῦ ζῴου, τὴν τοῦ παντὸς ἀναγκάζεται μιμεῖσθαι φοράν· πρὸς τὸ συγγενὲς οὖν φερόμενον ἕκαστον τῶν ἐντὸς μερισθέντων τὸ κενωθὲν τότε πάλιν ἀνεπλήρωσεν. ὅταν μὲν δὴ πλέον τοῦ ἐπιρρέοντος ἀπίῃ, φθίνει πᾶν, ὅταν δὲ ἔλαττον, αὐξάνεται.

The manner of this replenishment and wasting is like that movement of all things in the universe which carries each thing towards its own kind [...] the substances in the blood, when they are broken up small within us and find themselves comprehended by the individual living creature,

---

46 My discussion in the following paragraphs owes much to Karfík, "Human Body," esp. 177 and 178.
47 Cf. also Pelavski, "Physiology," 71.

framed like a heaven to include them are constrained to reproduce the movement of the universe. Thus each substance within us that is reduced to fragments replenishes at once the part that has just been depleted, by moving towards its own kind.

81a2–81b6

Human metabolism is thus an imitation of cosmic metabolism. This is in a way exactly what we have expected. Just as the motions of the human rational soul ought to emulate the perfectly orderly motions of the world soul in order to get closer to the truth, the human body must imitate the internal processes of the cosmic body in order to be, and remain, healthy, and thereby let the rational soul perform its proper activity as far as possible undisturbed.

My third, connected point is that, as Filip Karfík has convincingly suggested, the respiratory organ shows faint but intriguing resemblance to the world soul. Most importantly, Timaeus likens the motion of the air and the fire of the respiratory organ to the motion of a wheel. However, this wheel does not go in full circles, but swings back and forth (κύκλον οὕτω σαλευόμενον ἔνθα καὶ ἔνθα, 79e7–8; cf. 79c1). The swinging of this roughly spherical organ is a faint echo of the circular motion of the soul; but the image also suggests that this pendulum-like motion will necessarily come to an end, whereas proper circular motion is eternal.

Be that as it may, the two completely unified activities and functions of the world soul—i.e. its cognitive activities on the one hand and its regulation of the metabolism of its body on the other—come to be distributed between two distinct parts of us: our rational souls created by the Demiurge from the residues of the same stuff and according to the same ratios as the world soul, and the respiratory organ created by the lesser gods, made out of fire and air. Strange as it might seem, I think that at the end of the day the key difference between the functioning of the divine cosmic and the mortal human organism is that in human beings cognitive activity and the maintenance of metabolism cease to be unified, and get split between these two organs.

Now the respiratory organ is not an intelligent soul. It imitates the movements of the cosmos not by reason, but by necessitation (τὴν τοῦ παντὸς ἀναγκάζεται μιμεῖσθαι φοράν, 81b1–2). Moreover, it cannot in and of itself counteract what, according to Timaeus' general description of illness, the ultimate cause of the breakdown of the balance of metabolism is: the unnatural *pleonexia* and deficiency of the four elements (τούτων ἡ παρὰ φύσιν πλεονεξία καὶ ἔνδεια, 82a2–3).[48] And this is where we ultimately have arrived back also to

---

48 Let me only signal that despite the deflationary translations and interpretations adopted by most translators and commentators, I am certain that *pleonexia* is a normatively highly

pleasure and pain. For as Timaeus famously claims, the illnesses of the soul are dependent on, and caused by, bodily conditions (86b2–4).[49] The greatest of these, he explains, are excessive pleasures and pains, which in turn are the origins of both madness and ignorance (86b5–c4). Lack of moderation in sex and food themselves are also caused by bodily conditions (and not a malfunctioning of the lowest soul part), and in turn aggravate the imbalance in our metabolism, and exacerbate the illness. At the end of the day, all the ills of the body and the soul are thus derivable from the breakdown of our metabolism. Alas, this is not something that we could regulate simply by making the revolutions of our rational soul more regular. Contemplation in and of itself will not make us healthier. This is why, in order to remain healthy, or to regain our health, and thereby to allow our rational soul to perform its proper cognitive activity, we occasionally have to stop contemplating. In view of all the above, it does not come as a surprise that Timaeus offers fairly detailed advice about how to keep the body in good health, and how to restore health in cases of bouts of illness. And just as we have expected, the key to prevention and cure is to imitate the cosmic body as far as possible: "the individual parts also should be cared for on the same principle, in imitation of the frame of the universe" (κατὰ δὲ ταὐτὰ ταῦτα καὶ τὰ μέρη θεραπευτέον, τὸ τοῦ παντὸς ἀπομιμούμενον εἶδος, 88c7–d1). And this we can achieve by emulating the motions of the cosmos:

> τοῦ γὰρ σώματος ὑπὸ τῶν εἰσιόντων καομένου τε ἐντὸς καὶ ψυχομένου, καὶ πάλιν ὑπὸ τῶν ἔξωθεν ξηραινομένου καὶ ὑγραινομένου καὶ τὰ τούτοις ἀκόλουθα πάσχοντος ὑπ' ἀμφοτέρων τῶν κινήσεων, ὅταν μέν τις ἡσυχίαν ἄγον τὸ σῶμα παραδιδῷ ταῖς κινήσεσι, κρατηθὲν διώλετο, ἐὰν δὲ ἥν τε τροφὸν καὶ τιθήνην τοῦ παντὸς προσείπομεν μιμηταί τις, καὶ τὸ σῶμα μάλιστα μὲν μηδέποτε ἡσυχίαν ἄγειν ἐᾷ, κινῇ δὲ καὶ σεισμοὺς ἀεί τινας ἐμποιῶν αὐτῷ διὰ παντὸς τὰς ἐντὸς καὶ ἐκτὸς ἀμύνηται κατὰ φύσιν κινήσεις, καὶ μετρίως σείων τά τε περὶ τὸ σῶμα πλανώμενα παθήματα καὶ μέρη κατὰ συγγενείας εἰς τάξιν κατακοσμῇ πρὸς ἄλληλα, κατὰ τὸν πρόσθεν λόγον ὃν περὶ τοῦ παντὸς ἐλέγομεν, οὐκ ἐχθρὸν παρ'

---

charged concept here. Cornford: "prevalence"; Zeyl: "increase"; Miller: "excess"; Brisson: "excès"; Fronterotta: "in quantità troppo grande," etc., cannot quite capture the connotations of the term. The political and ethical connotations and ramifications of this expression, as well as those of Timaeus' language in the subsequent description of illnesses, are brought out well by Lloyd, *Grip of Disease*, 154–158.

49 On the point that the crucial sentence at 86b2–4 should mean that *all* psychic illnesses are derivable from bodily states, see most recently Lautner, "Diseases of the Soul," Sassi, "Mental Illness," and Jorgenson in this volume.

ἐχθρὸν τιθέμενον ἐάσει πολέμους ἐντίκτειν τῷ σώματι καὶ νόσους, ἀλλὰ φίλον παρὰ φίλον τεθὲν ὑγίειαν ἀπεργαζόμενον παρέξει.

For our body is heated and cooled within by the things that enter it, and again is dried and moistened by what is outside, and suffers affections consequent upon disturbances of both these kinds, if a man surrenders his body to these motions in a state of rest, it is overpowered and ruined. But if it will imitate what we have called the foster-mother and nurse of the universe and never, if possible, allow the body to rest in topor; if he will keep in motion and, by perpetually giving it a shake, constantly holding in check the internal and external motions in a natural balance; if by thus shaking it in moderation, he will bring into orderly arrangement, one with another such as we described in speaking of the universe, those affections and particles that wander according to their affinities about the body; then he will not be leaving foe ranged by foe to engender warfare and disease in his body, but will have friend ranged by the side of friend for the production of health.

88d1–89a1

And finally we learn that:

τῶν δ' αὖ κινήσεων ἡ ἐν ἑαυτῷ ὑφ' αὑτοῦ ἀρίστη κίνησις—μάλιστα γὰρ τῇ διανοητικῇ καὶ τῇ τοῦ παντὸς κινήσει συγγενής—ἡ δὲ ὑπ' ἄλλου χείρων [...]

Of motions, again, the best is that motion which is produced in oneself by oneself, since it is most akin to the movement of thought and of the universe [...]

89a1–2

The outcome is that we don't need to be helpless victims passively waiting for the onset of bodily illnesses. We do have the means to prevent, and if we don't succeed, treat ailments. But for this, we ought to study and understand the movements and processes of the body of the cosmos, and how a non-static equilibrium is maintained in that. We ought to study cosmology and physics in order to keep our bodies fit, just as we ought to study mathematical astronomy and the cognitive function of the world soul to bring our rational souls to a good condition. All in all, by studying cosmology, physics, and astronomy, we can become our own Asclepius. Timaeus and his friends have to make sure that the fourth, unnamed guest learns about all this so that he can regain his good health again, and can make sure, as far as possible, not to miss such fascinating discussions in the future. The study of physics and cosmology turns out to have immediate practical ramifications not only for our intellectual advancement, but also for our bodily well-being. This is something that readers of the *Phaedo* and the *Republic* could hardly have expected.

It's time to conclude. I have argued that Timaeus fully agrees with the Socrates of the *Phaedo* and the *Republic* that bodily illness can be the source of major bad for us in so far as it can hinder us from pursuing philosophy, and indeed is the source of all kinds of psychic dysfunction. On the other hand, in contrast to these earlier dialogues, the *Timaeus* presents us with the image of a well-functioning body, that of the cosmos, which does not fall ill, and does not create an obstacle for an intelligent, contemplative life. Timaeus, however, makes it clear that retaining health requires attention and care for the body. The bodily, in and of itself, is disorderly, and has an inherent tendency to lose any ordering imposed on it—just as we see in the myth of the *Statesman*. This is why we should also take care of our own bodies, trying to imitate, as far as possible, the way in which the world soul takes care of its own body and maintains its metabolism. Timaeus even mentions the possibility that a human being can reach death without falling ill, simply because after a while the triangles which build up the elementary particles of the marrow wear out. But this is a painless, natural death:

> πᾶν γὰρ τὸ μὲν παρὰ φύσιν ἀλγεινόν, τὸ δ' ᾗ πέφυκεν γιγνόμενον ἡδύ. καὶ θάνατος δὴ κατὰ ταὐτὰ ὁ μὲν κατὰ νόσους καὶ ὑπὸ τραυμάτων γιγνόμενος ἀλγεινὸς καὶ βίαιος, ὁ δὲ μετὰ γήρως ἰὼν ἐπὶ τέλος κατὰ φύσιν ἀπονώτατος τῶν θανάτων καὶ μᾶλλον μεθ' ἡδονῆς γιγνόμενος ἢ λύπης.

> For whereas all that is against nature is painful, what takes place in the natural way is pleasant. So death itself, on this principle, is painful and contrary to nature when it results from disease or wounds, but when it comes to close the natural course of old age, it is, of all death, the least distressing and is accompanied rather by pleasure than by pain.
>
> 81e1–5

This passage, I would suggest, offers no less than a further important supplement to the *Phaedo*: a description of the bodily, physiological conditions of a good death.

Whether or not one finds Timaeus' story about the cosmic organism and its metabolism compelling, or even remotely plausible, I think we would all agree that his attempt at understanding and philosophically domesticating illness leads him to recommending a regimen that results in a healthier life, in which, on balance, our soul is less likely to be distracted, and our most important projects thwarted, by illness and pain.

Works Cited

Abel, Karl H. "Plato und die Medizin seiner Zeit." *Gesnerus: Swiss Journal of the History of Medicine and Sciences* 14 (3/4) (1957): 94–118.

Ayache, Laurent. "Est-il vraiment question d'art médical dans le *Timée*?" In *Interpreting the* Timaeus-Critias. Edited by Tommaso Calvo and Luc Brisson. Sankt Augustin: Academia Verlag, 1997.

Betegh, Gábor. "Tale, theology, and teleology in the *Phaedo*." In *Plato's Myths*. Edited by Catalin Partenie. Cambridge: Cambridge University Press, 2009, 77–100.

Betegh, Gábor. "Cosmic and Human Cognition in the *Timaeus*." In *Philosophy of Mind in Antiquity: The History of the Philosophy of Mind*. Vol. 1. Edited by John Sisko. London: Routledge.

Boorse, Christopher. "Health as a Theoretical Concept." *Philosophy of Science* 44 (1977): 542–573.

Boorse, Christopher. "A Rebuttal on Health." In *What is Disease?* Edited by James M. Humber and Robert F. Almeder. Totowa NJ: Springer, 1997, 1–134.

Brisson, Luc. *Platon*: Timée/Critias. Paris: Flammarion, 1999.

Broadie, Sarah. *Nature and Divinity in Plato's* Timaeus. Cambridge: Cambridge University Press, 2011.

Broadie, Sarah. "Corporeal Gods, with Reference to Plato and Aristotle." In *ΣΩΜΑ. Körperkonzepte und körperliche Existenz in der antiken Philosophie und Literatur*. Edited by Thomas Buchheim, David Meißner and Nora C. Wachsmann. *Archiv für Begriffsgeschichte Sonderheft* 13. Hamburg: F. Meiner, 2016, 159–182.

Burnet, John. Plato *Phaedo*. Oxford: Oxford University Press, 1979.

Butler, Travis. "A Riveting Argument in Favor of Asceticism in the Phaedo." *History of Philosophy Quarterly* 29 (2012): 103–123.

Carel, Havi. "Can I be ill and happy?" *Philosophia* 35 (2007): 95–110.

Carone, Gabriela Roxana. *Plato's Cosmology and Its Ethical Dimensions*. Cambridge: Cambridge University Press, 2005.

Cornford, Francis MacDonald. *Plato's Cosmology: The* Timaeus *of Plato*. London: Routledge, 2010.

Ebrey, David. "The Asceticism of the *Phaedo*: Pleasure, Purification, and the Soul's Proper Activity." *Archiv für Geschichte der Philosophie* 99 (2017): 1–30.

Evans, Matthew. "Plato and the Meaning of Pain." *Apeiron* 40 (2007): 71–93.

Freudenthal, Gad. "The Theory of the Opposites and an Ordered Universe: Physics and Metaphysics in Anaximander." *Phronesis*, 31 (1986): 197–228.

Fronterotta, Francesco. *Platone: Timeo*. Milano: BUR, 2003.

Ferrari, G. R. F., ed. *The Cambridge Companion to Plato's* Republic. Cambridge: Cambridge University Press, 2007.

Gallop, David. *Plato: Phaedo*. Oxford: Oxford University Press, 1993.
Gertz, Sebastian Ramon Philipp. *Death and Immortality in Late Neoplatonism: Studies on the Ancient Commentaries on Plato's* Phaedo. *Ancient Mediterranean and Medieval Texts and Contexts. Studies in Platonism, Neoplatonism, and the Platonic tradition, 12.* Leiden: Brill, 2011.
Gill, Christopher. "The Body's Fault? Plato's *Timaeus* on Psychic Illness." *Reason and Necessity: Essays on Plato's* Timaeus. Edited by M. R. Wright. London: Duckworth, 2000, 59–84.
Gill, Mary Louise. "Plato's Unfinished Trilogy: *Timaeus-Critias-Hermocrates*." In *Styles and Characters*. Edited by Gabriele Cornelli. Berlin: De Gruyter, 2015, 33–45.
Grams, Laura. "Medical Theory in Plato's *Timaeus*." *Rhizai* 6 (2009): 161–192.
Guthrie, W. K. C. A History of Greek *Philosophy. Volume 3: The Fifth Century Enlightenment*. Cambridge: Cambridge University Press, 1969.
Johansen, Thomas K. *Plato's Natural Philosophy: A Study of the* Timaeus-Critias. Cambridge: Cambridge University Press, 2004.
Jorgenson, Chad. *The Embodied Soul in Plato's Later Thought*. Cambridge: Cambridge University Press, 2018.
Joubaud, Catherine. *Le corps humain dans la philosophie platonicienne: étude à partir du* Timée, Paris: Vrin, 1991.
Kanayama, Yahei. "Socrates' Last Words" (unpublished). Online version: https://nuss.nagoya-u.ac.jp/index.php/s/kZZwdP4tpqKcSX7#pdfviewer.
Karfík, Filip. *Die Beseelung des Kosmos. Untersuchungen zur Seelenlehre, Kosmologie und Theologie in Platons Phaidon und Timaios*. München/Leipzig: De Gruyter, 2004.
Karfík, Filip. "The Constitution of the Human Body in Plato's *Timaeus*." *Croatian Journal of Philosophy* 12 (2012): 167–181.
Lautner, Péter. "Plato's Account of the Diseases of the Soul in *Timaeus* 86B1–87B9." *Apeiron* 44 (2011): 22–39.
Levin, Susan B. *Plato's Rivalry with Medicine: A Struggle and its Dissolution*. Oxford: Oxford University Press, 2014.
Lloyd, G. E. R. *In the Grip of Disease: Studies in the Greek Imagination*. Oxford: Oxford University Press, 2003.
Mackenzie, M. M. *Plato on Punishment*. Berkeley: University of California Press, 1981.
Miller, Harold W. "The Aetiology of Disease in Plato's *Timaeus*." T*ransactions and Proceedings of the American Philological Association* 93 (1962): 175–187.
Most, Glenn W. "A Cock for Asclepius." *Classical Quarterly* 43 (1993): 96–111.
Pelavski, Andrès "Physiology in Plato's *Timaeus*: Irrigation, Digestion and Respiration." *Cambridge Classical Journal* 60 (2014): 61–74.
Prince, Brian D. "The Metaphysics of Bodily Health and Disease in Plato's *Timaeus*." *British Journal for the History of Philosophy* 22 (2014): 908–928.

Reeve, C. D. C. *Philosopher-Kings: The Argument of Plato's Republic*. Indianapolis: Hackett, 1988.

Russell, Daniel C. *Plato on Pleasure and the Good Life*. Oxford: Oxford University Press, 2005.

Schofield, Malcolm, ed., and Tom Griffith, trans. *Plato, Laws*. Cambridge: Cambridge University Press, 2016.

Sassi, M. M. "Mental Illness, Moral Error, and Responsibility in the Late Plato." In *Mental Disorders in the Classical World*. Edited by W. V Harris. Leiden: Brill, 2013, 413–426.

Sedley, David. "The Ideal of Godlikeness." In *Plato 2: Ethics, Politics, Religion, and the Soul*. Edited by Gail Fine. Oxford: Oxford University Press, 1999, 309–328.

Sedley, David. "*Timaeus* as Vehicle for Platonic Doctrine." *Oxford Studies in Ancient Philosophy* 56 (2019): 45–71.

Sedley, David and Alex Long, eds. *Plato: Meno and Phaedo*. Cambridge: Cambridge University Press, 2014.

Taylor, A. E. *Plato: Timaeus and Critias*. London: Routledge, 2012.

Vegetti, Mario. *La Medicina in Platone*. Venice: Cardo, 1995.

Wilamowitz-Moellendorff, Ulrich von. *Platon*². Berlin: Weidmann, 1920.

Woolf, Raphael. "The Practice of a Philosopher." *Oxford Studies in Ancient Philosophy* 26 (2004): 97–129.

Zeyl, Donald J. *Timaeus*. Indianapolis: Hackett, 2000.

Responsibility, Causality, and Will in the *Timaeus*

Chad Jorgenson

Abstract

This paper explores a tension in the account of human responsibility given in the *Timaeus*. In his description of divine causality in the first section of the dialogue, Timaeus denies that the gods bear any responsibility for the evils that befall human beings, arguing that the responsibility lies rather with them. However, in his account of human badness in the third part of the dialogue, Timaeus appears to contradict himself, claiming that environmental and genetic factors are responsible for an individual becoming bad, rather than their own agency. In fact, a close analysis of Timaeus' language reveals that he is proposing a nuanced theory of causality and responsibility that goes beyond a simple opposition between free will and determinism to give a rich account of the various ways in which we can be held causally responsible or not for our actions.

Keywords

Plato – *Timaeus* – responsibility – will – action – determinism

Although the *Timaeus* is known first and foremost as Plato's contribution to cosmology, its scope extends beyond natural philosophy in the narrow sense to cover a wide range of topics, including ethics and politics. Plato brings the Socratic revolution full circle, not only by reinvigorating the Greek cosmological tradition—from which Socrates had famously turned away in despair (*Phaed.* 95e–102a)—with a robust injection of teleology, but also by blurring the margins between the inquiry into the structure of the natural world and the Socratic quest for the good life, thus paving the way for the radical naturalization of ethics undertaken by the Stoics.[1] At the same time, the *Timaeus* presents us with a cosmological perspective on a number of central themes in Plato's ethical and political thought. Tripartition, which was introduced in purely psychological terms in the *Republic* and the *Phaedrus*, is here given a

---

[1] For a fuller discussion of the relationship between the practice of cosmology and ethics in the *Timaeus* and its influence on the Stoics, see Betegh, "Cosmological Ethics in the *Timaeus* and Early Stoicism."

physiological foundation. The lower "mortal" soul parts (*thymos* and the appetitive soul) are described as necessary ancillaries to the activity of the rational soul in its embodied condition, and the activity of each part is connected to the functioning of particular bodily organs, especially the brain, the heart, and the gut.

This move towards a naturalization of the tripartite soul, which connects it not merely to embodiment in general, but to the differentiated organic structures of the human body, sets the stage for a curious passage in which Timaeus claims that all human badness (*kakia*) is the product of the joint action of two causes: a defective bodily constitution and a bad upbringing (86b–87b). This passage, tucked away in the comparatively little-read third part of the dialogue has been the subject of a slow-moving scholarly controversy for almost a century. Taylor, author of the first major English-language commentary on the *Timaeus*, cites this passage as a key piece of evidence for his widely rejected thesis that, rather than being an exponent of Plato's own views, Timaeus is, in fact, presenting a pastiche of outdated Pythagorean and Empedoclean ideas.[2] On Taylor's view, not only does the attribution of a physiological origin to human badness undermine the Socratic-Platonic insistence on individual responsibility, by making our character a product of biological determinism, it also introduces a flagrant contradiction into Timaeus' account.[3]

The contradiction that Taylor has in mind appears to be the following. At 42d5–e4, Timaeus explains that, having created the immortal souls destined to animate terrestrial life, the Demiurge deputizes lower-level divinities, the so-called "young gods," to create mortal bodies to house them, along with "what remained to be added of the human soul" (ὅσον ἔτι ἦν ψυχῆς ἀνθρωπίνης δέον προσγενέσθαι, i.e. the mortal parts of soul described at 69a–d), instructing them "to guide the mortal animal as nobly and as well as possible, *except insofar as it should be a cause of evils to itself*" (κατὰ δύναμιν ὅτι κάλλιστα καὶ ἄριστα τὸ θνητὸν διακυβερνᾶν ζῷον, ὅτι μὴ κακῶν αὐτὸ ἑαυτῷ γίγνοιτο αἴτιον).[4] The upshot of this passage, which echoes Socrates' assertion in *Republic* x that "the chooser is responsible, god is blameless" (αἰτία ἑλομένου· θεὸς ἀναίτιος, 617e4–5), appears to be that the individual is wholly responsible for the evils that occur to them. The gods have structured the world in such a way as to be conducive to our living a good life; if we fail to do so, the onus is squarely on us.

---

2 Taylor, *A Commentary on Plato's* Timaeus, 18–19. Against this interpretation, see the introduction to Cornford, *Plato's Cosmology*.
3 Taylor, *Commentary*, 110–114.
4 Emphasis mine. All translations are my own.

However, at 86a–d Timaeus abruptly reverses himself, attributing the existence of human badness to the joint influence of our physical constitution and our upbringing, neither of which are under our control. He concludes "for these [i.e. the causes of badness] we should always lay the responsibility more on those who beget than on those who are begotten, and more on those who rear than on those who are reared" (ὧν αἰτιατέον μὲν τοὺς φυτεύοντας ἀεὶ τῶν φυτευομένων μᾶλλον καὶ τοὺς τρέφοντας τῶν τρεφομένων, 87b4–6). If we are bad, Timaeus seems to be saying, it is in the first instance our body, our parents, and our society that are at fault, not ourselves. We need not share Taylor's idiosyncratic views about the *Timaeus* as a whole to wonder whether there is not a genuine contradiction here. Does the physiological and sociological account of the origin of badness at 86b–87b not wholly undermine the concentration of responsibility in individual human beings at 42d–e?[5] Moreover, if biology and social conditioning, rather than the exercise of autonomous agency, determines the goodness or badness of an individual, how can the gods, who are ultimately responsible for the world being arranged the way it is, be absolved of blame for the evils that we do?

1 Physiological Defects and Human Badness

I propose to begin at the end, by examining 86b–87b, in order to determine how strong a causal connection between badness and bodily defectiveness is actually drawn, before turning back to consider to what extent this account can be harmonized with what is said about divine and human responsibility at 42d–e. There is, of course, a first, uncontroversial sense in which the human body is the cause of badness. In order to navigate an environment constituted of dynamic material powers, the embodied rational soul is endowed with two mortal soul-parts, the *thymos* and the *epithymētikon*, which are necessary for nutrition, procreation, and self-defence. Although indispensable for survival, given the finitude and fragility of the human body, these sub-rational

---

5 Cornford, *Plato's Cosmology*, while critical of Taylor's interpretation, does not explicitly address this contradiction. Commenting on 42d–e, Cornford claims "If [the soul] does not reduce to order the consequent turbulence in the bodily members, the fault will be her own. Her will is free to follow after righteousness and the created gods [...]" Later, in relation to 86b–87b, while acknowledging the pervasive influence of bodily constitution and upbringing on character, he claims that there is nonetheless room for "moral purpose," (Cornford, *Plato's Cosmology*, 347–348). His idea seems to be that the behaviour of the embodied soul is not completely determined by physiological and social causes, leaving room for an element of free choice in which resides our moral responsibility.

motivational centres can also corrupt or even wholly supplant the rational soul as the ruling principle within us, if their characteristic affections come to unduly influence our behaviour. In this sense, familiar from the *Phaedo* and the *Republic*, embodiment is a necessary, if not, perhaps, sufficient condition for our becoming bad.

Timaeus seems to be saying something more, however, namely that within the broad range of existing human bodies, some possess acute physiological defects that, on a weaker reading, make them more inclined to badness or, on a stronger reading, constitute a necessary condition for the development of a bad character. It is this latter idea that has been rejected, on various grounds, as un-Platonic. Thus, Taylor, while accepting that the stronger reading of the passage is correct, attributes it to the character Timaeus rather than to Plato himself. Cornford, by contrast, endorses the weaker reading, arguing that Timaeus is speaking here only of a particular sub-set of psychic disorders and is not claiming that all cases of human badness necessarily have a physiological foundation.[6] It is true that the opening line of the passage is ambiguous: Καὶ τὰ μὲν περὶ τὸ σῶμα νοσήματα ταύτῃ συμβαίνει γιγνόμενα, τὰ δὲ περὶ ψυχὴν διὰ σώματος ἕξιν τῇδε (86b1–2). The first clause clearly states: "Illnesses of the body come about as we have described." The second clause, however, can be read in two very different ways. The first possibility is to take διὰ σώματος ἕξιν ("through the condition of the body") as restricting the scope of the τὰ δὲ περὶ ψυχήν ("diseases of the soul"), in which case Timaeus will be announcing a discussion of a particular subset of psychic disorders, namely those that come about as a result of the condition of the body, in contrast to those that do not. The second possibility is to take διὰ σώματος ἕξιν as qualifying τῇδε ("in the following way"), in which case Timaeus will be saying that "[all] psychic disorders [come about] through the condition of the body in the following way."

Be that as it may, the conclusion of the passage removes any doubt about the intended scope of Timaeus' claim:

> πρὸς δὲ τούτοις, ὅταν οὕτως κακῶς παγέντων πολιτεῖαι κακαὶ καὶ λόγοι κατὰ πόλεις ἰδίᾳ τε καὶ δημοσίᾳ λεχθῶσιν, ἔτι δὲ μαθήματα μεδαμῇ τούτων ἰατικὰ ἐκ νέων μανθάνηται, ταύτῃ κακοὶ πάντες οἱ κακοὶ διὰ δύο ἀκουσιώτατα γιγνόμεθα.

> Furthermore, whenever individuals who are so badly constituted live under bad regimes and corresponding discourses are pronounced in public and in private, and, moreover, no studies capable of curing these

---

6 Cornford, *Plato's Cosmology*, ad loc.

are pursued from a young age, in this way, all of us who are bad become so on account of two most involuntary causes.

87a7–b4

This passage clarifies two points. First, Timaeus is not restricting the discussion to a sub-class of psychic disorders, but is describing the way in which *all* those who are bad become bad. Second, the corrupting influence of society is understood to play a secondary causal role, since the existence of "badly constituted individuals" (οὕτως κακῶς παγέντων) is, as the genitive absolute construction indicates, a condition for everything that follows.

Gill has attempted to make this passage more palatable through a comparison with the doctrines of Galen and the Stoics.[7] Emphasizing the general theme of the need for proportion between body and soul that runs throughout this section, he argues that Timaeus is closer to the Stoics than to Galen. Whereas Galen propounds a "mechanistic" theory, in which there is a unidirectional causal influence running from the body to the soul, the Stoics emphasize the right proportion between these two elements.[8] Yet, as Gill himself acknowledges, although Timaeus does mention the importance of the proportion between body and soul (87c–88b), he does so only after the section on psychic disorders (86b–87b), in which his approach is unmistakably much closer to that of Galen.[9] Although Timaeus nowhere advocates a reductive physiological determinism, he does identify the unidirectional influence of bodily defects on the soul as a necessary condition for the development of a bad character, with social and educational factors only subsequently determining the extent to which this disposition towards badness is realized in practice.

While somewhat counterintuitive, I do not believe that this position is as outlandish as it has been made to seem. Rather, it is a natural consequence of the *Timaeus*' commitment to two claims about the relationship between body and soul: 1) the operation of the lower soul parts are co-constituted by physiological processes; 2) the human body and its organs possess a fundamentally rational structure. Thus, before even acknowledging the existence of mortal parts of soul, Timaeus describes, in general terms, what occurs when the soul enters into contact with a body in a state of flux (τὸ μὲν προσίοι, τὸ δ' ἀπίοι τοῦ σώματος),[10] namely the generation of a series of different kinds of affections:

7   Gill, "The Body's Fault? Plato's *Timaeus* on psychic illness."
8   Gill, "The Body's Fault?" 70.
9   Gill, "The Body's Fault?" 71–72.
10 The terminology here both mirrors and contrasts with the earlier description of the body of the cosmos, where Timaeus explains that the cosmos does not need sense organs or any capacity to take in nutrition: "For nothing left it, nor did anything enter it – for there

1) sensation (*aisthēsin*); 2) desire (*erōta*) mixed with pleasure (*hedonē*) and pain (*lypē*); 3) fear (*phobon*) and anger (*thymon*); 4) "everything that follows on these or by nature stands in opposition to them" (ὅσα τε ἑπόμενα αὐτοῖς καὶ ὁπόσα ἐναντίως πέφυκε διεστηκότα, 42a3–b1). In other words, the mere fact of the soul entering into contact with the body is sufficient to give rise to the affections (*pathēmata*) characteristic of both the appetitive soul (desire, pleasure, and pain) and *thymos* (fear and anger).

How this works in the case of pleasure and pain is explained in more detail at 64a–65b, where Timaeus claims that pain arises from damage to the body's natural structures, while pleasure corresponds to their restoration, insofar as these disruptions and restorations are transmitted to the "mind" (*to phronimon*). This account of pleasure and pain in terms of the transmission of alterations of bodily states to the perceiving soul is fleshed out in the *Philebus*, where it is expanded to cover desire, which is defined as a pain accompanied by an awareness of the object that will relieve it.[11] Central to the constitution of such affections as desire, pleasure, and pain is the perception by the soul of the condition of the relevant bodily organ. The account of the generation of the various affections is thus simultaneously an account of the ontological structure of the corresponding soul parts.[12] For instance, Timaeus explains sexual desire in terms of the descent of marrow from the brain through the spinal cord into the genitals, causing a painful buildup of semen that produces pleasure when it is excreted, as the natural equilibrium of substances in the body is restored.[13] This suggests that the phenomenon of sexual desire, which is associated with the appetitive soul, cannot be understood without reference to the underlying physiological structures (i.e. the reproductive system) in which it is grounded.

But if the pleasures, pains, and desires associated with the appetitive soul are anchored in this way in the natural condition of the body and if the body has a rational structure, permitting it to fulfill certain necessary functions, then why do these affections represent such a threat to the well-being of the soul? That the body and the lower parts of soul should constitute a danger is understandable if we consider it to be fundamentally unstable and irrational, along

---

was nothing [outside of it]" (ἀπῄει τε γὰρ οὐδὲν οὐδὲ προσῄειν αὐτῷ ποθεν—οὐδὲ γὰρ ἦν 33c6–7).

11 *Phil.* 32e–35b. On this passage, see Frede, *Philebos*, 235–238.

12 On the association of the mortal parts with bodily movements perceived by the soul, see Karfík, "What the Mortal Parts of the Soul Really Are."

13 *Tim.* 86d–e; 91a–d. Incidentally this allows him to produce an account to which sexual desire has an appetitive element, while at the same time being an expression of the rational soul's *erōs* (in line with the *Symposium*), since the marrow is the seat of the rational soul.

the lines of the murky, unstructured bodily flux of the *Phaedo*. It is less comprehensible if we understand the body and, by extension, the lower parts of soul, to possess a rational structure. The appetitive soul, in particular, alerts us to the condition of our body, thus enabling us to take the measures necessary to avoid sickness and death.

It is in order to lessen this tension, I believe, that Timaeus attributes to bodily defects a central role in the dysregulation of our emotions and desires, especially in the form of "exaggerated pleasures and pains" (ἡδονὰς δὲ καὶ λύπας ὑπερβαλλούσας, 86b5–6), which are identified as the greatest threat to the project of rational self-government. If healthy pleasures, pains, and desires arise from natural fluctuations in a healthy bodily constitution, then it is reasonable to look for the origin of unhealthy pleasures, pains, and desires in abnormal alterations to our bodily constitution, especially those that result from structural defects in the body. For instance, in a perfectly healthy individual, the natural functioning of the reproductive system would not engender the obsessive pursuit of sexual pleasure. In those cases where sexual desire takes on a pathological character, this is to be explained, in the first instance, in terms of a disfunction in the underlying physiological structures, namely an abnormal porousness of the bones which leads to the excessive production of semen. This unnatural excess of a particular bodily substance is experienced as persistent, painful sexual desire, which Timaeus calls an involuntary "disease of the soul."[14] Sexual incontinence, a classic form of appetitive vice, is thus rooted in the abnormal intensity with which certain individuals experience sexual pleasures, pains, and desires, a form hypersensitivity that has underlying physiological causes.

This conclusion may be rendered more palatable by the observation that Plato is, on the whole, quite pessimistic about the possibilities of things going right on our level of existence. Timaeus' point, I take it, is not that a minority of individuals are condemned to badness due to their abnormal physiological defects—in the manner of a proto-Lombrosian criminologist—but rather that such defectiveness is present to some degree in everyone. After all, Timaeus is careful to stress that his theory concerns how "all of *us* who are bad become so" (87b4). This would leave open the possibility that certain exceptional individuals may possess a form of natural moderation in virtue of their unusually healthy bodily constitution. In the *Symposium*, to take a notable example, Socrates is described as exhibiting abnormal resistance to the intoxicating effects of alcohol (214a, 220a), physical hardship and cold (219e–220b), sleep deprivation (223d), and sexual desire (218c–219d). Of course, the most obvious

---

14   *Tim.* 86d–e.

explanation for this imperviousness to bodily affections is the insulating effect of Socrates' wisdom. But the *Timaeus* suggests that the explanation might run in the other direction as well, in the sense that an inclination towards intellectual pursuits might be encouraged by the possession of an unusually robust constitution that makes us less responsive to bodily pleasure and pain, and therefore less inclined to blindly pursue the former and flee the latter.

Such a theory is far from advocating a form of physiological determinism, however, because whether or not these physiological vulnerabilities exercise a decisive influence over the development of our character depends on the extent to which they are indulged or curbed. Timaeus' insistence on the influence of "bad regimes" (*politeiai kakai*) and "discourses that correspond to them" (*logoi kata poleis*), as the second cause of badness, recalls Books VIII–IX of the *Republic*.[15] The vicious regimes ruled by appetitive soul, such as oligarchy and democracy, are characterized not merely by the dominance of particular classes or social groups, but, more fundamentally, by the hegemony of a value system that takes particular objects of appetitive desire—in this instance, wealth and pleasure respectively—to be the highest good. These societies do not merely open up space for bad desires to develop; they actively foster their growth, encouraging our inchoate physiological predisposition towards vice to crystallize into a bad character. Faced with the possibility of such corrupting influences, the chief remedy that Timaeus proposes is "therapeutic studies" (*mathēmata ... iatika*, 87b2), which are to be pursued from a young age. These studies are designed to bolster the hegemony of reason within the soul and to bring our lower drives under control, taking us back onto the terrain of the more purely ethical and political dialogues. Our physiological defects do not unilaterally shape our character, but they do mark out the boundaries within which it can develop and determine the forms of excess to which it is prone. It is our education, in a broad sense, that determines how our character develops within these boundaries and the extent to which our innate predisposition towards vice is realized.

2   Responsibility and Will

If a bad character is the result of the joint action of our biology and our upbringing, how are we to understand the earlier affirmation (42d–e) that we, rather than the gods, are responsible for the evils that befall us? On Timaeus' account, the opposite would seem to be true, since the causes of our having

---

15   Following the interpretation of *logoi kata poleis* suggested by Cornford, *Cosmology*, 345n.

a certain character, while not wholly biologically determined, nonetheless lie outside of our control. It is the gods who are responsible for creating the human body, and it is even suggested that they exercise a form of providential rule over us. In what sense can they absolved of blame for the condition of our souls?

In attempting to answer this question, we must be careful to avoid importing foreign notions of moral responsibility or divine providence into the text. For instance, when the gods are enjoined "to guide the mortal animal as nobly and as well as possible" (κατὰ δύναμιν ὅτι κάλλιστα καὶ ἄριστα τὸ θνητὸν διακυβερνᾶν ζῷον ... 42e2–3), there is a *prima facie* temptation to interpret this passage in line with a Stoic or Christian conception of providence, as saying that the world is ordered in all of its details in such a way as to enable us, as individuals, to live the best life possible. The use of the verbs *archein* (to rule) and *diakybernan* (to steer) at 42e3–4 suggest an active engagement of the gods in human affairs.

Despite this talk of ruling and guiding, however, the actual description of the causal influence that the gods exert over human beings suggests that it is restricted to the level of the species, rather than the individual. Thus, the Demiurge is absolved of responsibility for human badness on the basis of three claims:[16] i) all souls have the same structure; ii) all souls possess knowledge of "the nature of the whole ... and the laws of destiny" (τὴν τοῦ παντὸς φύσιν [...] νόμους τε τοὺς εἱμαρμένους, 41e2–3);[17] iii) all souls are incarnated for the first time in the same form (γένεσις πρώτη μὲν ἔσοιτο τεταγμένη μία πᾶσιν, ἵνα μήτις ἐλαττοῖτο ὑπ' αὐτοῦ, 41e3–4). The last condition, in particular, highlights the limits of divine power and responsibility as Timaeus defines them. The equality of starting conditions for which the Demiurge bears responsibility concerns only the *class* of body that a soul inhabits. The concept of a "birth" (*genesis*) common to all is directly connected to the notion of a specific bodily "nature" (*physis*), which tracks the distinction between human beings and other animals, but also between "male" and "female," which are considered two separate forms of human nature (41e–42c). Initially, all souls are embedded in male bodies and only in subsequent births can they become attached to other "natures," including female bodies. There is no suggestion in this passage that the Demiurge's influence extends beyond the level of bodily forms to determine the specific way in which a particular form or "nature" is realized in concrete

---

16   "[He] ordain[ed] all of these things for them, so that he would not be responsible for the subsequent badness of each of them" (διαθεσμοθετήσας δὲ πάντα αὐτοῖς ταῦτα, ἵνα τῆς ἔπειτα εἴη κακίας ἑκάστων ἀναίτιος, 42d2–4).

17   The notion that all souls possess knowledge of the nature of reality calls to mind the doctrine of anamnesis, although the term does not appear here.

instances. Unlike in Stoicism, divine providence here concerns only universal structures common to particular species or sub-species (in the case of male and female humans), and not individuals *qua* individuals. The claim that he orders everything "so that no one is disadvantaged by him" (ἵνα μήτις ἐλαττοῖτο ὑπ' αὐτοῦ, 41e4) is comprehensible only if we deny that the bodily variations responsible for human badness can be ascribed to his causal agency. And, in fact, this passage is carefully worded to avoid such an ascription, stressing the identity of bodily "natures" in a general sense rather than the actual equality of individual human bodies.

But if the gods are not causally responsible for physiological defects, then where do these variations between bodies come from? The obvious culprit is the second main element of Timaeus' ontology, namely "necessity" (*anankē*), a countervailing principle to reason, which is both the recipient of rational structure—i.e. the material to which the Demiurge gives form to create the cosmos—and a limiting condition on what can be accomplished. Considered as a limit, necessity manifests itself in two main ways. The first is as a general constraint on what can be accomplished on the level of material reality. Certain trade-offs are made necessary by the fact that particular properties cannot be co-instantiated on the physical level. For instance, the thinness of the skull and the flesh that surrounds it is the result of a trade-off between the conflicting demands of robustness and sensitivity. Longevity is sacrificed for the sake of intelligence, on the grounds that the thick layers of flesh and bone that would afford greater protection would also dull our senses and intellect.[18] In such cases, necessity limits what reason can accomplish, but because of the general character of this limitation, it can be deliberately incorporated into the rational design of the human body.

But necessity also makes itself felt in another way, namely as a "wandering cause" (*planōmenē aitia*), an apparent residue of the disorderly motion of the elements that precedes—whether ontologically or temporally—the imposition of rational, mathematical structure by the Demiurge.[19] The continued operation of irrational mechanical causation within the cosmos enables us to account for localized breakdowns in order, without making it necessary to explain how this is beneficial from the point of view of the whole. It is no coincidence that the humours that randomly invade the different seats of the soul and engender various psychic disorders are described as "wandering" (*planēthentes*).[20] While Timaeus does not explicitly evoke this chaotic motion

---

18   *Tim.* 74e–75e.
19   *Tim.* 48a7; *Tim.* 52d–53c.
20   *Tim.* 86e6–7. Note too that at 43a, the soul's circles are said to "wander" under the influence of bombardment of sense impressions.

in describing the origin of the excessive porousness of the bones—the other physiological cause of psychic disorders that he identifies in this passage—it is unclear what else could be responsible. This porousness cannot be the result of the sort of rational trade-off found in the construction of skull, since it occurs only in some bodies and not others.[21] If such defects are ultimately due to the operation of a non-rational cause that falls outside of their power, then the lack of responsibility of the gods for the evils that befall an individual can be straightforwardly explained in terms of the limitations of their agency. That is, an appeal to divine causality cannot account for why one person possesses a particular bodily defect and another one does not, but can only explain why the human body, in general, has the form and nature that it has. In this very literal sense, we can say that the gods are "not the cause" (*anaitioi*) of human badness.

But if this is so, what are we to make of the corresponding claim that the individual is responsible for the evils that befall them? Here again, we should pay careful attention to Timaeus' exact wording. First of all, he is careful to specify that it is not the soul itself that is "responsible for the evils that occur to it" (κακῶν αὐτὸ ἑαυτῷ γίγνοιτο αἴτιον), but rather the "mortal animal" (τὸ θνητὸν [...] ζῷον, 42e2–4). This distinction is subtle, but significant, because the physiological defects that are the ultimate cause of these evils are external to the rational soul, considered in itself, but are constitutive of the human animal *qua* composite of body and soul. For instance, if a concrete human being is embroiled in misfortunes brought about by his excessive sexual appetites, it is perfectly reasonable to say that he is the proximate cause of these misfortunes, because his desires and corresponding actions, are an expression of his individual character, which is defined by a confluence of psychic and physiological causes. But attributing responsibility in this sense is not incompatible with giving a further explanation of the antecedent biological and social factors that led him to have the character that he does. There is a contradiction here only if we take *aitios*—as Taylor, Cornford, and, to a lesser extent, Gill do—to refer to some form of autonomous moral responsibility, grounded in free choice, that is undermined to the extent that our actions can be further explained by antecedent physiological and social causes.[22]

---

21   On the status of disease as purely negative in the *Timaeus*, see Betegh's contribution in this volume. This is in stark contrast to the Stoics who place particular events within the scope of providence and who see disease, in particular, as fulfilling a positive function.

22   Both seem to fall victim to the retroactive projection of later notions of choice and freedom of the will criticized by Frede, *Free Will*. This is true of Cornford more so than Taylor, since Taylor is careful to deny that Plato (or the Greeks in general) are interested in the problem of free will, while still trying to make the notion of choice central to Plato's account. Cornford, by contrast, openly speaks of "free will."

At the same time, to say that we are causally responsible for the evils that occur to us, as the result of our own vicious character, is not to say that we should be *blamed* for them. Timaeus remains faithful to the Socratic maxim that no one does evil voluntarily. Although we are responsible for the evils that we do, this does not mean that they express what we truly want for ourselves. The bad desires that we have are undeniably ours, but they are not a direct and spontaneous expression of our original nature, but rather a product of bodily infirmity and of a misguided education. As such, they are more deserving of pity than of blame. At the same time, it is not merely that *we* cannot be blamed for our badness, but that the notion of blame itself makes little sense, at least at this lofty level of analysis. This point seems to be missed by most commentators, who take Timaeus to say that blame is transferred from the child to the parents.[23] In fact, there is a subtle, but significant difference in meaning between the words Timaeus uses in the two cases. Initially, he says that no one does wrong willingly and hence that those who are bad are "wrongly blamed" (*ouk orthōs oneidizeitai*, 86d7) for their actions. But when he attributes responsibility to parents and educators he uses not *oneidizeitai*, but *aitiateon*. The latter term can mean "to blame" someone for a fault, which is how it is generally interpreted here, but it also has the more neutral sense of "identify as the cause." Not coincidentally, this usage of *aitiateon* is found in *Republic* II, where Socrates claims that god is good and hence not "responsible" (*aitios*) for evils, but must rather be "identified as the cause" (*aitiateon*) of all good things (379c2–7).

If we take *aitiateon* in this more neutral sense, it explains the otherwise puzzling fact that our parents are "blamed" insofar as they beget us, and not only insofar as they educate us.[24] After all, if we are not to be blamed for our badness, on the grounds that "no one is willingly bad" (κακὸς μὲν γὰρ ἑκὼν οὐδείς, 86d7–e1), then the same will hold of our parents and educators. What the

---

23   Cf. Cornford, *Plato's Cosmology*, 346, "blame must fall upon the parents rather than the offspring," Taylor, *Commentary*, 618, "these [defects], T. thinks, are not our own fault, but those of our parents," Gill, "The Body's Fault?" 61, "people should not be blamed (*aitiateon*) or held responsible for [these failings]. More precisely, any blame should be attached to those who 'implant' such failings, through social influence, rather than those in whom they are implanted."

24   Gill, "The Body's Fault," does not mention the fact that our parents are held responsible not only for our bad upbringing but also for our physical defects. Taylor, *Commentary*, 618, attempts to explain this by saying that our parents married unwisely, while Cornford, *Plato's Cosmology*, 346, refers to a passage in the *Laws* about the possibility of bad actions having an effect on the souls and bodies of our offspring. In both cases, the assumption that responsibility must be attached to choice leads them to overlook the most obvious and immediate sense in which our parents are the cause of our bodily defects.

choice of the word *aitiateon* is intended to stress, I take it, is that it is not really a question of transferring blame, but rather of individuating the causes of our having a bad character. These include the imperfect bodily constitution that we inherited from our parents and the harmful beliefs we absorbed from our surroundings, both of which play a clear causal role in the development of a bad character. They do not, however, include the gods whose causal influence, as we have seen, covers only what is natural and good, and who thus play no role in our aetiology of vice, as an unhealthy—i.e. unnatural—condition of the soul. If we wish to understand why we are bad and, more important, what can be done to correct this badness, then we must identify the antecedent causes of our character being the way it is, rather than attributing it to some power of autonomous self-determination. Reading into these passages a notion of moral responsibility linked to free choice muddies the waters, obscuring the fact that Timaeus is attempting to demonstrate precisely the opposite. This is not merely a theoretical point, but has practical consequences, since if we misidentify the causes of bad character—by treating it as the result of an autonomous choice independent of biological and social influences—we will propose the wrong treatment for it, making the situation worse rather than better.

This does not, however, mean that the concept of blame is devoid of uses in other contexts. In the *Laws*, we encounter blame (*oneidos*) presented as a "a more severe penalty than a large fine for the reasonable man" (πολλῶν χρημάτων νοῦν κεκτημένῳ ζημία βαρυτέρα, 926d6–7). Taylor seizes on this as evidence that what we find in the *Timaeus* is fundamentally at odds with Plato's own positions, pointing out that the distinction between voluntary and involuntary harm (*blabē*) plays a central role in *Laws* IX.[25] But even a cursory examination reveals that the *Laws* passage complements rather than conflicts with the *Timaeus*' account of responsibility and blame. The Athenian Stranger pointedly contrasts the notion of "harm" with that of "injustice," precisely in order to allow for what he takes to be a juridically important distinction between voluntary and involuntary *acts*, without compromising the claim that injustice, as a *condition* of the soul, is always involuntary. The Athenian Stranger is somewhat vague about what the voluntariness or intentionality of harm consists in, but the specific examples of involuntary killing that he gives—namely as a result of sporting accidents, friendly fire, or medical treatment (865a1–865b4)—suggests that the distinction is fundamentally one of intentionality, that is, of whether or not the killing in question was the intended result of the action that brought it about. His point is that the injustice of an agent is, in itself, not sufficient to establish that a particular harmful act is an injustice.

25   Taylor, *Commentary*, 616–617.

Nor is it sufficient that the act itself be harmful for it to constitute an injustice. In order to establish that a harmful act is, in fact, an injustice, it is necessary to establish a causal connection between the act and an unjust disposition of the soul, which is done by means of the concept of intentionality. For instance, from a juridical point of view, it makes a significant difference whether an unjust man kills a fellow soldier in the heat of the battle because he genuinely mistook him for an enemy, a mistake that a just man could just as easily make, or to settle an old score. The question is not whether or not the killing was the result of a genuinely free choice—this does not enter into the picture at all here—but whether or not the killing was motivated by an unjust desire. The voluntariness of the killing—at least, in the absence of a legitimate justification like self-defence—*reveals* the injustice in the killer's soul, an injustice that the Stranger defines as the tyranny of thumotic or appetitive motivation over reason (863a7–864b4). This is, however, perfectly compatible with saying that the injustice of the soul in which these (voluntary) unjust actions are grounded is itself involuntary, albeit in the slightly different sense of not reflecting our innate desire for the good.

Not only does this two-tier approach save the phenomena by reconciling our ordinary intuitions about the distinction between intentionally and unintentionally causing harm with the Socratic maxim that injustice is always involuntary, it also clarifies the scope and function of punishment, which is not discussed in the *Timaeus*. Out of all of the forms of harm or injury that humans can inflict on each other, only one can clearly be identified as injustice, namely the intentional harm caused by an unjust agent as a result of their unjust character. This is also the only case in which the function of justice is punitive rather than restorative (in the sense of compensating the harm caused and reconciling the parties). An unjust act, as opposed to a merely harmful one, reveals an unhealthy disposition of the soul in need of treatment, and not merely for the sake of society as a whole. As the Athenian Stranger puts it "no punishment that conforms to law aims to harm, but, on the whole, accomplishes one of two things; for the person who is punished is made either better or less bad" (οὐ γὰρ ἐπὶ κακῷ δίκη γίγνεται οὐδεμία γενομένη κατὰ νόμον, δυοῖν δὲ θάτερον ἀπεργάζεται σχεδόν· ἢ γὰρ βελτίονα ἢ μοχθηρότερον ἧττον ἐξηργάσατο τὸν τὴν δίκην παρασχόντα, *Laws* 854d5–e1). For this reason, the concept of intentionality is so important from a juridical point of view. An intentional act lays bare the underlying motivational structures in an agent's soul in a way that an unintentional one does not, helping us to determine what response will lead to the most desirable outcome.

The use of blame as a punishment, whose severity for the "reasonable man" no doubt derives from its appeal to *thymos* rather than to the baser appetitive soul, as in the case of corporal punishment or monetary penalties, can therefore be understood in pragmatic terms, as an instrument of political pedagogy that can be employed to help promote a just disposition in the soul by curbing unjust desires. But none of this requires any substantive notion of free will or even of choice. On the contrary, the aim is to draw our attention away from the notion of autonomous action and towards a more scientific analysis of the causes of bad behaviour. To the extent that we blame others for their injustice, as if it reflected a spontaneous, voluntary decision, we risk making the problem worse, since by misidentifying the causes of their injustice, we will apply the wrong remedies. Seen in this light, Timaeus' goal is not to make space within the causal nexus that determines our behaviour for an element of indeterminacy that would underpin a robust conception of moral responsibility, but on the contrary to dispassionately identify the various physiological and social causes of human badness, paving the way for a genuinely scientific approach that treats blame as a pedagogical tool whose use is restricted to the political sphere.

Works Cited

Archer-Hind, R. D. *The* Timaeus *of Plato*. London: Macmillan, 1849–1910.

Betegh, Gabor. "Cosmological Ethics in the *Timaeus* and Early Stoicism." *Oxford Studies in Ancient Philosophy* 24 (2003): 273–302.

Brisson, Luc. *Le même et l'autre dans la structure ontologique du* Timée *de Platon*. 2éd. Sankt Augustin: Academia Verlag, 1994.

Cornford, Francis. *Plato's Cosmology*. London: Routledge and Kegan and Paul, 1937.

Frede, Dorothea. *Platon, Philebos: Übersetzung und Kommentar*. Göttingen: Vandenhoeck & Ruprecht, 1997.

Frede, Michael. A Free Will: *Origins of the Notion in Ancient Thought*. Berkeley: University of California Press, 2011.

Fronterotta, Francesco. "Anima e corpo: immortalità, organicismo e psico-fisilogia nel *Timeo* di Platone." *Études platoniciennes* II (2006): 141–154.

Gill, Christopher. "The Body's Fault? Plato's *Timaeus* on psychic illness." In *Reason and Necessity: Essays on Plato's* Timaeus. Edited by Wright, M.R. London: Duckworth, 2000.

Johansen, Thomas K. *Plato's Natural Philosophy: A Study of the* Timaeus-Critias. Cambridge: Cambridge University Press, 2004.

Karfík, Filip. "What the Mortal Parts of the Soul Really Are." *Rhizai* II.2 (2005): 197–217.

Taylor, A. E. A Commentary on *Plato's* Timaeus. Oxford: Clarendon Press, 1928.

Index Locorum

Anaxagoras (Diels-Kranz)
A 78   121

Anaximander (Diels-Kranz)
B 1   242
A 27   242

Antipho (Diels-Kranz)
B 13.42   180

Archimedes
Stomachion (Mugler)
III 71.18   180

Aristoteles
Categoriae
1, 1a25–27   154

De anima
I 5, 410b28–30   80
II 4, 415a26–b7   100

De caelo
II 12   107
III 1, 299a1–5   177
III 1, 299a5–10   177
III 1, 299a25–b23   177
III 8, 306b3–9   182
III 8, 307b18–20   177
III 8, 306a23–26   176

De gen. an.
IV 1, 764b32–33   14

De gen. et corr.
I 2, 315b24–32   176
I 2, 315b30–32   141
I 2, 316a3–4   176
I 8, 325b25–34   176
II 1, 329a13–24   142
II 1, 329a15 ff.   178
II 10, 336a14–18   246

Metaphysica
I 6, 987b14–18   187
XII 5, 1071a11–17   246
XII 10, 1075b37–1076a4   189
XIV 3, 1090b13–20   189

Meteorologica
II 1, 353b6 ff.   242

Physica
II 2, 194a13   246

Boethius
Consolatio
V vi.9–11   95

Empedocles (Diels-Kranz)
B 3   23

Euclides
Elementa (Stamatis)
III dem. 32.13   180
VII–IX   206
VII 30–32   204–205
X   207

Euripides
Ion
266–274   8

Hippocrates
De aere locis aquis (Jouanna)
12–13   11
5–16 (§ 1–2)   11
23–24   11

Herodotus
II 77,3   11
IX 122,3   11

Homerus
Ilias
II 546–551   8

Iamblichus
In Timaeum
fr. 64 (Dillon)   109

Orphica
Fr. 27 (Kern) 81
Fr. 421 (Bernabé) 81

Parmenides
B 8.50–61 (Diels-Kranz) 225

Philo
Heres (Wendland)
34, 165 (III 38.159) 95

Philoponus
In De gen. et corr. (Vitelli)
210.12–16 177–178

Plato
Alcibiades I
108 232

Apologia
17a ff. 26
19c 24
34a1 228
38b6 228

Charmides
164a–b 232
165c–d 232

Cratylus
399e–400a 245

Critias
106a f. 40–41, 43
106c ff. 43
109b1–5 5
109b6–7 5
109c6–d2 10, 11
110d4–111e5 16
110d4–112d3 11
111e1–5 10
112e2–6 10

Crito
47c–48a 233

Epistolae
VII 342d4–8 225

Eryximachus
397a–b 232

Gorgias
454e 27
461d f. 24
465e f. 30
478a–b 232
486a ff. 32
493b3–7 85
495e–497a 235
503a ff. 26
511e–512a 233
521c ff. 32

Hippias Ma.
297b–c 55

Laches
191d–e 232

Leges
I 625e5–626a5 15
II 678e–679e 5
IV 713c2–e3 5
V 728d–e 232
V 737c1–738b1 201–202, 211
V 738b2–e8 209–210
V 739a1–e7 191–192, 194, 211
V 746d–747b 202–203
V 747d–e 11
VI 771a–c 203–204
VI 738a2 197
VI 739e1–7 198–199, 201
VI 741b2–3 197
VI 782e3 81
VII 819a8–820d2 207
VII 822a–b 120
VIII 837c7 80
IX 854d5–e1 272
IX 857e10–858a6 200
IX 863a7–864b4 272
IX 865a1–865b4 271
X 893b–895a 72, 85
X 896b10–d4 169–170
X 897b8 80
X 897c4–9 170
XI 926d6–7 271
XII 969c4–d3 197

INDEX LOCORUM

Menexenus
234c f.	26
237c2–3	14
238c1	9

Meno
76a7	143
81c–d	59
86e	27

Phaedo
59b10	229
60b–c	235
64d	232
66b5–c5	235
66c1–2	235–236
75b	157
79b–d	59
83c	232
97b ff.	24
100a ff.	27
102d5 ff.	135
111b1–6	237–238
114c	232

Phaedrus
237a	44
237c	29
240d1	81
245c–246b	79
245c5	78
245c9	72
245d–248c	87
246a7–b3	79
246b1–4	83
246c5–d2	241
246d1–2	77
248a–c	59
248c–e	87
250c	85
259e	27
260a1 ff.	27
260a2–3	43
260c6	27
261a	27
263a9	27
264c	26, 28–29
265b	29
265d f.	28, 29–30
267a6 f.	24, 43
267b	30
269a	30
269b7 f.	28
270c	31
271b3 ff.	31
271d	31–32
272a	30
272d5	27
272d8	43
272e2 f.	43
273b1	43
273e f.	32
273e2	27
274b ff.	33
276d f.	33
277e f.	33
278a3 f.	27
278c	33

Philebus
32e–35b	263–264

Politicus
269d–e	245
271d–e	5
273b	245

Protagoras
320c ff.	23
334c ff.	25

Respublica
II 368c7–369b4	2
II 369b5–371e11	4
II 372a–373e	4
II 372a5–372d3	4
II 372d4	4
II 372d7–e1	4
II 372e8	4
II 373a–c	4
II 373b3–4	4
II 373d4	4
II 373d9–10	4
II 378b8–e3	5
II 379c2–7	270
III 402e–405a	237
III 405c8–d4	237
III 406c3–5	233

Respublica (cont.)		220a	265
III 406e2	234	223d	265
III 407a1–2	234		
III 413a–414a	238	*Theaetetus*	
III 414b8–415d2	7	143d	127
V 478d	151	154–156	160
VI 496c2	234	155b7	158
VI 503a	238	156–157	166
VI 510b ff.	27–28	156a3–157c2	80
VII 523c	127	156e	155
VII 527d	114, 115	172c ff.	32
VII 529d–530b	114–115	182a3	80
VII 530d	115		
VII 530c1	80	*Timaeus*	
VII 530e ff.	116–117	17a–20d	213
VII 531c	114	17a1–5	230
VII 531d	116	17c1–19b2	2–3
VII 539e1–3	195–196	17c6–8	9
IX 577e2	81	18d8–9	9
IX 586d7	80	19b4–e8	3
IX 591b	232	19e8–20b7	4
X 597a1–2	157	20a	39, 113
X 604e2	80	20d7–8	6, 16
X 605a	115	20d7–21a3	16
X 611d–e	59	21e1–7	17
X 617c–d	119	21e1–25d6	6
X 617e4–5	260	22a4–b3	7
		22b4–23d1	6
Sophista		22b4–25d6	6, 7
247d–e	65	22c	43
248e	65	22d5–6	17
248e–249a	65	22e2–4	17
248e–249d	60–61	22e4–23a5	17
249a	151	23b	8, 43
249b5	151	23c6	11
249b–d	65	23d4–24d6	6
251e	66	23d4–e2	17
252d	66	23d4–25d6	16
254a–b	62	23d6–e2	8
254d–259b	71	23e5	9
262d–264c	77	24a2	9
		24a4–d3	9
Symposium		24c4	11
198b ff.	26	24d6–25d6	6
207d	100	25a6	16
210a ff.	85	25b5–d6	15
214a	265	25d7–26c5	7
218c–219d	265	26c ff.	43
219e–220b	265	26c5–26e1	7

INDEX LOCORUM 279

26c7–d5	8, 17, 18	37d	38, 94, 95, 96–97, 109
26e4	45	37d1–38b5	97
27a	34–35, 112, 214	36d7–e5	240
27a2–b6	2, 11, 18	37e	95, 97, 123
27c	23, 40	37e3–38b5	98–99
27c1–47e2	12	38a3–b5	107–108
27d–28b	49, 54, 55	38b6–c6	100, 101
27d5–6	36, 132	38b8	109
28a	38, 166	38c	107, 108, 119
28a2–3	214, 215	38c–39e	75, 105
28b	52, 213, 215	38d f.	38, 118
28b ff.	38	38d–e	117
28b–29a	55	38e5–6	103
28b–29b	51	39a	120
28c	41, 42, 138, 166, 215	39b–c	104, 121
29a	38	39c	121–123, 125
29b–d	53	39c2 ff.	124
29c	23–24, 42, 42	39c–d	118
29d	23, 38, 42	39d1–2	96, 103
29d2	19, 44	39d4–7	125
29e	38, 56	39d8–e2	103, 109
29e–30a	102	39e–40b	12, 123
30a–d	56–57	40a	117, 119, 123
30a2–6	172	40b	118
30b4–8	42, 215	40b9–10	246
30d1–2	12	40c	102, 123
31a–b	58, 102, 188	40c–d	117
31b3–6	173, 214, 215	40d	74, 117
31b4–32c4	133	41a7	138
32b3–8	173, 214, 215	41b–c	104, 118
32c5–33a6	242–243	41b6–44d2	216
33b–d	76	41b7–c2	77
33c3–d3	243–244	41c2–d3	216
33c6–7	263–264	41c7	83
33d1–3	145, 220	41d1–e1	77, 89, 216, 246
34b3–37c5	216	41e–42c	267
34b10–35a1	70	41e2–5	105, 267–268
34c–36d	59	42a3–b2	78, 82, 220, 263–264
35a1–b1	71, 89		
36b5–c2	72–73	42b	59
36c7 f.	126	42d5	103
36d–37c	59	42d–e	261, 266
36e4–5	101, 107, 216	42e2–6	145, 267, 269
37a–c	76, 107, 128, 225	42e4–44d	247
37b6–8	214, 216	42e5–43a6	216
37b6–c4	225, 241	43a–44a	226
37c1	214	43a3–5	216
37c6–d1	93		

Timaeus (cont.)

43a4–44c7	80, 216
43b5–c5	220
43b5–44b1	225
43b7	220
43c6	217
43c6–d2	221
43c7–44c4	225
44a8	220
44a1–c4	78, 82, 85
44b1–c1	216
44c1	248
42d2–4	267
44d3–5	106, 216
46a2–c6	139
46c7–47c4	100
46e–47a	117
47a–c	127–128
47b–c	119
47b6–c4	105
47c–e	116
47e4–48a5	220
48a–51b	133, 140
48a–53b	132, 135
48a7	268
48a7–68d7	7, 12, 16
48b5–6	152
48b5–c2	133
48c	41, 42
48d	19, 40, 42, 43
48e	151
48e–49a	53, 55
48e2–49a6	7, 135
48e5–6	35, 165
48e6–49a1	174
48e7–53a8	12
49a	38
49a1–2	151
49a4–6	14, 16, 132, 133
49a6–b5	152
49a7–b7	135
49b4–e4	153
49b7–c7	133, 135–136
49c7–50a4	134, 136, 137
49d–e	174
49d5–7	153
49e	134, 135
49e ff.	150
49e–50b	141, 150
49e7–8	154
50a	154, 157
50a1–3	154, 223
50a4–b6	136, 156
50b6	132, 137
50b6–c6	155
50b8–c2	139
50b5–e5	137
50b5–51b6	136–137, 138, 140
50c–d	53, 135, 137
50d	14, 55, 137, 138, 141, 156
50d4–e4	138
50e1	37, 138
51a	38, 137, 138
51a4–5	14, 138
51a7	174
51b	38, 135, 137, 140
51b–c	55
51b–52a	55, 145
51b6–e6	209
51b7–8	174
51b6–e6	140
51d4–6	174, 215
51e–52c	54
51e6–52a4	146
51e6–52d1	140
52a	141, 157, 162, 215
52a8–52d4	7, 14
52b	141
52c7	215
52d	54, 151
52d–53c	268
52d2–53a7	140, 141
52d4–5	14
52d4–e1	137
52d2–53b7	132
52d4–53a7	13, 15
53a–b	55, 174
53a8	13, 16
53b	13, 16, 55, 144
53b1–68d7	12
53c	39, 178, 179
53c–55c	180
53c–56c	171–172
53c4–54d7	208–209
53c4–56c7	13
53c4–57c6	217
53c6–56b6	142

INDEX LOCORUM 281

53d	35, 41, 42, 178	58e7	220
53e	180	59a3	143
54a1–b2	144	58a2–b5	15
54b5 ff.	133	59a5	14
54c	180	59c f.	41, 42
54c8–d2	181	59c5–d2	224
54d1–3	181	59c6	19
54d6	179	60c1	15
54d–56a	180	60e5	143, 182
55a8	179, 180	61a–b	143
55b4	179, 180	61a5	182
55c	180	61a7	179
55c–d	188–190, 209, 211	61b1–4	182
55d5	42	61c3–68d7	80, 142
55d6–56b6	215	61c5	220
55e1–56c7	142	61c7–8	84
56a1	42	61d	35, 80, 145, 221
56b4	42	61d–65b	215
56b5	14	61d5–64a1	221
56b7–c3	179, 217	62a–b	80
56c–57c	166	62a6–7	80
56c2–7	217, 220	62b5–7	80, 220
56c8–57b7	15, 142	62b6 ff.	145
56d5–e1	143, 219	62c5–8	143
56e1–4	15, 219	62d2–7	224
56e2–57b7	142	62d6–8	143
56e8–57b7	218–219	63a–d	80
57a4–5	220	63b1–2	35, 143
57a6–b4	15	63c3	220
57b6–c6	15, 142	63d2–6	143
57c1	220	64a–65b	264
57c2–6	132	64a1–6	221
57c3	142	64a2–3	80
57c8–d3	217	64a2–65b6	78, 221
57c9	179	64a4–7	80, 220
57d2–6	42, 217	64a6–c7	216
57d7–c4	218	64b2–6	80, 220
58a2–c4	142, 144	64e5–6	220
58a4	182	65b4–c1	221
58a5	245	65b4–67a6	215
58a4–c4	245	65b5	220
58a7	143	65b7	220
58a7–b8	143	65b6–68d7	221
58b3–5	182	65d6	220
58b4–c4	245–246	65c2–3	80
58b8	15, 143	65d4	221
58c5–61c2	142	65e3	221
58d1–5	215	66a–c	80
58d–60d	80	66b	241

Timaeus (cont.)

66b5–c5	229–230
66d1–2	80
66d1–67a1	223
67a1–68b5	80
67a7–c3	80
67c4–68d7	80
67d2–e4	222
67e6–68b1	80
68d2	19, 42
68d2–69c3	220
68e3–4	145
69b	26, 37
69c2–8	216
69c5–d6	79, 83, 88
69c5–77c5	214
69c7–8	84
69c7–72b5	216
69d4–5	81, 81–82
69e4	84
69e5–70a2	216
70b3–4	83
70d7–8	83, 216, 249
71a3–72b5	83
71a7–e2	139
72d	35
72d4	83
73b–76e	88
73b1–c6	81
73b6	179
73c6–d2	216
73c7	83
73d3	84
74a4	81
74b7–c5	243
74e–75e	268
75e–76d	243
76a6–b1	85
76e6–77c5	88–89
77a2–3	248
77a3–c5	216
77b3–6	215–216
78b2–c1	250
78b4	250
78d1–e2	250
78e2	250
78e4–79a4	249
78e6–80d7	251
79c1	143, 252
79c7–e3	251
79d5–6	15
79e7–8	252
80c3	143
80e1–4	80
81a–87a	240
81a2–81b6	251–252
81b–e	242
81c2–d7	179, 183–184
81d4–e5	216
81e1–5	255
82a1–b7	246–247
82a2–3	252
82b2–4	253
82d6–7	179
86b1–2	262
86b5–6	265
86b–87b	260, 261, 263
86b5–c4	253
86c3–d5	81, 82
86c3–e3	82
86d–e	264, 265
86d7–e1	270
86e6–7	268
87a7–b4	263
87b2–6	261, 265, 266
87c–88b	263
88c	127
88c7–d1	100, 253
88d1–89a1	132, 254
88d6	14, 142
89a1–2	254
89c1–4	179
90a–c	239, 242
90a8	83
90b–d	128
90c4–8	83
90c6–d5	106
90e	37, 39, 42
91a–d	82, 264
91d–e	128
91d–92b	77
91d–92c	226
91e	127, 216
91e8–92a1	86
92c7	213

INDEX LOCORUM

Plotinus
Enneades (Henry-Schwyzer)
I 8.8.13–16	165
II 4.8.23–30	163
II 6.1.6–8	165
II 7.3.3–14	162
III 8.2.18–25	164
IV 7.2.22–25	162
VI 3.8.20 ff.	161
VI 3.10.14–20	161
VI 3.15.26–36	163–164

Plutarchus
De Stoic. repugn. (Westman)
1040d1–3	232

Proclus
In Timaeum (Diehl)
I 20.7–9	231
I 23.4–11	229
I 236	35
I 383.1–22	173
III 3.29–4.6	109
III 27.18–21	109
III 57.15–27	109

Ps.-Apollodorus (Wagner)
Bibliotheca
III 14.6 (§ 187–190)	8

Ps.-Aristoteles
De lin. insec.
970a9	180

Ps.-Timaeus
De nat. mun. et an. (Marg)
215.12	184

Simplicius
In De caelo (Heiberg)
421.7–33	106
646.21–24	179
648.19–22	177

In Phys. (Diels)
789.16–18	109

Theon
In Synt. math. (Rome)
637.20	184

Theophrastus
Metaphysica
5a23–28	109

Xenophon
Memorabilia
II 1.21–34	23

Printed in the United States
By Bookmasters